Love & Renewal

A Couple's Guide to Commitment

Larry A. Bugen, Ph.D.

NEW HARBINGER PUBLICATIONS, INC.

Edited by Barbara Quick
Typeset by Gayle Zanca
Illustration page 257 by Shelby Designs & Illustrates, Richard W. Sams

First Printing July 1990 11,000 copies

Table of Contents

ACKNOWLEDGMENTS

Love and Renewal had to be written. I have been stirred by its calling for almost a decade. Yet the process has not been straightforward. There have been occasions when I have hit a wall so imposing that I thought I would be stuck forever. On one occasion, I was so burned out that I put the whole project away for six months. In retrospect, I realize that the book may never have been written without the help of very special people who reached out to me during these very special times.

First and foremost I am forever indebted to my loving wife, Claire, who so patiently put up with my endless retreats—up the spiral staircase, to my always beckoning word processor. Claire, your emotional support helped to motivate me when I hit the wall, while your honest critique—though sometimes painful—helped me realize when I had wandered too far astray from my points. What a courageous warrior you are in allowing me to go public about our lives! Thanks to you, Erik, and Jessica for all the lost weekends.

Next, I am indebted to Sheila Henderson, whose editing skills are superb gifts. I found Sheila through the Austin Writer's League at a time when I needed a comrade in arms who not only had the capacity to straighten out my twisted sentences, but more importantly to challenge my concepts—my coherence. Sheila, you accomplished both quite well and I shall always appreciate your wise guidance throughout the project.

How can I thank you, friend, The Reverend Chuck Meyer, for all your encouragement along the way? Chuck, you have believed in me for years and have empowered me to speak out with confidence. There were days, even weeks at a time, when you would direct me to structure my time more appropriately or to write even one sentence at a time—just to make some headway. Thank you, Chuck, for helping me to transcend some of my worst moments.

My deepest appreciation to all my clients and friends whose struggles are my struggles—whose disenchantments are my disenchantments. I have been so encouraged by your response to RENEW, as well as your consistent support behind me in writing the book. Since your problems are so immediate and so real, you are undoubtedly the very best critics of all. A special thank you to each of you who may find yourself somewhere on the pages that follow. Know that I was moved by your story and that I hope and pray I have been sensitive and compassionate in my retelling of your story. And to so many other friends—WHAT GREAT SUPPORT!

And thanks to so many who have reviewed drafts of the manuscript and helped to technically shape up this book. Kate McKenna helped in the early going, while Kirk Johnson, from New Harbinger Publications, was wonderfully attentive to readability and flow of the entire manuscript. There is quite a family at New Harbinger, and I am so grateful to have found you. Thank you Pat, Matt, and Gayle.

Preface

My personal and my professional vision has too often been clouded over by the disappointments of everyday existence. (Disenchantment blinds just as much as enchantment does.) This was especially true during the idealistic and innocent years of my twenties and early thirties, when I often found myself disenchanted with inadequacies in people, inefficiencies in educational programs, power politics in work settings, and a general malaise within our society as a whole. Perhaps I was a product of the times. If you are one of the 76 million Americans born between 1946 and 1964, perhaps you will recognize the thoughts that I have when I glance back in time.

You must remember that I have suffered the growing pains of being a Baby Boomer. I am a member of that 1968 college class that *Time* has called "the most conscious-stricken, moralistic, and perhaps, most promising in US history." I was a member of the "Spock generation, the Now generation, the Woodstock generation, and the Me generation. Baby Boomers were expected to remake the world ... but, a lot of shadows have fallen between the dream and reality" (*Time*, 19 May 1968).

As each of you have done, I have taken pleasure from and struggled with love, work, leisure, health, finances, and spirituality (the six domains that make up what I call the pillars of happiness). My struggles to have, to hold, to love, to achieve, and to be have all been compromised to some extent. This book was intended to be my catharsis—a bloodletting of sorts—for each of these unmet needs and expectations, these shattered illusions that have given birth to an endless parade of disenchantments.

The first draft of this book, entitled *Dream Making—Dream Breaking*, was devoted equally to each of these six pillars of happiness. Two editors told me that I was trying to tackle too much. How could one book hope to embrace so many complex areas? Reluctantly, I agreed to narrow my focus to one domain. Paring down my six options to a choice between love and work, I decided on the more enchanting topic of love— even though my early skirmishes with disenchantment were more clearly in the domain of work. (And I still remember the painful jolts I felt whenever I ventured into a new employment setting. How can so many reasonable expectations come to be shattered so quickly? Those experiences helped me to formulate the Bugen Rule of Three—the law that kept me from lasting longer than three years in any organization!

My decision to write about love represents a heartfelt conviction that there is no endeavor more worthy, no element of happiness more pivotal, and no process of renewal more misunderstood than the process of love. Most of us don't even know what love is. We can't love ... because we never learned how.

- We never learned how to distinguish romantic love from mature love ... how to distinguish passion from intimacy from commitment.
- We never learned how to distinguish the illusions of our beliefs and expectations from the reality of our lovers and our lives.
- We never learned how to view disenchantment as a natural, inevitable process in relationships ... an opportunity to learn and grow.
- We never learned how to cope successfully with adversity, grabbing instead for quick fixes that trap us in a cycle of continuing pain and frustration.

We never learned these things because our parents never learned them. They simply didn't know how to show us a mature, loving, adult relationship. Nor did they know how to give us the kind of parental love we needed in order to experience what mature love feels like. They couldn't help it ... but we can.

We must challenge the common myths that have been perpetuated by recent books on romance and relationships:

Myth: Most of our love relationships fail because we have chosen someone who is immature, impaired, addicted, or "neurotic." We must get rid of this loser and fix ourselves before we can expect to have a successful long-term relationship.

Truth: We can learn to love only within the context of a loving relationship. Our current partner represents our very best chance for learning how to do so.

Myth: If we are mature adults, we do not need love to be happy or seek good about ourselves.

Truth: We are normal to need and want someone else in order to seek wholeness. Our loving partner must become, and must remain, our most important source of affirmation and worth—after ourselves.

Myth: If we truly love each other, we accept each other just as we are, warts and all.

Truth: We are absolutely justified in wishing our partners to change in order to meet our needs. Unconditional love is a standard which works for less than 1 percent of all loving couples and probably creates more harm than good.

Myth: If we are truly in love, we show our commitment by giving unselfishly to each other.

Truth: True love is based on *quid pro quo*—something for something. It is only when we are getting our own needs met that we are open to meeting our partner's needs.

Myth: If a relationship doesn't work, it's because we weren't "right" for each other. We should keep looking for our "perfect" match.

Truth: We will never find "perfect." In truth, each of us is potentially compatible with thousands of people who are "just fine," people who can give us a lifetime of pleasure and meaning—if only we know how to RENEW our relationships once disenchantment occurs.

This book's focus is directed toward the attainment of those skills necessary for renewal. While most of you will be able to acquire many of these skills on your own, there are often points along the way where outside help is needed. Don't hesitate to contact a professional in your community who is experienced as a couples therapist. In choosing a therapist, keep these considerations in mind:

1. Many therapists prefer to work only with individuals. My advice is to avoid any therapist who proposes to do couples therapy on an individual basis. No matter what the rationale for doing so, couples cannot learn how to renew their bonds unless they are working collaboratively.

2. Many therapists prefer to work only in a group format. One pitiful couple came to me on the brink of divorce after having worked with a therapist who preferred to see clients in a group format only. This professional had actually placed the husband and wife in separate therapy groups. For over a year, the husband went to a Wednesday night group while the wife went to a Thursday night group. When their marital problems worsened during the year, they thought their relationship was truly beyond hope. They soon learned that it was the group format they had been asked to conform to which was beyond hope!

3. Many therapists do not follow a clear course for couples therapy. The focus may be on immediate feelings or crises of the week, or the therapist's attention may be restricted to communication skills, fair-fighting strategies, or some other narrow band of skill building. After a while, you may feel as though you are on a fishing trip with no clear destination.

4. Many therapists do not have a clear-cut bias toward the renewal process. And let's be clear: we therapists do have subjective views which guide our work. We are not value free. In seeking out a couples therapist, I believe you should try to find a professional who believes that the disenchantment you are feeling is inevitable and necessary for mature, convenant love—and not a sign that your relationship has failed or is over. Though divorce is often a necessary passage in its own right, you will want to know that your therapist helped you to explore every conceivable avenue toward renewing your bond.

The course that I propose for you is a structured renewal process that I call Structured Couples Therapy (SCT). I make the assumption that disenchanted couples need a very clear path to follow when confused, resentful, hurt, or angry. (To this end I hope that I have spoken in a clear voice in the chapters ahead.) I believe that Structured Couples Therapy is the right path because:

1. Most transformations in the natural world are *continuous* and *sequential*. Each step in the process builds on the steps before it.

2. All relationship changes require *tasks* to be accomplished at each level in order for enduring transformations to occur.

3. All relationship changes require new *behaviors* to be learned which can then be observed.

4. All relationship changes require the *dynamic integration* of the past within the present.

5. All relationship changes require stated *goals* which permit the future to be objectified.

Structured Couples Therapy incorporates each of these principles in an *eclectic* manner. That is, I have not hesitated to borrow different components from diverse therapeutic approaches. Though cognitive and behavioral in many respects, SCT also embraces the more dynamic views advocated by family systems therapists. Explorations into childhood origins—as an unconscious framework for disenchantment in adulthood—reflects this integration. At the same time, SCT takes a pragmatic approach in focusing on immediate needs and wants—a level of awareness that gestalt therapists have espoused for decades. And existentialists will certainly find meaning in SCT's emphasis on perspective taking (as exemplified by the proposition that no loving relationship can endure unless we learn to reconcile wholeness with incompleteness).

As diverse as these approaches to change may be, each offers us a needed element for lasting renewal—so long as they are proffered in a structured manner. No step in the RENEW process can be omitted, and progress from one level to the next is not advised until the prior levels of transformation have occurred *to each partner's satisfaction*.

There is little that is mysterious about Structured Couples Therapy. This may be considered a weakness by those of you looking for esoteric change models. I simply find no need to inundate you with the rhetoric of unconscious object relations theory or other views that usually take years of therapy to understand, let alone use in any constructive manner. Change in your relationship can occur much faster than that!

Most of you will do well in the RENEW process so long as your commitment to one another is not negotiable (see chapter 3). Others will need professional assistance. I urge you again not to hesitate to find a qualified professional or any other source of inspiration throughout the RENEW process.

Mature love will always be unattainable as long as we believe we are entitled to it. Mature love is not something which can be demanded, or even expected. There is only one way to get it—the old-fashioned way. YOU HAVE TO EARN IT! Whatever your path to that love may be, I hope that this book will help you find your way.

DEDICATION

To Claire
... Your commitment to maturity has led the way.

To Erik and Jessica
... In the hope that each of you will be able to renew your most cherished commitments.

Introduction

... being to timelessness as it's to time,
love did no more begin than love will end ....

e e cummings

As I approach my twenty first year of marriage, I can remember a glowing November day in 1969 when I met a gorgeous young blonde and fell madly in love. Claire was beautiful and bright. She worked in Manhattan and lived in Greenwich Village, a lifestyle that seemed utterly exotic and glamorous to me. Our romance bloomed in the rarefied atmosphere of The City, charming restaurants in the Village, Broadway shows, the Staten Island Ferry, the Sunday *New York Times*. Our cherished moments together were all the more precious to us since we couldn't be together all the time—I lived in Philadephia in those days. I would struggle through the week, yearning for Friday afternoon when I could catch the commuter train to New York and my wonderful Claire.

Nine months later, we went on our honeymoon, three weeks in beautiful Nova Scotia. Like many young newlyweds we were on a tight budget, so we decided to cut expenses by staying in motels only part of the time; the rest of the time we would camp out. Being an outdoorsy guy, I thought our ideal itinerary would alternate six nights camping with one night in a cheap motel. Claire, on the other hand, thought that one night in a tent was really roughing it and six nights in a Holiday Inn were necessary to recuperate from the ordeal. In the end, of course, we compromised: for every three nights spent camping out, we would spend one night in a motel.

If I'd been paying attention, I would have realized that Claire and camping didn't mix. But it wasn't until we were spending our first night together under the stars that I discovered that my beautiful bride would not make love in a tent! Sex in a tent made Claire paranoid. She believed that wild animals (raccoons and owls were particularly likely candidates) were spying on us. The underbrush was full of little beady-eyed voyeurs chuckling and drooling over our nakedness. So further compromises had to be made. Very quickly Claire and I fell into a pattern of making love every fourth night.

Toward the end of our second week, I found an incredibly beautiful campsite overlooking the Atlantic Ocean—dramatic coastal cliffs, roaring waves below us, a refreshing saltwater breeze, lush pines hovering close to the ground, and a thicket of greenery separating our campsite from the others. A more romantic place could not be found! Surely Claire would respond to the glory of this private paradise, this Garden of Eden made just for us. As I pitched our tent, I began to fantasize about the extraordinary sensual experiences we would share in this exhilarating setting. This was to be the backdrop for our ultimate union, our most profound expression of passion and commitment, the place where Claire and I would burn our intense love into the side of an entire continent enveloped by the eternal sea.

I had to wait for the dark of night. (By this time I knew that daytime lovemaking was not even a remote possibility.) As the sun began to sink behind the mountains, I romantically suggested to Claire that we should retire early that night. But she quickly deflated my expectations. "Larry! What if someone needs a match for their Coleman stove? Can you imagine how embarrassed I would be for the rest of my life?"

"But Claire, we would hear them approaching and have plenty of time to pretend that we are looking for snails in our sleeping bags," I pleaded.

"My God! If we can hear them approaching our tent, that means they can hear us making love! I knew the animals could see us, but now everyone on the North American continent will get a peep show! Forget it, Larry. I can't believe you would put me through such misery. Let's wait until we get to the Holiday Inn next week."

That evening I tried every strategy I could think of to dispel Claire's fears. I stood thirty, forty, then fifty feet away from our tent and moaned in an ecstatic voice, asking Claire if she could hear me. I went inside the tent and conducted unusual shadow experiments, designed to demonstrate that two passionately undulating bodies would not create silhouettes on the tent walls in the moonlight. I even suggested that we could make love without moving! None of my strategies worked. The omnipresent guilt of a Catholic upbringing had won over my passionate vision of union.

That night I crawled miserably out of our tent and sat alone in the moonlight. Feeling in total harmony with nature (if not with my fellow man), I imagined all the animals around us uniting spontaneously and freely, responding fully to the rhythms of life. I longed to live in the same natural way and bleakly concluded that I would never have the chance with Claire as my wife. Gazing down at the ocean glistening below, I numbly thought back to those exciting moments when I first met that young, gorgeous blonde now sleeping so peacefully nearby. I struggled with her fall from grace. How could this wondrous woman, this shining free spirit living in Greenwich Village, *not* like to make love in tents?

Though I wondered how I could possibly endure this ordeal much longer, I felt grateful that we were scheduled to be at a motel in only three more days. I knew that fresh linens, closed drapes, and concrete walls would make all the difference to Claire.

In Nova Scotia, where endless sea met rugged coastline under the shimmering moon, I began learning my first important lesson in love: *Love must end before it can truly begin.*

This Thing Called Love

What is this paradox called love, this crazy thing that must "end" before it can "begin"? Love may be our greatest hope, yet it remains our greatest mystery. "Falling in love" is a time of wondrous beginnings, of joining and celebration. "Being in love" is a process of bonding and fulfillment, of building a life together, of taking care and being taken care of. But what do we experience when we experience this thing called *love*? To understand the experience of love, we must explore the patterns of thoughts and feelings that we call "falling in" and "being in" love.

Somehow, through a miracle of destiny, you meet him (or her). Maybe you know right away that this is the special "one" for you, or maybe the realization grows slowly. But however it happens, you begin to fall in love. Fascinated by this amazing creature who has magically entered your life, you focus all of your energy and attention on him or her. The world around you blurs and, in fact, you develop psychological "tunnel vision." Concerns about family problems, car payments, or career difficulties seem to simply evaporate. Nothing else matters but you and your beloved and this incredible unfolding and enfolding that is transforming your lives. You are driven by the compelling desire to be locked alone in time, place, and feeling with this wonderful being, just the two of you, no one else allowed. Your life is electrically charged with high-voltage expectation and excitement. Your needs, your dreams, and, most implicitly, your childhood yearnings all become grounded in these expectations and feelings of excitement.

As you fall in love, your tunnel-vision focus narrows from your world to your lover and then to only certain specific characteristics of your lover. By selectively focusing your emotional attention on the qualities and traits that you find most fulfilling, you begin to paint a highly personal "portrait of desire" of your new romantic partner, an idealized image colored by your inner palette of hopes and needs. Without realizing it, you begin to think in absolutes:

"He is so powerful, always so sure of himself."

"She is the most sensual lover I have ever had."

Of course, because he or she is *more* than your image portrays, eventually he or she will do or say something that seems out of character with the person you think you know. In these inevitable moments of doubt, you may ask yourself: Is what I see in my lover real? Is he really so self-assured? Why did he seem to get so flustered in the restaurant last evening? Is she really this sensual? Why did she turn off so quickly last night? Will he always be there for me when I'm hurting? Will she always put me ahead of children and career?

Confronted with these doubts, you narrow your focus even more, further distorting your lover's image in order to sustain the new sense of fulfillment that seems to have changed your life. You not only ignore the traits you don't want to see, but you also magnify the traits that you prefer and even manufacture characteristics that you believe, at some deep level, are important or necessary for your happiness together. Unconsciously, in your imagination, you create the romantic illusion of a perfectly loyal friend, sensitive sexual partner, hardworking provider, devoted mate.

And, of course, your lover is doing the same thing—narrowing his or her perceptual and emotional focus on you to include only specific qualities, traits that he or she finds desirable because of deeply felt needs and deeply held beliefs; ignoring or downplaying the significance of traits or qualities that you have which seem undesirable or problematic; and even making himself or herself believe, out of intense but unconscious need, that you have qualities or traits that you do not have. And you and your lover consciously and unconsciously reinforce each other's portraits of desire in order to please each other. Your behavior helps to confirm his or her perceptions—and vice versa.

This is what new romantic love is all about: exaggerated images fueled by intense emotion. Smoke and mirrors. There's nothing inappropriate or neurotic about it. This is just the way human beings fall in love.

That's the way it was for Jim and Ann, a couple that I met in my therapy practice. Here's how Ann described their romantic beginnings:

> I remember feeling so much anticipation it almost made me light-headed. Oh, how I waited for the sound of his Bug coming up the driveway in second gear! I could hardly wait to tell him everything. We would talk for hours. He was the most brilliant person I ever met. He also had a great tenderness and warmth, a power that radiated everywhere and eased all my concerns. Those love letters, poems, touches, hugs, caresses, kisses, all were so bountiful. Anytime was the right time. Sexuality permeated everything.
>
> Like a stone thrown into a still pond, Jim broke the surface and went deep, sending out waves into all aspects of my existence. Tremendous joy permeated everything connected to him. He was my center, my source, my point of reference. I would look into his eyes and never have to look away.

Jim had romantic recollections as well:

> I really fell for Ann right off—tiny, petite, and so obviously smart and fun. I felt that she was really very, very different. After she went

home that first summer, I couldn't believe how much I missed her. I saw other girls that summer, but soon gave them up because of how I felt for Ann. Her letters kept me going, and her voice when I called. I still remember the first time I took her clothes off. We were in my bedroom and she was wearing a pink and gray kilt. I knew no one had ever been that close to her before. God, I felt great. She was so sweet. Such a cute ass. And then there was that special dinner at McCloud's Charcoal Hearth. What a romantic evening! And we made it last all night.

I trusted her so much. I thought she would be great to have a life with. I thought she would be steady, someone I could always count on, my partner in life. I put her on a pedestal.

When they came to me, Jim and Ann had been married for thirteen years. Together they had given birth to three beautiful children and built up a successful computer software business. They lived in a lovely home and were well regarded in the community. From all appearances, they seemed to be the ideal couple. But, of course, they wouldn't have shown up in my office if that was the case. In fact, Jim was on the verge of leaving Ann for another woman. Clearly, something had happened to the powerful romantic love Jim and Ann started their lives together with. But what?

Why the Bubble *Must* Burst

By the time we reach adulthood, most of us understand that in love relationships we eventually have to pull our heads out of the clouds and put our feet firmly on the ground. If we are sensible, we accept that no one person, not even this marvelous and fascinating person, can be expected to meet all of our needs forever. And we realize it is to be expected that each of us will have different priorities, different preferences, different points of view from time to time, and that compromise is both valuable and necessary in getting along day to day.

But even after years of marriage, when we think that our relationship has successfully grown beyond the hearts and flowers of romance, we can still actually be operating under the influence of romantic illusions, illusions based on the deeply embedded needs and beliefs that we have regarding our partners and love itself. Part of the paradox of love is that the same needs and beliefs that draw us together and bond us to each other actually prevent the real intimacy and commitment we seek. They are destined to pull us apart as our relationship continues through time.

The romantic forces which attract and bond two lovers inevitably must encounter resistance. I call this painful experience *disenchantment*. Disenchantment is a painful but necessary process that *all* relationships (not just romantic ones) must pass through in order to enter maturity. The passage from romantic love to mature love isn't a simple, one-step transition. Disenchantment arises in progressive cycles of increasing frustration and disappointment, anger and resentment, apathy and withdrawal that can blitz a brand new relationship in just a few months or gradually grind down a marriage over many years.

There are four basic relationship realities which guarantee that disenchantment *must* occur. First, our early romantic illusions about our lovers naturally lose focus and force as time passes. I call this "the tarnishing effect." The heightened sexuality that Jim and Ann experienced early in their relationship faded in intensity over the years. The expressions of affection that Ann had come to believe were integral to Jim's nature came less frequently. Ann described how this experience felt to her:

> At first Jim put me in the limelight. He was so affectionate—always holding me close, whispering sweet things in my ear. After we got married, he gradually stopped holding me as much, calling me during the day, even fondling me as much before we made love. He somehow seemed to be more in a hurry, taking me for granted.

Second, we begin to realize that our lovers lack certain personal qualities that we wish they had. At the beginning of our relationship, we are so busy enjoying, and even sanctifying, the special qualities they do have that we often are blind to these missing pieces. Or we may be aware our partners don't possess these missing qualities but unaware that these qualities are (or will be) important to us. I call this "the missing pieces effect." When Jim fell in love with Ann, he believed that she was steady and reliable, someone he could count on. He didn't recognize that her "reliability" precluded a sense of spontaneity, a quality he came to value over time. Here's what Jim had come to see about Ann:

> Ann obsesses over everything to the point of ruining a good time. I'll suggest that we go swimming, to a friend's house, or to the movies—often on the spur of the moment. I work too damn hard not to have more fun. When I suggest these things to her, she always tells me to slow down. She'll say, "What about our unfinished errands?" or "I need to write that letter!" or whatever. Even when I attempt to make love, she'll first need to check the lights, the front door, or clothes for the kids the next day. Let's get with the program! She is so wrapped up in being Superwoman, she can't seem to just enjoy being alive.

Third, the "business" of life, such as children and careers, seriously interferes with the exclusivity we once enjoyed with our partner as a couple. When Ann and Jim's relationship was new, they both put their relationship with each other ahead of the other things in their lives, family, friends, school, and career. But over time, they began to shift their priorities. Ann experienced "the distraction effect" with Jim in this way:

> We have created a wonderful and successful business together. Each week, more and more people sing our praises. But Jim doesn't seem to realize that we have enough success already. He feels obligated to work so many hours, to travel to so many conferences, to make

himself so available to customers. As a consequence, he spends less and less time with our family. We can't count on him for dinner, social engagements, or even bedtime for the kids.

Finally, there is "the existential effect." We eventually have to deal with the fact that our lovers will never completely fill the parts of us that are incomplete. In our hearts, we realize that we are ultimately alone and must eventually die, separated from those we most love. This factor is particularly powerful for those who grew up without a secure sense of being appreciated and loved. This was true of Jim, whose mother died when he was very young. His father was too aloof and impersonal to meet Jim's starved emotional needs. Years later, Jim said of Ann:

> I resent that I can hardly remember her dropping what she was doing, looking into my eyes, touching me, and saying "I love you" or "I love your eyes" or "I love your hands" or "I love to hear your voice" or "I love to see you walk across the room" or "I can still feel you inside me." This stuff may seem superficial, but it's important to me. I feel significant in those moments. I resent all the times she hasn't really been there for me.

From the intense ecstacy of their early romance, it was just a matter of time before Jim and Ann accumulated a list of bitter grievances against each other. Over the years, Ann fell off the pedestal that Jim had placed her on, and Jim clouded Ann's open gaze into his eyes. Jim's affair was not merely a mid-life crisis born of a sudden eruptive urge to be free. Fractures had been developing in the foundation of their relationship for some time.

Individually and as a couple, Jim and Ann experienced the effects of disenchantment in their own singular way, just as they experienced the beautiful illusions of romance in a way that was unique to them. But their experience was also typical. These are not the shattered dreams of crazy people. Their concerns are our concerns. Their passage from romance to disenchantment is our passage. As loving couples, we may hit different bumps in the road, but we all are destined to have a rough ride on the way to a mature loving relationship.

The Impasse of Disenchantment

As divorce statistics show all too clearly, many of us experience disenchantment as an *impasse:* ashes and ruin. Faced with the violation of our romantic illusions, we begin to suffer through the process called falling out of love—losing trust, then hope, then interest. In the hard, cold light of disenchantment, we come to see with bitter clarity how stupid, neurotic, or naive we were to fall for that jerk, that bitch. What we don't realize is that the "hard, cold light of disenchantment" isn't any more real than the rosy candlelight of romance. They are both based on illusions—

the illusions of our beliefs and expectations—not on the reality of our lovers and our lives. But all too often we choose to relinquish our love instead of our illusions about love.

Most of us experience disenchantment as an impasse to love because we've never learned how to distinguish romantic love from "real," or mature, love. Romantic love is an immature phase of love, the infancy and childhood of love—as necessary as the tadpole is to the frog or the caterpillar is to the butterfly, and just as important to leave behind. Butterflies must stop being caterpillars in order to become butterflies. In the same way, romantic love must undergo a transformation, must end, in order for mature love to arise. Mature love is not without romance, it is simply more than romance. Much, much more.

However, confronted with the pain and confusion of disenchantment, we think that we are facing love's worst obstacle rather than its greatest opportunity. Just when we get the chance to learn how to give and receive mature love—love that is well-grounded, deeply fulfilling, self-renewing—we think that we have failed at love again. And our mistaken attitude toward disenchantment is matched by the ineffective strategies we use to cope effectively with it. We end up grabbing for "quick fixes" that trap us in a cycle of continuing pain and frustration.

At many points in their relationship, Jim and Ann experienced cycles of disenchantment. They coped with some more effectively than with others, but overall they never got *past* disenchantment—past the illusions that people "in love" should always meet each other's needs, should find loving easy, should remain (at heart) the utterly charming creatures they were in the beginning, and should have an unerring, undying devotion to each other.

When I met Jim and Ann, they were struggling with one of the ultimate disenchantment illusions: If a relationship doesn't work, it's because we aren't "right" for each other. We must move on and keep looking for our perfect match. As Ann said during our first session:

> It is hard to believe what I have put up with. I have been knocking my head against a wall for years, hiding our misery from the world, and basically living a lie. I can't do it anymore. I have never felt so compromised or so painfully unloved in all my life. Nothing I have done has made a difference for Jim. I feel helpless. And I don't believe anyone else would have endured what I have for as long as I have.

Jim also felt like they had reached the end of the line:

> Whenever I feel this angry, I know that Ann is wrong for me, maybe she never was the right one for me! When we met, I never would have imagined that two people could argue as constantly and bitterly as we do. I would never have guessed that I could lose interest in someone, become so numb, so apathetic, toward someone I once loved. If it gets this bad, can I be such a jerk to want to be with someone else?

The truth is, neither they nor we will ever find "perfect." Each of us is potentially compatible with thousands of people who are "just fine," people who can give us a lifetime of pleasure and meaning—if only we know how to *renew* our relationships once disenchantment occurs.

The Passage to Love

Mature love is covenant love. It reconciles the illusions of romance and disenchantment in a way that opens our relationships to a vast range of possibilities. This love is "mature" because it ripens with time; it is "covenant" because it is built upon a mutual bond, a shared agreement, a deep pact which emerges from our emotional struggles. No matter how many times in the past we have tried and failed to sustain a loving, committed relationship, *we can learn how to give and receive mature, covenant love ... love that fulfills, that lasts, that changes our lives.*

Through therapy, Jim and Ann were able to renew their relationship. In the midst of their shattered dreams, they were able to experience tolerance, forgiveness, and caring toward and from each other. Together they created a mature covenant of love that will nurture and protect them in the years to come. They not only saved their marriage from falling apart, but transformed it into a real-life version of the "happily ever after" that we all dream of.

After only a few months, Jim and Ann had very different perspectives on their relationship. Jim was able to open his heart to Ann and share his belief in their life together:

> It's hard for me to believe that we have come so far from where we were. I feel your understanding of me, your tolerance and devotion. And I believe I understand your needs so much better now, too. I don't resent you the way I did. Can you feel how much I care for you? I hope so, because I'm trying so hard to show you. It's hard to know who changed whom, but I'm convinced we've got something between us now that can survive those crazies that will probably still come up between us. In some metaphorical way, I feel we have replaced a wooden bridge between us with a concrete span—something which will endure exposure to the elements. Ann, I love you dearly.

Ann was able to look clearly into Jim's eyes once again with her own confession of love:

> We've been working so hard on our relationship, Jim, and I know it's going to take more work. But where we are now is like a miracle to me! I feel so much more able to stay in touch with your feelings, and I can see I'm getting better at expressing my own feelings, too. Jim, I feel such a deep commitment to us, apart from all the other events in our lives. Sometimes I'm afraid I'll lose the energy to please you or that I'll forget how to show you that you are so special to me. I want the things

we've learned about how to get back in balance to become second nature to us. I know we'll make mistakes, have setbacks, but I am dedicated to going forward and not turning back. I love you, too.

If you are experiencing (or have experienced) the pain and confusion of disenchantment, this book can help you. No matter how alienated from your partner you may feel, it is possible to release your resentments and reestablish the flow of caring between you. It is possible to renew your loving bonds with one another—if you possess the *will to love*, the will to submit your romantic illusions to the transforming power of disenchantment.

This book will show you:

- The natural psychological processes that cause us to need and expect more from love relationships than they can give
- The patterns of disenchantment that couples go through and why we get stuck in them
- The tremendous costs of disenchantment for our physical health and what we can do about it
- Concrete techniques for getting past the negativity of disenchantment and building mature, covenant love

I dedicate this book to the renewal of your love.

PART I

GETTING TO LOVE

Before we can truly understand the "paradox of love"—that after we fall *in* love we must fall *out* of it in order to experience a truly loving, committed relationship—we must understand the meaning of this complicated and misused word ... "love." What is this mysterious process of falling in love? Of breaking up? Of experiencing a broken heart? Of building a successful marriage? This section of the book describes in detail the three phases of love: romance, disenchantment, and mature love.

1

Romantic Love

Romantic love is the single greatest energy system in the
Western psyche. In our culture it has supplanted religion
as the arena in which men and women seek meaning,
transcendence, wholeness, and ecstasy.

Robert A. Johnson

Most relationships are thrust into being by one great force or another. In
more traditional Eastern societies, these forces are often religious, economic, or political in nature. Marriages are often arranged by parents or
ruling families. The perpetuation of blood lines, societal structures, spiritual beliefs, or financial holdings determines who will marry whom. The
bride and groom in such cases may not even meet one another until the
wedding day. In other societies, marriage can be a different kind of
strategic game. For instance, emigration from certain Communist-bloc
countries might depend on marriage to a citizen of a "free" country. People
in such situations often desperately advertise in the classifieds for a
"suitable" bride or groom. Love is irrelevant.

Religious structures also influence who marries whom—both in the
East and in the West. Despite the growing number of intermarriages, a
Christian is still encouraged to marry a Christian, and the same is true
with a Jew, a Muslim, or a Hindu. If God is to bless the marriage, or even
be a part of it, then certain sacraments or covenants must be adhered to.
We take vows or commit ourselves to sacred promises which are to last
until death do us part or, in the case of the Mormon temple, for eternity.

To many people in Western societies, such meddling by outside
forces—secular or religious—is practically blasphemous. We indignantly
believe that there is only one great ruler, one majestic force, that can (or
should) unify two disparate souls—romantic love. Only love can elevate
us from our lonely, desolate state to one of joyful majesty. Only love can
provide the glue to hold us together. Only love can justify committing our
bodies, our property, our lives to another person. But only recently in

human history have we been so daring to combine love, sex, and marriage in one institution. Most prior civilizations knew better!

In his wonderful book *We*, Robert Johnson reminds us that our Western culture has been replaying the myth of romantic love since it was first introduced in our literature during the Middle Ages. In his retelling of this romantic tale about two lovers, Tristan and Iseult, we learn that:

> Romantic love doesn't just mean loving someone; it means being "in love." This is a psychological phenomenon that is very specific. When we are "in love" we believe we have found the ultimate meaning of life, revealed in another human being. We feel we are finally completed, that we have found the missing parts of ourselves. Life suddenly seems to have a wholeness, a super-human intensity that lifts us high above the ordinary plain of existence. For us, these are the sure signs of "true love." The psychological package includes an unconscious demand that our lover or spouse always provide us with this feeling of ecstasy and intensity. (Johnson 1983, xii)

We are perhaps the only culture to have marketed romance as a "mass phenomenon." Romance is a media event. Our society bombards us with images that glorify romance. Our favorite movie idols teach us how to seduce and be seduced in one torrid scene after another. Then, as if this is not enough, weekly tabloids fuel our fantasies further by revealing the "real life" affairs of these same actors and actresses. TV soaps and commercials subtly or blatantly remind us that something very mysterious and fulfilling is just around the corner—if we project the right image, wear the right clothes, and use the right deodorant.

Some people experience romantic love as a flood of powerful emotions —burning excitement, exquisite yearning, profound joy. For others, the experience is more cerebral—constantly whirring thoughts about their lover, memory reruns of special moments, elaborate plans for the future. And for some, romantic love is experienced as both gushing emotions and spinning thoughts. Regardless of whether romantic love is experienced more as feelings or as thoughts, it is marked by eight characteristics:

1. Intense passion
2. Ecstatic loss of judgment
3. Obsessive focus on the beloved
4. Desire for exclusivity
5. Self-centered preoccupation with oneself
6. Selective focus on positive qualities
7. Exaggeration of real or imagined qualities
8. Secret codes, private meanings, special language

Although these characteristics of romantic love are sustained in some fashion throughout the course of a mature, covenant love relationship, they are destined to shatter as the foundation for love. They must shatter because they are built upon a fluid base of emotions, feelings which by their very nature are vacillating and momentary. They must also shatter because the attitudes that accompany them are too brittle, too absolute, and too extreme to serve as the foundation for a love that can endure the bumps of everyday living.

Two reciprocal sets of needs seem to underlie all love relationships: (1) self needs versus other needs and (2) need for novelty versus need for familiarity.

	NOVEL	*FAMILIAR*
SELF NEEDS	ROMANTIC LOVE	
OTHER NEEDS		MATURE LOVE

Romantic love is characterized by *self-oriented needs* that require the stimulation of *novelty*. In our heightened physical and emotional state, we clamor for more and more supercharged experiences to perpetuate the high we call "romance." Candlelight dinners, passionate love in the morning, and sentimental mementos of places where we spent time together develop into a pattern of intensity that we expect to sustain over time. However, although romance itself can certainly endure, this level of idealized intensity is destined to wane. If our appetite for intensity is stronger than our sense of satisfaction in our current relationship, then our pursuit of novelty can become addicting as we flit from one "new" relationship to another.

Eventually, if we are to experience the fulfillment we yearn for, we must come to appreciate the "paradox of love"—the paradox that after we fall *in* love we must fall *out* of it in order to experience a truly loving, committed relationship. We must learn that something equally wonderful—mature, covenant love—can augment and enrich the fading intensity of romantic love. We must learn to cherish the needs of *others* within a life structure which is *familiar* to us. Here we find the security, predictability, and rootedness that we need to be truly happy. Later chapters will explore this process of evolution in our loving relationships. But to understand the process of reaching mature love, we must understand the eight characteristics of romantic love.

Romantic Love

Romantic love is characterized by intense passion. Courtship is driven by powerful hormones that are felt as intense emotional and physical passion. And lovers become even more passionate to overcome any obstacles (real or imaginary) that threaten to prevent union with their beloved. Sex! It exhilarates our moods and excites our imaginations. Richard Burton, upon meeting Elizabeth Taylor by a swimming pool, effused: "She is the most astounding, self-contained, pulchritudinous, remote, inaccessible woman I have ever seen. Her breasts were apocalyptic. They would topple empires down before they were withered" (Stein 1977).

The word *passion* originally meant "to suffer." Lovers suffer because there are obstacles to overcome. Physical separation due to school or military service, religious or cultural differences, and parental objections may create immense barriers to romantic fulfillment, yet lovers will strive passionately to overcome these barriers. Even other men or women—the "competition"—can present obstacles, yet passionate lovers can be quite creative in establishing a special status above the rest.

There are times when the competition can actually be the husband or wife of the beloved. This was certainly the case in the Middle Ages when knights would charm a lady by doing a great feat and troubadours would travel from castle to castle to entertain and woo these women. It was this extramarital passion that was defined as love. (In fact, it was not until the Middle Ages that the word "love" came in vogue.) Perhaps the most symbolic obstacle of the time was the chastity belt, which the lord of the castle hopelessly believed would deter the penetration of a passionate lover. Today's version of this chastity belt is, of course, the wedding band.

These passionate women of the Middle Ages would actually gather in small groups to discuss their extramarital affairs, since sex outside marriage was fashionable. Their groups, called Courts of Love, defined the then current norms and traditions of "loving." Under the leadership of the Countess of Champagne, in May 1174, one group of women created a code of love. Their list of 31 principles included these five tenets (Langdon-Davies 1927, 266-267).

- Marriage is no good excuse against loving.
- Whoever cannot conceal a thing, cannot love.
- Love that is known publicly rarely lasts.
- An easy conquest renders love despised, a difficult one makes it desired.
- The true lover is haunted by the co-lover's image unceasingly.

These passionate lovers had to overcome the rather unique obstacles of their time. As do we. Dual career marriages, changing gender roles, and evening soccer leagues may all sabotage our desire to be "unceasingly haunted" by a co-lover's image. Certainly, waiting for the kids to go to bed hardly encourages spontaneous passion. Perhaps the first principle listed above should read "Kids are no good excuse against loving"! Yet it is these very obstacles that make us wonder "Where did all our passion go?" Waiting for the reappearance of those rare delicious moments is hardly the basis of a solid relationship. Spent passion usually gets washed away in the laundry the next day.

Is nature duping us? Courtship may be a biological lure that allows us to perpetuate ourselves as a species. Once we copulate, nature's aims have been fulfilled. Erotic love, driven by powerful hormones within the body, is nature's gift to enjoy, but we must be careful not to marry for this gift alone. When our initial attraction for a person's height, legs, or breasts diminish in intensity—when the novelty wears off—our relationship may disintegrate if nothing more holds it together. Erotic feelings, when they are most important to us, may seem to be absolutely vital to our relationships, but they never will be sufficient for continued loving. In fact, for some couples erotic feelings are actually unimportant, perhaps even unnecessary.

Romantic love is characterized by ecstatic loss of judgment. Ecstasy, from the Greek *ekstasis*, originally meant "deranged"! In many ways, lovers are actually "out of their minds" when they fall in love, blinded by a montage of compelling images and sensations. Early love is powerfully fueled by the smell, the taste, the sight, the touch, and the sound of one's lover. Our responses are beyond reason and self-control. We may not know what we are doing or we may be in such a stupor that we are unable to make sound judgments. Blinded by ecstatic desire, we may repeatedly choose lovers who are unable to make a living, who abuse us physically, who fear commitment, or who cling to mommy or old friends. Not only are our responses beyond reason, but we may be driven by unreasonable motivations as well. Our ecstatic love may be based on unconscious needs for dependency, approval, or safety. Perhaps we have a desperate urgency to cling or bond which shows our inability to be alone or self-sufficient. Or we may be unable to stand feeling bored or restless.

These powerful, primal urges blur the distinctions between reason and emotion, thought and feeling, mind and body. However, these distinctions actually are artificial. Both reason and emotion envelop one another as they dance together throughout a love relationship. Though emotion may take the lead in the early going, the presence of reason determines how long the dance will last!

Obsessive focus on the beloved. Often lovers are distracted from their normal thoughts and activities by constantly intruding thoughts about their romantic partner. We become preoccupied with every aspect of our lover's personality, history, current life, and so forth. Our capacity to concentrate on important tasks may be impaired by constant romantic daydreams. The more complex the task, the worse this condition can be. Some of us become so distracted by thoughts of our lovers that even our most basic cognitive functions seem to be on vacation. We can handle only the most routine, rote tasks—mindless chores that require no thinking, planning, or decision making. In other words, we can handle the grocery shopping, but somebody else has to prepare the list.

Our thoughts are preoccupied with what might be called "rendezvous work." Rendezvous work can be a full-time job. Schedules must be juxtapositioned, excuses found, and rationales provided. We devote tremendous amounts of thought and energy to figuring out when, where, and how we might meet with our beloved—either by design or by chance—and we often exhibit great creativity and cunning in pulling off our romantic plans.

Obsessed with our beloved, we may consciously make "risky" choices that previously would have seemed unthinkable. Meeting for an early morning rendevous may seem a higher priority than attending an executive planning session. Giving a special expensive gift may seem a better choice than replacing the bald tires on our car. Going away together for the weekend may seem much more important than attending our child's awards banquet.

Obsessive preoccupation with our beloved is often exhilarating, but can also be an energy drain. Our sleep patterns are often disrupted, our appetites suppressed, and our normal routines disturbed. But none of this seems to matter at the time. All we want is to submerge ourselves in the depths of our beloved.

Romantic love is characterized by a desire for exclusivity. Romantic lovers feel a need to merge with their beloved, a need to lose their separate, individual identities and "become one." The presence of other people in our lover's life—other romantic contenders, best friends, even children—interferes with this experience of union. Our hunger for exclusivity can be understood in light of our deep need to feel completed in some sense. In union with another we hope to find a missing part of ourselves that we desperately need to fulfill our human experience. And, truly, when we are in love, we experience ourselves as more complete, more whole.

Exclusive love is exhilarating, as if we are somehow lifted above the average plane of life. We soar to new heights. This transcendence beyond our normal, ordinary life drives us to seek such fulfillment in love. Is it any wonder that we would so cherish time spent alone with our beloved? Can there be any doubt that such a meaningful union—such exclusivity—is likened quite often to a religious experience? Robert Johnson reminds us:

> If we ask where else we have looked for these things, there is a startling and troubling answer: religious experience. When we look for something greater than our egos, when we seek a vision of perfection, a sense of inner wholeness and unity, when we strive to rise above the smallness and partialness of personal life to something extraordinary and limitless, this is spiritual aspiration. (Johnson 1983, 52)

Herein lies a bitter truth: What we have been taught to seek in others, by way of romantic love, cannot be found there. The exclusivity we cherish is supposed to provide us with a bottomless vessel, an ever-flowing source of emotional and spiritual sustenance to nourish us all our lives. This is a fantasy. The lover we seek this exclusive bond with is not a real person but instead a projection of our most basic needs. Whether the need be nurturance, attention, affection, assertiveness, or playful sexuality, we see in the other the hope of getting what is sorely missing within ourselves. This, as we will see in chapter 3 on mature love, is impossible—for enduring love requires that we find unity and wholeness more in the transformation of ourselves than in the projected fantasies that we create about one another. Robert Johnson goes on to say:

When a man's projections on a woman unexpectedly evaporate, he will often announce that he is "disenchanted" with her; he is disappointed that she is a human being rather than the embodiment of his fantasy. He acts as though she has done something wrong. If he would open his eyes, he would see that the breaking of the spell opens a golden opportunity to discover the real person who is there. It is equally the chance to discover the unknown parts of himself that he has been projecting on her and trying to live through her. (Johnson 1983, 108)

We see then that exclusivity, though a normal part of romantic love, often blinds us to the "real" person we must discover and know if mature love is to emerge—if indeed love is to endure at all!

Romantic love is characterized by self-centered preoccupation with oneself. This may be surprising, but the fact is that we receive far more than we give during romantic love. This phenomenon is rooted in the similarities between romantic love relationships and parent-child relationships. Most of us came into this world with an attentive parent-figure who attempted to meet our burgeoning narcissistic needs. We had to trust that our needs would be met in order to progress in a normal psychological manner. We cried and someone fed us or held us. We walked and someone applauded our every step. We stumbled and someone caught us. The more our needs were met, the more we believed that the entire universe was in harmony with us. We were somehow complete because of this oneness with our parents. Youthful narcissism is like this. But we outgrow this narcissism, don't we? I'm not sure we do.

We bring this self-absorbed preoccupation with ourselves with us throughout life. Many of our courting behaviors that appear to be loving are really selfish. During candlelight dinners we glow with warmth from all the "loving" attention *we* get. Passionate lovemaking reminds us of how desirous *we* are to others. The more special we feel in these moments, the more our basic needs appear to be met, the more we want to love. According to psychiatrist Don Jackson (1965), even the distress and misery that romantic lovers typically suffer when separated is caused by "selfishness of the most egocentric type."

Unfortunately, this self-centered sense of fulfillment is sure to fade once our work routines, children, and other life-style choices complicate our daily schedules. If our selfish preoccupation requires megadoses of undivided attention, we are in for a rude awakening. The average American couple probably spends less than fifteen minutes together per week gazing into each others' eyes. Furthermore—and this point will be made repeatedly throughout this book—most of us have never taken enough time to truly know what our basic needs actually are.

An ideal partner can complement our ego ideal. (We all have an unconscious desire to improve ourselves by choosing the right partner. In this way, we feel more complete.) But in this search for an ideal are we finding romantic or mature love? Erich Fromm, in his book, *The Art of Loving*, points out:

> Infantile love follows the principle "I love because I am loved."
> Mature love follows the principle "I am loved because I love."
> Immature love says "I love you because I need you."
> Mature love says "I need you because I love you." (Fromm 1956, 36)

We may become so preoccupied with all that we are getting that we love only because we are loved or give only because we receive.

Romantic love is characterized by a selective focus on positive qualities. If you were asked, in the heat of your passion, what attracted you to your lover, you might point out that she or he was disciplined, bright, perceptive, spirited, silly, creative, energetic, gentle, confident, and certainly sexy. If you were then asked what negative qualities you find in your lover, this second list of adjectives would certainly be most sparse compared to the former list. This is the nature of romantic love. From 240 million potential partners in the United States alone, we choose one person. Then from thousands of adjectives and adverbs we choose less than ten (usually less than five) to describe this one person out of millions.

Certain positive qualities have actually been found to be more culturally embedded, perhaps more significant than others. "Warm" versus "cold" is one such dimension. Most of us put warmth right at the top of our positive quality list. Research shows that we are attracted to people who exude warmth, perhaps as a reflection of our incessant quest to find warm acceptance or a safe harbor.

Romance serves to focus our attention on positive qualities while blurring our vision regarding more negative qualities. We only get part of the picture. But there's more. The bad news is that the positive qualities that initially attract two lovers are seldom sufficient, or even apropos, to meet the long-term needs of mature love. Disenchanted clients tell me so each day.

Romantic love is characterized by idealized exaggeration of real or imagined qualities. What we see in our lover is not what we get. Like two used car salespersons, each of us is presenting our very best features. Notice my exterior finish, my flashy undercoating, my acceleration and pickup. What we don't see are bent wheels, grinding gears, and leaky bottoms!

The two key words here are *idealized* and *imagined*. In our hunger to find what we are looking for, we do more than just notice positive qualities. We *sanctify* these qualities. We exaggerate their presence and their importance. Physical attraction may prompt us to idolize her golden hair, his rounded chin, her svelte slimness and firmness, or his towering height. All positive qualities, in the beginning, will appear more pronounced than they really are.

Romance is also based on imputed qualities that we wish our partners had. If we want to be taken care of, we will somehow find some measure of caring in our lover. The observation that he feeds his dog once a day may be enough for us to assume that he will nurture our needs as well. Only later do we begin to notice that his dog has fleas and tangled fur. Only later do we discover that our nurturing lover refuses to talk to his alcoholic father, believes his controlling mother is a bitch, and prays that his Ivy League brother will be crushed by fourteen cars at the Port Jefferson branch of the Long Island Railroad. And this is the guy we believe will care for us!

Therapist Muriel James has said, "Being in love with a person is quite different from being in love with love. The romance in loving a person involves recognizing and treating that person as someone special and wonderful—but not someone adored or idealized. Romance is for real; romanticism is not" (James 1979, 38).

Romantic love is characterized by secret codes, private meanings, and special language. As lovers we sustain our fantasies about our beloved—and the special relationship we share—by communicating with each other in a personal, exclusive language, especially when we are in the company of others.

The intensity of romantic love is marked by very personalized communications. We use the blandest of words—words like peanut, treasure, or dewdrop—to connote very special meanings. We refer to body parts, a sexual act, or a sexual setting by a secret code. This allows us to build fantasies about one another while in the company of others. The clandestine nature of these communications is deceptive and adds to the intensity of the relationship.

Virtually all of the senses might, in some way, be part of a secret code. A certain glance or wink, a certain dress or shirt, a certain aromatic meal, or a certain way of touching or massaging may send a message. During our courting days, we spend much time and money creating interludes where our senses can be titillated. An evening out may build in intensity as we dress for one another, perfume for one another, and begin to touch one another. Usually the dessert for such a romantic evening will be the richness of sexual passion.

Though many codes will die away during the course of a love relationship, mature lovers will delight in finding new ways to enchant and to entreat. This is not the case with romantic lovers, who never grow beyond their original codes.

Many of these characteristics of romantic love can be found in love letters. One of my clients shared this past lover's note with me. It captures the illusory power of romantic love quite well.

Dear Sandy,
    I am delighted that you came by the other day—twice! Nothing like doubling your pleasure, doubling your fun! I only wish that we could discard all that intrudes in our lives so that we could totally immerse ourselves in one another. [*Exclusivity.*]

When I saw you at the door the other morning, I don't think it was chance or irony which explains how just before you arrived you were firmly set in a dream which often comes to me. [*Obsessive focus—not to mention divine intervention.*]

It is strange how events occur which change our lives. Some for the better, some for the worse. And some keep you right where you are, making you wonder if this is really what I envisioned. I am not sure what you have in mind or have up your sleeve (or elsewhere—ha!) but I think you know the consequences that could result from our "special encounters" [*secret codes, private meanings*], but I want you to know that I am always here for you—no matter what—whenever you need me day or night. This will ALWAYS be true! [*Ecstatic loss of judgment.*]

When I saw you the other morning I was quite stunned! I couldn't believe that you were there—radiating that incredible essence of yours. Then we talked for a while and you let me kiss you—one of those long "special" kisses with those very "special" lips. Well I felt too good to be true—and many great memories started to flow ...oh!! what a morning. [*Selective focus on positive qualities.*]

I often think about making love to you again and again. When we do, these are surely some of the sweetest and most erotic times in my life [*intense passion*]. Why is it that even though we're not together, people I meet cannot compare to you. Feelings I get just cannot be compared in any way. It's going to be very hard, maybe impossible, for me to find someone that can fit those shoes that I keep by my bed for that someone "special" (guess who) whenever she comes by. [*Idealized exaggeration of real or imagined qualities.*]

Well, I shall try again to go back to sleep. Since I can't have you next to me now, I'll do the next best thing, I'll dream about you—perhaps a nice wet one! I LOVE you very, very much.

Sam

Sam's love note to Sandy is not unusual. All the components of romantic love are evident in just these few words. Sam is experiencing the real thing—he is truly in love. He is in romantic love. He has found not only the right woman, but the right *experience*. If he insists on preserving Sandy and this profound romantic experience—as they are—he will go down in the very flames that have ignited his current passion. He will crash and burn unless he understands much more about loving relationships.

Romance: Its Promise

Romantic love, as a magic potion, has been with us for many centuries. Its wondrous status as "the greatest force in the Western psyche" reflects its high performance ratings by consumers over the years. As we know from supply and demand economics, products and services that perform poorly are not wanted, resulting in less demand and value for those commodities. This is hardly the case with romantic love.

Romantic love has been "selling and trading" quite well in most national and international exchanges. Its market "highs" are noteworthy and its market shares are growing at a rapid pace. Consumers are obviously very interested in its upward cycle of growth and are willing to invest huge sums of capital and personal reserves in its behalf. Remarkably, romantic love seems to be the one investment people take "stock" in where it is not necessary to buy "low." Buying in when "high" seems to bring greater dividends to the average consumer—at least for a while! Even though people "crash" and burn daily in the marketplace of love, investors are as persistent as ever in betting it all on a bluechip winner!

TV talk shows make this point daily. While recently tuning in to "Donahue," I actually heard one member of the audience disdainfully put down one of the guests who clearly was not as intoxicated by love's magic as she had been: "How can you talk of financial security, family background, and career goals as important qualities to look for in another? What we need are more sparks, more flames, and more dreams to live by. That other stuff really doesn't matter. In fact, it's boring!"

This consumer, obviously taken with romance, is willing to "invest" the quality of her life, her most cherished goals and dreams, in a man who meets one essential criterion: he somehow evokes an intensity—a captivating beam of light—that she experiences as romance. Nothing else matters. Though she has certainly found the promise of romantic love, she has regrettably been blinded by it. The inevitability of disenchantment will rock her out of her senses.

Romance does have its place so long as we do not attempt to bottle it—to preserve it over time. This is precisely what we attempt to do in romantic love. We idealize our most intense experience of "falling in love." We project our most cherished images of perfection onto the beloved. We turn a wonderfully human experience into a divine one. We attempt to transform a delightful human being into a revered king or queen. We rigidly encapsulate a breathtaking, but fleeting, experience of romance by creating molds that must eventually fracture or break.

Romance is that sometimes intense, often tender, experience when two souls taste the wonders of oneness, when for the briefest of moments we transcend our lonely status as individuals and instead find ourselves immersed in another. Romantic lovers worry and fret that this experience will dissipate—a sure sign that "love" has ended. It is this notion that one should be able to drink the everlasting love potion *at all times* which underlies the absurdity of romantic love. Such a notion implies both insatiability and a belief in a perpetual flame that never goes out. Such abundance is certainly implied in our rituals of faith (such as Chanukah candles), but is, at best, a divine notion that only destines us mortals to despair when the light flickers out.

Mature lovers know better. In fact, the irony is that mature lovers know more about romance than romantic lovers do. Mature lovers know that romance has its seasons—its springtime passion and its wintertime repose. They know that romance waxes and wanes as do most natural things of beauty. Romantic lovers, in contrast, begin to pack their belongings when winter clouds start rolling in. But no amount of shoring up can prevent this intrusion. No wall, no moat, can hold off the inevitable—that disenchanting interlude when the intensity of romantic love fades and renewal has yet to commence.

Mature lovers know how to maintain romance as a power pellet in a loving relationship. Mature lovers know how to tap into romance as a fluid source of energy that sustains a relationship over time. Each of the eight characteristics of romantic love, described earlier, can be transformed into this special promise of renewal.

Intense passion can become genuine intimacy where we truly risk being known. We learn to reveal our true nakedness which we entrust to another's tender touch. We learn what turns each other on and take great delight in doing so. We learn that passion can be driven by an other-directedness that enjoys seeing the other so satisfied. Erotic intensity may also be transformed into a deep, abiding pleasure in the other's company and presence. We finally learn how to care about another by demonstrating effective communication, warm, loving affection, and reflective intuition.

Ecstatic loss of judgment can become a generosity of judgment in which we accept those of each other's flaws that aren't destructive to the relationship. This tenderness and tolerance of one another, in the face of obvious shortcomings, promotes the creation of a safe, loving environment where we can lose our self-consciousness as well as our harsh judgments of self and others. By providing a safe harbor for our beloved, we offer a fertile setting where mutual growth can occur.

Obsessive focus on the beloved can become thoughtful reminders of love which convey our caring. Flowers, cards, surprise notes on the bathroom mirror are all ongoing ways to demonstrate our feelings which, in turn, trigger romance in our relationships. Mature lovers learn to create endearing moments when specialness is celebrated, instead of clinging to an illusion that specialness should be unflagging.

Desire for exclusivity can become the special night out, the lunchtime date, or the planned weekend for two (no kids allowed) that allow us time to renew our focus on each other, as well as the "we-ness" we have come to share. In daily life, our time together is eroded by children, work demands, or other independent activities. Mature couples, within the context of these "interruptions," learn to stoke their romance on a more time-limited basis. When we learn to accept the complexity of our lives beyond one another, we are well positioned to enjoy the quality of our exclusive time together—even when the quantity of time is limited.

Self-centered preoccupation with oneself can become our intrepid dedication to attending to the demands and needs of the relationship while maintaining our own independence. We are solitary beings by nature and must accept this in order to be fully mature. Sometimes we try to shield ourselves from this truth by possessing one another in our quest for oneness. Yet, we must remember that we are born alone, we die alone, and we must live a portion of our lives alone—separate even from those we feel most close to. Mature lovers, knowing this, come to embrace each other with more devotion and romance as each cherishes the miracle of sharing that which can be shared by two separate individuals.

Selective focus on positive qualities can become the framework for healthy confrontation. By recognizing the many good qualities in our partners, we are actually more free to point out those that trouble us. Confrontation is an invitation to look at oneself honestly. This process is always easier when we know that our positive qualities have not been forgotten by our partner who confronts. Now, instead of idealizing the beloved or his or her qualities, we learn to prize the commitment we have made to a life together. By reassuring one another that our focus is on a lifelong journey, more than on personal qualities frozen in time, we are each free to find romantic renewal over the seasons of our relationship.

Exaggeration of real or imagined qualities can become the dreams and life-planning of the future. Loving couples know how to dream real dreams. They know how to envision their first home, their first child, a special trip, or retirement way down the road. Romance is largely a state of mind. If we can unintentionally exaggerate the imputed qualities of a beloved during romantic love, we can surely create intentional visions of the future during mature love. These visions may change, but mature lovers seldom fret, for the meaning in creating a dream, more than the dream itself, marks true love.

Secret codes, private meanings, and special language can become the memories, words, and phrases which make our relationship unique. Romance continues over time when we discover new nicknames and special touches for one another. Love relationships that endure do not need to lose their reliance on symbols to convey meaning. If anything, we expand our common base of facial expressions, favorite TV shows, and rituals to signal feelings and thoughts to one another. There are signals for dinner and there are signals for lovemaking. There are signals for "it's time to go home" and there are signals for good old-fashioned flirting. Romantic feelings are often ignited by these special codes and language.

If romance can truly be refueled and renewed in this fashion, why do so many loving couples crash and burn—often ending up in a therapist's office? Why do so many people find themselves wounded and bedraggled and wondering what went wrong? How could something so wonderful suddenly be gone?

In these painful times, we actually grieve the *loss of an experience* much more than the *loss of a person*. In romantic love, we believe that we are entitled to a romantic experience that will mysteriously endure on its own. We shouldn't have to do anything ourselves to sustain this bliss. What a deal! We do nothing, yet expect our partner to do it all. Then, when we slam into the wall of disenchantment, we end up blaming the other person for somehow taking away the experience. In these somber moments, we learn a number of important caveats about romantic love.

Romance: Its Sorcery

Romantic love is an enchanting experience. Like any land of enchantment, romantic love offers us a movie screen upon which we can create our wildest scenes, idolize our favorite actors, project our most cherished dreams, and edit out our worst fears. However, we are destined to discover that these experiences are only strips of celluloid in a can, no matter how real they may seem to be when they feed through the projector and the light casts them as larger-than-life images:

1. Romantic love is destined to fade in intensity. Disenchantment in love in inevitable. It is appropriate. And it is required ... as a necessary developmental phase in every important relationship. Disenchantment is not a sign that a love relationship has failed. In fact, any relationship is guaranteed to fail without the transformation of disenchantment. Even after years of marriage, when we think our relationship has successfully grown beyond the hearts-and-flowers of romance, we can discover that we have been operating under the influence of romantic illusions—those deeply embedded needs and beliefs that prevent real intimacy and commitment. Disenchantment is the shattering of these illusions.

2. People often fall in love with love. As a culture, we have come to idealize the process of falling in love with love rather than actually loving the beloved. We are enthralled with the experience itself. Not to have been in love by age twenty is painful; by age thirty, catastrophic; and by age forty, cataclysmic! Some of the most tortured individuals I see are those who have not experienced the sense of enchantment that we call being in love.

We somehow fail to see that romance is a separate dimension from love itself. Romance is on its own track. Though they may be heading in the same general direction, and even overlay one another for short periods of time, romance is quite distinct, quite separate, from love. But although our pursuit of romance is natural, our pursuit of romantic love is ridiculous.

Romance is exciting, even for the briefest of moments. Our need for romance, for this spark of excitement, cannot be denied. If we cannot create it with our beloved, we will seek it elsewhere. Affairs offer us either the hope of reexperiencing romance or the hope of finding a new romantic partner. In the former case, it is necessary to shift this natural need for romance back toward the "truly" beloved one. In the latter, it is necessary to debunk the notion that true love lies elsewhere. Such lovers waste years searching endlessly for the perfect romantic experience which they erroneously believe depends somehow on the perfect partner! They never find it, of course.

3. Romantic love perpetuates extreme polarities in our attitudes about life, people, and human events. When we idealize one another, we usher in the divine with all of its polarized truths. God is all loving ... as is our beloved. God is all righteous ... as is our beloved. God is all goodness ... as is our beloved. It is one thing for a divine being to live up to such grand notions and quite another for a human being to do so! Yet we set ourselves up in the everyday dialogue of romantic love. Take time to read another love note by one of my clients:

> Bill, you are the most special person in my life. It scares me to realize how much I love you. This is all so new and exciting. I never knew I was capable of feeling this way about another person. You are truly an inspiration ... a wonder to behold. You have a supreme presence which comforts me and gives me hope. You are absolutely the most intelligent, beautiful, and gifted man I have ever met. Thanks for coming into my life! You *always* seem to make me happy and smile, no matter how down I might be. This is something Sam [her husband] was *never* able to do. Pretty amazing, don't you think?

> Lyla

Romantic love is "pretty amazing," don't you think? Look how divine Bill appears to be. He is an "inspiration ... a wonder to behold." He possesses a "supreme presence" and is the "most intelligent, beautiful, and gifted man" Lyla has ever seen. As if these divine ascriptions are not enough, Bill has an uncanny ability to *always* make her happy. Will he *always* be capable of doing so? Fat chance!

Lyla is destined to crash and burn, just as she has done with her husband, Sam. She will continue to crash and burn as she loses herself in extremisms about life, people, and human events. We will learn more about these processes in the chapters ahead.

4. Romantic love, as an involuntary and conscious experience, cannot possibly sustain the most conscious institution of our time—

marriage. Romantic love *happens* to us. It is a powerful visceral experience that hurdles us into an altered state of consciousness. Whether we consider this to be a trick of nature or a case of divine intervention, we are nonetheless caught by surprise by its intensity. We do not placidly say, "This man is a likely candidate to sweep me off my feet, absorb my every thought, and turn my heart into a 350 cc V8 engine with overhead cams." We don't choose to fall in love. We are catapulted into love.

Romantic love is storybook love which has been passed down to us, unconsciously, as a culture. But what do we do in the face of vacillating careers, indebtedness, and children? What force drives us then? This is where romantic love fails miserably. Romantic love offers few resources as we attempt to fashion strategies to deal with the awesome complexity of our lives. This is when we realize that we need conscious love, that mature commitment to one another in the face of great responsibilities and challenges. Love cannot be maintained without this conscious commitment. If we are merely content, or conditioned, to play out our prescribed roles, we will discover a bitter truth: love must end before it begins.

5. Romantic love will never serve as a reasonable basis for the renewal of wholeness which we all desparately seek. Each of us enters any new relationship with an inherent incompleteness. We may not be loved enough, bright enough, assertive enough, or courageous enough. Our beloved offers us hope that we may somehow be completed. If we can capture her attention, ensnare her affection, and compel her devotion, we will somehow get all the love, raw intelligence, assertiveness, and courage we will ever need to face life. Then we will feel complete!

In this way love is like a religious experience. Curiously enough, the word *religion* actually means "to join" or "link" (from the prefix *re*, meaning "again," and *ligere*, meaning "to join, to connect, to unite, to blend, or to couple"). We are convinced that by linking up with our beloved we will gain the necessary molecular mass to freely orbit in a world of opposing forces. This power, this strength, this mass can only come from linking up. Through romantic love, the banality of our lives is somehow transformed into something exciting, even mystical. Our mundane world is somehow "linked" once again to a blissful world which usually belongs only to the Gods.

We must awaken from this dreamlike world. Though the seeds for personal growth and harmony may lie in this vast realm of unconscious dreams, true germination and development does not occur until we wake up to experience a mature loving relationship. Our deep desire to know a peak religious experience can never be fulfilled by romantic love. Only mature, covenant love can do so.

As I'm sure you can tell, I have grown skeptical about our fascination with romantic love. Perhaps I have had to get "down and dirty" with my clients too many times. Perhaps I have seen too many victims ... too many people who believed they had it all and then lost it all. Perhaps I have seen too many people repeat their errors over and over and over again. Not just plunging into one relationship after another for the wrong reasons—it's worse than that! The big error is *leaving* one relationship after another for the wrong reasons. Just when mature love can be discovered, we leave, believing that everything has been lost. We leave psychologically and, eventually, we leave physically. We don't know how to stay and make things better.

Paraphrasing T. S. Eliot's *Four Quartets*, we might describe the reality of love as "A condition of complete simplicity, costing not less than everything!" "Costing not less than everything" implies work. All work implies conscious effort ... being awake ... having a deliberate focus ... having control. Mature love requires work, romantic love does not. Perhaps part of the lure of romantic love is that we are not expected to do very much ... We are not expected to be very conscious, to be in control. Indeed, romantic love may be the one last opportunity Western man allows himself to be out of control. As Robert Johnson points out:

> The one power left in life that destroys our illusion of control, that forces a man to see that there is something beyond his understanding and his control, is romantic love. Formal religion and the church have long since ceased to threaten Western man's illusion of control. He either reduces his religion to platitudes or ignores it altogether. He seeks his soul neither in religion nor in spiritual experience nor in his inner life; but he looks for that transcendence, that mystery, that revelation, in woman. He *will* fall in love. (Johnson 1983, 58)

As a culture, we have learned to "consciously" value the experience of romantic love, but once the process begins to unfold, we are "out of our minds" until we "come to our senses." We "willingly" allow ourselves to be overcome by the passion of romantic love. But for love to endure, we must be "willfully conscious" ... we must be willing to demonstrate mastery of this great mystery.

To move beyond the inevitable impasse of disenchantment, each partner in a loving couple must employ a powerful arsenal of skills. These are learnable skills which not only will bring us greater satisfaction in love, but are guaranteed to help us solve other problems in life as well. There is only one criterion for learning these skills: We must be willing to make a conscious commitment to our partner. Unless we do so, we will continue to crash and burn in the painful fires of disenchantment.

2

Disenchantment: Ashes and Ruin

The universal human yearning is for something
permanent, enduring, without shadow of change.

Willa Cather

Change is constant ... Life is cyclical ... To everything there is a season. Nothing stays the same, yet there is a natural human tendency to cling to anything which is known, be it blissful or painful. When we learn to let go of things as they are and anticipate the inevitable changes that will occur, we are infinitely more free to live each moment more fully.

The starkness of winter gives way to the colorful blooms of spring. Menopause signals the inevitable "change of season" that women are destined to experience. Our days follow the inevitable pulse of circadian rhythms and lunar tides. Tadpoles become frogs and caterpillars transform into magnificent monarch butterflies. And how awesome to consider the powerful forces that exert evolutionary changes upon the planet itself—not to mention our species! Who can doubt that nature—that life itself—has its cycles?

We can't hold on to spring, menstruation, childhood, or lunar tides for very long—nor can we preserve the idyllic wonders of romantic love. Love also must follow rhythms, experience cycles, change seasons. The romantic forces which attract and bond two lovers *inevitably* must encounter resistance ... the painful experience that I call disenchantment. Our illusions must shatter!

For many of us, disenchantment is an impasse. Our relationships, once a source of such delight and hope, end in confusion, hurt, and anger. But disenchantment need not signal the end of a loving relationship. In fact, it can be the catalyst that transforms the ephemeral pleasures of romance into the deep fulfillment of a well-grounded, enduring, committed love. In truth, romantic love *must* end before mature covenant love can begin.

There are four inescapable reasons why romantic love cannot go on indefinitely. I call these:

- the tarnishing effect
- the eye-opening effect
- the distraction effect
- the existential effect

The Tarnishing Effect

The tarnishing effect demonstrates how our thoughts are distorted by the powerful force of our emotions. The *singularity* of our hearts during romantic love actually creates *duality* in our minds, a polarization of our perceptions and beliefs that secretly sets the disenchantment process in motion even when we are just falling in love. Our beloved is not just a sensitive man—he is the most sensitive man we have ever known! She is not simply hard-working—she is the most industrious woman we have ever met! We somehow find the best, the most, the fastest, the smartest, or the funniest person around.

These extremes arise from our deep longing for wholeness and perfection. They are the unconscious projections of our most important unmet needs, the sum total of our unfinished life experiences. At a profound, visceral level, we expect our beloved to complete all the incompleteness of our lives. To do so, he or she must be cast in idyllic terms—extreme terms–which somehow convince us that we are making the right choice.

Of course, the "right choice" is the evocation of an *illusion*—a vision created about someone else from which loving feelings and actions flow. In beginning love, we create positive illusions that may describe either our beloved ("She is the most beautiful woman I have ever known") or ourselves ("I am a great lover; I am a gifted communicator"). These illusions may be central to self-concept and identity ("She is a person of integrity") or more peripheral ("He is a wonderful dancer"). But such illusions are destined to waver and fade—to become tarnished as we experience the true complexity of this other human being that we have chosen as our beloved.

It is ironic that during the process of disenchantment we come to believe that our most prized "other" is actually the *absolute opposite* of who or what we previously believed. We swing on the pendulum of extremes from the idyllic to the blasphemous. That same most responsible person is now the most irresponsible S.O.B. we have ever known! That most attentive lover is now the most inattentive, aloof iceburg we have ever met! In truth, both extremes are illusions. In the former case, the bliss and rapture of romantic love create an overly positive perspective. In the latter case, the hurt and anger of disenchantment create an overly negative perspective. With mature, covenant love we learn to create a more moderate perspective that is fashioned from more substantial data than our projected fantasies about one another.

The Eye-Opening Effect

As love matures, we not only realize more about our real partners, but we also learn more about our real needs. It is inevitable that we eventually realize that

- Our partners *possess* certain obnoxious qualities or traits that we were not aware of in the dawn of our relationships.
- Our partners *lack* certain constructive qualities or traits that we need for an enduring love bond.

Somehow these qualities—or the lack of them—either weren't noticed or didn't seem important during romantic love. We discover these things only after the first flush of romance has passed. Truly an eye-opening experience!

Has this ever happened to you? You are sitting in a movie theater, deeply engrossed in a suspenseful and dramatic scene. Suddenly, your stomach gurgles, first quietly, and then with the gusto of a Hawaiian volcano. You start fantasizing about roast beef or cheesecake and lose track of the movie's plot. What you experience during the next ten minutes is a vacillating shift in attention. One moment the movie actors are *figure* (that is, they are your focal point) while your hunger pangs are *ground* (meaning in the background of your awareness). The next moment, figure and ground reverse in your attention. This process continues, of course, until you get up and buy yourself a jumbo bag of popcorn.

This shifting perceptual focus from figure to ground occurs with all our senses as well as our higher levels of cortical functioning. What we perceive or believe always occurs within the context of other perceptions or beliefs. We hear our child's cry, even though many other people are talking, or pick out the melody of a violin over the rest of the orchestra. We notice our friend's beautiful turquoise rug and miss the lovely backyard view through the plateglass window. We see the disfiguring scar on a new acquaintance's cheek, but only notice his smile when we have become friends.

What do you see when you look at the figure on the next page? If you are like most people, you will first notice a young woman looking over her right shoulder. Now, if you concentrate a bit more, you will discover an older woman, commonly referred to as the "mother-in-law." Notice that you are actively selecting what features of this drawing to pay attention to: first, the feather, then the hair, then the chin, and so on. Now that you have found both the wife and the mother-in-law, can you hold onto the image without flip-flopping back and forth? This is difficult because our perceptions are not static. *Perceiving is an active search for the most meaningful interpretation of information.*

Our beliefs about one another are not static either. What we believe about one another is also an active search for the most meaningful interpretation of information. As loved ones spend more time with one another, they collect more data and use it to form interpretations about one another. When a boy hears his father say "I love you," he must sort through the hugs and the spankings, the smiles and the frowns, and the baseball games with and without Dad in the stands before he accepts this belief for himself.

Lovers must do the same. What we notice about one another during early love is dramatically different from what we focus on during disenchantment—or even mature love, for that matter: Our attention is drawn by sparkling eyes during romantic love, dirty laundry during disenchantment, and tender forgiveness during covenant love. Each phase of love is a truly wondrous discovery, an eye-opening experience, which welcomes the curious traveler who is patient enough to make the journey.

The Distraction Effect

Like morning dew, the exclusivity of early love is destined to evaporate before our eyes. The business of life dramatically interferes with the quality time we once enjoyed as a romantic couple. In our drive to build homes, families, and careers, we end up driving ourselves apart. Our human relationships are being pushed and pounded by technological advances, accelerated lifestyles and what has colloquially been termed the "rat race." Since 1971, leisure time has shrunk by 37 percent and the average workweek has jumped from 41 to 47 hours. As *Time* magazine notes:

> If all this continues, time could end up being to the '90s what money was to the '80s. In fact, for the callow yuppies of Wall Street, with their abundant salaries and meager freedom, leisure time is the one thing they find hard to buy. Their lives are so busy that merely to give someone the time of day seems an act of charity. They order gourmet takeout because microwave dinners have become just too much trouble. Canary sales are up (low-maintenance pets); Beaujolais nouveau is booming (a wine one needn't wait for). "I gave up pressure for Lent," says a theater director in Manhattan. If only it were that easy. (24 April 1989, 58)

My clients Tim and Ann provide a perfect example of this phenomenon. Only their financial success makes them untypical of the couples I see. Tim is a twenty-eight-year-old entrepreneur who started one clothing store that soon mushroomed to three. Ann, a top executive in the cable industry, earns a hearty six-figure salary and receives bonuses of as much as $40,000 at a pop. They drive fast cars, take lavish trips, and have more bank accounts than most people have friends! Yet, as a couple, they are miserable.

"I never see her!" grumbles Tim as he considers the fact that Ann travels around the United States twelve to fifteen days a month. But Ann retorts, "If Tim would stop spawning clothing stores as if they were million dollar fisheries, maybe we could get something going. We never have time for love, and I doubt if he still finds me attractive any more."

Most American marriages are in a tragic state. For 57 percent of all married couples in the United States, both partners must work to eke out a living. We are no longer keeping up with the Joneses—we are just trying to keep up with each other! When we sluggishly pull into the driveway at day's end, we order pizza with pepperoni and extra cheese (assuming our eight-year-old, latchkey kids haven't already prepared dinner for us) and pay our "family helper," who has managed to shop for our groceries, sort our laundry, pick up our dry cleaning, take our kids to soccer practice and ballet, and even turn down our beds. Single-parent households and couples who can't afford a "family helper," are really up the creek.

Inevitably, the counseling process reveals a couple who have forsaken their time together for a lifestyle that pushes and presses and demands entirely too much of them. Intimacy becomes a scheduled event, rather than a naturally occurring experience. We plan our sexual encounters, evenings out with friends, and yearly vacations to fit into a blurry-eyed blitz of soccer tournaments, summer camps, and professional commitments that never seem to end.

The way out for some is to sell the home, give up the careers, grab the kids, and head for Colorado—without jobs in hand—as a couple I know are doing. This is too daring for most of us, who must be content with carving out time for Sunday brunch and private evening walks. We must constantly dam back the distractions that dilute our values and drown out intimacy. And very few elements of mature love can be expressed if we are limited, by our own hellish lifestyles, to milliseconds of interaction with one another!

The Existential Effect

Ultimately, all of us must come to realize that we are alone and mortal. At its best, marriage is a safe harbor within which we can attempt to reconcile life's most painful incongruities. However, the inevitable realization of our individual human dilemma may estrange us from one another as we search for the meaning of our separate lives.

In the beginning, we enter our love bonds with the infinite hope that all our dreams will be met in an exclusive arena created by God himself. We see marriage as an opportunity to reconcile all of the crucial dichotomies of our lives—man versus woman, mind versus body, good versus evil, autonomy versus dependence, thinking versus feeling, love versus hate, controlling versus controlled, and included versus excluded. Where else can we risk being known to such degree? Where else can we find ourselves, discover who we are? Where else can we allow our thoughts, feelings, and actions to run their full course, through the seasons and cycles of our lives?

Yet we are destined to realize that no person, regardless of his or her special powers and gifts, can complete what will never be completed within us. When we cannot synthesize or reconcile the emotionally charged dichotomies of our lives, we crash and burn. When ambiguity cannot be reduced to certainty, we withdraw our commitments from one another, believing that our sense of neglect and abandon mandates such action. Wanting it all, we desperately fear a profound psychological and spiritual death. That unspoken and unconscious yearning for wholeness or completeness that pervades our psyche is now revealed for what it is—a pipedream, a tunnel-vision, an illusion. Thinking we have been duped, we blame each other and believe the perfect union must be elsewhere. Instead of working on the integration of cherished hopes and shattered dreams, we seem wrecklessly programmed to throw them away and start all over again—someplace else with someone else.

But no matter who we turn to, we cannot stop attempting to reconcile opposites. There is an inherent quest for order, purpose, and predictability in our lives. Our salvation as individuals, as well as a species, depends on our capacity to balance meaning with confusion, harmony with disharmony, love with hate, aloneness with togetherness, and life with death.

Marriage, I believe, is our most sacred haven—a special place in which we create a union to reconcile life's extremes. There is no clear path. We must each be pathfinders. We must each be willing to transcend our solitary uniqueness in order to find a place of balance and reconciliation in our coupled lives. We must each be willing to give in order to receive, to receive in order to give, to hate in order to love, to love in order to hate, and so on. And if our disenchantment leads us to turn away from each other, we miss the chance to find what Sheldon Kopp describes as life's "amalgam of compromises," which is the very best any of us could possibly hope for! The search will be hard work. For a start, we must begin to see things for what they are! We must rip off our blinders, hold up our mirrors, and take a long, honest look at the hurt, anger and resentment that underlie our disenchantment.

A Case in Point: The Nine Signs of Disenchantment

What does disenchantment look like? What are the telltale signs of a couple in distress? A number of such signs can best be explained by telling you about one such couple: Gail and Don.

I still remember Gail's first visit. She appeared for her appointment wearing a crisp white blouse and ankle-length plaid skirt. She seemed eager to tell her tale.

"Don and I have been married for about three years, Dr. Bugen, and I am depressed as hell. I don't know why I am so depressed, and I don't know why I am in this damn marriage."

Gail told me that in the beginning she was attracted to Don's upward mobility. His architectural firm was booming. He seemed stable, secure, and devoted to his career. Surely he would be devoted to her as well. And, in sharp contrast to her first husband, Don was very attentive.

As I got to know more about them, I learned that in the spring of their relationship Don saw Gail as bright, articulate, and vivacious. Always agreeable, she was eager to please. She seemed able to charm anyone she met. These traits made her a highly successful salesperson. A clever entrepreneur by day; a wanton sex goddess by night! Don figured he had it made.

Within two years of tying the knot, Gail came to see Don as an undependable con artist. He was slick and silver-tongued with others, but strangely distant from her. The more she protested his avoidance, the more he seemed to withdraw. He insisted that his long hours away from home were necessary in order to sustain his success as an architect. This physical and emotional vacuum only reinforced Gail's long-standing belief that she was excluded, shut out of other's lives. This belief had taken root during her first marriage to a physician, who had also created a work schedule that gave him little time at home.

On his part, Don grew to see Gail as a runaway freight train. She was constantly nagging him about too little time together, too little money, too many possessions, too many drugs, and too many friends. She was as demanding as his father had been many years before, when he ran away from home at sixteen. He had learned very early on that he couldn't please anyone. Escape, away from people, would be the answer—escape into drugs, escape into sailing, escape into work!

At that first session, Gail brought along an audiocassette tape: "I knew I would have difficulty telling you about Don and me, so I talked Don into letting me tape one of our Sunday bitch sessions. I think this is typical of what happens to us, and I'd like you to listen to it."

That evening I settled comfortably into a lounge chair with tape recorder in hand and once again found evidence of the deep disenchantment so common in troubled relationships.

1. A specific triggering event. Disenchantment begins when one partner doesn't fulfill the other's expectations, causing frustration and disappointment. Every love relationship, no matter how compatible the partners are, encounters countless situations that may trigger frustration or disappointment. This is inevitable, since no lover can be a man or woman for all seasons!

"Don, I found a glass in the car which reeked of alcohol," Gail said in the first part of their taped Sunday bout. *"Drinking and driving is one of the worst things you can do ... YOU don't think that there is anything wrong with it. Drinking and driving is a part of your life ... You had parents who abused the stuff and you abuse the stuff yourself ... You didn't learn that drinking and driving is bad. If anything, your parents encouraged drinking."*

"Uh-huh. I agree," Don responded.

Finding Don's glass in the car triggered Gail's *disappointment.* Disappointment is a thought, while frustration is a feeling. Both may characterize our response to a disenchantment-triggering event.

For instance, how do you feel when you prepare a wonderful meal and your spouse is three hours late? How do you feel when he or she forgets your birthday, an anniversary, or Valentine's Day? Do you ever get frustrated when your amorous advances are rebuffed? And let's not forget the weekend porcupine who sticks his face in the TV during a football game when you need some feedback to work through an employment crisis.

It may help to remember two important phrases in conflict management: "I am disappointed that ... " and "I feel frustrated that ... " If you are able to identify triggering situations early and talk them out using these two expressions, you will not build up to the volcanic eruptions which typify most lovers' spats. We'll talk more about disappointment and frustration in chapter 7.

2. Reciprocalness. Disenchantment is mutual. Both partners experience it, although one may experience it before the other does. In fact, disenchantment in one partner can trigger disenchantment in the other.

"I'm not going to be on your case all the time about drinking," Gail tried to back off. *"But it's just that I feel differently about drinking than you do."*

Don reacted: "Gail, I feel the same about people bitching and swearing at me. See, my parents discouraged that. But in your house it was 'damn' this or 'damn' that."

"Bullshit!" Gail snapped. *"I don't like bitching or swearing!"*

"One other thing," Don returned. *"Every one of you would go into the room and slam the door. To you, that's normal! I was just drunk!"*

Gail hears her disappointment; Don hears his own. Neither truly understands the other's plea for help. Instead, they are caught in an enmeshed web of hurt, which becomes more entangled over time.

When patterns of frustration and disappointment reoccur in love relationships, it is likely that both partners are keeping score. If couples are to untangle their reciprocal patterns of disenchantment, each partner must own up to three assumptions:

First, if I have been disenchanted for some time, it is likely that my partner has been as well.

Second, if my partner is partly responsible for not meeting my needs, it then follows that I am partly responsible for not meeting his or her needs.

Third, it is absolutely necessary to recognize unmet needs in a relationship in order to sustain the well-being of the bond.

3. Underlying themes. Ninety percent of the hurt and anger that disenchanted lovers experience mirror deeper resentments or "themes" in the relationship which have little or nothing to do with the immediate situation. Together, we might refer to hurt, anger, and resentment as the "disenchantment triad."

Hurt and anger are the "big gun" emotional byproducts which result *after* repeated frustrations and disappointments have occurred and noticeable behavior *patterns* have emerged. However, resentment is not a feeling, as many believe. Anger and hurt are feelings, but resentment, like disappointment, is a *thought*. We commonly say, "I feel resentment about such and such." But think about that for a second. Our resentments are actually well-memorized storage centers.

Gail: "Well, you get mad, too! You've ruined many an evening when you just walked out of a room after having one drink and hearing my protest, particularly when you ask me to drive so you can drink some more!"

Don: "I'm the one who came back into the room ten minutes ago and told you I just thought about me and my drinking and realized how destructive it was. I'm admitting it! I'm the one who brought it up! I'm the one who said, 'Hell, I just saw this lousy pattern which branded these two people ... The pain, the anguish, the distance in this house, instead of dealing with it.' I'm aware of this! That's why I brought it up!"

Gail: *"So you want to control your drinking?"*

Don: *"Hell yes, I want to control my drinking."*

Gail: *"Are you recognizing that you have a drinking problem?"*

"Oh God, Gail, YES! But do you recognize that you have a problem with arguing?"

"NO!" she shouts back.

Resentments mean not giving in.

Men are often very good at remembering their resentments, but very poor at identifying their feelings. Although Don recognizes the anguish and pain of their relationship, it is more common for men, when they do identify a feeling, to express it as anger. Very rarely will a man admit that he feels hurt because of something his lover did or didn't do. This is quite significant, since hurt underlies all anger. Until both men and women can identify—and discuss—their painful hurts, lovers are likely to remain stuck with their angry barbs.

Once you have stored up enough anger, you can play the "I remember" game. "I remember when you ripped the upholstery with your hunting knife." "I remember when you left me sitting in a hotel bar for four hours." "I remember when you went fishing for two weeks during my ninth month of pregnancy."

People often tell me that they have the right to express anger when they feel it. This is a ridiculous notion, since anger only shocks, devalues and alienates the other person. If we would be more assertive in expressing our frustrations and disappointments earlier, the intense build-up of anger might be avoided. Fortunately, when we finally allow ourselves to become vulnerable by sharing our hurts, something remarkable happens—anger melts away.

4. Negative cycles of behavior. Disenchanted lovers often engage in self-defeating cycles that feed off one another. Coming home late leads to loss of sexual desire, which leads to coming home late, and so on.

"Do you realize," Don pointed out, *"that these two things feed each other? The more we argue, the more I drink, the more we argue."*

These negative cycles are all fueled by the disenchantment triad of resentment, anger, and hurt. Each cycle is a modern day corollary of biblical metaphors: an eye for an eye, a tooth for a tooth. Such cycles may have represented justice in our biblical past, but hardly heal our present-day heartaches and despair. Instead of working toward harmony, lovers will often begin to play the tit-for-tat game. From other couples I have worked with I've heard: "If you don't pick up the kids, I won't make dinner." "If you don't stop smoking, I won't stop drinking." "If you continue to work overtime, I'll make a showing at every happy hour I can find." "If you choose to sleep rather than make love, I will find another lover."

5. Caricaturization. When caught up in a negative cycle, disenchanted lovers polarize their attitudes toward each other, deliberately distorting their mental images of each other.

George Kelly, a one-time engineer who later migrated into psychology, espoused the idea that all human beings strive to make sense of their personal experience, and that their success in doing so largely depends upon the language structures they adopt. Each of us labels our experiences, in a positive or negative direction, along a continuum. Each continuum is best understood as a polarity. Note how Gail's experience of Don has polarized:

Gail screamed at Don: "I think you misinterpret me a lot. You never really talk to me."

"Oh, this should be good," Don bellowed.

"It's that ... that ... I mean it's like ... well, not arguments. You just always misinterpret. When I am on the phone, you always know why. You are always drunk when you talk to me. You never remember what we talk about," Gail said.

Don *never* really talks. He *always* misinterprets. He *never* remembers. To break the disenchantment cycle, we must shatter our polarized views of one another, and rediscover that gray is okay.

6. Scientific research. Like mad scientists, disenchanted lovers look for any data that support their negative beliefs about each other. It is never enough to merely label our lovers in negative terms. We must be able to support this belief with new data. Each of us, on a daily basis, is conducting countless experiments—just like scientists, well-trained in the scientific method. Each experiment attempts to support a hypothesis or theory:

Theory 1: My lover does not like my body.
Theory 2: My wife cares more about the kids and her job than about me.
Theory 3: My husband is an alcoholic.
Theory 4: My wife is insensitive.
Theory 5: My husband only appreciates me after we make love.

Each of these theories requires close observation over time. Theory 1, for instance, was recently put forth by one of my clients, who first informed her husband of this belief during a counseling session. (This hidden-theory technique is quite handy, since our partner, without feedback, can continue to unwittingly support our biases without knowing what he or she is doing.) This client was able to provide voluminous data. She told her husband how far away he slept, how often he had initiated love-making during the prior month, when he had touched her breasts, and actual dates and times that he "stopped reading the newspaper to notice those Hollywood hussies on TV," instead of her.

"Aren't you the wonderful party animal!" Gail asserts.

"What are you talking about?" Don wonders.

"Don, you know damn well that you have been putting moves on any of my

friends who would be stupid enough to listen to your garbage. I've actually watched you pour drinks for Mary and Stephanie and then, for an added nightcap, give each of them a hug."

"Gail, if I had your fantasy mind, I'd become a movie producer. What a bunch of crap."

Note the evidence that Gail has compiled to support her case that Don is flirting with her girlfriends. Her theory helps us understand her plight more clearly. Don has been avoiding her, turning instead to his booze. Gail is not feeling very special to Don, and her jealousy regarding other women reflects her hurt and distrust.

Beware that your observations may be too selective, so that you see only what you want—or fear—to see! We will learn more about this process in chapter 8 on getting stuck.

7. Personal indictments. Disenchanted lovers often attack one another with "You are ... " statements rather than admit their own needs. Every therapist knows how difficult it is for clients to say "I feel ... ," "I need ... ," "I want ... ," or "I am...." We feel so vulnerable when we reference ourselves by saying "I." How different it could be! Instead of preparing for war, we might instead prepare for clarity and understanding. We might say, "Bill, try to hear me out. I need more affection from you. I want to feel you hug me when I come home. I feel frustrated when you don't ... ," Instead, anger and resentment build to a crescendo that obliterates good communication. Lovers go on the attack:

- We negatively label our partners with statements like: "You are a callous son-of-a-bitch!"
- We ignore feelings.
- We show boredom when he or she is talking to us.
- We do not give eye contact.
- We change the topic.
- We use incomplete sentences.
- We give irrelevant responses.
- We show inappropriate affect (like laughing).
- We make frequent judgments.
- We point our finger, fold our arms, sit rigidly, lean away, stare away, or sit far away.
- We say, "I didn't hear a word you said!"

Without a clear understanding of Gail's need for reassurance about his matchmaking, Don simply packages the feelings that he sees in her and labels them as anger.

"Don't you understand," Gail pleaded, "I know you won't, but don't you understand what you are doing? You don't even know what you are doing!"

"Do you know what I'm doing?" Don responded. "I don't think so."

"I don't know what you are doing," she returned.

"I don't even think you know how this came about. I think that it's just your anger ... ," he replied.

8. Mistaking symptoms for real problems. Excessive drinking, eating, spending, sleeping, and arguing aren't the real problems in a disenchanted relationship. They simply mask the real issues. We escape into activities like these in order to somehow numb ourselves to an unbearable pain—the pain of unmet needs.

Escape patterns usually emerge after we have created "themes" about our lovers. These themes express the polarized and negative generalities we use to caricature our loved ones. Familiar themes I have heard include: "She doesn't care!" "He is totally irresponsible!" "He lacks ambition!" "She smothers me with demands or complaints!" Rather than work through these themes, which are always lying in wait, people go shopping, get drunk, watch too much TV, read excessively, make chocolate cakes, or go to sleep!

For Gail and Don, the alcohol and the arguing mask underlying pain that they dance around rather than examine with clarity. Their themes are "Gail, you control too much of my life!" and "Don, you are neither responsible nor loving as my husband!"

9. Mutually exclusive blame. Disenchanted lovers blame each other for screwing up the relationship, rather than recognizing that both are responsible for mending it. Blaming, like anger and resentment, only separates lovers from one another. Blaming our partners, if that is our style, entitles us to be part of the problem rather than the solution. Until we are willing to accept our role in making things worse, we will never accept our role in making things better.

Couples have esteem, just as individuals do. Successful love relationships are successful over time because of mutual esteem. Mutual esteem is the capacity to share, not only in life's blessings and joys, but its misfortunes and hassles as well. Relationships continue to grow over time, not because they lack their share of problems, but because they mutually resolve their share of problems. Often, after a bitter-sweet argument, couples find themselves making passionate love, an excitation partly aroused by the satisfaction of having intensely worked through a problem. When we experience mutual esteem in our bond, we are truly sharing in all that binds us close. If we forego this collaborative view, simply because we think we are "right," then we are "wrong" in our estimation of closeness.

Gail made the first move by lowering her voice and letting her real feelings come to the surface: "I don't have a sense of myself anymore. I don't really have a sense of me and that's real scarey, and I don't … I don't feel real secure."

And Don, instead of taking advantage of his opportunity to move in on Gail's vulnerability, tenderly acknowledged her fear and his own responsibility. "Why don't we do this, Gail. Why don't we plot a course. That will give us a sense of security so we'll know where we are going."

Ernest and Julio Gallo have assured us that they will serve no wine before its time. Lovers, too, must learn not to serve solutions before their time. Only when we fully recognize the barbs of resentment and bitterness that have poisoned our relationships will we be ready to grow into mature, covenant love.

Expressing our resentments is the first precondition for working through disenchantment. Understanding each other's resentments allows us to forgive. The second precondition is the willingness and capacity to express caring. Receiving each other's caring motivates us to improve our relationship. Unless we and our partner can meet these two preconditions, we will not succeed.

Couples can love only when they learn how to forgive one another and begin to care for one another. The "portraits of desire" that we desperately cling to in the beginning can be fashioned anew if we know how to do so. Certainly, there are difficulties along the way. Our resolve to continue this journey will require ingenuity and solidarity of purpose.

3

Mature Love: The Covenant

Two roads diverged in the woods,
And I took the one less traveled by,
And that has made all the difference.

Robert Frost

Commitment is nonnegotiable.

Everything in a loving relationship is up for grabs except for that special pact that each of you will not abandon the other. Such a pact or covenant is easily threatened by the consuming outrage, quiet desperation, or detached numbness of disenchantment. For many of us, commitment is like a winning hand, a full house or royal flush that we play close to the vest on the condition that our partners give us what we want. But this puts the cart before the horse. It is perfectly normal to expect our partners to change, but *commitment must precede expectation.* We must extend to our partners the reassurance that, although we may have painful grievances about our relationships, we are going to stay in order to work them out. Since many of us are secretly afraid that we are not worthy enough to be loved, it is most comforting to know that we won't be abandoned as soon as disenchantment begins to take its toll on our relationships.

In most relationships, the signs of broken commitments inevitably surface. I am not thinking of the more dramatic events, like affairs or trial separations. Usually commitment dies more slowly than this—not with a bang but a whimper. Our commitment dies in those daily moments when we meet our partners with bland indifference, passive resistance, or more open rebellion. In each of these quietly decisive moments, we make the choice *not* to commit. We say to ourselves:

"Why *should* I come home right after work?"

"I know she is worried about driving in the snow, but I sure as hell won't go out of my way for her!"

"She puts her career and the kids before me, so why should I respond to her lovemaking?"

I am amazed at how perceptive, vigilant, and imaginative spouses can be in detecting broken commitments, even when an objective accounting by a Big Eight firm wouldn't justify the claim. Examples are often subtle; we leave the kitchen light on, we stop attending church, we only call home once on a two-day conference trip. Less subtle examples include maintaining a separate checking or savings account or staying late at Happy Hour with co-workers every Friday.

One female client, who had been rip-roaring mad for the preceding three years, could isolate the event when her husband actually "abandoned" her. She remembered her shock at discovering her multiple pregnancy, a feeling that mushroomed into fear and anger when her husband advocated keeping the pregnancy viable. Such a decision not only had implications for her physical health, but would lock her into a domestic role for many years. She had wanted an abortion, but his advocacy and eagerness in behalf of the two unborn fetuses won out. To her it was obvious that this meant that he was choosing the welfare of two strangers over her well-being. Given the risk factors associated with multiple births and her career aspirations, his insistence was an outrage which could not be forgiven.

For my client, this "clear abandonment" on her husband's part easily justified her own withdrawal from him—a response which perpetuated the inevitable downward cycle of disenchantment. The "less traveled road" in this instance, as with most disenchantments, is to transcend our immediate, intense *reaction* in order to find a more balanced, fair-minded *response*. This point seems reasonable enough ... unless we feel so wronged that we cannot shift our attention from the evil wrongdoer or the knot of resentments that harden our hearts and stiffen our necks. We insist on blaming our partners for all our pain and thereby missing an opportunity to look beyond—to look inward—to find something better. This chapter is about finding "something better" and is tied together by three premises:

Premise 1: Mature committed love begins when romance has palled and we find ourselves glaring daggers into each other's eyes.

Premise 2: Our capacity for mature, committed love is well established within our families by the time we reach eighteen.

Premise 3: Our commitment to renew our love is our most profound opportunity for personal and spiritual growth.

Let me comment briefly on each of these premises. First, I do not believe that a mature commitment can exist at the time of the marriage ceremony. The wedding vows we agree to—"for better or for worse, in sickness and in health, for richer or for poorer, till death do us part"—are blanket commitments based on illusions and blind faith. We can't possibly know about mature commitment until we experience the "worse," the "sickness," and the "poorer." On our wedding day, we actually are committing ourselves to the state of our love *at that time*. Marriage is a commitment to an already known and shared time and space; covenant love is a commitment to the kind of bridge building that can arch into the unknown and span both time and space.

Second, I believe that the psychological maturity needed for committed love results from the capacities that people bring to their relationships. Unfortunately, many of us are stuck in a developmental dead end—cornered by our biological impulses, our reflexive biases, and our fragmented experience of life. When we marry, most of us have not developed the characteristics of maturity. Most significantly, we are incapable of mature love because of wounds we experienced in our families during childhood. Most of us don't know how to love because we never learned how to love. We never saw mature love between our parents and never experienced it as children within our families. Our own parents didn't know how to love, and so were unable to teach us.

Third, the wounds of childhood can be healed when we use our love relationships as a context for renewal. This is a profound notion: *By committing ourselves to our partners when romantic love has faded, we actually can reclaim our own original wholeness.* We can embrace and cultivate those characteristics within ourselves which, though atrophied by early family life, allow commitment to take place. Unless we have these characteristics of personal wholeness, our relationships also cannot be whole. Thus, when we commit, we nurture our own spiritual healing as well as the healing of our relationships.

The Eight Characteristics of Committed Love

The capacity to love can be learned if we are willing to move through the immediate pain of disenchantment and evolve beyond our romantic longings. Mature, committed love begins when we shift our emphasis from meeting *personal* romantic needs to meeting *relationship* needs. Rather than continuing to seek out the novelty, excitement, and self-gratification that characterize romance, we must also focus on our equally important needs for familiarity, trust, and self-fulfillment. Novelty, excitement, and self-gratification need not be sacrificed to the "ho-hum" of a long-term relationship—"ho-hum" is evidence of disenchantment, not covenant love! Lovers in a mature, committed relationship simply shift their emphasis to create a balance between passion and affiliation, between attachment and interdependence.

For a loving relationship to endure, it must embody the following eight characteristics of covenant love:

1. A mutual balance of met needs
2. Other-directedness
3. Realistic values and expectations
4. Tolerance
5. Yearning to be known

6. Freedom to express all emotions
7. Separate identities
8. Transcendence of two separate selves into one identity

Let's take a closer look at each of these characteristics.

1. A mutual balance of met needs. *Both partners have needs of equal importance, both understand and accept those needs, and both are willing to meet those needs as often as possible.*

Loving couples find ways to meet each other's needs in an equitable fashion. Equitable does not mean *equal*, it means *fair*. One partner may have compromised more than the other—not because he or she is an inferior in the relationship, but because a fair resolution required compromise. Loving couples find equitable ways to share affection ("Can I have a massage tonight?"), vacation planning ("Since we went to Mexico last year, I'd like to go to Colorado this year!"), exercise schedules ("If you jog on Tuesdays and Thursdays, I can do aerobic dance on Mondays and Wednesdays"), household tasks ("Would you do the dishes tonight since I'm so tired?"), financial obligations ("I can put an extra $50 a month into savings; can you handle an extra $50 out of your salary, too?"), childrearing ("If you take the kids in the a.m., I'll be able to get them in the p.m., okay?"), and spiritual pathways ("I know you don't like organized religion, but it means a lot for you to go to Sunday services with me"). Each couple works out its own formula for sharing.

2. Other-directedness. *Each partner experiences meaning or pleasure from the other partner fulfilling his or her own needs—and actively helps him or her to fulfill those needs.*

Other-directedness implies celebration. We are pleased, touched, and even ecstatic that our partners seem so happy. Perhaps she received a promotion, a raise, or an award of some kind. Perhaps he competed in his first 5K run and you stood in the cold drizzle and watched it all. Perhaps she lost ten pounds or kicked some other habit. Or perhaps he is having a playful moment with the children or the cat. The bottom line is the same—*you* have the capacity to smile, clap your hands, and celebrate the moment.

Often we must stretch ourselves in order for our partners to meet their needs. If your partner is on a diet, you make the considerate decision to not buy gallons of Blue Bell ice cream for the freezer. Or you realize that your partner will need an extra pair of sweatpants on race day and drive the ten miles to deliver them. Or your wife is frolicking with your daughter and you grab the video camera in order to capture the moment for all to share later.

In each of these moments, you are giving your partner a gift—empathy. You deeply understand the significance of his or her moment of self-expression or accomplishment, and you even serve as a power booster to propel him or her further. Relationships endure because partners delight in each other's delight!

3. Realistic values and expectations. *Both partners jettison stereotypes about men and women, husbands and wives, love and marriage. They make their assumptions explicit to each other and avoid extreme points of view.*

Why would a nurse who understands the demands of medicine marry a physician and then bitterly complain that he or she is never home for dinner by 6:00 each evening? Call schedules, emergency office visits, and hospital rounds obliterate the best laid plans of any physician to be home on time. Yet resentment often breeds in this familiar scenario in which cold soup, bedraggled children, and sarcastic remarks all are thrown at the unwitting doctor as he or she enters the house—late again! Realistic expectations are flexible, not rigid, and flexibility requires a moderate point of view. After years of doing therapy, I am convinced that there is absolutely no place for absolutes in marriage. Fixed mindsets about men, women, and marriage can only lead to conflict. Real men do eat quiche, do cry real tears when emotionally moved, and do even need to be cuddled. Real women do like standing on their own two feet, do relish being physically challenged, and do take pride in their careers outside the home. Rigidly insisting that the children be put to bed by 9:00, that your wife make love every night, or that your husband visit your mother with you every Sunday afternoon will inevitably result in disenchantment.

Though needs may be reasonable, expectations often are not. Mature couples put more stock in the *process* of getting their needs met than in investing in a single expected *outcome*.

4. Tolerance. *Mature loving partners do not expect to find perfection in each other. Instead, they accept each other's attitudes, beliefs, and actions. They discuss problems on a situational level, rather than on the level of personal indictment.*

During romantic love, we often think that we have found it all—everything we need to fill our own void. Then we discover the flaws, the incompleteness, and the very real differences that naturally distinguish one person from another. It is at this point that our capacity for acceptance, forgiveness, and true appreciation is revealed.

Surely our tolerance is tested weekly, if not daily. One partner likes to make love as the sun rises, while the other prefers the stillness of moonlight. One partner is meticulously clean, while the other can step over unpacked suitcases and dirty socks for weeks at a time. One partner likes two cats and a dog, while the other resents the intrusion of a goldfish. Beyond these natural "compatibility" differences, there are other situations in which things simply go wrong. Your wife tells an embarrassing joke at a neighbor's party or forgets to pick up your suit at the cleaners before you must fly out on a business trip. Your husband arrives a half-hour late for your son's soccer game or has a headache one night and rebuffs your seductive overtures.

You have a choice in these situations. You can trigger the long-lasting themes of disenchantment ("You're so incredibly thoughtless." "You're such a boring sexual partner.") or you can treat the behavior as *situational*

("I wish you had thought about my position before you told that story about me." "I really wanted you to see this game with me, and I feel frustrated that you missed it."). With mature tolerance, we do not indict the *person*, no matter how much we may deplore the *situation*.

In thinking about mature, self-actualized persons, psychologist Abraham Maslow once said, "One does not complain about water because it is wet, nor about rocks because they are hard. ... As the child looks out upon the world with wide, uncritical and innocent eyes, simply noting and observing what is the case, without either arguing the matter or demanding that it be otherwise, so does the self- actualizing person look upon human nature both in himself and in others" (Maslow 1970, 156). This mature capacity for tolerance and acceptance can short circuit our resentments and allow us to work through problems, not get stuck in them.

5. Yearning to be known. *Both partners value the safe harbor of their relationship, the place where they can put aside their societal masks and truly be themselves. Mature relationships nurture this process of becoming fully known.*

In order for love relationships to sustain their vitality, they must be based on trust and openness. Both partners must believe that each can express his or her feelings, beliefs, and actions with relative impunity. We must have a sense of being in a protected place in which we can let down our guard and open up.

For many of us, this kind of trust is not easy. One of my clients recently accounted for his quietness with this observation: "If I wasn't being teased by my friends for being too fat, I was humiliated by my parents for the twitch in my eye or the cowlick in my hair." Silence became the best policy in all relationships for this man— until he met Jan. Suddenly, this sensitive man was thrust into a different world where a special woman invited him to look deep within himself and then open up, to disclose to her all that he was. In time, he learned to trust.

Soren Kierkegaard, the Danish philosopher, believed that our most common despair was in not choosing, or willing, to be ourselves; but our worst despair is in choosing to be *other* than ourselves. The will to be our true selves, as we truly are, is a deep responsibility that can be achieved in a healthy love relationship. What is required is our mature capacity to put aside our masks, which we often mistakenly think are a part of our real selves, and find instead a new freedom to think and feel and be.

6. Freedom to express all emotions. *Both partners encourage each other to express all of their feelings, including sadness, remorse, anger, and embarrassment. And each is open about expressing these feelings.*

Psychiatrist Fritz Perls has said, "In any plant, any animal, ripening and maturing are identical. You don't find any animal—no natural animal and no plant exists that will prevent its own growing. So the question is how do we prevent ourselves from maturing? What prevents us from ripening?" (Perls 1971, 30). In my opinion, not expressing our feelings stunts our emotional and psychological growth.

Perls (like other Gestalt therapists) believes that "awareness" by and of itself can be curative. But awareness of what? In large, he is talking about awareness of our emotions, our feelings. Both awareness of feelings and the expression of feelings are utterly natural. Maturation depends on such expression. As infants, we would not get nourished if we had no tears. As adults, we would not be assertive if we had no frustration, nor would we be sexually satisfied if we had no desire. Maturity depends upon our willingness to listen to the natural wisdom of the organism—of ourselves—without interfering or interrupting this process.

Some couples express their emotions very well. Partners allow themselves to cry when there is loss, to be scared when out of control, to be embarrassed when personally humiliated, to be frustrated or angry when promises are broken, to be joyful on a sunny day, to be excited before a trip, or to be sexually excited when the senses are aroused. How appropriate for Perls to remind us to lose our minds and come to our senses.

7. Separate identities. *Maturely loving partners recognize that each has a unique set of personality traits, skills, and aspirations. They give each other freedom to explore their separate interests and friends without judgment or undue restriction.*

Mature love offers us our most profound opportunity for regaining wholeness—not because our partners will fill all of our emptiness, but because we can use the embrace of a loving relationship to nurture ourselves toward greater maturation and ripening. An eagle or hawk, when taken airborne by a warm summer breeze, does not claim the breeze as its own. In a similar manner, lovers who are carried airborne by their own magical experience of love, must not claim their partner as their own. We must allow ourselves to be inspired, comforted, and renewed without trying to possess and control the source of our sustenance.

In his book, *The Road Less Traveled*, M. Scott Peck defines dependency as "the inability to experience wholeness or to function adequately without the certainty that one is being actively cared for by another" (Peck 1978, 98). When we are so concerned with our own nurture, we cannot possibly encourage our partners to nurture themselves. Instead of smothering or restricting one another, mature lovers learn to encourage each other to pursue their unique paths. Our encouragement both validates and facilitates our partner's yearning for growth.

Mature lovers help each other find ways to grow. I have seen this done in so many ways: by urging one another to take courses at a local college or university, giving photography or art lessons as a gift at Christmas, or encouraging one another to develop new friendships with colleagues at work. Recognizing that your partner has a unique identity that must have its own space to bloom is intrinsic to mature love.

8. Transcendence of two separate selves into one identity. *Both part-ners in healthy relationships enjoy celebrating their "we-ness" through time spent together in shared activities, creating a shared identity. And with this shared identity comes a joint sense of worth, a shared feeling of esteem as a couple which goes beyond individual self-esteem.*

The marital whole is much greater than the sum of its parts. A love relationship endures because both partners have learned to conceive of their bond as serving a higher purpose than the gratification of individual needs. Mature love is an abstraction built upon principles, values, shared beliefs, and common goals. Couples who have matured to this point want to grow old together because they have learned to take pride in a life they have built together.

Couples who love maturely have learned to gauge their happiness by more than the concrete satisfactions of well-prepared meals, clean rooms, sexy nightgowns, and balanced checkbooks. Instead, happiness becomes a pride in, or perhaps a celebration of, the less tangible accomplishment of being superb dancers, gracious hosts, loving parents or grandparents, sageful mentors, or well-seasoned voyagers of life. Mature lovers tran-scend petty conflicts between themselves as *individiuals* by focusing on more meaningful qualities they share as a *couple*.

Nathaniel Branden has stated that "no value-judgment is more impor-tant to man—no factor more decisive in his psychological development and motivation—than the estimate he passes on himself" (Branden 1969, 103). The same is true of loving couples. For a love relationship to mature, both partners must experience a deep feeling, a tacit belief, that there is something quite special about them which would never have happened had each not contributed to its creation.

These eight characteristics underlie maturity and commitment in lov-ing relationships. Each may seem reasonable enough—perhaps even too obvious to put much stock into! Yet, every couple who struggles with the impasse of disenchantment seems to have an incapacity in one or more of these characteristics. During such an impasse, each partner will insist on blaming the other for repeated failures to perform as a loving husband or wife should. In time, I am usually able to convince each partner to look inward, to introspect a bit, in order to scrutinize his *own* capacity to love or her *own* capacity to commit.

At this point, *each partner inevitably recognizes his or her own wounds from childhood—the experiences that left him or her incapable of fully relating, fully loving, fully committing.* Each begins to understand how his or her family life *then*, decades before, has impaired his or her capacity to demonstrate the eight characteristics of mature love *now*. Each now confronts a some-times bitter truth: Our current unhappiness with love has more to do with our own incapacity than it does with our partner! As we face this uncom-fortable reality, we must be kind to ourselves, remembering that this incapacity is *not our fault*. Like our parents, we are only capable of relating as we have been taught to relate. Our partners face the same uncomfortable reality—and for the same reason. We must be tolerant of ourselves ... and of them.

Wounded Origins

You may remember the biblical story of Abraham and Isaac. If you were like me, you probably heard this story of commitment and sacrifice from Abraham's perspective. Abraham, as God requested, agreed to sacrifice his own son, Isaac, as a measure of his faith. With a devotion greater than most could demonstrate, Abraham tells Isaac to lie on his back and tethers his arms and legs securely. Then, raising a sharpened knife high above his head, Abraham prepares to slay his loving son. Moments before the sacrifice can be made, God tells Abraham to put the knife down, to abandon this act of devotion. With his faith tested and his mettle proven, Abraham is now instructed to find a Paschal lamb to sacrifice instead of his son.

But what of Isaac? What of his mental health and well-being? After all, he had thought that his father loved him. What kind of loving father would kill his own son? Surely there could be another sacrifice worthy of God's countenance! Isaac had to be a wounded young man after this painful life experience. Think about his losses. He lost his innocence in this frightening moment when love could not provide a safe haven. He lost his dignity as he lay weak and helpless beneath his father's knife. And he lost his trust in life's fairness and in human kindness. Would he ever allow himself to be so vulnerable again, to enter into a loving relationship again?

The wounds we suffered as children may not have been as dramatic or as brutal as Isaac's—though I have seen worse. But most of us, perhaps all of us, were wounded in some way within our families during child-hood. These wounds usually go relatively unnoticed until disenchant-ment tests our will to truly commit, our capacity to fully love. If we are wounded, this capacity is impaired—as Isaac's capacity had to have been.

Each of the eight characteristics of mature, committed love is based upon an *interpersonal* dimension—a trait or ability that is measurable on a scale from full presence to total absence. Our childhood wounds result from the degree to which these interpersonal dimensions tended to be absent in our family dynamics.

Equitable versus Unfair

We are wounded by parents who were "unfair" in meeting our needs as children. They denied our developmental right to participate in shared decision making, to express our points of view, and to have reasonable privileges. This denial limits our ability to create a *mutual balance of met needs*.

Ideally, parents are equitable in balancing their needs with those of their children. Unfortunately, many parents are quite unfair in this regard. These parents "rule the roost" in a very dominant, autocratic manner. Growing up in these families is like being in boot camp where some calloused drill sergeant barks orders for the day. This control can be quite coercive at times, leaving children with the clear impression that it is much better, and safer, to be seen and not heard!

In other families, parental dominance may be more subtle. Routines may be so well established that children rarely have an opportunity to make suggestions or experience change. Children quickly learn that an open forum does not exist and begin to develop their own private world where they make their own decisions unimpeded by parental control. One's siblings or peer group may become the preferred reference group.

Here is a sampling of what some wounded clients recall about their early family life.

Mary: I don't remember making decisions. Everything was scheduled. Up at 6:00 a.m., catch the bus at 7:00 a.m., home at 3:30, dinner promptly at 6:00 p.m., and bed at 8:00 p.m. There was simply no spontaneity.

Jean: What strikes me is not only did we not have any privileges, but Mom didn't as well. Dad would never go out with Mom because he didn't like movies and didn't believe in babysitters.

Bill: Whenever we went for a ride in the car, whether a cross- country family trip or a short drive to the grocery story, they *always* got to pick the radio station and pooh-poohed anything we wanted to hear.

Beth: The Christmas my grandfather died, my parents asked me to do all the shopping and preparation for my brothers and sisters. This I did, so on Christmas morning there were presents and trapping just like other Christmases. For me, there were no gifts because my parents were too tied up with Mom's dad. They never said thank you and they never gave me a gift.

If we rarely experienced mutuality while growing up, we may become either very self-serving or overly compromising as a result. In the former case, we may want to make up for lost time: "Since I never got my needs met as a child, I sure as hell am going to make sure I get them met now!" If you live with someone like this, you know how difficult it is to get this person to compromise. And without compromise, it is impossible to achieve mutuality.

In the latter case, we may never know how to ask for what we need: "Since I never got my needs met as a child, I guess I'm not worthy of having them met as an adult." We will continue to over-compromise in the same way we did growing up. We may not even *know* what our needs are and only very rarely will say, "I need such-and-such from you." Once again, mutuality is impossible because the ability of the partners to identify and express needs is so out of balance.

Empathy versus Aloofness

We are wounded by parents who are indifferent or aloof, incapable of celebrating our special moments of joy and pleasure. This hampers our own capacity for other-directedness.

Imagine your excitement as a twelve-year-old when a friend invites you to the movies. Then, in a predictable moment of despair, you hear your father refuse to drive you since he has other things to do. Didn't he always have other things to do? In this painful moment, you knew once again that your father did not have the warmth and empathy he needed to understand your needs. Regrettably, he always seemed too removed to appreciate you.

Parents who regularly do not show up for soccer games, school plays, piano recitals, or swim meets send a painful message to their children: "You are not special enough for me to drop what I'm doing to spend time with you. Nor do I particularly care about your joyful moments." Children are seen as a burden or a distraction by such parents who, on the whole, are too selfish to give of themselves. They lack an ability to stretch—to extend themselves—toward their children in a caring, involved way. Every turned shoulder, hurried answer, or denied request was yet another reminder that we did not have an audience to celebrate our lives with. Here's what some of my clients remember about their childhood wounds.

Robert: I wrestled competitively for four years during high school and eventually won the district championship. I realized just recently that during that time my Dad never come to one match!"

Eric: My Dad didn't play games with me. I would sit for hours and play games against an imaginary opponent. I'd come upstairs and say "I won" and they would just laugh at me.

Marge: My parents just didn't understand our need to fit in with our peers. They would not let us buy fad clothes, they sneered at popular music, and they didn't allow us to watch TV on week nights.

Sue: My Dad had a large medical practice and was very well-known throughout the state. He would arrive home late at night and quickly retire to his private office where he would play the violin for two hours. We rarely saw him.

These recollections reveal more than a loss of celebration. They show a loss of attention and, in some instances, even parental neglect. If we did not receive enough attention or fanfare as children, we may keep our distance from others, including our mates. We may retreat behind newspapers or immerse ourselves in television programs. We may use work, fatigue, or illness as excuses for not getting more involved with others. Though we may be sending the message that we don't care, the truth of the matter is that we simply never learned how to applaud the happy times of others. We never learned how because we never experienced this approval from our own parents.

Flexible versus Rigid

We are wounded by parents who set standards and express expectations that are too absolute or categorical. This damages our own ability to develop *realistic values and expectations*.

In mature love, we must maintain moderate attitudes, avoid extreme points of view, and make implicit assumptions explicit. This is often not the case in our early family life. As we acquire receptive language skills, we are all bombarded with parental messages that shape our lives forever: "Treat people with respect." "Always dress nicely for church and school." "No dinner, no dessert." "It is a man's job to support the family." "Never allow a boy in this house if one of us is not here." "If you hurt, suck in your gut and be strong."

Some messages that espouse a strong work ethic seem reasonable enough—until "working hard" mutates into "being perfect." Other messages that espouse love and devotion also seem desirable—until "devotion" comes to mean giving up every sign of independence for fear of "breaking your mother's heart." These messages are the seeds for a distorted perspective later in life.

Marshall McLuhan reminds us that the medium can sometimes be the message. The form and packaging of a message may often become the message itself. Parents who dogmatically insist on one rule after another often become a symbol of dogma itself. Parents who insist on the role of rule makers abdicate their role as conversation makers. Rather than getting to know what their children really think and feel, these parents are content to define human experience in very stark, black-and-white terms. This is foolish, since all human relationships depend on a willing capacity to negotiate, compromise, and embrace the gray. Moderation works, absolutes don't! Here's what some clients remember about the rigidity of their parents.

Carla: Because of my mother's religion, I was not allowed to wear makeup, watch TV, dance, cut my hair, or go to the movies. I finally ran away at age fourteen, which was about the same time I found out that my father had been having serial affairs. I guess we both wanted more pleasure than Mom would allow!

Jim: If I make a bad grade, which in my family meant a B, I got cut to shreds by my father for failing. His rejection was devastating to me.

Thomas: I liked to lie on my stomach on the floor and read the newspaper. Whenever I had my toes pointed inward, Dad told me to point them out, since "only sissies" pointed them in!

Donna: When I think back to it now, I always wanted to go into medicine, but my parents were dead set against it. They repeatedly told me that it was too hard a life for a woman. So I acquiesced and studied biology instead.

We must grow our own values in our own gardens. Some must be fertilized, some pruned, and still others weeded out. As one client put it,

"Patently accepting my parents' or society's values is the same as not having any at all!"

Everything in a love relationship is—and must be—negotiable, *except for commitment itself.* We are very likely to damage our relationships if we persist in maintaining rigid points of view on anything from finances to food to sexuality. Rigidity traps us, actually exiles us in the Siberia of the 1st or 100th percentiles, when we have freedom to explore the other 98 percentiles between those two extremes. We must learn to meet our partners in this warm gray zone where life's compromises weave our relationships together.

Accepting versus Rejecting

We are wounded by parents who are rejecting, who impose guilt, and who lack a loving capacity to forgive. This wound leads us to have an incapacity for *tolerance* toward others.

In mature love, we *expect* imperfection—and discover it without surprise or dismay. We learn to smile and joke about flaws in character or physique. Our relationships endure in spite of our partner's eccentricities, just as Edith loved Archie Bunker in spite of his less-than-charming mannerisms and unenlightened opinions. Our capacity to be tolerant is well established by the experiences we have growing up.

I remember a female client whose intolerance for her husband was so extreme that we could not begin any therapy session until she had given me an update of his failings during the previous week. Everything was up for grabs. "He embarrassed me at a party because of that stupid outfit he was wearing ... He is not doing the therapy homework as rigorously as I am ... He still came home late on Tuesday." (By seven minutes!)

Closer scrutiny revealed that intolerance was endemic in her birth family. She remembered the day the police came to haul off her brother. It seemed that her father had discovered a roach clip used in smoking marijuana in her brother's dresser drawer. (What was he doing rummaging in the drawer anyway?) Without consulting his son, this man called the police and insisted that they arrest his son for illegal possession of drugs. This same parent disowned another daughter and insisted on opening the entire family's mail! This kind of intolerance and rejection wounds us for years to come, as other clients show us:

Linda: When I had my first pelvic exam, I told my mother I had a strange new feeling when the doctor examined me. Mother told me that she was ashamed of me and never to tell another person about this experience.

Mark: My dad was a champion diver when he was in college. One day, when I was nine, he urged me to go off a high dive. When I told him I was too scared, he laughed at me, called me a crybaby, and walked off.

Claire: Anytime I screwed up, my father and stepmother took long rides with me, preaching at me that I would be a failure. I just sat silently the entire time.

What we need from our parents is acceptance, forgiveness, and praise. What we often get instead is rejection, personal indictment, and guilt. It is one thing to express disappointment about a situation and quite another to judge the whole person as being a sinner, a sissy, or a failure. A child coming home late is not necessarily "irresponsible." A child expressing sexual feelings is not a "tramp." A child too fearful to ride a roller coaster is hardly a "coward." These labels, whether stated or implied, leave children with self-doubts, guilt, and low self-esteem. When rejected in childhood, we often replenish our self-esteem by denigrating and humiliating others (like our husbands or wives).

Forgiveness is more an act than a sentiment. Though we often experience feelings of warmth or compassion when we forgive, forgiveness is really more a demonstration of commitment—an act of will. When we choose to forgive and accept, we actually set ourselves free from the triad of resentment, anger, and hurt that underlie so many negative cycles of behavior. In fact, the refusal to forgive is what I have called resentment—that storehouse of unforgotten memories of hurt or bitterness. As mature lovers, we must learn how to accept and forgive, for the real victims of resentment are those who carry it.

Emotional versus Stoical

We are wounded by parents who squash our spontaneity and prevent us from expressing our true feelings. This injury can damage our capacity to *freely express emotions* in our adult lives.

Our natural state is expressive. Deep within our brains lie two areas, the hypothalamus and the limbic system, which essentially control all of our emotional responses, from rage to pleasure to fear. These basic physiological systems are prepared to fire up whenever appropriate, whether the source of stimulation is the sight of someone scantily dressed, the sound of a parent being critical, or the presence of a nighttime intruder coming through a bedroom window. As natural as these emotional states are, we often are not permitted to express them within our families. For various reasons, many parents develop the suffocating notion that it is better to suppress these human emotions rather than to spontaneously express them. This is counter to our natural state and usually will result in psychological problems that seriously harm our love relationships later in life. The following clients recall this wound well:

Robert: Mom and Dad showed very few feelings. They were too busy with too many kids, it seemed. At any rate, they never hugged us or each other. Touching and being affectionate just weren't done in our family.

Betty: My brother was humiliated for crying once and never did it again. As a matter of fact, he decided to go into therapy during college because he felt so shut down emotionally.

Claire: I really don't think that expressing feelings was encouraged. I was always so compliant. I do remember a period of time in early adolescence when I began to show my feelings and preferences—and the comment back to me several times was "We want the old Claire back!"

Larry: My parents always bragged that they had a great marriage, yet I would often hear my mother go down into the basement and cry and cry. Then I would cry as well, but would never let anyone know, just like Mom.

Our parents aren't solely responsible for this tendency to stoicism. Socialization certainly contributes to this restraint of emotions. The usual gender distinctions of "emotional" women and "logical, rational" men only perpetuate a cultural myth unsupported by our physiology. In fact, I have often discovered that male clients who present themselves as very much "thinking types" are in truth some of the most extreme "feeling types" of all—only they aren't *expressing* their feelings.

Mature love is seriously impaired by this loss of spontaneity. Observe any healthy family and you will see normal people responding emotionally and naturally throughout the day. They will express frustration when they can't find something, fear about a presentation the next day, anger about an insulting remark, affection when greeting each other, laughter when being teased, and so forth. All of this emotion is natural. If you are wounded in this dimension, you can learn to heal yourself within your loving relationship simply by learning to express your emotions more spontaneously.

Open versus Closed

We are wounded by parents who are too secretive about revealing themselves and do little to encourage others within the family to do so. This damages our capacity to allow ourselves to truly know our intimate partners and to be know by them.

As children, we have a natural capacity to reveal ourselves. We twirl ourselves into dizziness, we incessantly nag until we get what we want, we cry and talk about our fears until we are soothed, and we ask endless questions until our thirst for knowledge is satisfied. We seem to have a natural yearning to be known during our earliest years. Then, as we twirl and nag and cry and probe ourselves into our family circles, we often learn a bitter truth—openness makes you vulnerable. We are either ignored or rejected. For some, having no audience at all or having one that only boos means only one thing—never going on stage again (or only when you know that the role you've chosen will receive applause).

I am reminded of a man that I only met twice. His wife asked him to come in after he announced that he was going to leave her for another women he had met thirty years before. She was stunned, bewildered. Where did all of this comes from? "Haven't we had a good marriage?" she asked him. The reply was affirmative. They had lots of fun, good friends, great careers, and super sex. Neither could put their finger on any major disenchantments with one another. Then, in the two sessions I was given, both admitted that they lacked a capacity to "truly be ourselves—to tell it all to each other." He in particular felt strongly that he must first work things through in his own mind before going public. In fact, sometimes he wouldn't even work it through privately, but would simply go with the urgency and immediacy of the moment. And thus he had to leave her.

When I offered the husband psychotherapy or bibliotherapy to help him work through this important decision, he looked at me quizzically, almost as if I were crazy to even think of "wasting his time" with such hogwash. He obviously thought it was hogwash to discuss this minor matter with his wife as well! I later learned that he had indeed been wounded in a family where harsh consequences accompanied openness. Such consequences are not rare, as these clients report:

David: With my mother, my mask never came down. She was such a prying person—it was another way for her to have control over you. Knowledge is power, so to speak. I'm not sure that once I reached twelve whether my mask ever came down at home.

Bill: I took a risk and told my Dad that I was going to get a C in junior high school, and that I thought it was all right to be average in history. He went into a rage, saying "No children of mine are average!"

Harvey: I remember telling my mother that I had a crush on a neighbor's daughter. Two hours later, I overheard her tell three of the neighbors in one big powwow on our front lawn. That was the last thing she ever heard.

Marty: When I was four years old, I told my parents and sister, "This is my beautiful little penis!" I was humiliated by them for years following that.

Though openness is similar to the freedom to express emotions, this capacity is more reflective, more considered. When we choose to be known, we make a conscious decision, more than a spontaneous one, to reveal ourselves. When wounded in this way as children, adults tend to search for "safe" things to talk about. It is much safer to talk about activities and responsibilities than feelings and thoughts. From dinnertime to bedtime, how many couples only discuss unfinished chores, make arrangements for the kids the next day, or gossip about friends, neighbors, and family members? Relationships like these become very superficial, lacking introspection, meaningful disclosure, and trust.

The real tragedy here is that mature love offers us the wondrous gift of a safe harbor—a haven where we can truly be ourselves, fully open, and natural. To lose this capacity for openness—to hide behind our personas—is to sentence ourselves to a lifetime of silence. We must learn to heal ourselves by becoming more introspective, more trusting of our partners, and more open with our thoughts and feelings. This responsibility is ours alone, not our partners. In the familiar words of an anonymous writer:

Don't be fooled by me,
Don't be fooled by the mask I wear.
For I wear a mask,
I wear a thousand masks,
Masks that I'm afraid to take off,
And none of them are me.
Pretending is an art that is second nature to me!

Unity versus Isolation

We are wounded by parents who lack a capacity to celebrate the fullness of union. This hinders our ability as adults to *transcend our separate selves into a joint identity.*

Mature love brings with it the promise of abundance—a realization that our lives are more full, more connected, more expanded, and more empowered than ever before. We have a clear sense that our life, by virtue of this connection, has become more substantial—that it has evolved into something different that would have been impossible had we not connected with another. Through this celebration of connection we learn to take pride in the "we" that we have become. Our capacity to celebrate "we-ness"—to experience pride and increased esteem because of it—is clearly established within our original families.

Think back to your youth and seek in memory those moments when your family took pride in being a family—when unity seemed far more important than separateness. Perhaps it was during Christmas or Chanukah celebrations, perhaps summer vacations at a lakehouse, or perhaps a special family reunion where everyone was a great cook and had gorgeous children! Although these were special moments, they might be just crumbs and scraps of what was possible. Perhaps your family, like so many, lived most of the time as a collection of individuals rather than as a unit with a shared identity of its own. Quite often a family's sense of togetherness—its pride in connectedness—atrophies or dies following a family tragedy or as a result of long-term conflicts. Consider the following examples:

Ellen: Family identity and pride was once very strong until my brother died. Then my family as I had known it disintegrated. My mother withdrew into a bottomless depression and my father buried himself in his work. My dear little brother obviously took more than his precious little self when he died!

Sam: I don't remember my Dad ever going shopping with me for a present for Mom. And I don't remember Mom and I ever shopping for a gift for Dad. They'd just give something in my name, even though I didn't share in the joy of buying it.

Louis: In fourth grade, I was asked to represent my native country of Spain by sharing momentos and describing the culture. I was so proud that our family seemed so unique and special. When I asked my parents to come and join me in class, they both sort of laughed and told me they "had more important things to do."

Sissy: I remember that our neighbors had a great pride in decorating their house together at Christmas time. Their outside lights would actually back cars up for blocks at night. How envious I was, especially when I realized we did nothing together as a family.

Couples, like families, avoid connectedness for two reasons: (1) a fear of being engulfed and (2) busy schedules. In the former case, we learn to distance ourselves from others, to fear intimacy, and to insist on personal boundaries. We may be overly concerned that if we become too close to another, their demands and expectations will swallow us up. In the latter case, busy lifestyles place so many demands on couples and family members that it seems nearly impossible to be in the same place at the same time very often. Fortunately, some families have a capacity to transcend each member's busy schedule in order to share in each other's joys—to take pride in being a unified team. You can't transcend yourself without giving up your fear of losing yourself. This healing often takes time.

Independence versus Dependence

We are wounded by parents who restrict our need to distinguish ourselves as individuals with unique personalities, needs, and wants. This can damage our ability to establish a *separate identity*, or to allow our partner to do so.

As important as transcendence appears to be, we also have an equally important need to separate at times—to actualize our own uniqueness as individuals. Some experience their uniqueness as God-given, while others sense that they must cultivate their uniqueness over time. How can there be any doubt that loving couples must learn to give each other space, not to mention encouragement, to expand themselves individually? Yet we often cling to one another, imprisoned in our own world of fear—somehow hoping that this prize possession we call our love will protect us, nurture us, and heal us. Regrettably, this suffocating dependence can only result in that which we fear the most—being abandoned.

We learn—or don't learn—the importance of being separate individuals within our birth families. Many of us may recall parental encouragement to play with neighborhood children, to develop our musical talents by taking piano lessons, or to discover other hobbies of special interest. As one client recalled, "My Dad always said if he could afford it, we could have anything we wanted that was educational to improve our minds and skills—and this was extended to all of us." Regrettably, this affirmation of individuality is not always the case, as the following clients reveal:

Sheila: I remember that I was required to babysit all day Saturday, every Saturday, from age thirteen to fifteen, while my mother and father pursued their own interests. They would not let me participate in sports or have friendships.

Don: My junior year in high school, I was offered the opportunity to take two advanced science courses, as well as participate in an after-school science project. Both of my parents refused to give me permission. They told me that my chances for college admission would be better if I took easier courses with a guarantee of a top grade.

Paul: In my family, everyone started to study at 7:00 p.m. and finished studying at 9:00 p.m. We all had to conform to family rules, no matter if we were in elementary school or high school.

Wounds in this area are most likely due to family "master plans" that are rigidly enforced by one or both parents. These parents have a vision of ideal developmental growth and are in a position to vigorously shape this growth over the years by demanding conformity from their children. In truth, however, these parents were most likely severely wounded in their own personal growth and are the least likely to know what ideal developmental growth looks like. Regrettably, our natural need to in-dividuate as uniquely special persons may be squashed over the years— leaving us impoverished in self-esteem and frightfully dependent on others to define our worth for us. Needless to say, this dependency can be a deathblow to any loving relationship.

Toward Maturity and Renewal

Charles Hampden-Turner, in summarizing the work of Erich Fromm, says that we human beings are "freaks of the universe. We are part nature and subject to her laws, yet we also transcend nature through culture, lan-guage and symbolism. We are set apart from each other, as Adam and Eve realized in their nakedness, yet we yearn for the harmony from which we are cast out. We plan and try to empower ourselves, yet we were thrown accidentally into this world and will be pulled inexorably out of it. We have vast potentials, yet in the course of our short span on earth, we can hope to realize but a fraction of our endowments. Reason is then our blessing and our curse, enabling us to solve the more superficial issues until we reach the impasse beyond" (Hampden-Turner 1982, 48).

Confronted with contradictions of this magnitude, we often tend to claim or affirm one end of the spectrum while negating the other. That is, in our need to reason our way through our dilemmas, we often force a choice between two extremities when an integration or reconciliation of the two is more appropriate.

What better dilemma to try to reconcile than that of love? We are each faced with the contradictions of novelty and famililiary, of romantic sparks and meaningful covenants, of nascent yearnings and numbing impasses. In our need for finitude, we may repeatedly choose novelty over familiarity, or romance over covenance, or new beginnings over impasse resolution—but what do we really learn about ourselves, as well as life itself, by doing so? The mature personality, the mature lover, instead chooses to *reconcile* contradiction and impasse. If our capacity to reason underlies our freakish status in the universe, then we must use this capacity to transcend the difficult contradictions of our lives.

The resolution of contradiction within marriage is no easy matter, as author Adolph Guggenbuhl-Craig points out. We must learn to reconcile our needs for happiness and well-being, on the one hand, with our equally strong need for salvation, which entails the antithesis of happiness—suffering! Guggenbuhl-Craig states: "every path to salvation leads through hell. Happiness in the sense that is presented to married couples today belongs to well-being, not to salvation. Marriage above all is a soteriological institution, and this is why it is filled with highs and lows; it consists of sacrifices, joys *and* suffering" (Guggenbuhl-Craig 1977).

He goes on to say that "marriage is not comfortable and harmonious; rather it is a place of individuation where a person rubs up against himself and against his partner, bumps up against him in love and rejection, and in this fashion learns to know himself, the world, good and evil, the heights and the depths." We thus can *learn* from our suffering—from our disenchantments in love. Renewal can reconcile.

Recently I described the contents of this chapter to an old family friend whom I hadn't seen in years. In discussing our early family wounds, my friend told me that her own upbringing had been abominable. She experienced both poverty and neglect. There never seemed to be enough clothing, food, or attention for eight children—particularly after her father died at a young age. Yet she sat before me with her Ph.D. in hand. And she was not alone—many of her brothers and sisters possessed graduate degrees as well.

I also was aware that her marriage had had difficulties as well. During her doctoral course of study, she and her husband lived in separate states for part of the time so that she could complete her coursework. This almost split up their family, with the inevitable likelihood that their children would be split in different directions. Theirs was a dual-career marriage which almost didn't survive. Yet they did survive and seemed to flourish beyond their early dreams. She mused kindly over her years of suffering and pain as she thought how far they had come. I watched her smile and breathe deeply as she spoke lovingly of her husband, children, and career.

Yet I was puzzled. How could she bring so many elements of mature love to her marriage when she had been so obviously wounded in her birth family? Now, within her current marriage, she was so clearly equitable, empathetic, flexible, accepting, open, emotional, independent, and transcendent. By comparison, her parents had been oriented in exactly the opposite direction on these dimensions.

This presented no quandary to my friend. She remembered a day when she was twelve years old, a day she was helping her mother bus tables in a local restaurant. Watching the dinner guests holding hands, laughing, and appearing to be content with their lives, she made a vow to be among them one day. This was not an emotional moment. It always seemed matter-of-fact to her as she recalled her vow: "I simply made a decision that my life would be significantly different from what I had experienced so far. My pattern of relationships, as well as my quality of life, would be vastly different from the misery I had known." And so it was!

Consider this for a moment. My friend could not have made her vow had she not first experienced the hardships and turmoil that marked her early family life. From the depths of her pain, she was able to envision something better, a life worth having for herself. She used her knowledge, as painful as it was, as a backdrop for a new audition. This is also true of love.

Mature love can begin only when we have come to know our partners as they truly are, not as we had imagined they were. Only at this point in a relationship can we begin to like and care for them as human beings. Only at this point can we demonstrate our own capacity for love. Erich Fromm has described this capacity as "productivity"— meaning the creative synthesis of our most human powers in a way that fosters an active expression, or pouring out, from within us. It is this active pouring out that has led writers like M. Scott Peck to suggest that love *is* as love *does*. Love is willful, love is a demonstration, love is a decision or choice based on knowledge and experience about another person. Love cannot mature otherwise.

Romantic love is characterized by a need to suspend our partners in a timeless prison so that our projected images of them as gods and goddesses can endure. In contrast, mature love allows for the natural evolution of two disparate souls to occur in a mutually satisfying manner. Mature love is that process by which we learn to *integrate* the differences, rather than try to *eliminate* them. Only those who possess the eight characteristics of mature love are able to participate in the evolution of what Fromm calls "unified separateness."

This chapter has been about conscious love—that mature commitment to another person which reflects our seasoned and reasoned experiences in life. Our ability to make and sustain a commitment must be based on a real knowledge of what we are committing ourselves to, as well as a recognition that we have the capacity to do so. On the one hand, we actually make a vow to embrace the imperfection we find in our partner; on the other, we recognize the imperfection, or wounds, within ourselves. This integration and acceptance of inner and outer imperfection is what mature love is about. With our distinctly human gift of reason, we may indeed learn how to reshape, rewrite, and renew our lives.

PART II

ILLUSIONS
The Roots of
Disenchantment

Disenchantment is an inevitable dilemma of loving because we come to our love relationships "enchanted" by illusions about love, our lovers, and happiness in general. Our choice of lovers and our expectations of them and ourselves are usually distorted by these false notions which have nothing to do with our actual partners or our real lives. This section of the book examines our romantic illusions, their sources and consequences.

4

The Imprint of Childhood

When two persons marry, they are "in love." This usually
means that two adults ... see in the opposite adult the promise
of fulfillment of past longings. Then, either gradually or
suddenly, each marital partner comes face to face with the
"child of the past" of the other—the childish part of your
spouse, the part that seems so unreasonable.

Hugh Missildine

Deep inside us, intricately entwined in the fabric of our being, resides an
"inner child." We carry this little child, this homunculus of raw emotion,
with us wherever we go. Our illusions of the perfect partner are largely
created by the experiences our inner child has had in relationships with
our mothers, fathers, and other caretakers. There is a little Larry, a little
Claire, and a little you. The hurt and anger we express as adult lovers are
largely the unresolved pain of this little child within.

As adult lovers, we hope to find in one another the fulfillment of past
longings. These longings arise from three fundamental human needs: (1)
the need to belong, (2) the need for control over our lives, and (3) the need
for affection. When we were children, if one or more of these needs was
not met by our parents, we felt deeply angry or hurt. That angry or hurt
"child of the past" still lives within our adult bodies and minds, emerging
years later when triggered by six patterns in our adult relationships:

- Too many demands or expectations
- Too little attention
- Too much imposed control or criticism
- Too little appreciation or approval
- Too much smothering or overprotection
- Too little affection

Ninety percent of our emotional reactions as adults typically have
nothing to do with the immediate situation. Instead, our anger and hurt
reflect the buried pain of childhood whenever our basic needs for belonging, control, and affection are frustrated. In our need to find a perfectly

divine partner, we usually find instead an imperfectly human partner who will frustrate one or more of these needs.

As I began explaining this concept to a client one afternoon a few years ago, she asked me if I had ever read *Your Inner Child of the Past* by Hugh Missildine. Twenty four hours later I was eagerly reading her copy of this 1963 classic, nodding in agreement as I read Missildine's apt characterization of this usually unrecognized but nevertheless powerful figure in our inner world.

> The child you once were continues to survive inside your adult shell. 'Thrive' would perhaps be a better word than 'survive', for often this inner child of the past is a sprawling, bawling, brawling character— racing pell-mell into activities he likes, dawdling, cheating, lying to get out of things he doesn't like, upsetting and wrecking others' lives—or perhaps this child is the fearful, timid, shrinking part of your personality. (Missildine 1963, 14)

Couples must realize that because *each* has "an inner child of the past," love requires that four persons, not two, share a bed together. Though this may sound ridiculous, it is true in every love relationship. Two little people, each bringing to the present moment his or her needs from the past, carefully scrutinize all interactions that take place between loving partners.

Let me convince you that this is not so far-fetched. Imagine that your father was overcritical and overbearing (perhaps you don't have to imagine!). As a budding adolescent, you felt under the gun constantly. Everything you did seemed to be a target for review and vicious critique by Dad. Reveille, diet, fashion, etiquette, social life, and curfew were family issues that Dad controlled with an iron hand. You eventually learned to avoid conflict by any means, usually by avoiding Dad.

Years later, in the course of your marriage, your husband discovers that he cannot be too opinionated or you will stalk off to the den or, more explosively, retreat to a friend's house. He learns that you are devastated by the slightest hint of disapproval. He had surmised that he married a logical, rational human being who could discuss ideas without popping a cork. What he discovers is that your inner child is filtering experiences through a twenty-year-old strainer. The presence of this little girl within you may often be felt, but rarely is seen.

The tap roots for adult disenchantment are always buried deeply in the fertile soil of childhood. We learn all about relationships during these early years. We learn what we need—and what we *don't* need—from others:

- We *do* need enough attention. We *don't* need too many expectations.
- We *do* need enough appreciation. We *don't* need too much criticism.
- We *do* need enough warmth. We *don't* need too much smothering.

If we received the right amounts of attention, appreciation, and warmth as a young child, we unconsciously want the same from our adult lovers. We want to achieve the same secure feelings as an adult that we had as a child. We want to replicate the same emotional atmosphere that existed decades before. By the same token, if we experienced too many expectations, too much criticism, or too much neglect as a young child, we unconsciously want to avoid these experiences with our adult mates. We want to bury these painful memories several miles below the surface of our current bond.

The odds of our lovemate knowing about these things is next to nil. Who goes looking for such wounds during the dawn of a budding relationship? Instead, we notice her legs, his eyes, her lips, his status, her degree, his aspirations, her social grace, his sense of humor, her ability to initiate, his interest in photography, her interest in wilderness adventures. As important as these qualities might be, we miss the substrata of our partner's personality. We miss the neediness of our lover's inner child.

Our early illusions—what I have called "portraits of desire"—convince us that what we see is what we get. But it just isn't so. The attractive, bright, energetic lover we embrace in the light of today is also a hurt and angry child of a twilight past.

Each of these unmet childhood needs is a veritable landmine that can explode in our faces. You will see how this process works for one couple—Bo and Shana—and have an opportunity to identify *your* inner child, but first let's clarify a few points.

Inclusion, Control, and Affection

William Schutz (in his 1966 book, *The Interpersonal Underworld*) was the first to postulate that all relationships can be understood in terms of three interpersonal needs: *inclusion, control,* and *affection.* Inclusion refers to association between people. Unlike affection, inclusion does not invoke strong emotional attachments to individual persons. It is also unlike control in that the preoccupation is more with prominence than with dominance.

I believe these three basic interpersonal needs are especially pronounced in love relationships. In love relationships, two things are certain: First, these needs are *always* operating throughout the course of the relationship. Second, the strength of these needs is determined very early in our lives through the attachment experiences we have had with our parents or other caretakers.

Two lovers engage in a mirrored dance. In order for you to be happy in love, you must elicit certain inclusion, control, and affection behaviors from your partner. Likewise, in order for your partner to be happy you must demonstrate certain inclusion, control, and affection behaviors for him or her. If this ongoing, mutual exchange of behaviors does not occur to everyone's satisfaction, disenchantment is sure to follow. When two people first meet, inclusion and affection behaviors are unusually high. We must belong and be loved! Exclusivity and passion, two powerful urges which mark early romantic love, ensure that inclusion and affection needs are met. Later, when these same couples arrive for counseling, control behaviors are quite high, with one partner out-maneuvering the other in a reciprocal dance of anger.

Let's take a closer look at how inclusion, control, and affection are reflected in a loving relationship:

Inclusion. When we are included we belong, we interact, we mingle, and we join. We are members in good standing. We feel accepted. If your style is more outgoing and social than your husband's, you know the difference between high and low inclusion. Just think back to the last party you dragged him to, the one where he wanted to go home at 9:30, just when you were beginning to rock-and-roll! Or recall your wife's answer when you asked if you could join her on her annual trek to San Francisco: "No way, Josè!"

Repeated exclusions hurt! No one likes rejection—a process that regrettably begins very early in life. I only have to remember back to fourth grade softball when I was the last to be selected, or Amy's seventh grade party that I was never invited to. Jerry Gruber and Ronnie Ralph were, though!

Control. Inevitably, all loving couples must come to terms with the *equitable* distribution of control and power. Very seldom do two people in a loving relationship have equal, 50-50 say in most matters. This is true of child rearing, checking accounts, and leisure activities. A wife in one relationship may take responsibility of children 80 percent of the time, while the husband takes responsibility for fiscal matters 70 percent of the time. So long as both partners consider this arrangement fair, it works. They have learned to distribute power and control *equitably*.

When this is not the case, it is often because of poor communication between partners or the excessive needs of one partner to be in control most of the time. When one partner becomes too dominant in decision making, the other will no doubt harbor resentments. All decision making between two people has to do with their respective control needs. If you have no input, you have no control. The process of working through differences of opinion is an ever present, ongoing consideration in all love relationships.

Affection. Compliments, acts of caring, sensitivity to our lover's feelings, holding hands, hugging, smiling, touching, emotional closeness—all come to mind when we think of affection. Affection is the glue that seals a loving relationship. All healthy love relationships have an adequate sharing of warmth and caring. The gift of affection is important in that it affirms our beloved's special status in our life. We must be able to give and receive affection in order to sustain a healthy relationship. Yet the amount of affection—and the manner of expressing it—is a tapestry woven together differently by every couple.

Some people avoid close affectionate ties with others by becoming equally close with everyone. High *inclusion* behaviors may thereby mask low *affection* needs. This helps to explain how someone who appeared so friendly can be so emotionally distant when you get to know him!

Whereas inclusion needs are often critical to the formation of a relationship, control and affection are usually more relevant in relationships already formed. Inclusion signals whether a relationship actually exists, control signals to who has the power in the relationship, and affection signals the emotional closeness of the relationship. Here's a simple way to remember these relationship dimensions:

Inclusion = in or out
Control = top or bottom
Affection = close or far

Each of us has a "personal preference plan" for the amount of inclusion, control, and affection we want in a love relationship. Our personal preference plans are well established during our formative years and represent the needs and wants of our inner child. A personal preference plan can be mapped out as follows:

Dimension	Expressed Behavior	Wanted Behavior
Inclusion	I initiate interaction	I want to be included
Control	I control people	I want to be controlled
Affection	I get close to people	I want people near me

These dimensions—and the behaviors that represent them—are a veritable marketplace for disenchantment in our everyday lives. Consider the case of Bill: Bill's alarm goes off at 6:00 a.m., as usual. He rolls over to kiss his wife, Hanna, who sleepily finds an unassailable position under the blanket to ward off the expected assault. Unperturbed, good-natured Bill saunters into the kitchen, where he begins preparing omelets and muffins for the family's breakfast that morning. Half an hour later, both kids grab a banana and head for the door to catch their schoolbus. Later, finishing his second cup of coffee, he hears Hanna's hurried yell "Goodbye, Bill, I'm late," as she dashes to the car. As Bill peers at two fluffy omelets, one purring cat, and a coffee pot brewing nearby, he begins to sense a sinking feeling in his gut—a reminder of other hurts gone by.

Bill's day has not started well. His unstated need for warmth and togetherness have been violated by the actions, or inactions, of others. Let's take a closer look at his expressed and wanted behaviors, as well as the nonreciprocated behaviors from others.

Expressed Behaviors	*Response Behaviors*
1. I initiate interaction with others. (He made an omelet.)	Nobody ate my omelet!

2. I am affectionate toward others. (He hugged his wife.)

My wife curled up away from me!

3. I want others to get close to me. (He set the table for the family.)

I am sitting alone at the breakfast table after I prepared it for four!

Notice that Bill's disenchantments can be understood from the current exchange of behaviors. When his expressed and wanted behaviors are reciprocated, we can suppose that he will be quite pleased. When they are rebuffed, as in this situation, he is on the way to disenchantment. However, to fully understand the situation we must look a bit deeper. We must go below the surface and explore yet another layer—the layer represented by his inner child. If we were to discover that Bill has been wounded as a child in the areas of "belonging" and "affection," we would be more able to understand his adult hurt and anger.

We all must do this for ourselves in order to sort out the unfulfilled dreams of our childhood (which may never be able to be met) from the needs and wants of adulthood (which can be met). To understand this process more fully, we turn now to the case study of Bo and Shana.

A Couple in Disguise

Bo is an engineer whose practice, though quite successful, is very demanding. Shana is a corporate manager whose career, though upwardly mobile, is also time demanding. Though they had been married seven years, they were separated when they came to me for counseling.

When I asked Bo to describe his problem, he stated: "I am hypersensitive to criticism and rejection, easily hurt when others appear to be ignoring me, and I have some difficulty getting close to others." Shana believed that she had a "problem with perfection, resentment, and an inability to forgive." Both felt that they cared for one another very much but that the constant arguing was taking a toll on them and their fourteen-month-old infant. They seemed to be competing with one another. As they put it, "Whose needs will be more important today?"

Initially, each of them had been taken with very special qualities in the other. Bo had found Shana particularly gregarious, honest, friendly, and a good listener with a great sense of humor. Shana had found Bo to be intense, sensitive, fun-loving, humorous, and very creative and intelligent. They enjoyed many of the same interests, such as traveling, movies, and afternoon drives. Each had felt very comfortable with the other. So, I wondered, why were they separated and seeing me for therapy?

Deeper probing revealed that Bo's father had died when he was three, leaving his mother with the tremendous responsibility of raising a family by herself. The only way she could manage was to work two jobs. Even so, Bo and his family lived close to poverty level. Shana was the adult child of an alcoholic father. She willingly admitted that her perfectionism and need for control might have something to do with her family background, but she was confused about the connection.

I asked each of them to describe their parents. Bo described his mother as "having high expectations, but giving little guidance due to her work schedule. She was a strong-willed and very independent individual. If I didn't do something right, I heard about it in a big way. I guess her life was so stressed that she really depended on me to help with much of the work. I was, and still am, a source of tremendous pride to her."

From Bo's description we can see that his inner child experienced many demands and expectations (high inclusion) as well as his share of parental influence (high control). We can also guess that because she worked two jobs, his mother was probably not around enough to appreciate Bo on a day-to-day basis. The absence of a father added to his feelings of neglect. Bo's inner child was prewired to respond to any person who demanded too much, controlled too much, or did not appreciate him enough. The magnitude of Bo's anger toward Shana attested to the hurt and anger he often felt as a child when these triggers were pulled.

Shana did not let him down. Her need to control and be perfectionistic led her into a critical mode just often enough to push Bo's buttons. Additionally, when Shana traveled professionally, or had too many evening commitments, Bo often felt unappreciated or abandoned—left to take care of their small child for days at a time. Not until therapy did Bo learn to understand that the anguish he felt when Shana traveled was linked to the pain he felt when his mother worked two jobs decades ago—only then he could not risk further loss of his mother by protesting too loudly.

Shana described her father as a "very private man who did not easily share his thoughts. I resented him as a teenager. I have learned to see that he loved us very much and tried to provide the best. He was not a very affectionate man." She added, "I remind myself of my mother, which does not make me happy. She was uptight, pushed too hard, made us conform to her whims, and was somewhat cold and removed. Mom was definitely the disciplinarian." We can see that Shana's inner child experienced many demands and manipulation from her mother and very little affection or attention from her father. As an adult, she was primed and ready to respond to any person who demanded, criticized, or did not care about her in an affectionate way.

Bo did not let her down. By his own admission, he was angry and critical. Fueled by the reciprocal nature of disenchantment, Bo was an active participant in their dance of anger. This further triggered Shana's anger, which escalated their skirmishes into a full-blown war.

It is easy to see how two basically caring and loving persons can find themselves thrashing about in a bloody sea without understanding how or why it is happening. The emotional volatility of our inner child cannot be overstated. We must learn to identify and accept these parts of ourselves with an eye toward controlling them. Though we must live with our inner child for the rest of our days, we need not be ruled by him or her.

Are you ready to identify your inner child?

Identifying Your Inner Child of the Past

To remove a mask which you had thought was part of your real self can be a deeply disturbing experience, yet when there is freedom to think and feel and be, the individual moves toward such a goal.

Carl Rogers

Covenant love offers us an opportunity to freely think and feel and be. A mature love relationship requires that we express a broad spectrum of emotions while valuing the safe harbor in which we can be truly known. It is also within this safe harbor that we can reintegrate that part of ourself which represents the hurt and anger of a childhood past—our inner child.

Unless you take the time to identify your inner child, you will not be able to understand why you get hurt, angry, or resentful. You are very likely to blame your partner—wrongly—for *all* the anger and hurt you feel. Though he or she may be responsible for 10 percent of it—by triggering it—you still have the responsibility to account for the other 90 percent. Such an accounting will require that you recall how your own parents wounded you many years ago. What you learn will help you identify and understand the buttons or triggers that seem to set you off now.

We are wounded by parents who are in some way *extreme* in their child rearing practices. I believe that parents can be extreme in any of the following six ways:

1. Parents may be extreme in providing *too much inclusion* by demanding or expecting too much. These parents are interested in imposing their values and their rules upon you implicitly or explicitly. Your business becomes their business when they get *too* involved.

2. Parents may be extreme in providing *too little inclusion* by not paying attention to you. These parents may be too busy working or may simply refuse to bend over to find out what is happening in your world. They cannot provide the undivided attention you need.

3. Parents may be extreme in providing *too much control* by being critical, manipulating, or overpowering. Criticism is a direct means of controlling, while manipulation is less direct. These parents may use very stern voice tones, threaten physical harm, or more subtly influence your every decision. You may not feel accepted.

4. Parents may be extreme in providing *too little control* by not appreciating your input or not approving of your ideas. Whether you make a suggestion or perform well at some task, your contribution simply goes unnoticed. These parents may actually abdicate their role as parents.

5. Parents may be extreme in providing *too much affection* by being smothering or overprotective. In the name of love, these parents are constantly warning you of all the dangers in the world, whether they be physical, biological, or interpersonal. As a result, you may have been restricted from doing many things you wanted to do.

6. Parents may be extreme in providing *too little affection* by not demonstrating love with hugs or saying "I love you." These parents may be cold, unfeeling, emotionally numb, and distant. Worse yet, some parents are emotionally and physically abusive, which truly impairs a sense of lovability.

With the above in mind, settle back comfortably in your chair. Recall a period of time when you were a child growing up in your hometown or city. Be little. Be small. See yourself in the old neighborhood surrounded by the familiar scenes that filled your childhood years on a daily basis. What were Mom and Dad doing? Where were they? Were they happy? Were you happy? As you recall these early years, get an image of Mom in your mind. Keeping this image of Mom very vivid, respond to the following statements according to this scale:

	Not True	Somewhat True	Generally True	Usually True	Very True
	1	2	3	4	5

1. Mom, you demand or expect too much from me.
2. Mom, you criticize, manipulate, or overpower me.
3. Mom, you smother or overprotect me.
4. Mom, you don't pay attention to me.
5. Mom, you don't appreciate me or approve of me.
6. Mom, you don't care about me.

Now, I would like you to do the same with an image of your father. Be little. Be small. Experience your father as if you were a child.

	Not True 1	Somewhat True 2	Generally True 3	Usually True 4	Very True 5

1. Dad, you demand or expect too much from me.
2. Dad, you criticize, manipulate, or overpower me.
3. Dad, you smother or overprotect me.
4. Dad, you don't pay attention to me.
5. Dad, you don't appreciate me or approve of me.
6. Dad, you don't care about me.

If a parent died, or a stepparent lived with you, or some other caretaker raised you, consider substituting this person or persons for your mother or father. You may still be able to get a profile of your original family.

I have noticed that three patterns emerge from the above questions. First, people usually feel *anger* in response to too much inclusion, control, or affection. It just seems to be human nature that we often get angry when others are demanding, controlling, or smothering us. Second, people usually feel *hurt* in response to too little inclusion, control, or affection. It is very painful when loved ones do not attend to us, appreciate us, or care about us. Third, as people recall these early hurts and anger, they often tend to distort their recollections in extreme ways. We are more likely to use words like *always* or *never* to describe these early experiences, as if there were few good exceptions.

Being a hurt or angry child does not mean you expressed your hurt or anger. It often was not safe for you to do so as a child. Adult children of alcoholics know this quite well. Many parents will physically or emotionally pulverize children who express anger and other intense emotions. In other families, there is always the threat of physical or emotional abandonment by parents if we express our pain too loudly. How fragile our homes can be! So we sadly grab our pillows, pull them over our heads to drown out the yelling in the other room, and then cry ourselves to sleep. Perhaps it was also true that your parents did not know how to assuage or work through feelings of their own—let alone your feelings. This usually means that your inner child carries a dammed up reservoir of feelings that can burst forth if you don't have any constructive outlets for these emotions.

Try to remember that you are no longer that frightened child. It is now safe to learn how to express these emotions in your loving bond.

Interpreting your profile is relatively straightforward. Since I have used this technique only for clinical purposes, there are no statistical norms with which to compare your scores. Keep the following points in mind:

1. Any 4 or 5 indicates apparent dissatisfaction.

2. Any 3 may also indicate dissatisfaction if all your other scores are 1s or 2s. (You may simply be more reserved about admitting that you are dissatisfied.)

3. Your inner child will likely erupt with any other person who evokes these dissatisfied needs.

4. You are likely to spit forth anger whenever you experience too much inclusion, control, or affection.

5. You are likely to sink into despair whenever you experience too little inclusion, control, or affection.

6. You are likely to experience both hurt and anger if you are dissatisfied in more than one need area.

7. You may be more likely to express anger when you are actually hurt. This is particularly true of men who feel too vulnerable expressing hurt.

8. It is not necessary that your memories of your parents be perfectly, or even remotely, accurate. What matters is your subjective impression.

Do you recall Bo and Shana from the prior section? Let's take a moment to review their scores. As you may recall, Bo described his mother as high on expectations, low on guidance, and absent from the family by working two jobs. His profile for his mother was as follows:

MOTHER

	Inclusion	Control	Affection
High	5	5	3
Low	5	3	1

Bo, as you can see, is likely to have anger triggered whenever he experiences too many demands or expectations (high inclusion) or too much criticism or manipulation (high control). He will also be hurt with too little attention (low inclusion). This was exactly what happened in his relationship with Shana. By comparison, Shana's profile for both her parents is as follows:

	MOTHER				FATHER		
	Inclusion	Control	Affection		Inclusion	Control	Affection
High	5	5	1		5	5	1
Low	3	2	1		4	3	5

Shana, as you can see, is likely to experience either anger or hurt, depending on whether she experiences too many demands or expectations (high inclusion), too much criticism or manipulation (high control), or too little caring (low affection). Her inner child was as prepared to respond to triggering situations as was Bo's. (I might also note that I have found that perfectionists usually have high scores in both inclusion and control. This was certainly true in Shana's case with both parents!)

Bo and Shana learned to appreciate each other's sensitive inner child more fully by using the RENEW model. Each learned to become more tolerant and more tender regarding the other's past. Trust and love were replenished, and they soon began living together again.

We will carefully analyze how this process occurs later in the book. For now, we must recognize that the resentments which ooze out during adulthood are largely the seepage from infected wounds incurred many years before during childhood. Though your partner may appear to be blameworthy, you must learn to look inward rather than outward, backward rather than forward. This is the only way you will truly know and understand your anger and hurt.

As uncomfortable as this process may be, we must look more thoroughly at the attachment process that shapes all human relationships. This process begins during infancy and affects every bond we create for the remainder of our days.

Early Wounds

Parent-Infant Attachment

A woman, shopping in a food store, stops to pluck an item off the shelf. With her, nestled comfortably in one corner of the food cart, lies her three-month-old infant. As she carefully places a bag of flour in the cart, a fast-paced businessman stops in his tracks to respond to the familiar cooing sounds coming from among the shortening, peanut butter, and bread. As he bends over to make better facial contact with this adorable child, he experiences a *deja-vu* of when his own children once uttered these same beguiling, universal sounds.

For such a common life event, this situation is quite profound. Here we find a helpless three-month-old infant somehow getting more of a response out of a top level executive than his own subordinates sometimes do. Not bad for a fourteen-pound baby!

Of course this is precisely the same process which is occuring with the infants own parents—hopefully. Four points are noteworthy about this situation.

First, it is quite apparent that communication between parent and child is a two-way street. Infants are not merely responding to parental messages, they are also creating them by their own behaviors.

Second, these delightful infant behaviors, which stop us in our tracks, are prewired. Such behaviors as "smiling" or "visual following" are actually inborn. Our infants are quite prepared from day one to influence us unsuspecting parents.

Third, the manner in which parents respond to these innate invitations will determine the social and emotional development of the child for years to come.

And fourth, the survival of the infant, as well as of our species, depends upon an adequate response from parents or appropriate caretakers. It is this emerging attachment between parent and infant that buffers the infant from risk during the long years of immaturity. No other species on the zoological scale has such a long period of development and family care.

Parent-infant attachment is largely established within the first year of life and serves as a secure backdrop for all subsequent human development. The importance of a warm and secure attachment to a loving caregiver in the first year of life cannot be overstated. It is this base that allows our toddlers to begin their explorations into their brave new world.

Studies have clearly shown that physical contact between parent and infant is necessary in order for this attachment to occur. For instance, it is necessary (but not sufficient) to feed your child well. Holding your infant close to you, so that both of you feel warmth and softness, is also required in order for normal attachment to occur.

Facial contact facilitates this process as well. This leads us to appreciate yet another delightful, built-in capacity of infants—an inborn capacity to selectively focus on facial expression. Human emotion can be predominantly viewed as a facial experience. Can there be any doubt that the formation of healthy attachment between parent and child depends on a parent's willingness, or capacity, to respond to this visual exchange?

Let me clarify the relation of attachment to inclusion, control, and affection. The healthy formation of inclusion needs depends on undivided attention from parent to child. This occurs when a parent bends over, looks a child in the eyes, expresses a smile, and says, "You're the best baseball player in the family. Do you want to hit a few?" It is only when a child receives this total commitment, even for the briefest period of time each day, that he or she begins to feel important and worthy of attention. When love and physical affection are added to this formula, we have the right chemistry for the healthy formation of a self-identity.

Many writers in child development make a distinction between "attachment behaviors" and "attachment." Attachment behaviors characterize the very early years. They are the infant's repertoire of behaviors directed to caregivers—the looking, cooing, crying, smiling, clinging, and other "approach" behaviors that are intended to bring mommy or daddy closer. These are often considered to be proximity seeking or contact maintaining behaviors because they are intended to secure comfort in the presence of a special caregiver, such as a parent.

When a parent continues to be responsive to a child's attachment behaviors, the child gradually realizes that he or she feels good when the parent is close by. In a sense, the child feels *empowered* by his or her ability to bring a parent near. Eventually, children also realize that they can feel safe when mom or dad is away from them, which usually occurs toward the end of the first year. Such trust in a huge, uncertain world can occur only when children develop positive feelings—and eventually beliefs—

that they are so securely attached to another that this love-bond actually transcends space and time.

It is this *inner representation* of a safe, loving, and responsive world which we call "secure attachment." Once secure attachment is established, a child will more actively explore the world around. It is a paradox of human development that we must first become securely attached to someone before we are free to become autonomous. Attachment always precedes detachment. Remember that attachment and detachment are not polar opposites. They represent *separate dimensions*. The daring expeditions of young explorers are successful experiences when they carry within themselves an undeniably secure base of affection and celebrational support from significant others.

Detachment continues throughout life, well beyond the wobbly first steps of an uncertain toddler. Subsequent phases occur when a child enters school around the age of six, whenever a child enters a peer-group activity such as camping or sports, and certainly during the hormone-driven years of adolescence. The creation of all this autonomous functioning does not need to diminish the strength of the original attachment bond at all.

However, if the attachment process is too extreme, too possessive, children will never take the initiative to courageously strike out on their own. Detachment won't occur. Children who are "insecurely attached" to their parents feel anxious because of inconsistent nurturing, overbearing control, or psychological or physical absence. They demonstrate either angry protest or apathetic withdrawal.

I believe adult disenchantment themes often have their roots in early childhood attachment patterns. And there is evidence that positive behaviors and social interactions, once established, do hold up over time. An infant's positive social relationship with his or her parents is likely to generalize to a positive social orientation toward other members of a larger social network. When studies over time are conducted, securely attached children display the following behaviors at three to five years of age:

- Engage in more imaginative play than anxiously attached children.
- Be more enthusiastic.
- Comply with maternal requests more frequently.
- Ignore the mother less.
- Display less frustration.
- Display more positive feelings.
- Cry, whine, or say no less.
- Spend more time on a task.
- Be more sociable.
- Be more peer-oriented.
- Present fewer problem behaviors in social settings.
- Be less dependent on their preschool teachers.
- Be more socially competent.
- Be more empathetic.

Healthy signs of inclusion, control, and affection are evident in these these securely attached children. They enjoy being included in activities and are certainly peer-oriented. Regarding control, they have a well-balanced need for autonomy, they can spend self-directed time on a task, and can work independently in a preschool setting. And most impressive of all is their healthy display of affection. They are enthusiastic, playful, empathic, emotionally expressive children.

Parents clearly have a tremendous impact on the healthy development of inclusion, control, and affection needs throughout human development. This is true particularly during the first few years of life. Research has shown the following characteristics to be significant:

Parents of Securely Attached Children	*Parents of Insecurely Attached Children*
1. Respond quickly to their crying infant.	Delay longer in responding to their crying infant.
2. Are very responsive in acknowledging their children when they interact.	Are much less responsive in acknowledging their children when they interact.
3. Are very affectionate during bodily contact.	Are physically distant.
4. Are tender when they pick up their children.	Are abrupt and interfering when they pick up children.
5. Give undivided attention while holding children.	Devote themselves to routine activities while holding children.
6. Are rated more sensitive, accepting, cooperative, and psychologically accessible to their babies.	Are rated insensitive, rejecting, interfering, and ignoring.
7. Are supportive in aiding their children in their tasks.	Are impatient or intrusive while aiding children in their tasks.
8. Have more mutual support for each other.	Lack support from a significant other.
9. Perceive wider social support.	Perceive themselves as detached and alone.

Generally, parents of securely attached children know when it is important and appropriate to be involved in the caregiving needs of their children. And when they do get involved, they do so in a sensitive, attentive, and truly affectionate manner which conveys to the child that he or she truly is significant. Good consistent parenting is a wondrous thing to behold. Its effects can last a lifetime. Unfortunately, the ill effects of poor parenting can last just as long.

Dysfunctional Families

I grew up believing that all the world was like Sherman, Texas. I also grew up thinking everyone else's family was different from mine. Other families surely did not experience what I experienced in a family where alcohol was the dominant factor. I would later learn that my situation was not unique. I simply could not talk about the situation. So we lived in a conspiracy of silence. We lived alone, and we hurt alone, and believed no one could possibly understand.

Rev. C. Ray Burchette, Jr.

Many of us are the products of dysfunctional homes. Some of us are Adult Children of Alcoholics. Others are victims of mental, physical, or sexual abuse. And still others were wounded by parents who were workaholics—parents whose addiction to achievement as an escape was as damaging as addiction to any other drug. The results are usually the same.

If we grew up in a dysfunctional family, we are likely to feel abandoned—because we *were* abandoned! If we were not physically abandoned, we were definitely emotionally abandoned. We were left to fend for ourselves, to figure ourselves out, to find our place in a world which often seemed too frightening and overwhelming. We often felt like we were burdens to others—excess baggage. We might have thought, "I'm not really wanted here," or "I am not very special," or "No one really cares about me." Given such abandonment, can there be any wonder that adult children and other wounded inner children feel so worthless, hurt, and angry?

This chapter has explored the inevitable hurt and anger which result when our developmental needs are unmet. But we must see that a deeper, more primal emotion underlies all the anger and hurt—fear! As adults, we often don't know where our fear comes from. Usually we can't identify a single event as the source. Yet, if we are honest with ourselves, we can admit that our entire adult lives have been shadowed by a feeling that something uncertain, something remote, perhaps something cataclysmic threatens our entire being—our very survival!

We may have phobias, panic attacks, and generalized anxiety. We may have tense shoulders, stomach troubles, or sexual difficulties. Getting close feels scary, so we learn to withdraw, to hide, to run away—to manifest symptoms. But we can avoid intimacy for only so long. Ultimately, in the course of a love relationship, we must come to terms with the buried wounds of our painful childhoods.

You might assume that functional families don't experience the problems that dysfunctional families experience. This simply is not so. Problems are inevitable in life. But in functional families, the problems which do occur are dealt with differently. Communication is open. Feelings are expressed. Needs are honestly stated. As stress develops and crises occur, they are dealt with until they are resolved. Such resolution does not occur in dysfunctional homes. Problems are avoided, feelings are buried, and the truth is never told.

We have seen how important it is to belong, to have control, and to receive warmth. When these needs are repeatedly violated, we begin to develop roles to cope with the dysfunctional patterns that threaten us so.

We may become "enablers," "heros," "scapegoats," and so on. The purpose is the same, no matter the role. Provide a cover-up! Make sure that the sickness which pervades the family is not openly confronted or revealed. To do so would be too embarrassing, too frightening, too overwhelming. So we hide until we must look at ourselves, years later, when disenchantment has pryed open our previously sealed tombs.

Our need to face our own histories is often an urgent one. In my practice, I use a letter-writing exercise to help my clients work through the hurt and anger of their childhood wounds. Here are some descriptions of the childhood wounds that others have experienced.

Too Many Demands and Expectations (High Inclusion)

Mom, none of the ways I have disappointed you have been deliberate attempts to do so. Indeed, for me not to have disappointed you, I would have had to meet some very strict requirements that only you have the key to. Had I met these, I would not be a better person—only a more submissive one, even a spineless one! I wish you could have loved seeing me develop into something of you but apart from you. I am not what you expected me to be. I am not a scientist. I am not great. But I am O.K.

Karen

Too Little Attention (Low Inclusion)

Mom, I have always felt like the fifth wheel of a car. Necessary in case of an emergency, but for the most part in the way. By the time I was growing up, you were ready to develop your career. It was like you didn't have time to be involved with me or the things I was interested in. You never *tried* to guide me or get me involved. You were never present unless absolutely necessary at any of my school functions or sporting events. And when you did show up, I felt like a huge burden. I was always afraid to ask you and Daddy to come to something for me, because I didn't know if you would enjoy it. In addition, I always felt responsible if everything wasn't just so. Why wasn't I good enough for you to take pride in?

Susan

Too Little Appreciation or Approval (Low Control)

Mom and Dad, I spend my whole life doing something. There is a penalty of death for doing nothing, for relaxing and enjoying something. Any accomplishment I made was accompanied by subtle hints that I could do better or I was not doing enough. Mom, this was particularly true of you if I encroached on your territory! I recall, when I was sixteen, there was a lot of financial pressure because of all of Mom's illness. You both mentioned that money was tight and there would not be much for Christmas. I had wanted to save my money to learn to ski, but I wanted more to help the family.

I spent most of the money I earned to buy a nice gift for each of my brothers and sisters. You knew what I was up to because I showed you everything I bought. I had spent a lot of time and energy choosing gifts that would be valued by everyone and I approached Christmas with a good feeling. When Christmas morning came, every effort that I made had been overshadowed by one of the most lavish and expensive displays of Christmas giving that you two had or will ever know. The memory of that Christmas still bothers me, for Mom was not outdone that year by my efforts at giving!

Phillip

Too Little Caring (Low Affection)

Mom, I remember going up to you and wanting a hug or a kiss. You would push me away. I remember wanting to lie with you and wrap my arms around you and you would push me away. I remember you telling me one scripture after another in your effort to direct my life. Yet you never seemed to be there when I had real problems. You never seemed to want to listen to me when I had a worry. I remember when I was going through my divorce you came to visit me, and with all the agony I was experiencing all you could do was quote one passage after another from the Bible. What I really wanted you to do was to hold me and reassure me.

Margaret

I want to close this chapter with a short story written by one of my clients. It painfully documents the characteristics of too much control and too much smothering. The result is an angry inner child whose experiences of being manipulated affected the author for many years.

Bertha's Elusive, Guilt-Free Christmas

Bertha hovered above the jewelry display case like a buzzard on carrion. It was December 24th, and Royce didn't have that special gift. Not just any gift. Not what he asked for; not what he needed. No, a special gift. One that costs at least as much as the videotape camera and recorder that his sister will be getting.

"We've always given you and Jessie things that were equally as nice," said Bertha, wanting oh-so-much for me to be six again. "You need a pretty watch."

Emmet, my father, stood at a distance, mute and neutered. Christmas depression had begun to settle down around him, and he disappeared into a shuffling bundle of navy blue cashmere. Bertha was at her height, her peak. She was in a buying frenzy. And it was the best kind of buying, too. Guilt free.

No bargain-hunting here, boy. No going out of her way to save that much-bragged-about buck. Nope. This was for Royce. Her pride and joy. Her "little brother." Her life. Of course, she'd never spend the money on herself.

I know that because she tells me so.

"It's not the money," Bertha was braying at a distance. "He just won't let us get him anything too expensive." The clerk feigned understanding and placed a watch back in the window display. A questioning glance in my direction queried whether the watch was for me or her. I turned away from him and whispered to my father:

"Daddy, I guess the thing is, I really don't want a watch. I mean, it's a wonderful gift, and I would use it, but I just can't get excited about one. I don't want to get just any watch, just so I'll have something for Christmas. When you buy something this expensive, you should love it right away, and nothing we've seen has really been the watch I'd like to have."

"No, I don't like that rough gold. It's not shiny and pretty. It snags your clothes. See here? Feel it. No, no, like this ... " Bertha was imparting her metallurgical savvy to a twenty-year veteran of the jewelry business as I tapped her furred shoulder.

"Let's look around a little more," I said.

"Oh, Emmet, oh, Royce, look at this one. This is a beauty," she stammered as she blew a bleached curl from her well-lifted brow.

"Uh-huh, I saw that one. It's too much."

"No, it isn't."

"Mama, it's eight thousand dollars."

"Nooo! How much is this one?" she asked the weary salesman.

"Seven-thousand five hundred, ma'am."

"See? It's not too much."

"Yes, it is, Mama. Let's look around. Thanks anyway," I called as we moved towards the door.

"Royce, I'm just heart-sick," whined Bertha on the crowded sidewalk. Her eyes welled with tears. I felt bad for wanting to laugh.

"I just haven't found one I really want, Mama."

"Oh, you just don't want to spend the money. It would give me so much pleasure to see you get a pretty watch ... "

(My hands were around her throat.)

" ... You're the only joy Daddy and I have ... "

(Her surgically-altered skin yielded beneath my fingers.)

" ... We love to give you pretty things ... "

(Veins collapsed in violet goo as the arms of my coat filled with blood.)

" ... I want you to have something really special ... "

(Her bulging eyes abandoned their dilated sockets.)

" ... Something you'll always remember as a gift from Mama ... "

(Her useless head fell from her body and mingled with gutter debris.)

"Bertha, you don't want to get him something he doesn't really want," Daddy finally offered. "He's told us just exactly what he's looking for, and when we find it, we'll buy it. And don't worry about the money, Royce," he added, "if you like something, let's get it."

Please, God, let us find something soon, thought Daddy and I.

Please, God, let him get what I like, thought Bertha, but this is what she said: "Well, let's not stand on a street corner arguing about it."

A tear escaped one eye, and she felt the pitying gaze of passersby. A crying woman was only curiosity, of course. This was New York.

Bertha walked ahead leaving Daddy and me behind. The game was on. The rules were set—oh, so long ago. Pass the guilt, shift the blame, and choose up sides. There was a time limit, too. Midnight, Christmas. God's birthday or something, and the symbol of our love for one another.

"Is that a jewelry store up there, Royce?"

And there was dinner still to be made, and the theater to attend. We'd be in fine shape by then.

"Isn't this nice?" she'll say, and no one will answer. "Wasn't that nice?" she'll say again next year, and no one will remember.

"Let's go in here, Mama."

The heavy brass door swung open, and a young saleswoman approached.

"May I help you?"

If only she could have been warned. If only she could have known the list of salespeople to which her name was to be added. Those poor bastards. For more than fifty years, unsuspecting shoptenders had been badgered, cajoled, slandered, reported, teased, loved, hated, and talked to death by Bertha. And now this young woman was to be among them. She never had a chance.

"May I help you?" she asked again.

Bertha surveyed the scene in an instant, looking for an available male salesperson. None was in sight. If given the choice, Bertha will take a man every time. Shopping is a primal act for Bertha—as rudimentary as self-defense, as life-supporting as eating, as instinctual as screwing. Her's is a world where a wink of an eye and a hand on the arm can spell the difference between retail and wholesale prices. Or once could. Who can say now whether the last time she avoided the sales tax was due to the intimate recounting of her first date, or because the salesman would have done anything to be rid of her.

"We're looking for a watch for my son," said Bertha coolly.

The saleswoman moved toward the watch counter and asked, "Any particular style?"

And there it was. The watch I was looking for. Absolutely simple. An elegant gold band with a slim rectangular face. But it was too easy. It wasn't perfect. I heard the question before it escaped her lips. God help me, I have learned some things from Bertha.

"But that's not 18-karat gold, is it?"

"No, ma'am," answered the woman. "It's 14 karat."

Bertha reacted as though the watch suddenly smelled very bad. I countered by placing the loathsome object on my wrist. She glanced away from this indiscretion and continued the search. The game wasn't over. Not by a long shot. But by taking my hideous prize to a nearby mirror, I had tilted the score in my favor. Bertha was down by two: I was looking at a watch that I had shamelessly confessed an attraction for, and I had been the one who picked it out.

"That old 14-karat stuff has a greenish cast to it," said Bertha just loudly enough for me, and everyone else, to hear. "It doesn't have the rich look of ... " Bertha stopped mid-sentence. Something had caught her eye. I knew it would, of course—anything but this fecal material that presently soiled my wrist. But this I was frankly unprepared for. She had found a watch that was not only more expensive and four karats heavier, but also one that she genuinely seemed to love. This would be tough. This would be hell. God help me, I began to weaken already.

"Oh, Royce," she breathed with a familiarity that made me sick, "look at this one!" I hated being spoken to like one of her effeminate companions. "Oh, Royce, now this looks like you to me."

If it hadn't been such an attractive watch, those words alone would have cemented the purchase of the lightweight abomination. But it was, unfortunately, a handsome piece, almost art deco in design with an unusual ten-sided face and an intricately woven band. It was also twice as much as I had wanted to spend, much more pretentious than the green turd, and probably better suited for an older man.

"Isn't this a beauty, Emmet?"

Daddy sat silently in the leather club chair like a pool player waiting to clear the table. Not calculating. Not contemptuous. Just waiting his turn.

"Yes," said Daddy mildly. And then, in a brighter tone, "Say, this is a pretty nice place! What time do you folks serve lunch around here?"

The pretty saleswoman smiled at the nice, quiet man and offered him some coffee. He declined with a laugh.

"How late are you open tonight?" Bertha was asking as I approached the counter.

"My God," I thought, "It's only 11:30!" This one promised to go the limit.

"Now see, Royce, you'll never find a watch prettier than this one. See how unusual it is? See how much prettier the color is? Let's look at it in the mirror."

Sotto voce at the mirror, I was once again made privy to the reasons for my mother's existence. Not the least of which, it seemed, was the purchase of this watch.

"This watch just looks like it belongs to you, Royce. Don't worry about the money. I want to buy it for you. You know, half of everything Daddy has is mine. And it would make Daddy so happy to see you wear this beautiful watch. He just got through saying to me, 'Oh, Bertha, that watch is really a beauty.'"

And on. And on.

There comes a time in this game of guilt and love when forces must be weighed and all elements taken into consideration. On one hand is the private battle—one on one. "I want what I want and not what you want for me." As a child, this can be dangerous, and losing can be advantageous in the long run. But as an adult—well, an adult simply doesn't play. But with Bertha in the game, the rules must be altered slightly, concessions made. Call it the "Special Olympics" of emotional competition, if you will.

And who takes joy in beating a cripple?

On the other hand, there are consequential concerns to be studied. For instance, if I buy the watch I want, will we ever be allowed to take pleasure in the Christmas decorations I painstakingly constructed, will we enjoy the Broadway musical I arranged for us to see, will we enjoy the ludicrous mound of food prepared for three depressed appetites?

Bertha extracted one foot from the shoe that she had bought on sale and shifted her weight. She brushed back her hair and braced herself for another filibuster if necessary. Her hand caressed my arm and her pleading eyes told me that she was doing everything in her power to make at least one of us happy. Her body swayed slightly, and there was just a hint of coquettishness—a coy "do-it-for-Mama" look that made me taste my own bile.

Love me! Love me! she cried.

But only I could hear. And I wasn't listening. "I tell you what," I said as I led her back to the counter, "since you want me to have this watch, and I want the other one, why don't you buy your favorite, and I'll buy mine?"

The solution was at once ludicrous and absolutely befitting of Solomon. Surely, not even Bertha would condone the expenditure for two watches. Surely, she would understand, without my being cruel, that if I accepted her watch at all, it would only be to keep peace in the family. Surely, when all was said and done, she would want me to have the gift that I truly wanted.

"Great!" exclaimed Bertha. "Let's do it!"

The poor saleswoman laughed good-naturedly, thinking it was a joke. And it was only after she had been asked her opinion of the solution that her countenance changed.

"He could wear one for everyday and one for dress, couldn't he? Lots of people have more than one watch, don't they?"

And then there was silence—very brief for anyone but Bertha—but a silence most complete. The kind of silence that follows a gunshot. Or a look of reproof.

"Now, you're mad at me, aren't you?" Bertha asked Daddy.

I lifted my downturned eyes to see what miniscule communication had escaped my notice. The cashmere-coated pool shooter was chalking up his cue.

"You think I'm making him get something he doesn't want, don't you?"

"Bertha, if you want a watch, why don't you pick one for yourself, and we'll buy it right now. I know which watch Royce wants, and it's the one I think we ought to get."

Eight ball in the corner pocket.

Bertha paced about the store as Emmet produced a credit card. The transaction was conducted in silence. A chore. Like the silent, long walk home.

"Thank you, Daddy," I later said when we were both alone. "I got the watch I wanted."

There was no pleasure in his response, not the slightest betrayal of triumph.

"It's a beautiful watch," he said blandly. And that was the end of that.

5

Through a Looking Glass

It was the best of times, it was the worst of times. It was the age
of wisdom, it was the age of foolishness. It was the season of
light, it was the season of darkness. It was the spring of hope, it
was the winter of despair. We had everything before us, we had
nothing before us ....

Charles Dickens
A Tale of Two Cities

This chapter addresses our most embedded beliefs about human relationships ... personal beliefs that color and distort our experience of the world.
These beliefs, often extreme in nature, guide all our reactions to people
and events in our lives, as well as all of our hopes and expectations about
the future. Our beliefs are the conscious and unconscious filters that strain
all human experience into enchantment or disenchantment. So integral
are these beliefs that we will distort the world around us rather than
change a deeply held conviction. In their book, *The Art of Being Human*,
Janero and Altshuler tell the following story:

There is a story about a scientific father who wanted his son to be
armed with the toughness required to face a harsh world. He decided
the fantasy of Santa Claus was nonsense, and on his son's fifth Christmas, he forced the boy to stay awake all night to observe the source of
the presents. The child, rubbing his eyes, watched as his parents
assembled the gifts under the tree. At dawn he pleaded to be allowed
to sleep. His father, however, insisted that he have breakfast and then
play with his toys. Before he was allowed to eat, the boy was required
to finish the sentence, "There is no ...." When the boy kept meeting the
command with silence, the father became angry and threatened to beat
the child if he did not comply. Wearily the little boy looked up and said,
"There is no father!" (Janero and Altshuler 1979, 123)

Our pattern of personal beliefs has an impact on all aspects of our lives,
including our love relationships. We pick lovers, keep, and discard lovers

because of the beliefs we use to evaluate people in our lives. Most of us take these embedded beliefs for granted—somehow believing they are suitable lenses through which to view the world. In fact, we will often maintain the same self-defeating beliefs while casting aside one suitable lovemate after another.

These embedded beliefs are always set up in terms of opposites and are arranged in a hierarchy of importance—some beliefs have a greater influence on our thinking than others. For instance, we might have an embedded belief that independence is important in life. At the same time, we have mental pictures of what independence looks like—in other words, how independent people behave. If our lover doesn't behave according to these pictures, then he or she must be dependent, a quality we disapprove of. The more strongly we value independence and the more narrowly we define it, the more likely we are to experience disenchantment with our lover.

We all have embedded evaluative beliefs about many other personal qualities, which we also polarized into extremes—for example, open versus closed, warm versus cold, generous versus selfish, frugal versus spendthrift, or outgoing versus aloof. The more rigidly we believe that our lovers (or our friends or children or parents) must conform to one of these qualities, the more destined we are to be disenchanted.

Romantic love is rigidly dichotomous—our partner is seen as *always* warm or *never* selfish. But in mature relationships, our evaluative beliefs can—and must—be flexible. For instance, while we may wish for warmth (however we define it), we can acknowledge and accept that at times our partner can only give us something that feels lukewarm. In committed love, our opinions and feelings can move back and forth *along the continuum* of our personal beliefs. Maturation of love brings with it the ability to see a full spectrum of shades between black and white. Unfortunately, in our need to ground ourselves, we often gravitate toward one end of the continuum, thereby negating the other.

The Missing Piece

Once upon a time there was a young woman who lived in a growing, dynamic city. She had seen the growing business sector, the new greenbelts which protected the environment, and the bustling entertainment district. These wonders provided little pleasure to her, however. She was quite sad. She had been sad for years and had shared her sadness with many helpers. Though she felt helped at times, she quickly forgot these moments as she gazed upon the whole of her life. Overall, she would say, nothing had changed. While visiting with her most recent helper, this woman described the vast emptiness that seemed to paralyze her morning, noon, and night—an emptiness which contrasted sharply with the fullness she yearned for.

"You don't know what it is like to be so empty," she moaned.

"But what of the masterful craftwork that you create?" remarked her helper. "What of the pleasure you bring to others through your work?"

"Their pleasure is momentary and my pleasure is even more short-lived than theirs," she responded.

"What of the coterie of friends who call upon you, who surround you with love, who seek out your warmth and expressiveness? What of these friends who say that your gatherings are among the most fun-filled in the land?" quizzed the helper.

"They are reflections in the sun who disappear at the end of the day. Each of them, in their own way, returns to the fullness of their own lives."

"Then what of the lovely home you own, the financial security you have, and your sound health and well-being?" asked the helper.

"These things are unimportant details; they are the dull, murky, gray background which contrasts with the sharpness of my daily pain."

"You have so much fullness in life," mused the helper. "I envision a sparkling wine goblet, full to the brim. Beauty, friends, artistry, creativity, compassion, financial success, economic security, and a beautiful city fill this goblet of life from bottom to top. All this is yours now. Things others dream of are yours *now*. Yet, you are sad. It is almost as if you gloss over these gifts, as though your focus is elsewhere. What more could fill this bountiful goblet?"

"A red rose floating at the top! My life would then truly be full," the young woman boldly proclaimed.

"With such fullness already available, what could a red rose, floating at the top, symbolize?"

"The loving relationship I have never had!"

Missing pieces represent our incompleteness—our lack of wholeness. They are the polar opposites of our lives. We all have a "red rose." It may be the perfect job, the perfect family, or the perfect love. What is your missing piece? This woman yearned for the emotional closeness of a loving relationship and discounted everything else she did have. With love she hoped to complete all that was incomplete about her life. She sought life's ultimate meaning and fulfillment in a beloved.

To view your life as half empty is to miss an equal truth—that your life is also half full. With extreme beliefs we are only able to see one side of the equation. When these exaggerated notions are then fueled by powerful feelings, such as sadness or fear, our beliefs become rigidly cast in bronze. We may believe that our lives have always been a desolate wasteland ... and always will be!

We are constantly searching for the most meaningful interpretation of information in our lives. Our views of ourselves, others, and the world in which we live represent this search for coherence and wholeness. Let's take a closer look at this:

Barbara, a twenty-eight-year-old woman, has contracted genital herpes within the last year. She now considers herself unlovable and destined to "an old maid's existence." She maintains this view in spite of the fact that two men have proposed marriage to her during the last year—men who knew that she has genital herpes.

Which view is accurate in the above scenario? Which belief is valid? Barbara has recurrent outbreaks of herpes, partly from her intense anxiety and guilt. Why, she wonders, would any man want to spend his life exposing himself to the risk of herpes? Her childhood dreams of blissful romance suddenly seem shattered. She begins to avoid social situations, refuses to date, and isolates herself from others. She describes herself as "dirtied" in spite of continued advances from two beaus who remember—and cherish—the frolicking, lovable Barbara she had been. Barbara acts "as if" she is tainted, while her lovers act "as if" she is pristine. In her need to be perfectly whole and complete, she obsessively focuses on one physical imperfection. If she does not learn to alter this belief, Barbara's quality of life will be affected for years to come.

Barbara has also allowed her beliefs to influence her behavior. Her belief that she is tainted has altered her actions and reactions with others. Now that she has withdrawn from others, she has begun to notice that the phone is not ringing, that she has fewer dates, and that the expressionless face she presents to the world is matched by others around her! Once Barbara labeled herself as tainted, she began to:

1. Limit her interactions with others
2. Focus on the behaviors of others that reinforce her own beliefs
3. Evoke congruent behaviors from others that reinforce her own beliefs
4. Distort or misinterpret the behavior of others
5. Present behaviors that are consistent with her beliefs
6. Misinterpret her own behavior

We will learn more about these processes in chapter 8 on getting stuck. For now it is important to understand that once we label ourselves or others we act "as if" our labels are appropriate and true. Our labels are constantly evolving and usually represent the missing pieces we yearn for. Thus, when two people meet, the relationship between them—and the behaviors of each of them—are constantly changing as their relationship develops. The words used to describe one another during romantic love are very different from those used during mature, covenant love. The meaning given the labels is constantly evolving as well. Communication is interactive. Yet, our language, both spoken and unspoken, seems to suggest a static world unaffected by time and experience.

Putting on Our White Coats

We are adept at actively constructing beliefs about ourselves and others. These beliefs have been called "personal constructs" by psychologist George Kelly. Beliefs represent an active searching for the most meaningful interpretation of the information we have at hand—even if this information is false, misleading, and misinterpreted!

For instance, if my mother-in-law describes herself as *outgoing*—which she does—how do we account for her barricading herself in her bedroom during numerous social engagements over the years *or* her peering silently from the kitchen window rather than personally greeting her neighbors. Even if she behaves differently at other times and places, are these behaviors enough to support her personal view of herself? And how do we account for such a discrepancy between her view of herself and the view of others?

We are talking about a biased, subjective process. We selectively receive information, interpret it, store it, and then retrieve it, using our own private logic. We form beliefs about ourselves, others, and the world around us in this way. Somehow, within our mysterious "black box," we filter all of our human experience into a hierarchical structure of beliefs. Understanding these beliefs as they relate to our choice of a beloved is not so mysterious, as we will see in the next section. But first, let's look at how one person filters her own experience in a way that creates much personal pain.

This is a personal journal entry from one of my clients, Jean. As you read about her trip to visit her cousin in Los Angeles, notice the personal constructions, or beliefs, that she generated about both herself and her cousin. Take time to consider how accurate these beliefs may be.

April 21

I knew before I went to Los Angeles how I might feel when I returned. I have experienced it before. The depths to which I fell when I came home! Is it worth it? Should I ever go again? Why am I so terribly affected by my visits to Betty? What happens to me? Is my life that empty, that unsatisfying? I had a wonderful time. I loved being there. But the comparisons between us are just too great.

Betty is glamorous, capable, confident—fantastic! Jim is too good to be true. The kids are too good to be true. Their life is too good to be true. Their house is so beautiful. Betty looks gorgeous in her gorgeous, elegant clothes. Her life is so exciting. And they are so happy! Then I came back home to my average life. My average days. Dull. Boring. Nothing to look forward to. My dull husband. My dull kids. I have no purpose. No work. I am selfish and self-centered.

And ... we are the Poor Relations. That hurts. I do not want to be the Poor Relations!

I want some of what Betty has—but I do not have it. Kids with promise. A husband who puts her first. A confident husband. But I am not smart either. And I am jealous as well. I wish I could have some of her flair and her confidence. I would like to look terrific. Life with Leonard is definitely never going to be in the fast lane. Sometimes he is even in reverse. I would like more action and I don't know how to get it.

I am pretty slow myself. Too introverted, too detailed—no ambition really. I want things to happen, but I am not very good at making them happen. I'm lazy and I'm pampered. Spoiled. Sheltered? I want to be a lady. Sort of. God, am I depressed!

Is is so wrong to just want to have a pleasant life? Security! Why does being loved and being taken care of, supported financially by someone else, make me feel so guilty?

Jean uses these personal constructs to describe herself and her life:

Empty	Frustrated	Purposeless	Poor
Unsatisfying	Average	Selfish	Slow
Sad	Pampered	Self-centered	Lazy
Spoiled	Sheltered	Introverted	Dull
Depressed	Boring	Guilty	Detailed

She uses these personal constructs to describe her cousin, Betty:

Glamorous	Exciting	Capable	Confident
Gorgeous	Elegant	Happy	Fantastic
Wealthy	Flair	Fast lane	A lady

Are these beliefs, these descriptive adjectives that Jean uses to describe herself and Betty, absolutely true? *Absolutely not*! For all we know, Betty may view herself as empty, unsatisfied, depressed, poor, and so on. Betty's friends may view her as a selfish bitch rather than elegant, confident, and fantastic!

Jean is doing three common things that people do when they are disenchanted with themselves or others. First, Jean is *filtering*. She has successfully excluded every positive description of herself from this painful epistle. All we find are twenty indictments against herself. She has selectively creamed herself while she has sanctified her cousin.

Second, Jean uses *polarized thinking* with deftness. She thinks in terms of opposites. She is dull, Betty is glamorous. She is poor, Betty is wealthy. She is depressed, Betty is happy. Her life has no purpose, Betty's life has promise. When beliefs become this rigid or categorical, they lack what psychologist Jerome Bruner once called *veridicality*, or truth. How can such extremes be true?

Third, Jean seems to *concretize abstractions*. She takes subjective appraisals of herself, as well as others, and gives them the same credence as the Ten Commandments. She states them "as if" 100 percent of the population would agree with her. For instance, we are led to view her husband as so dull that life with him is akin to watching a tree grow. Leonard must hardly be breathing by her account!

This chapter is about those "looking glasses" through which we peer, those lenses we construct that help—or hinder—our view of the world. What you are about to discover are your most embedded beliefs about love relationships—those beliefs that shape your very selection of a love-mate.

Settle back comfortably in order to complete the following survey instrument. Answer honestly. The data you provide will help you understand the cognitive map you follow in picking and discarding the men and women in your life.

A Relationship Survey

Below, you will be given an opportunity to think about a number of people in your life who have been very special to you in some way. You are to consider what qualities you perceived in these people that made each person special or appealing to you. You may have been engaged to, married to, or just infatuated with these people, or—in the case of parents—you may have been significantly shaped, as a person, by them. What is important now is that you recall that certain quality which distinguishes each person from another. Please remember that it is not necessary for you to have dated each "previous love" for very long—if at all—to write his or her name below.

On lines six and seven, write the name of your mother and father, or the two caretakers you consider the most responsible for your upbringing.

1. Your name _____

2. Your current partner _____

3. A previous love _____

4. A previous love _____

5. A previous love _____

6. Your mother (or surrogate) _____

7. Your father (or surrogate) _____

On the next page, you will see a diagram that you should complete in the following manner:

1. Begin by writing the names of the same people listed above in the seven spaces provided along the top of the diagram. In the first space, you should write your name; in the second space, the name of your current partner (if you have one); and so on.

2. When you have written in the seven names, look at the first row. Three X's appear under your name, your current partner's name, and your first "previous love." Think of some way in which two of the three persons are alike, but different from the third. Be sure to give yourself time to think

of an *important* difference. Now place a circle around the X's of the two who are alike. Do *not* circle the X for the person who is different. Do the same for each row of X's on the diagram.

3. Under the heading SIMILARITY, write the word or phrase that describes how these two persons are alike. Use any adjective or adverb that describes their personality, values, or attributes. Then, under the heading CONTRAST, write the *opposite* of this word or phrase. (Note that there is an extra space in both columns, in case you think of two ways that these same two persons are different from the third.)

N
a
m
e
1 2 3 4 5 6 7

	SIMILARITY	CONTRAST
X X X	(1) _____	_____
	_____	_____
X X X	(2) _____	_____
	_____	_____
X X X	(3) _____	_____
	_____	_____
X X X	(4) _____	_____
	_____	_____
X X X	(5) _____	_____
	_____	_____
X X X	(6) _____	_____
	_____	_____
X X X	(7) _____	_____
	_____	_____

4. Now that you have decided on the similarities and contrasts that apply, let's go one step further and rate your current love partner on each *set* of opposites listed above. But first you will need to decide which is the more positive or desirable end of the continuum. For instance, if your first SIMILARITY was "warm" and your first CONTRAST was "cold," you would pick "warm" as the positive end and "cold" as the negative end. Then you would choose a number from one to seven to describe your current partner, with seven representing the positive end of the continuum:

Cold   1   2   3   4   5   6   7   *Warm*

Use the diagram below to rate your current partner. Simply write the *negative* quality to the left and the positive quality to the right and then circle the number that best reflects how much your current partner possesses this quality.

	−		+
1._____	1 2 3 4 5 6 7	_____	
2._____	1 2 3 4 5 6 7	_____	
3._____	1 2 3 4 5 6 7	_____	
4._____	1 2 3 4 5 6 7	_____	
5._____	1 2 3 4 5 6 7	_____	
6._____	1 2 3 4 5 6 7	_____	
7._____	1 2 3 4 5 6 7	_____	

If you have more than seven polar opposites, use these additional rating scales.

8._____   1   2   3   4   5   6   7   _____

9._____   1   2   3   4   5   6   7   _____

10._____   1   2   3   4   5   6   7   _____

5. In the space below, list the ten characteristics that describe your ideal love partner—a partner who could last a lifetime. After listing these ten characteristics, decide whether your current partner, as well as each of your three prior loves, possesses these characteristics. Again, rate each person from one (low) to ten (high) on each characteristic.

CHARACTERISTICS OF IDEAL LOVE	CURRENT LOVE	PREVIOUS LOVE	PREVIOUS LOVE	PREVIOUS LOVE
1. _____	_____	_____	_____	_____
2. _____	_____	_____	_____	_____
3. _____	_____	_____	_____	_____
4. _____	_____	_____	_____	_____
5. _____	_____	_____	_____	_____
6. _____	_____	_____	_____	_____
7. _____	_____	_____	_____	_____
8. _____	_____	_____	_____	_____

9._____ _____ _____ _____ _____

10._____ _____ _____ _____ _____

Understanding Your Personal Constructs

If you want to know what you look for in a new love relationship, take the time to understand what you have valued in prior love relationships. These crucial bonds can help you to understand your personal "looking glass" through which you color and distort your perceptions of others. This looking glass is represented by the set of seven to ten dichotomies that you have chosen to evaluate your prior personal relationships.

I believe that the seven to ten dichotomies you reported in the first part of the questionnaire are more basic, more embedded, and somehow more important than the ten characteristics of an ideal love relationship that you listed at the end of the questionnaire. These dichotomies represent the *unconscious* templates that you use to judge the suitability of others. This is key. It is almost as if an inner voice from the past calls forth—beckoning, beguiling, commanding!

Perhaps it is warmth that beckons! We have learned to cherish warmth from mom or dad or someone else along the way. Whoever these path-finders may have been, they have left behind a reminder of their presence, their connection to us. Deep within us, we have preserved a set of visual memories, tacit assumptions, and dichotomies that we will attempt to replicate forever.

Often we are not even aware why we value one person over another. Once again, this is due to a continuing process we all engage in. Each of us relentlessly interprets the meaning of events that occur throughout our lives. When these events involve close relationships with others, we are likely to chronicle these positive and negative experiences by transforming them into stable belief systems. These belief systems may be understood as including three types of beliefs. Let's take a look at each of them.

Type I Beliefs

Short versus tall	Available versus unavailable
Poor versus rich	Beautiful versus ugly
Good looking versus plain	Large versus small breasts
Faithful versus unfaithful	Center of attention versus one of
Hairy versus hairless	the crowd.
Dark featured versus light	
featured	

What do you notice about these personal constructs? They seem rather shallow, concrete, and superficial, don't they? How would you like to be a beloved who is selected on the basis of these criteria? Imagine calling home and telling the folks that you are madly in love and about to get engaged to a man who values you because you are a "tall, hairless, dark-featured beauty, who has big money out the wazoo!" Yet each of these constructs was reported to me by one client or another during the past year or so. People really do select one another on the basis of Type I constructs and then wonder why their bonds seem so empty, such a wasteland, months later!

Type II Beliefs

Smart versus not so smart
Selfish versus unselfish
Cooperative versus
  uncooperative
Low morals versus high
  morals
Spontaneous versus
  unspontaneous
Honest versus dishonest
Powerful versus powerless
Successful versus
  unsuccessful
Musically gifted versus
  unmusical

Ambitious versus unambitious
Jerk versus not a jerk
High self-esteem versus low
  self-esteem
Materialistic versus
  nonmaterialistic
Realistic versus unrealistic
Sensitive versus insensitive
Aggressive versus unaggressive

What do you notice here? These beliefs are certainly more abstract than Type I beliefs. They represent a more complex thinking process that prizes culturally valued beliefs. It is a good thing to be cherished as someone who possesses high morals and self-esteem, or as someone who is cooperative and sensitive. We tend to judge those who have low morals harshly and we prefer not to associate with those who are uncooperative or insensitive. Yet something is still lacking in these personal constructions.

Each is stated as a negation. That is, if you are not what I want—powerful, successful, or honest—then that must mean that you are the opposite —insensitive, powerless, unsuccessful, or dishonest. These examples lack the complex thought process needed to create well differentiated stops along a continuum of thought and reason. This means that evaluations based on beliefs like these are much more likely to rigidly swing from one end of a polarity to the other.

Type III Beliefs

Stable versus impulsive
Giver versus taker
Tolerant versus unforgiving
Introspective versus
  superficial
Encouraging versus critical
Open versus guarded
Affectionate versus
  undemonstrative
Thinking versus feeling
Short-sighted versus long-
  term minded

Creative versus analytical
Outgoing versus introverted
Eloquent versus simplistic
Humorous versus morbid
Self-absorbed versus altruistic
Playful versus stodgy
Judging versus perceiving
Compassionate versus aloof
Emotional versus logical

Do you see the differences in the these examples? For one thing, these examples, all provided by clients, reflect a grasp of language that exceeds that in the constructs we saw earlier. Though you might argue that we are just looking at an IQ factor, I would suggest that the language skills we develop provide us with the tools we need to function in personal relationships as well. The more complex these skills, the more adept we are at selecting, understanding, and influencing one another.

Once again, consider yourself the beloved of someone who views you as "emotional." If your partner is at the level of Type III beliefs, she demonstrates a level of abstraction, uses the full continuum of thought and reason, and has a well-ordered hierarchy of personal constructs which support this evaluation. For instance, if you ask her how you appear to be emotional, she might say that she enjoys the fact that you cry easily, that your body shudders with excitement when you make love, that you have an expressive face when you talk, and that you are physically affectionate. What we see is a superordinate construct—emotional versus apathetic—supported by four subordinate constructs:

1. Tearful versus repressed
2. Physically intense versus physically inhibited
3. Expressive versus stolid
4. Affectionate versus undemonstrative

Notice how much more clearly this person's needs are stated. She is saying: "I need you to be tearful on occasions, to be physically intense, to be facially expressive, and to be physically affectionate. I will therefore view you as emotional, and since this is so important to me, I will therefore be a happy camper."

Let's review how one couple completed their relationship survey so that we can understand this process more clearly.

Peggy and Bob

The relationship survey allows us to monitor at least two of the factors in relationships that inevitably cause disenchantment—the tarnishing effect and the eye-opening effect. Relationships do fade in intensity as time goes by. This can be easily noted on the survey when prior partners are compared with current partners. Though you may now hang an old partner in effigy, you cannot avoid admitting that you once held this person in much higher esteem.

You will also discover that each person rated on the questionnaire usually has one or more low scores! This is particularly true of prior partners. These low scores reflect our being "blind-sided" in three eye-opening ways:

1. You may discover that your partner lacks a quality which you thought he or she possessed.

2. You may discover that your partner possesses a quality which you wished he or she did not possess.

3. You may discover that there are certain qualities which are consistently absent—with all partners—which affect your overall happiness in some way.

Peggy and Bob are in many ways typical of a couple just falling in love. When I first met Peggy she was separated from her husband and "very much in love" with a new beau named Bob. I strongly recommended marriage counseling to Peggy but she refused, indicating that there was nothing left between her and her husband. All attempts on my part to persuade her to consider the RENEW program proved fruitless. Instead, Peggy wanted me to meet with her and Bob in order to "check him out," so to speak. She did not want to simply rebound from one relationship to another without understanding what she was "really" looking for in a man.

This was a difficult situation for me since I am so biased toward working on existing relationships. Her situation also pointed out to me, once again, how difficult it is to work on a relationship when we romanticize a new partner who is waiting in the wings. This is why couples counseling is practically impossible when one or both partners is having an affair during the counseling process.

I explained my reservations to Peggy, who stated that she understood my biases but still wanted to know more about the "personal constructs" she used to select and reject her partners. She also stated that her new beau, Bob, was more than willing to participate in the counseling process since he was committed to "personal growth." I agreed to meet with them both and to administer the relationship survey.

The lists of similarities and contrasts on Peggy's questionnaire reveals all Type II and Type III beliefs (I'll let you decide which ones are which). Peggy also gave Bob a seven rating on most of them. Let's look at her scores.

Unexpressive	1	2	3	4	5	6	**7**	Expressive
Analytical	1	2	3	4	5	6	**7**	Creative
Introverted	1	2	3	4	5	6	**7**	Outgoing
Nonwriter	1	2	3	4	5	**6**	7	Eloquent
Nonhumorous	1	2	3	4	5	6	**7**	Humorous
Hides feelings	1	2	3	4	5	6	**7**	Very open
Passive	1	2	3	4	5	6	**7**	Very active

You will note the idealism of early romantic love. Bob possesses practically everything that Peggy wants in a relationship. We will take a closer look at this positive polarization in a moment, but first let's review what Peggy said about her Mom and Dad. On her life history questionnaire, she described her Dad as:

Highly energetic, youthful, proud of me, interested in achievements, and a real worrier. We are close, but aware of each other's need for privacy.

Mom is:

... very sweet, worried about things even more than Dad. She is very tense and could fly off the handle for little reason. No ability to joke or play.

We get a sense of Dad's energy level influencing Peggy. Dad was probably very expressive, creative, outgoing, and active—each a personal construct that Peggy values. She also values humor, which neither Mom nor her current husband possess. So we see that prior relationships can and do influence our way of viewing others. But let's go further by reviewing Peggy's ten characteristics of ideal love:

Characteristics of Ideal Love	Current Love	Previous Love	Previous Love	Previous Love	Sum
1. Expressive	10	4	8	9	31
2. Creative	8	1	7	9	25
3. Active	10	4	6	5	25
4. Sensual	10	3	9	7	29
5. Affectionate	10	7	6	7	30
6. Thoughtful	10	2	8	10	30
7. Wants to grow	10	5	8	7	30
8. Adaptable	9	3	6	7	25
9. To be intimate	10	3	8	8	29
10. Strong interests	10	3	7	9	29
TOTALS	97	35	75	78	

You will notice how high her total ratings are for Bob (a whopping 97). Her romantic bliss has not only succeeded in identifying positive qualities in her beloved, but then gone on to exaggerate these qualities. Her belief that Bob possesses these qualities to this extent is destined to fade. After all, notice what happened to the next guy over—her husband! He is getting creamed with a total score of 35. You can bet he didn't start off there.

Peggy's other two "previous loves" were relationships that ended after six to twelve months of dating. These bonds lasted long enough to provide Peggy with positive memories, but not long enough for her to experience the inevitable disenchantment process—the process that drives us into polarized, negative views of one another. Her marriage lasted long enough for disenchantment to set in.

You will also note that Peggy's total score is 25 for "active," 25 for "creative," and 25 for "adaptable." I am particularly interested in horizontal totals of 25 or less, since these low scores reveal chronic dissatisfaction in more than one relationship. We already knew that Peggy valued being active, but these scores show that every previous lover had disappointed her in this regard. This means that Bob will need to know this in order to meet her needs in the relationship. In their case, this is not likely to be a problem, since Bob is an outdoorsman who enjoys hiking, climbing, and other daredevil, sensation-seeking activities.

At this point, we don't know much about what Peggy means by "creative" or "adaptable," but it will be incumbent upon Bob to find out. We can suspect that she may mean "creative writing," which is what Bob does for a living—again, a potentially good match. Before we turn to Bob, we should note that Peggy admitted, in her description of her father, that she needs private space—but we do not see this need anywhere on her form. Perhaps a potential eye-opening experience awaits her if Bob's level of activity does not allow her to claim an opportunity for private space. Let's see what we find by looking at Bob's similarities and contrasts:

Uncommunicative	1	2	3	4	5	6	7	Communica-tive
Emotionally needy	1	2	3	4	5	6	7	Emotionally healthy
Emotionally unaware	1	2	3	4	5	6	7	Emotionally aware
Controlling	1	2	3	4	5	6	7	Cooperative
Unaware of relationship dynamics	1	2	3	4	5	6	7	Aware of relationship dynamics

Bob stated that his ex-wife was too involved with the children. Seldom did she "communicate or spend time with me!" As the demands of parenthood sapped her strength, she became more and more "emotionally demanding" and "controlling," according to Bob. You may wonder why these demands became so one-sided. I know I did!

At any rate, we do see evidence of the distraction effect as well—the business of life, such as children and careers, which can seriously hamper our hunger for exclusivity with one another. This was true for Bob. Bob was into encounter groups in the 60s, personal growth in the 70s, and holistic health in the 80s. Getting trapped by domesticity did him in! Peggy was the answer to his prayers. She was "communicative," "emotionally healthy," and very aware of her personal, as well as interpersonal dynamics. Nor did she desire children! Notice Bob's perfect ratings for her. Oh how smitten we are by romantic love!

Two concerns I expressed to Peggy were (1) that her own needs for private space would be difficult to achieve given Bob's intense desire for closeness, and (2) that her career aspirations might prove disenchanting to Bob if she were not fully available to him. These concerns can be better appreciated by sharing Bob's ten characteristics of ideal love:

Characteristics of Ideal Love	Current Love	Previous Love	Previous Love	Previous Love	Sum
1. Open	8	3	4	5	20
2. Communicative	10	2	4	3	19

3. Very sexual	9	2	4	3	18
4. Caring	10	6	5	7	28
5. Physically beautiful	9	6	6	5	26
6. Emotionally aware	10	2	3	3	18
7. Well-read	8	4	2	8	22
8. Physically fit	8	4	6	7	25
9. Playful/humorous	9	1	7	8	25
10. Creative	9	8	3	8	27
TOTALS	90	38	44	57	

What do you notice about this list? For one thing, Bob is a pretty intense guy when it comes to intimate bonding. When you are in a relationship with Bob, you had better be able to invest time and energy! Moreover, Peggy is certainly the recipient of ideal projections, while Bob's ex-wife is clearly shredded in comparison. You will also notice how disenchanted he has become in *all* his prior relationships. We exaggerate not only the natural illusions of romance, but also the shards which remain after the illusions of early love have shattered.

Remember that romantic love is often rigidly dichotomous. The more rigidly we believe that our lovers must conform to our embedded beliefs, the more likely we are to become disenchanted. I wonder about this when I see Bob gravitating as he does between poles of belief.

As of this writing, I can tell you that Bob and Peggy have married, left their jobs, moved to another state, and report that they are still very happy one year later. They live in a remote, rural setting sharing a small house, two cats, and a business they jointly created and manage.

When East Meets West: A Reconciliation

Each of us struggles to reconcile our voices of the past. This section of the book addresses this struggle. One of my clients expresses her struggle in this dialogue with herself:

> You are a little girl! You never got to develop—you got thrown in with the snakes and the sharks and had to learn to swim and find your place among them—to protect yourself from getting eaten alive. You had to survive. Some very precious time and experiences were stolen from you. You never got to experience them—sweetness, innocence, innocent love, and excitement were stolen from you. Your integrity and pride in yourself were stolen—your self-esteem was ripped out!
>
> I want to pick you up and hold you and try to put you back together. There may be scars, but we can do some pretty miraculous things these days. I promise you that I am going to do it—somehow!

We have seen how our visions of an ideal partner are fashioned by the early experiences we have had in our relationships with our mothers and fathers. We have seen how we hope to find in one another the fulfillment of past longings in three major need areas: (1) the need to belong, (2) the need for control, and (3) the need for affection. The price we pay—when these needs are not met—is the primal hurt, anger, or fear internalized by our inner child of the past.

It is clear, however, that our early wounds are not just represented by emotional triggers. We also record these early wounds in the cognitive imprints that I call embedded beliefs. We value one belief over another— one polarized extreme over another—because of these early emotional experiences.

I can demonstrate the connection between early emotional wounds and embedded beliefs by introducing you to Tom, a husband who was ready to call it quits after seventeen years. Tom felt smothered, manipulated, and overwhelmed by his wife's demands. His anger was to the boiling point. He felt wronged by Jill and would not forgive her. He believed that he had clearly given up numerous professional options because Jill wanted to be closer to her family here in Austin. Tom's resentments sounded something like this:

1. Jill, I resent you for being so close to your parents.

2. Jill, I resent you for always including your parents and excluding friends on weekend trips.

3. Jill, I resent you for planning every Sunday lunch with your parents.

4. Jill, I resent you for not moving to Beaumont in 1980, willingly, as a team.

5. Jill, I resent having to give up golf because your father would never have been away from your mother for so long!

Tom's natural father died when he was two years old. He lived in a fatherless home until age seven, when his stepfather arrived on the scene. According to Tom, his mother—who never stopped grieving for his natural father—would cling to him, cry on his shoulders, and demand that he take care of her needs. He was afraid to say no to her, fearing that she would feel even greater pain. His only hope was to escape his home in order to free himself from these emotional entanglements—just like he was hoping to do now!

His mother's expectations were ever-present and restricting. He had to fulfill her image of his deceased father. He was made to feel obligated to solve problems—to be the real man of the house! His stepfather, soon realizing that he had been displaced by Tom, withdrew his attention and devotion from the family. Tom was thereby abandoned, with nobody paying attention to him—nobody who might come to his baseball games or his school plays. No one really cared about *him*. Instead he felt continuously obligated to care for others, in particular his mother.

So you can better understand Tom's resentments, let me show you his portrait of his inner child. Notice the significant anger he felt in regard to his mother and the hurt he experienced in regard to his stepfather, who was not available for him. (Please refer to earlier pages in this chapter for any help you might need understanding the profile.)

	Mom			Stepdad		
	Inclusion	Control	Affection	Inclusion	Control	Affection
High	5	4	5	1	1	1
Low	2	4	1	4	4	5

There is too much *inclusion, control,* and *affection* from mom and too little from stepdad. Tom experiences his mother as "too demanding," "too controlling and manipulating," and "too smothering and restricting"—all of which strikes quite an angry chord. He also believes his stepdad did not "pay attention," "appreciate his needs," or "demonstrate enough affection." He felt much hurt about these omissions, which were evident in his tearfulness during the early weeks of therapy.

Tom also clearly experienced anger and hurt with his wife, Jill, as well. He obviously believes that Jill demands, controls, and manipulates him, just like his mother did. He also obviously believes she does not support him or understand his needs, just like stepdad. Yet there is more here than meets the eye. Let's look at Tom's personal constructs in order to understand how these emotional wounds have influenced the very language structures that guide his thinking and his behavior toward others. His similarities and contrasts are as follows:

Restricting	1	2	3	4	5	6	7	Enabling
Unsupportive	1	2	3	4	5	6	7	Supportive
Not loyal	1	2	3	4	5	6	7	Devoted
Unattractive	1	2	3	4	5	6	7	Attractive
Inconsiderate	1	2	3	4	5	6	7	Considerate
Cold	1	2	3	4	5	6	7	Warm
Unsympathetic	1	2	3	4	5	6	7	Compassionate

What do you notice here? It seems that Tom filters people through a mental strainer on the basis of how his control and affection needs are met. When others are "enabling" or "supportive," Tom feels in control because his input, his ideas, and his needs have merit in the eyes of others. What more could any of us want than to have a friend or beloved actually help us attain our goals? Perhaps this is what Tom means with his personal construct, "devoted"! When people are devoted to us, they are connected in an *inclusive* sense as well. We belong. We are valued members of a relationship in which we can influence the opinions of others. Tom wants this for himself.

Tom also looks for "warmth," "consideration," and "compassion" in his relationships with others. Once again, we can see how his wounds in the area of affection have shaped this search. (Tom gives Jill a low rating of three in these qualities!) Stepdad did not provide enough affection while mother smothered him with her own needs for affection. The ironic consequence for Tom is that he has conflicting needs in the affection area.

On the one hand, he seeks to escape from anyone who gets too close (because they may become too smothering or manipulating). On the other hand, he desperately seeks closeness if the boundaries are flexible and within his control.

In counseling, Tom realized that he was not the only one with grievances. Jill was disenchanted as well. By going through the RENEW process, each was able to find a more mature commitment to the other. It was imperative for Jill to understand Tom's childhood emotional wounds as well as his embedded beliefs of adulthood. She was then able to modify her behavior toward Tom appropriately. Furthermore, both realized that the problem was not merely Jill. Tom had to recognize the rigidity of his personal constructs and the vulnerability of his inner child.

In this chapter, we have seen how unconscious voices echoing from the past will dramatically affect our search for a perfect love in the present. There is even more to this picture. Our search for love often masks a more fundamental need—our quest for happiness. The concepts of love and happiness fuel one another and together account for most of what we consider to be our quality of life. In the next chapter, I attempt to answer the question, What is happiness, and how is it affected by our satisfaction with love?

6

The Pursuit of Happiness

Happiness is wanting what you want, getting
what you get, and hoping the two will coincide.

Howard Mumford Jones

Our search for love masks a more fundamental struggle we all engage in—the pursuit of happiness. We all want it but few of us can describe what it is, although we certainly can describe its opposite! We chase after happiness, make plans about it, wait for it, and agonize over it. Yet few of us will actually experience it because of three misguided notions that underlie our search:

Illusion 1: Happiness depends upon love. Consciously or unconsciously, many of us believe the illusion that love equals happiness. From this point of view, we can only be happy if we are "in love," which means not only loving someone but also being loved *by* him or her. Yet true happiness depends upon much more than love alone. It comes from an overall balance of all the important areas of our lives—love, work, leisure, health, finances, and spirituality. Though research suggests that love may be the most important to us, we have significant needs in the other areas which also must be met.

Illusion 2: Happiness results from having or doing. Without realizing it, many of us believe the illusion that happiness can be *owned* or *achieved*. In general, happiness arises from an experience of personal validation, a sense of "specialness," which we derive from four basic sources: ownership, achievement, self-appreciation, and self-expression. Too often we confuse these sources of happiness. For instance, we confuse *achievement* with *self-expression*, believing our "specialness" in relationships depends upon our performance—making love proficiently, keeping a clean and attractive home, buying the "perfect" gift. Yet happiness truly depends upon recognizing and appreciating our inherent qualities, the traits and talents that make us unique, and then expressing that uniqueness *through* our actions.

Illusion 3: Happiness is a continuous feeling of pleasure. Another illusion we have about happiness is that it is based on pleasure. Pleasure is obviously an element of happiness, yet happiness is more than just pleasure. Happiness is more rightly understood as an overall balance of pleasure and meaning in our lives. Fun, enjoyment, and excitement are vital elements of the good life. On the other hand, without a sense of significance, purpose, or fulfillment, "the good life" seems shallow or empty. Each represents a different pathway to happiness—through feeling (pleasure) and through thought (meaning). Not only must we balance pleasure and meaning in our lives, we must also balance the *sources* of our pleasure and meaning.

These illusions skew our perspective on happiness and send us in fruitless pursuit of something we can never find—because we're looking for the wrong thing in the wrong place! This chapter explores the disenchanting consequences of believing these illusions about happiness—and offers some tools to help you develop a new perspective.

Illusion 1: Happiness Depends Upon Love

Love Is Never Enough

Gloria, a wonderfully dynamic and attractive entrepreneur, had created one of the most highly regarded advertising firms in Austin. She possessed a flair for design and marketing her services. Her pizzazz won people over immediately. Yet, despite her enterprising, pathfinding lifestyle by day, Gloria felt miserably trapped at home by night.

Her husband of nineteen years, Chris, was still warm and affectionate, as he had been when love first bloomed between them. Gloria needed this warmth. Often she snuggled next to Chris as he worked in his study or watched TV. Chris filled Gloria's need for hugs—the hugs that she never seemed to get from her father during childhood.

Gloria's craving for affection was so strong that she was prepared to do anything to keep "that magic in those moments when Chris holds me." She was even prepared to ignore his fifteen years of serial affairs. Somehow, Gloria had endured these meaningless, one-night stands. But then Chris admitted that he was "hung up" on one woman he had met in Seattle three years before.

Loyally, Gloria stood by Chris as he went to visit his "new love"—infrequently at first, but more and more often as time went by. Eventually, Chris requested six months to live with his lover in Seattle. Gloria consented, never revealing the truth to a soul. She took care of the kids, her business, and Thanksgiving and Christmas—without Chris. She might have continued on this way forever had it not been for the irritable bowel ar d ulcer problems which sent her, wracked with pain, to her physician, who, in turn, referred her to me for "stress work."

On the surface, Gloria gave in to Chris's wayward style, not to mention his inability to commit, for what she called "security needs." What would happen to the children, their homestead, and her business reputation should their marriage end? But below the surface, Gloria had clung desperately to any semblance of family since her sister had drowned many years before—a tragic event that thrust her family into great disharmony and disarray. "Mom and Dad were never the same," Gloria told me. She feared the death of her own family. But there was more below the surface. Gloria had been taught:

- to honor marital codes *until death do us part*
- to cherish her *one true, God-given love*
- to value, nurture and sustain human bonds in *all times* of need
- to perpetuate the fragile notion of family at *all costs*

Gloria found herself loving Chris too much and not loving herself enough. She succumbed to a world of extremes—loving only one man, until death, at all times, at all costs. Her neediness blinded her to Chris's lack of commitment. She was unable to see that "loving too much" often meant not being loved enough!

By relying solely on Chris's warmth and affection to supply so much of her happiness, Gloria has set herself up for disenchantment. This "addicted" or "co-dependent" notion of love has been well described during the last few years, most popularly perhaps by Robin Norwood in her book, *Women Who Love Too Much* (1985). Although women typically fall into this kind of love-dependency more often than men, men may also be susceptible to the illusion that love is the key to happiness. The common ground appears to be in the realm of identity—in that glorious and personal space we call our "self." In order to understand love addiction, we must first understand that happiness requires a spirited and healthy acceptance of our "selves."

Self-esteem arises from this healthy acceptance and affirmation of ourselves. For men, self-esteem has traditionally been based on independent action, firm decision making, competitive striving, and sexual initiative. By contrast, women have previously been taught to find self-esteem in their capacity to create and maintain loving bonds. Women have been conditioned to value love and harmony, while men have been programmed to desire initiative and entitlement. Though research suggests that these worn-out gender differences appear to be changing, some women still find themselves mired in the old values. The problem for women who love too much is their reliance on one source of self-esteem—relatedness—at the cost of the other—independence. But healthy self-esteem must be based upon both.

In most traditional theories of human development, separation from significant others is seen as the ultimate milestone in reaching adulthood. Relatedness is often viewed as threatening and, in some mysterious way, diminishing to one's sense of self and the emergence of self-esteem. But there are problems with this perspective. Men have been socialized to separate from mother during childhood, from family during adolescence, and from mentors during young adulthood. As a result, they may eventually find themselves psychologically separating from their wives and families during middle adulthood for the sake of career goals and financial obligations.

When we believe that love is all we need to be happy, we fear risk. We fear change. We fear the unknown. We fear letting go of self-defeating, no-win routines. We fear being incomplete without him (or her). We lose touch with our own individuality, our sense of who we are. We experience little personal growth. And most regrettable of all, we experience little real intimacy—the cherished prize for which we barter ourselves!

We must base our self-esteem on experiences that further both our sense of "attachment" as well as our sense of freedom. As my friend and fellow psychologist, Alice Lawler, explains it to me:

> When we base our self-esteem only on freedom and independent action, we ask such questions as "Who am I?" "Where am I going?" and "How am I getting there?" By contrast, self-esteem may also be based on one's relationships and competence in caring for others (not just for taking care of others, but the more comprehensive notion which includes the skills, strengths, and challenges of caring for others). Developing one's identity means doing so in the context of relationships and answering such questions as "Who am I *and* who am I in relationship to others?" "Where am I going *and* how will that affect others?" and "How am I getting there *and* how will my getting there impact the other important people in my life?"

On the surface, the choice appears to be between love and independence or between relatedness and separation. However, this is not the case in successful, happy relationships. The answer lies in integrating our equally strong needs for attachment and freedom, balancing the two in a flexible, interdependent way that I call covenant love.

But Love Counts!

Making love our only source of happiness is obviously a mistake. But pretending that love isn't critical to our happiness is another. Love is clearly important to us. Study after study reveals that the most important values of Americans include love, friendship, and family life.

After years of study into "quality of life," researcher Angus Campbell (1976) concluded that the people who were most satisfied with their lives rated a "happy marriage" and a "good family life" as the main reasons for their contentment. *USA Today* conducted a poll in 1985 that scientifically measured the well-being and happiness of 1,504 American adults. Using a scale ranging from minus 100 to plus 100, they came up with an overall average rating of a very positive plus 61. From the results they found, *USA Today* concluded that marriage, a pay raise, a new job or promotion, and moving to a better place—more than any other events—make us satisfied with our personal lives.

Virtually every study of marital status and happiness has found married people to be happier than single people. In his book, *Happy People,* Jonathan Freedman found that 68 percent of married people and only 54 percent of single people were moderately happy with their lives. Single women get less and less happy as they get older, while married women of all ages seem to experience the same degree of happiness (Freedman 1978).

These studies, along with countless others, lead me to conclude that love is so important to us *not* because love equals happiness. Love is important because of its intricate link to the five other life areas that are important to our happiness: work, leisure, health, finances, and spirituality.

- *Love:* Being in an emotionally or sexually committed bond with another person. Bonds with parents, children, and other relatives are very important but represent icing on the cake.
- *Work:* Believing that one is making a contribution to the welfare of others, applying one's skills, and being recognized in either a social or financial way.
- *Finances:* Having enough resources to maintain one's desired standard of living and to obtain wanted goods or services.
- *Leisure:* Having sufficient interests, time, and companionship to enjoy pastimes unrelated to work or responsibility. Good friends enhance this life area.
- *Health:* Having enough mental or physical strength and stamina to participate in most activities one wishes to participate in. Being free of chronic health problems is particularly important.
- *Spirituality:* Having a conviction that one is part of a larger whole. Knowing that we are unconditionally loved by a power outside us may empower us to create, transcend, and endure in ways which would otherwise seem impossible to us.

Love enhances our quality of life because it increases our chances of being satisfied in these other areas. For instance:

- *Work:* Couples report more satisfaction with their career paths.
- *Leisure:* Couples have a wider network of friends, extended family, and social contacts than single people.
- *Health:* Couples have substantially lower rates of illness, accidents, and death than single or divorced comparison groups.
- *Finances:* Couples have a higher average income than the unmarried.
- *Spirituality:* Couples are more likely to develop a spiritual base for their families, which may include formal religious education or observance of traditional holidays and services.

Love relationships are empowering. Intimacy empowers us to find more positive satisfaction with work, leisure, health, finances, and spirituality. Although these combined elements comprise our happiness, they largely depend upon our ability to transform the transient high of romantic love into a deeper, more enduring covenant love. In turn, these six integrated quality of life areas (which undergird our happiness) become empowering in their own right. Combined, they serve as resources for us—veritable buffers that protect us from stressful encounters of the worst kind.

Resources are not what people do but what people have available to them in life. Some resources are within us, such as high intelligence, persistence, or hardiness. Other resources are more external, such as a secure job, solid bank account, network of family and friends, health club membership, or church affiliation. Together, these internal and external resources can either enhance our happiness and well-being or minimize our life stresses.

The noted Israeli writer, Aaron Antonovsky, in his book *Health, Stress and Coping*, describes these sources of life stress as "bugs":

> If bugs are ubiquitous, endogenic in human existence, and extremely resourceful; if we are all subjected to a constant barrage of what we ourselves would define as stressors or to those bugs that, though not in the forefront of our consciousness (such as microorganisms, unconscious conflicts, and strivings or social pressures), we would readily agree to call stressors were we aware of them; if levels of tension and imbalance range from moderate but real to unimaginably high for different individuals; and if the data indicate that a surprising number of us indeed manifest pathology at any one time—then the crucial question becomes, How do we manage tension and prevent it from leading to stress? What are the resources at our disposal that enable some of us or, rather, all of us, as long as we are alive, to resolve tension at least some of the time? (Antonovsky 1979, 98)

The answer, as I see it, is in the well-integrated fullness of our lives, which I am here calling "quality of life." Since this fullness seems to be so essential for our overall happiness and well-being, it is time to let each of you now measure your own happiness.

Measuring Your Happiness: Your Love Quotient

With my colleague Dr. Raymond Hawkins, I have developed a statistically valid and reliable questionnaire to measure happiness in the six quality of life areas. I have included this questionnaire so that you can discover how happy you are in each life area. As you answer the questions, please remember that there are certainly other aspects of living which are related to happiness. However, these areas are the most important.

Quality of Life Indicators

Directions: Below are a variety of statements about your job, your leisure activities and friendships, your love relationships, your health, your finances, and your spiritual life. Please indicate how true each one is by circling the appropriate number:

1 = Not at all true   2 = Not very true   3 = Somewhat true
4 = Mostly true   5 = Definitely true

I. WORK

1. The people I work with are competent and helpful.   1   2   3   4   5

2. My work is interesting.   1   2   3   4   5

3. My superior is good at his or her job.   1   2   3   4   5

4. I get recognition for my work.   1   2   3   4   5

5. I can influence important decisions made by my superior.   1   2   3   4   5

6. I have a great deal of freedom in deciding how to do my work.   1   2   3   4   5

7. If I had to make a choice again, I would choose the same work. 1   2   3   4   5

8. Overall, I am satisfied with my main job.   1   2   3   4   5

II. LEISURE

1. In general, I am satisfied with the way I spend my spare time. 1   2   3   4   5

2. Overall, I am satisfied with my leisure life.   1   2   3   4   5

3. I am satisifed with the way I get along with my friends.   1   2   3   4   5

4. The activities I participate in contribute to my satisfaction with leisure life. 1   2   3   4   5

5. My current leisure life activities add much to my quality of life. 1   2   3   4   5

6. At the present time, my leisure life activities are just right. 1   2   3   4   5

III. LOVE

1. All things considered, I am satisifed with my relationship.   1   2   3   4   5

2. The amount of love and affection I receive is extremely satisfying. 1   2   3   4   5

3. My love relationship continues to get better.   1   2   3   4   5

4. My love relationship satisfies my needs for friendship, understanding, and support. 1   2   3   4   5

5. If I had it to do all again, I would get involved   1   2   3   4   5
in this type of relationship with the same
person.

IV. HEALTH

1. Compared to others around me, I would have   1   2   3   4   5
to say my health is pretty good.
2. I would describe my state of health as   1   2   3   4   5
excellent.
3. I would describe the amount of energy and   1   2   3   4   5
endurance I have as excellent.
4. Medically speaking, I am in pretty good shape   1   2   3   4   5
for someone my age.

V. FINANCES

1. All things considered, I am satisfied with my   1   2   3   4   5
present financial situation.
2. I make enough money to meet my needs.   1   2   3   4   5
3. Financially speaking, I am in pretty good   1   2   3   4   5
shape for someone my age.
4. Compared to others around me, my finances   1   2   3   4   5
are quite satisfactory.
5. My finances allow me to live the kind of life I   1   2   3   4   5
want.

VI. SPIRITUALITY

1. I value a spiritual part of myself.   1   2   3   4   5
2. I have a soul from which I derive vitality,   1   2   3   4   5
comfort, and direction in life.
3. I live a life based on religious or spiritual   1   2   3   4   5
principles.
4. I find comfort in knowing that there are forces   1   2   3   4   5
greater than me which control my destiny and
well-being.

Scoring Your Questionnaire

First, add the point totals for each of the six life areas in the questionnaire. For instance, add up the point totals for all eight questions under "work." The possible range for work is from 8 to 40. Your score will fall somewhere in between. This will be your total work satisfaction score.

Second, divide the point totals for each of the six life areas by the actual number of questions in that section. (Work = 8, leisure = 6, love = 5, health = 4, finances = 5, and spirituality = 4.) For instance, if your work satisfaction total was 24, you would divide 24 by 8, giving you an average work satisfaction score of 3.

In general, the higher your score, the happier you are in that life area. However, happiness does not depend on a perfect score average of 5 or, for that matter, even a 4. Figuring out whether your score is high or low is somewhat similar to determining whether your blood pressure is borderline or normal. A general rule of thumb is that a systolic BP of 140 is borderline. But that depends on your age, life circumstances, organic illnesses, repeated measurements, and who your doctor is! Any doctor will tell you that a full physical and history must be taken before any interpretation can be made. The same is true of your quality of life scores.

Let us say that your average satisfaction score for love is 2.8. This is a low score which reflects the possibility of disenchantment, particularly if your other quality of life scores average 4.0 or more. Your score could be a signal of a deep chasm between you and your significant other. However, if your other quality of life scores average 2.0 or less, your 2.8 score for love may actually reflect a comfortable refuge for you at a time when the rest of your life seems to be crumbling. In general, however, average satisfaction scores above 4 clearly suggest overall happiness, while scores below 2 suggest overall disenchantment.

What do your scores reveal about you? In which life area are you the most satisfied or dissatisfied? Is there a sizeable gap between your most and least satisfied life areas? Do you have one life area, or more than one, which appears quite low? Some people, for instance, may be quite happy with many aspects of their life, such as love or leisure or health, and yet feel quite conflicted about work. This may be true of you if you view work only as a source of extrinsic monetary support rather than a meaningful extension of who you are.

A Quality of Life Profile

Here is a quality of life profile for Bert, an electrical engineer for a large firm in Austin. According to Bert, he had been happily married for thirteen years—until his wife, Julia, discovered her musical talent. What do you see in Bert's scores?

WORK	3.1
LEISURE	1.8
LOVE	1.7
HEALTH	3.3
FINANCES	2.6
SPIRITUALITY	2.8

Bert is crying out for help. Overall, he is not very happy. Love and leisure are particularly rock bottom. (These two areas are often associated, as are work and finances.) He is not particularly happy with work, finances, and spirituality, and his health is questionable.

Bert, I discovered, did not like to talk about his problems. Somehow he had learned to be a stoic about life, much as his father had been many years before. The only reason he ended up in therapy is because his personal family physician could not understand why his blood pressure had soared so persistently during the past year, when there were no organic reasons to explain it.

As Bert tells the story, his wife, Kim, had been quite satisfied for years with her own job as a computer programmer by day and her love of family by night. They had two children, David (age eight) and Lisa (age twelve). But there was more to Kim. She had played guitar since the age of ten, becoming very proficient with classical guitar by age sixteen. By college, however, she had discovered something even more fulfilling than guitar. Kim had a beautiful voice. She began to use her voice more, as a delightful escape during stressful periods or in more structured ways during Sorority Sing.

Many years later, a great opportunity—a wonderful dream—seemed to come sweeping down upon her. And she was more than willing to go for it. Cliff, a colleague at work, had a moonlighting operation that promoted rock bands and new talent in Austin. One night, during an impromptu talent contest, Kim took a shot in the dark and auditioned at a local club. She won! And Bert lost!

Cliff's support gave her a growing confidence in her ability to write, compose, and record her music. She attempted to balance both work and love, commitment and freedom. But she could only work on her music by night. She would leave her job as programmer by 5:00, return home to prepare dinner, supervise homework and bedtime until 9:00, and then exit stage left to meet Cliff, who was prepared to work with her until midnight or sometimes even 1:00 in the morning.

Though jealousy was an obvious issue for Bert, Kim tried to minimize it by inviting Bert to Friday and Saturday night jam sessions and calling home while she was away. Her best efforts to integrate personal ambition with devoted obligation were destined to fail with Bert. As he felt more and more neglected, Bert's resentments grew larger and larger, blocking any flow of caring to Kim. His accumulated hurt and anger became hot coals that burned his insides (and constricted his blood vessels).

When I asked Bert what he wanted out of therapy, he could only say "peace of mind." He admitted that he was committed only to his children, whom he loved very much. His devotion to his family meant loving them in Kim's absence. But the price he found himself paying was too great. His intimacy and leisure needs were now a void, his interest in work and spirituality were being sapped by an irritable depression that seemed destined to blunt his feelings even more, and his health was compromised by high blood pressure. Bert was so angry at Kim that he refused marital counseling for them and declined to go to church with her as well—a setting which, in the past, had offered him the peace of mind he had now lost.

Bert's profile is a telling reminder of how disenchantment with a major life area like love can overflow and color happiness in other quality of life areas. Strength in the different areas serves as a foundation for our overall ability to cope during major life crises, as well as during the usual trials and tribulations of everyday living. Imagine two friends who are getting divorced at the same time. One of them has a well-paying job in an exciting career, is active in the church, has many friends, and jogs three times a week. The other has an unrewarding job, stopped attending church years ago, has no friends or relatives living in the same city, and has a bad back. These friends may be going through the same situation in the life area of love, but they are not equally prepared to cope with their new life situations. Quality of life makes a difference.

Love may be necessary but will never be sufficient for our overall happiness. We must be careful. In our desire to order our lives, we often place needless emphasis upon one aspect of living, leaving other vital areas unattended—and setting ourselves up for disenchantment.

Illusion 2: Happiness Results From Having or Doing

Happiness Isn't What You Do

I recently had lunch with a physician friend who confided in me that he wanted a few "lunch sessions" with me as a personal birthday gift to himself. After reassuring me that he was content with his life as he approached his fortieth year, he explained why he wanted my counsel:

> It seems to me that nearly 95 percent of my worth, as a person, comes from what I do as a physician. Though I recognize that I am quite successful, make good money, and have a great reputation in the community, I am troubled by a realization that, aside from my professional role, I personally do not have other ways to value myself.

My friend's dilemma is no different from what each one of us faces on a continuing basis throughout our lives. By what formula, by what design, and by what criteria do we judge our worth as a person? Discovering our particular "specialness" is a continuing process which begins during the wobbly innocence of childhood and reaches its zenith when we risk being known within the dynamic union we call love. In this arena of love, we find our greatest opportunity to discover how special we really are. Our relentless search for affirmation, however, underscores a more basic human need than love alone. Nathaniel Branden, in his book *The Psychology of Self-Esteem*, states:

> There is no value judgement more important to man (kind)—no factor more decisive in his psychological development and motivation—than the estimate he passes on himself. Man(kind) experiences his desire for self-esteem as an urgent imperative, as a basic need. Whether he identifies the issue explicitly or not, he cannot escape the feeling that his estimate of himself is of life-and-death importance. (Branden 1969, 103)

Though related, there is a significant difference between self-esteem and pride. Self-esteem reflects our deeply held convictions about our capabilities, as well as our inherent worth as a person. In contrast, we experience pride during those fleeting moments when we acknowledge and celebrate our accomplishments. With self-esteem, we relish the notion that "I can," while with pride we rejoice in the fact that "I did." In our pursuit of happiness, our confusion between self-esteem and pride can lead us into a blind alley, a "you-can't-get-there-from-here" dead end that can cause us to experience disenchantment with our lives.

Being Special

As I pointed out earlier in this chapter, our sense of happiness arises from feeling personally validated—knowing that we are "special." The four ways that we can experience a sense of our specialness—ownership, achievement, self-appreciation, and self-expression—can each contribute to our overall sense of happiness.

When we find our sense of specialness in ownership or achievement, we are experiencing our validation *externally*—from things, events, and people. Standing in a spotlight of recognition, we feel good about ourselves because others admire or respect our homes, cars, appearance, baking, office management skills, leadership potential, or job title. The means may vary, but the outcome is still the same—we get stroked for our *efforts* and the strokes in turn enhance, at least temporarily, our appraisal of ourselves.

These external sources of validation cannot sustain us for long. They require constant replenishment. And we may become so addicted to this supply of strokes that we need an endless supply of possessions, continuous recognition, and positions of authority in order to feel personally valuable. Our identity becomes tied to *what we do* rather than to *who we are*.

When we identify with who we are, we receive our validation *internally*. We all have special, inherent qualities that set us apart from others. These qualities may be creativity, compassion, organizational skills, an ability to integrate, or mechanical aptitude. Whatever these jewels might be, it is not essential that others even know about them, for we do. What matters is that we acknowledge and value these personal attributes, knowing that nothing can ever take them away from us.

The goals we set for ourselves and the activities we pursue are merely choices we make to express what lies within. We may alter these choices as we please, because their true value lies only in how they promote the expression of our unique selves. A sense of specialness based upon appreciating and expressing ourselves is a limitless resource for experiencing happiness.

Although internal sources of validation are more enduring, I do not mean to suggest that external sources of validation are to be avoided as shallow or meaningless. All four sources of validation are appropriate avenues to happiness. Where we err is in depending too much on one, to the exclusion of the others. As with the six life areas I described in the previous section, balance is the key. Unfortunately, most people are imbalanced toward external sources of validation. In focusing on ownership and achievement, they neglect to recognize and affirm their inherent qualities and how they express those qualities.

I am reminded of a happily married but troubled client who was a superb tennis player. She was ranked second in Texas in her age group and was a perennial contender for the number one ranking. Each year, however, she would come up short of her goal. Somehow, she would lose her concentration just as the match was literally in hand. When I asked her if she believed that she was worthy of this illusive title, she retorted: "Of course I am worthy!"

"And would you be proud enough of your number two ranking to write to the editor of your high school newsletter in order to report your outstanding performances over the last few years?" I rebutted.

"Absolutely not. Tennis is the first thing I have ever done in my life in which I have experienced pride or notoriety. Yet, for some reason, I am ashamed. On the one hand, I don't think I have achieved enough. And on the other hand, I am ashamed of my 'celebrity status' because it means nothing compared to the contributions that my husband and so many others make to our community."

How could she possibly write to her high school editor and report such "insignificance"? (And, for that matter, how could she win a state championship with this self-appraisal?) So we see that when we base our happiness on external validation, we may get trapped in our own web of social comparisons. There is always someone who runs faster, makes more money, or influences more people. External validation seduces us into looking outside ourselves for that feeling of specialness, when the affirmation truly lies within.

The Validation Trap

Although it is dangerous to overgeneralize, men have traditionally tended to validate themselves through their achievements and possessions, while women have largely attempted to validate their specialness through self-appreciation and expression. And gender role stereotypes still typically portray men as decisive, independent, competent, and incapable of giving emotional support, while picturing women as dependent, loving, submissive, or gentle. Overall, men are often seen as powerful, while women are viewed as weak. These polarized views have influenced the way we actually define love and happiness.

Since love is so often identified with the stereotyped qualities associated with women—such as warmth, tenderness, empathy, compassion, and expression of feelings—love is usually linked with the "feminine" role. This identification results in the "feminization" of love, implying that women are responsible for the maintenance of relationships (if relationships are to be maintained at all beyond their romantic origins).

By the same token, self-development is usually associated with the "masculine" role. Men are socialized to become autonomous and independent in order to develop a healthy self-concept. Healthy adult development for men thus presumes that men must separate in order to achieve, and that attachments are actually impediments to their personal development. Since women are taught to emphasize attachment, they are actually penalized in their own growth and personal development. Francesca Cancian makes this point quite clear as she describes the impact of our inbred, social dichotomies:

> Most Americans have an incomplete, feminine conception of love. We identify love with emotional expression and talking about feelings, aspects of love that women prefer and in which women tend to be more skilled than men. We often ignore the instrumental and physical aspects of love that men prefer, such as providing help, sharing activities, and sex …. Our feminine conception of love exaggerates the difference between men's and women's ability to love, and their need for love. (Cancion 1987, 69)

Accepting that a very real split in gender roles does exist, the pivotal question is how do we close the gap? Dr. Lucia Gilbert describes this reconciliation quite well in her book, *Sharing It All*. I believe that men must clearly transform themselves more than women. The standard of giving, so needed for mature love, is more cherished by women because of our society's "feminization" of love. It is men who must learn that in order for romantic love to become more mature, covenant love, they must shift their values more from "owning" and "achieving" to "experiencing" and "expressing."

Experiencing Validation in Our Relationships

Our love relationships must become a safe harbor where shared intimacy provides comfort and renewal. If we are split off from one another, each competing to achieve or to find space, this succor will not be found. We must become transcendent enough to balance our own needs with our partner's and to pursue our own identities while recognizing our partner's quests. And we must learn to express our hurts and anguish while we learn to tolerate our partner's, who at times create this very anguish. These elements of mature love can be attained only when we learn to balance the notion of "what we do" with "who we are."

We are likely to experience disenchantment when we, and our partners, fail to value our inherent uniqueness and the expression of that uniqueness. When we are blocked in this effort, as when we are restricted by the expectations of others, a burning anger to be set free often exists. A client, Stephanie, states this exact point:

I believe that David has the traditional view of women in that he feels that doing the job of housewife and mother should be sufficient reward. That I should receive a feeling of worth from just doing the job. The satisfaction should be inherent in the job.

Am I warped because I find house cleaning and house minding so unfulfilling? Is it my perception which needs to change? I continue to rebel against the idea that there is something wrong with me and I need to change. I view the traditional role of housewife as that of a self-abrogating drudge. I find little satisfaction in knowing that my windows are shiny and my husband doesn't seem to have a ring around his collar. Why should my personal worth be judged by how orderly my laundry room is?

David often rates things in terms of the "hundred year plan." In other words, in a hundred years no one will know the difference. In a hundred years, no one will know that I, as a housewife, even existed. The fact that my house is clean will never be a factor in the greater scheme of things.

I want to be important to someone other than my children. Is that bad or warped to want to be important? Is it abnormal to want to be viewed as more than a fixture or a convenience or a pet that needs to be humored with an occasional pat on the head? I feel an anger building inside of me that I am viewed only as an *extension* of David, and a peripheral extension at that. I am a convenience to make his life more convenient. But where am I?

Stephanie is certainly more than just an extension to David, yet she believed that, in our society, all people are valued according to the general impression of value that is placed on the role they play or the job they do. If your work, or role, is not valued, then you have no value!

Furthermore, Stephanie believed that when she entered the role of "wife," she bought into the expectations and obligations which David had for that role: that to have value meant to "achieve" these expectations without much fanfare. It was her job to do so. As she relentlessly tried to "achieve" his expectations, a more basic question wracked her brain: "Have I a right to be happy and fulfilled, or did I abrogate that right when I accepted the role of wife to a traditional male?"

Her dilemma is our dilemma. We all must see ourselves as connected to yet separate from our significant others. We must meet some expectations of others—true! But we must also attempt to explore our own yearnings and desires as well. We must set ourselves free to discover that uniqueness within each of us which is inherent and has value simply because it is *ours*.

When we validate ourselves internally, we know that we do not have to control others to have significance. Nor do we have to fear that others will control us or limit our specialness. Our uniqueness already belongs to us. Others may control certain avenues by which we choose to express our uniqueness, but they can never prevent us from finding other avenues.

The form of our expression is always secondary to the subtance of our being.

Being Oneself

The Danish philosopher Soren Kierkegaard argued that the most common human despair was to be in despair at not choosing or willing to be oneself. But the ultimate despair lies in choosing to be someone other than onself! Being special entails a process of being who we truly are, without the socially sanctioned need to hide behind masks.

In his now classic 1961 book, *On Becoming a Person*, psychologist Carl Rogers describes this process of "being special" as a lifelong, unfolding quest:

> One trend which is evident in this process of becoming a person relates to the source or locus of choices and decisions, or evaluative judgments. The individual increasingly comes to feel that this locus of evaluation lies within himself. Less and less does he look to others for approval or disapproval; for standards to live by; for decisions and choices. He recognizes that it rests with himself to choose; that the only question which matters is, "Am I living in a way which is deeply satisfying to me, and which truly expresses me?" This I think is perhaps *the* most important question for the creative individual. (Rogers 1961, 119)

Being special within a love relationship always involves two simultaneous tasks. First, we adopt certain roles that satisfy our partners and fulfill certain societal expectations as well. These tasks represent the "achieving" aspect which underlies all commitments.

Second, we must learn to see ourselves as continuously evolving, persistently questioning, and relentlessly searching for meaning and a special place for ourselves in this world. This task is highly personal and requires much more risk-taking than the former task. It is in this context that we are so dogged in our search for a "safe harbor"—for a love relationship which comforts and renews us.

If our main task in life were simply to robotisize ourselves in order to fulfill roles and duties, we all might voluntarily elect electroshock therapy in order to still our internal conflicts. This is hardly the case for a species that has been destined to evolve more than any other. It is our incessant search for personal meaning which distinguishes our life plan from any other species. For one love partner to foolishly script this plan for us is ridiculous. To allow a partner to do this is tragic!

These issues are indeed timeless, as the noted "father of psychology," William James, pointed out nearly seventy years ago in a personal letter to his wife.

> A man's character is discernible in the mental or moral attitude in which, when it came upon him, he felt himself most deeply and intensely active and alive. At such moments, there is a voice inside

which speaks and says: "This is the real me!" ... Such experiences include an element of active tension, of holding my own, as it were, and trusting outward things to perform their part so as to make it a full harmony, but without any *guarantee* that they will. Make it a guarantee ... and the attitude immediately becomes to my consciousness stagnant and stingless. Take away the guarantee, and I feel a sort of deep enthusiastic bliss, of bitter willingness to do and suffer anything. (James 1920, 199)

Our best chances for "full harmony" lie within the relationships we form with others—most particularly our primary love relationships. It is here, where we become known for "who we are" rather than "what we do," that we find a mature love that can free us from the shoulds and oughts of this world.

Illusion 3: Happiness Is a Continuous Feeling of *Pleasure*

Happiness IS More Than Pleasure

It had been a high-risk pregnancy for Tim and Louise. Louise had spent the last two months of it in bed with her feet elevated, very apprehensive about labor and delivery. This was their first child—a meaningful extension of their five years together. For Louise, this first-born was to be the true foundation of their family, of their permanent nest. But for Tim, this child meant a loss of freedom and spontaneity that he had been brooding about throughout most of the pregnancy. He had seen their weekends transformed from the high-pitch excitement of Saturday night disco to the sedentary monotony of watching televised specials at home in bed.

Now, eight months later, Tim states that he is increasingly attracted to other women, that he contemplates divorce, and that his feelings for Louise have fallen to an all-time low. He notes that Louise is up all night, tired most of the time, and looks as haggard as his grandmother recently appeared during a holiday visit. He can't remember when Louise initiated sex and he believes her desire must be permanently gone.

His resentments have kept him from bonding with his son—a situation that mortifies Louise. She wonders how it is possible for a father to foresake these special moments when life begets life and love begets love. She urges Tim to hold, to wash, to feed, and to play with their child, but he angrily protests, telling her that she pampers and spoils the boy. She retorts that it is he who wants to be pampered and spoiled, it is he who is the real child needing attention and stimulation!

As these skirmishes continue to fuel their disenchantment, each wonders how they got into this mess. More desperately, perhaps, each wonders if they will ever get out. Tim, in particular, seems to have lost his perspective about happiness. He angrily protests the loss of fun and frivolity in their relationship, choosing only to grieve the loss of pleasure that once seemed to energize and weld their life together. This loss seems intolerable, even during these poignant and fleeting days when the innocence of his new son seems to reach out to him and beckon him to a higher calling.

Like Tim, some of us have become pleasure-bound in our search for happiness, somehow ignoring the call of a deeper purpose in life. We become so extreme, so urgent, in our need to find pleasure that we fail to sift life's wondrous surprises through the sometimes rigid strainer of our most embedded beliefs.

Paradoxically, our search for happiness may also lead us to pursue meaningful activities in such a way that life becomes too serious, too burdened with responsibilities, or too devoid of pleasure. We may forget how to laugh or how to play. George, one of my clients, had completely focused his life on being a responsible community leader and successful businessman. Working sixty hours a week, he had built up a million dollar enterprise that employed many Austinites. In the process, he gradually became so divorced from the natural sources of pleasure in his life—his wife, his friends, his hobbies and interests—that he began to lose his bearings, to actually lose sight of the values that were at the root of his sense of meaning in life.

When I met George, he had been arrested as a Peeping Tom. His wife was shocked and ashamed, unsure whether she could continue being married to a "sexual deviant." Her husband had become a stranger to her. In truth, he had become a stranger to pleasure. The only pleasure he would allow himself was a secretive glance, a momentary excitement watching others experience their excitement. He no longer knew how to be happy.

When we lose touch with the sources of pleasure in our lives, we lose touch with an essential ingredient for happiness. The children around us may be one remedy for this lopsided approach to life—or the "child within us" may be our best hope.

As I have said before, happiness is more than pleasure—and it is more than meaning. It arises from an overall balance of pleasure and meaning in our lives. Typically, sometime during midlife, this balance between pleasure and meaning becomes even more cherished. For men, this may become a major mid-life transition, as Daniel Levinson points out in his book, The Seasons of a Man's Life:

> The modest decline in the elemental drives may, with midlife development, enable a man to enrich his life. He can be more free from the petty vanities, animosities, envies and moralisms of early adulthood. His normal sexual capacity in middle age is more than enough for a gratifying sex life. The quality of his love relationships may well improve as he develops a greater capacity for intimacy and integrates more fully the tender, "feminine" aspects of his self. He has the possibility of becoming a more responsive friend to men as well as women. He can be a more facilitating parent to his adolescent and young adult offspring as he recognizes they are no longer children and that he is no longer the youthful controlling father. He can become a

more caring son to his aging parents, and a more compassionate authority and teacher to young adults. (Levinson 1978, 25)

Finding the Source

Not only must we have a balance of pleasure and meaning in our lives in order to be happy, but also the *sources* of our pleasure and meaning must be balanced. If we experience the pleasure and meaning in our lives primarily through our achievements (work), our time with friends (leisure), or our athletic pursuits (health)—and not through our love relationship—then we will experience disenchantment in love. One frustrated spouse put it this way during a counseling session:

> Jim seems happy enough. He works hard and he plays hard, *but never with me*! I know he loves his work. After all, he spends enough time doing it. I can see that, but why does he have to spend two evenings a week and one or two weekend days playing golf, sailing, or backpacking with *other* people? I want him to enjoy time with the family more than he does.

The route to both pleasure and meaning in our love relationships is intimacy. Intimacy is that meaningful expression of ourselves—mostly verbal but also nonverbal—which allows another person to know more fully who we are. It is a process of sharing our thoughts and feelings over time that grants another person a special status, an entitlement of sorts in which knowledge, trust, and risk-taking are to be expected. One of the most profound deficiencies of courtship is our failure to determine whether a prospective partner has this capacity to be expressive and open. Instead, we choose a partner in life based upon the pleasurable and exciting moments we have shared.

Intimacy in a loving relationship is the *meaningful* prelude for *pleasure*, particularly sexual pleasure. This is particularly true for women, according to many studies. It is the closeness, the sharing, the communication (both verbal and nonverbal) which facilitates the pleasure of sexual arousal. Without this meaningful part of a relationship, a gradual loss of sexual interest often precipitates a need for therapy. As one client sadly lamented:

> Our lovemaking once seemed so fulfilling, so right! It seemed to grow out of a certain closeness we had—a special feeling we would create. It just seemed to flow. We would be laughing, frollicking, talking, or just doing something together where we felt close and it would just happen. We'd be on the floor, in the bathroom, wherever! Now, he seems so grotesque. So demanding and insensitive. He wants it when he wants it … on his terms, never understanding how good it once felt when we really cared about each other. We just don't share ourselves the way we used to.

Once again, we can see the impact of gender roles. If, as noted earlier, men define meaning in terms of "owning" or "achieving" rather than by being close and emotionally open, their love relationships are destined to falter and erode in time.

Colorful sunsets and orgasmic release may be enough to fuel your flight into marital space, but repeated orbits depend upon an exchange of information which allows for meaningful, midcourse corrections. Without this wealth of sharing, your flight is destined to burn out before you know it. Intimate sharing is clearly the lifeblood for any relationship which endures the jolts of midflight disenchantment.

What Is Pleasure? What Is Meaning?

We need to experience pleasure and meaning in relatively equal proportions in order to be happy. Jonathan Freedman found this to be true in his surveys on happiness in his book, *Happy People*. Interestingly enough, this result held up throughout all age groups.

Agreeing on what is pleasurable or meaningful is no easy matter— even for professional psychologists, psychiatrists, and social workers! In an unpublished study I conducted some years ago, I discovered that a group of experienced professionals could not agree as to whether 38 out of 66 pleasant experiences were pleasurable or meaningful. They could agree that "playing tennis" or "going to a party" were pleasurable. They also could agree that "making contributions to a religious organization" was meaningful. And they could agree that "being in the country" or "going to a museum" were both pleasurable and meaningful. But 38 out of 66 eluded their consensus.

There are at least three reasons for this. First, a work ethic so powerful exists in Western cultures that we are actually duped into believing that work is pleasure. (I recently heard a client argue that cleaning toilet bowls and changing cat litter every day was pleasurable.) Second, self-worth, for many of us, is tied to accomplishments and not to fun, exuberance, and joy. We consequently feel guilty when we are not doing something constructive. And third, a great deal of confusion does surround the concepts of pleasure and meaning. How can pleasure and meaning be defined?

I believe that the concept of *pleasure* includes four related experiences: satisfaction, delight, joy, and ecstacy.

- *Satisfaction* is used to describe the most mild experience of pleasure. Generally, you are not physically active or emotionally aroused when you experience satisfaction. Examples include watching TV or listening to music.
- *Delight* is a poignant feeling which is sudden and transient. A surprise visit from your college roommate or flowers from your loved one are examples.
- *Joy* is deeper and more lasting than delight. Singing regularly in your church choir, sailing on a nearby lake, or playing with your newborn infant are all joyful experiences.
- *Ecstacy* is the most extreme pleasurable emotion. It connotes an "out of this world" experience which words somehow cannot describe. Sexual orgasm or winning a $10 million lottery both qualify.

The concept of *meaning* must be defined a little differently. Meaning can best be understood through the ways in which it *differs* from pleasure:

- *Meaning implies thinking rather than feeling.* We become reflective, intellectually stimulated, or introspective. A moving sermon, a thought-provoking movie, or an understanding talk with your husband are examples.
- *Meaning has more to do with significance or purpose than with fun and frolic.* A warm hug from your husband or smile from your child are significant moments in our day. Coaching your child's soccer team or participating in a church bible study are additional examples.
- *Meaning incorporates the past, present, and future.* Pleasure centers only on the present. Meaning is remembering your engagement party, beaming as your wife receives her first promotion, or recognizing that family planning in your childrearing years will give you opportunities for a secure and fulfilling life during retirement.

Looking for Pleasure and Meaning

I would like to conclude this chapter with an exercise which that clients have found useful in identifying and then affirming the pleasure and meaning in their lives. When practicing this technique, keep in mind that you can focus specifically on your love relationship or more generally on your overall quality of life.

Directions

Briefly note every experience you have during the next week which "feels good." Do not judge the experience in any way. Do not worry about its duration. If it lasts only ten seconds, still make a note of it. Write these "feeling good" moments in column one.

In column two, decide whether each moment is pleasurable, meaningful, or both. You may simply write P, M, or B.

In column three, write down an affirmation about yourself for each moment you have listed. Make sure that all your affirmations are positive, begin with the pronoun "I," and describe an inner quality, attribute, or strength. Keep a seven-day record in the following format:

Day One

Feeling Good Moment	Pleasure or Meaning	Affirmation
(1) _____	_____	_____
_____		_____
(2) _____	_____	_____
_____		_____
(3) _____	_____	_____

(4) _____   _____   _____

(5) _____   _____   _____

After a week of collecting information, you will be able to recognize your general state of happiness: (1) You may have a balance of pleasure and meaning in your life, (2) you may be high in pleasure and low in meaning, (3) you may be high in meaning but low in pleasure, or (4) you may be low in both pleasure and meaning.

One of my clients, Reva, used this exercise to clarify the amounts and sources of pleasure and meaning in her life. Reva has been married to Steven, an architect, for sixteen years. They have three children. Reva came to me because she was depressed, which she acknowledged had been ongoing for at least eight years. Nothing felt good to her. When I asked her to describe her relationship to Steven, she embarked on a ten-minute tirade about how he seldom lifts his face out of the newspaper or away from the TV set. Evenings, she complained, were often spent with Steven hardly uttering a grunt.

Reva actually remembered a specific incident that seemed to precipitate her depression eight years ago. She painfully recalled that she had lost twenty pounds in ten weeks—hoping to gain more attention from Steven. Since Steven had not said anything encouraging to her during the ten weeks, she asked him what he thought of her new vitality and appearance. He responded, "I never even noticed!"

Since Steven initially refused marital counseling, I asked Reva to collect data which she could present to him regarding her overall happiness. What follows is one day of her week-long entries.

Feeling Good Moment	Pleasure or Meaning	Affirmation
(1) Received a Halloween card from Lou Ann.	P and M	I am an important person to Lou Ann.
(2) Signed up for pottery class.	P	I delight in using my hands.
(3) Went to Bible study group.	M	I am a spiritual person.
(4) Driving home in the fog.	P	I am captivated by misty adventures!
(5) Exercise class.	P	I feel healthy when I sweat.

You will notice from just one day of records that Reva is experiencing both pleasure and meaning. This pattern held up over the course of seven days. However, she discovered at the end of a full week that Steven was not contributing to *either* pleasurable *or* meaningful experiences in her life! With this data in hand, she was able to persuade Steven to come in for counseling—a process that has saved their relationship.

Happiness is a matter of balance and integration. We must integrate disenchantment with romantic love, our "emotional inner child" with our "rational adult," and love with work, leisure, health, finances and spirituality. This same pattern is true for pleasure and meaning. Our ability to balance the complex elements of our lives is the key to our long-term happiness in all areas of our lives, and especially in our loving relationships.

PART III

DISENCHANTMENT
An Impasse

Most of the time, we experience disenchantment as a dead end. We see no way forward in our relationship ... we have reached an emotional impasse. The experience of disenchantment in love can be so powerful, so mentally and emotionally overwhelming, that we are only aware of our deep confusion and pain. However, disenchantment is a process that can be analyzed and understood. As we look more closely at the personal and situational elements of disenchantment, we can gain insight into how we are both responsible for and victimized by this experience. This section of the book examines both the psychological and physical aspects of disenchantment.

7

Right on Schedule

Couples who fear rocking the boat will never know if their
vessel can weather the storm.

Larry A. Bugen

At the dawn of the 20th Century, a gifted German artist named Paula
Becker married a well-known painter named Otto Modersohn. Before her
parents granted her permission to marry, they insisted that she attend two
laborious months of cooking school in Berlin so that she would be properly suited for her new role as wife. In a recently translated version of her
personal letters and journals, we are invited to view what the *New York
Times Book Review* described as "the tragic essence of Paula Modersohn-
Becker's great dilemma: How to live her life both as a woman and as a
serious artist." Her personal reflections are an early harbinger of our
modern-day conflicts surrounding work and love.

> *Marriage takes away the illusion that had sustained a belief in the pos-
> sibility of a kindred soul.* In marriage one feels doubly misunderstood.
> For one's whole life up to marriage had been devoted to finding
> another understanding being. And is it perhaps not better without this
> illusion, better to be eye to eye with one great and lonely truth? I am
> writing this in my housekeeping book ... sitting in my kitchen, cooking
> a roast of veal. (Wensinger 1984)

Each of us, like Modersohn-Becker, learns something about "a great
and lonely truth" during the course of our love relationships: We are
inevitably and predictably disappointed in our search to find a "soul mate,"
someone who will always understand us, someone who completes us. The
process of discovering this truth begins from day one of our relationship
and follows a predictable pattern over time. But the process is not a dead
end. As we follow disenchantment through its phases, we can gain insight
into our own experience and learn how to overcome the deep confusion
and pain of what appears to be an emotional impasse.

The Honeymoon Is Over

All disenchantments involve thoughts, feelings, and behaviors. Once the glow of romantic love has faded, these thoughts, feelings, and behaviors pass through three sequential phases. During the first phase, *reality shock*, we begin to experience countless situations that disappoint us or frustrate us. Birthdays or anniversaries are forgotten. Our partner shows up late for a date or shrugs off a sexual advance.

During the second phase, called *the moody black and blues*, these frustrating situations repeat themselves so often that they become patterns in our relationships. We experience intense reactions of resentment, anger, and hurt. Then we perpetuate our misery by polarizing our beliefs about our partners and indicting them with negative, resentment-based "themes." "You are a slob," we think. "You are too sensitive." "You are irresponsible." "You never support my goals." "You always put me down."

We experience phase three, *burnout*, when we cannot take the emotional pain any longer. At this point, we are disinterested and apathetic toward our partners. We may feel deeply weary or numb, as if we are just going through the motions. We may be clinically depressed as well.

Though the phases are sequential, we more often than not cycle in and out of them on a schedule all our own. It *is* possible to stay stuck in one of the last two phases, but never both at the same time. We either choose to stay in pain—the moody black and blues—or get out of pain through burnout. Beginning with the magic and romance of the honeymoon, the disenchantment cycle operates through our thoughts, feelings, and behaviors like this:

	THOUGHTS	FEELINGS	BEHAVIORS
THE HONEYMOON	Expectation	Excitement	Move Toward
REALITY SHOCK	Disappointment	Frustration	Move Against
THE MOODY BLACK AND BLUES	Resentment	Anger	Move Against
BURNOUT	Disinterest	Apathy	Move Away

The model is eloquently simple, yet it seems to describe the experience of all the couples to whom I have introduced it. Let me say at this point that it is crucial to distinguish among thoughts, feelings, and behaviors. People process their experiences and construe their worlds in very different ways. Some of us are more stoical, more intellectual, or more cognitively oriented than others. Consequently we express our disenchantment as disappointment, resentment, or disinterest. We don't lay claim to intense emotional feelings. We may even completely deny being pissed off when our partner smashes the car up for the third time this year!

On the other hand, some of us are much more emotional in our experience of disenchantment. We moan, bitch, or cry whenever we feel we have been wronged. Our style is more feeling oriented. Letting out our frustration or our anger is no problem for us at all!

Others of us deny being hurt, angry, or resentful about a thing. We may not display emotional upset and we may deny having disturbing thoughts—but our actions give us away! I know of one husband who, after twelve years of marriage, wanted to spend every weekend riding his Harley Davidson (and not spending time with his wife). And yet he consistently denied his disappointment (thoughts) or frustration (feeling), insisting that he was commited to the relationship. We must each understand our own individual pathways throughout disenchantment.

As I have said many times in this book, the high expectations and excitement of early romance are destined to fade in intensity. Each of the eight elements of romantic love must undergo some change. We may find that our passion has subsided, or that we no longer obsess over our beloved, or that our mutual desire for exclusivity has been eroded. For whatever reasons, we are destined to experience disenchantment. This was certainly the case with Ron, who had been married to Lois for well over six years. As Ron recalls:

We started going out because she was so much fun. She made me laugh. She seemed to enjoy my independence and my pride in it. I looked forward to her calls each night when we would talk endlessly for a long time. Once we started sleeping together, it seemed to get better each time. She was so sensual. We enjoyed cooking meals together. Whenever I would suggest an activity, she would throw herself into it with great enthusiasm. Since I was into jogging, she started jogging. She wanted to learn racquetball and she almost bought a racquet before she even knew if she would enjoy it. We planned a vacation together and shopped for camping gear like real outdoorsmen. Whatever I wanted to do, we did.

What a soul mate! Ron had found himself someone very special indeed. Lois appeared to be someone who would enthusiastically share leisure pursuits like camping and jogging as well as more intimate activities. What could possibly go wrong? How could two people who shared such high expectations, so much excitement, and so much pleasure spending time together possibly crash and burn? Predictably, after three years, they did. As Ron points out in a resentment letter to Lois:

Dear Lois,
    This letter is about being mad. Why am I mad right now? Why am I mad most of the time? No lovemaking in five months! That makes me angry. No dates by ourselves in five months! That makes me angry. No communication, no good times for just us, no shared interests, no shared dreams, no crying together, no laughing together. It just makes me boil. I'm a boiler just waiting to explode. I'm mad as hell and—you know how that one ends.

What in the name of heaven is the matter with you? Do you have to be sick all the time? Sleep all the time? Blame me all the time for the way you feel? Where are your friends? Who calls you? Who do you go see? Who do you have fun with? Why are you so sexually dead?

You told me once that you would never help support me in school or in looking for another job. The shock of that statement has worn off but the anger and resentment stays. I expect my wife to seriously consider my important wants and needs. As long as you won't ever listen to even a suggestion, I can only conclude that you really don't care about what's in it for the other half of this relationship. I think that you are incredibly selfish.

Finally, I am mad because you don't like my style. When I bring up a point in discussions at church or with my friends, you say I am too loud or that I embarrass you. I like to get away for some fun, so I am "irresponsible." I weigh alternatives and am slow to make important decisions, so I "can't make up my mind about anything." I like rock-and-roll and "heavy" movies which you consider weird. I like to sleep in the nude and take baths with my wife, or skinny dip. That is threatening to you. All you do is dress up in your bathrobe and wear long robes around the house. I guess that I am just kinky!

Whatever I am—I am. I'll do my best to compromise if you want to try, but I haven't seen any effort on your part. I can't continue in this armed camp that is our marriage. We can try to change it or give up. We've stagnated for too long. I am making a move. Hope you can reciprocate.

Love, Ron

It is painfully obvious that Ron's initial excitement and expectations have been zapped (as they have been for Lois as well). Ron's angry portrait of Lois suggests that she may be experiencing phase three of the disenchantment cycle—burnout. Through Ron's eyes, we see her as aloof, indifferent, and apathetic. In contrast, Ron is writhing in phase two—the moody black and blues. Yes, the honeymoon does end, but there are clear reasons why it must.

The Disenchantment Cube

If disenchantment is both inevitable and necessary, there must be a way to show the connection among the factors which cause it to occur. There must be some way to understand how we get washed away by stormy seas or isolated in quiet despair.

The previous section of this book has made it clear that we enter any love relationship with (1) early emotional wounds, (2) embedded beliefs, and (3) implicit values relating to happiness. Each of these elements can be the trigger for disenchantment later on, as the relationship develops. Let's review each of these components.

1. For your relationship to be satisfactory, it must be based on a healthy balance of inclusion, control, and affection needs. You, or your partner, will *not* be happy if there are:

1. Too many demands or expectations
2. Too much criticism or manipulation
3. Too much smothering or overprotection
4. Too little attention
5. Too little appreciation
6. Too little affection

Your dissatisfaction is almost guaranteed if you have been emotionally wounded in any of these areas during your earliest developmental years. Your partner will unwittingly fail you in some way, inevitably reminding you once again that your needs are "destined" to be sabotaged.

2. For your relationship to be satisfactory, it must be based on experiences which sustain your most important embedded beliefs about your soul mate. These beliefs are dichotomously organized into very special "personal constructs." Since you are looking to complete yourself in many ways within this love bond—to achieve wholeness—you need a partner who remains at the positive pole of each of your personal constructs.

3. For your relationship to be satisfactory, it must be based on experiences that reinforce your most valued assumptions about "the good life." Your happiness will depend upon having a partner who actively supports you in each of the pillars of happiness:

1. Love
2. Work
3. Leisure
4. Health
5. Finances
6. Spirituality

These three domains can be represented along the axes of a cube. In effect we have (1) six emotional needs interfacing with (2) a variable number of personal constructs which, in turn, interface with (3) six quality of life variables. For instance, it is possible that you married your husband believing that he was reliable (an important personal construct for you). Reliability may have been especially important to you in the area of finances, since you grew up feeling insecure amidst the poverty of your family. Since your fiancé was a law student, with potential for great income, you figured you had a valuable diamond in the rough!

Unfortunately, what you did not figure on was a nasty habit of gambling to which he soon became addicted! Now, years later, you painfully discredit him as *unreliable*, particularly in the area of finances. You are horrified to note (1) a threat to your emotional need for control (over finances), (2) a change in your evaluation of your partner (from reliable to unreliable), and (3) a dramatic shift in your quality of life (finances). Let's take a closer look at how these fit into a cube.

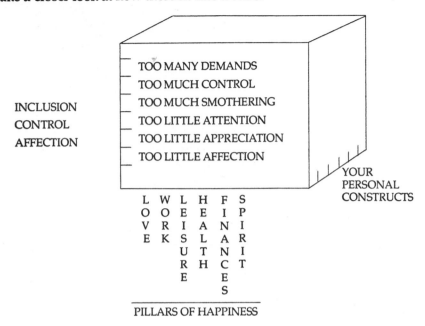

INCLUSION
CONTROL
AFFECTION

TOO MANY DEMANDS
TOO MUCH CONTROL
TOO MUCH SMOTHERING
TOO LITTLE ATTENTION
TOO LITTLE APPRECIATION
TOO LITTLE AFFECTION

YOUR
PERSONAL
CONSTRUCTS

```
L  W  L  H  F  S
O  O  E  E  I  P
V  R  I  N  N  I
E  K  S  A  A  R
      U  T  N  I
      R  H  C  T
      E     E
            S
```

PILLARS OF HAPPINESS

Remember Ron and Lois from earlier in this chapter? Ron was dismayed to discover that Lois had changed radically from the wondrous being she appeared to be early on in their love relationship. The cube helps us understand why this happened.

First, let's consider his wounded origins. Ron grew up in a father-absent family in which his mother had to work outside the home in order to make ends meet. She had no choice! This meant that Ron had to fend for himself, often asking a friend to invite him over for dinner or evening companionship. He would resent his mother's absence but always hesitated in expressing his hurt for fear that she would also abandon him like his father did. He desparately needed attention and affection as a child and, sadly, did not receive enough. He was emotionally wounded. As an adult, he was particularly sensitive to being hurt when these two needs were not met. Thus, we can see how devastating it was for him to find that Lois's sensual warmth and enthusiastic devotion faded after so short a time. Her apathetic withdrawal crushed him, and—in a style so characteristically male—he expressed anger rather than hurt.

Second, Ron's view of the good life clearly included "financial" security (he wanted Lois to support him in school if necessary) and "leisure satisfaction." At the beginning with Lois, he thought he had it all. They once shared the cooking, jogged together, played racketball, enjoyed camping, and delighted in mutually planning their vacations together. Now, a few years into this relationship, Ron's quality of life seems to be in the pits! Lois wants (1) no lovemaking, (2) no dates, (3) no communication, (4) no shared interests, (5) no fun, (6) no sensual baths, and (7) no changes in Ron's employment status. Ron's pillars of happiness appear to be crashing to the ground around him.

Third, Ron had created a number of personal constructs which framed his expectations for a loving relationship. These included:

- Fun versus boring
- Supportive versus unsupportive
- Communicative versus reclusive
- Sensual versus prudish
- Enthusiastic versus dull
- Thoughtful versus selfish

At the height of their romance, Ron obviously saw Lois as fun-loving, supportive, communicative, sensual, enthusiastic, and thoughtful. Now that Ron has crashed and burned, we discover that Lois has been trashed as well! He now categorically rejects Lois's position at the positive end of these continuums, and actually seems to reject the continuums themselves, choosing instead to polarize his views 100 degrees from what they once were. Now he views Lois as boring, unsupportive, reclusive, prudish, dull, and selfish.

Consider your own disenchantments for a moment. You may vaguely sense that the honeymoon is over and that your expectations and excitement have waned. Or you may have precipitously crashed and burned and may feel that your relationship is a living hell! No matter the degree of disquietude, you can trace the cause of your partner's fall from grace to each of the three domains of the cube.

Your natural inclination is to blame your partner for this predictable despair—convinced in your own right that he or she is the problem. Consider for a moment, however, the elements in the cube. Note that in each case the "real" problem may lie *within you*!

1. *Emotional wounds.* It may be your emotional wounds from early family life that compel you to respond so powerfully to your partner's commissions or omissions. You may demand too much attention, appreciation, or affection—more than any one person could possibly provide! Or you may require too much control— more than any other person could endure!

2. *Embedded beliefs.* It may be your categorical and absolute shift in perception—your extreme personal constructs—which have resulted in a critical and negative view of your partner. Unless you have learned to embrace the gray in life, the amalgam of compromise so necessary in any relationship, you may be doomed to view *any* partner as a despicable beast incapable of meeting your needs.

3. *Pillars of happiness.* It may be your inappropriate values and expectations regarding happiness that have contributed to the downturn in your relationship. If you have children, or a spouse who is

career-minded, it may be impossible to preserve the kind of leisure life or financial freedom you desire.

Whatever the case, disenchantment continues to unfold in a predictable and orderly fashion. Let's now take a closer look at the first phase in this process—reality shock.

Phase One: Reality Shock

The illusions that we create in the honeymoon of our relationships must begin to shatter sooner or later. Superlatives like "She is the most sensual," "He is the most generous," "She is the best …," "He is the finest …" begin to buckle under the weight of frequent experiences that seem to contradict these early notions. We begin to see that what we thought was true is not necessarily so. We encounter situation after situation that chips away at the early impressions we had formed about one another.

Making a snide comment about your outfit or not inviting you to a luncheon suddenly take on serious meaning. Or how about the forgotten hug on the way out the door in the morning after you concocted that special omelet for him. Oh yes, and let's not forget his refusal to attend the family picnic. Beliefs which once appeared to be unshakeable now appear to be as insecure as shifting sand.

Situations that create disappointment or frustration are unavoidable in every love relationship. When we experience these thoughts and feelings, we may begin to behave in argumentative ways. We may protest against our partner's actions or inactions. These are typically not angry protests so much as expressions of irritation or surprise. "How could you possibly forget the milk when I reminded you twice!" "You knew we had a social commitment with the Jacksons for Saturday night. How could you set us up for tennis doubles?" Notice that the protest in reality shock is directed more *to the situation* than *at the person*.

Let's listen to the complaints of a woman named Janice who began to notice questionable things about her new beau, Bill, a man who had a young son from a previous marriage.

> I remember the first thing I saw about Bill that turned me off was that he was not athletic. He was jogging down a trail with his son and looked funny doing it. I was also surprised that I had to wait for him every half mile or so.
>
> Another early realization was that I did not think he was disciplining his son very well. The boy always seemed to get what he wanted and no attempt was made to put an end to whining. I couldn't stand to hear him whining while Bill tried to reason with him instead of being stricter with discipline.
>
> One weekend I hosted an engagement party for a good friend. It was a large party and I was priding myself on the refreshments and organization of it. It was a "no kids" party, but Bill had his son for the

weekend, and elected to stay home with him instead of getting a babysitter. I think he worries too much about the effect of the divorce on his son. He does this to the extent that he ignores his own needs. He would really be providing a better role model if he showed his son that he put himself first sometimes.

Janice had initially noticed how successful Bill was as a businessman and community volunteer. She had also assumed that his prior marriage had taught him important lessons about life and love. The fact that he also owned a wonderful cabin on Lake Travis did not hurt matters either. Many a moonlit evening had been spent there. At first, she focused only on his successful career, community mindedness, and the house on the lake. Now she begins to notice cracks in the silver lining. She begins to shift her focus to Bill's reactions toward his son and his lack of athletic prowess. This is a good example of what I have called "the eye-opening effect."

Situations that might have been ignored during the honeymoon period now take on special meaning. The engagement party is noteworthy. She is clearly disappointed that he did not come and is beginning to feel frustrated about Bill ignoring his own needs—as well as hers! Individuation from children has now become a vital dimension in this relationship, when it was not even on the Top 20 chart during romantic love. This is the magic of perceptual shifts.

The hairline cracks of reality shock are not major faultlines in our lives. Rather, they are everyday tremors that occur randomly and regularly Sunday through Saturday. They are unavoidable. Every meaningful relationship we have is filled with them. When we cope constructively with these frustrating or disappointing *situations*, they remain inconsequential. However, if they are suppressed, or not effectively managed, they may evolve into the angry resentment of the moody black and blues.

While teaching at the University of Texas, I had an opportunity to do some research with a colleague, Dr. Sharon Humenich, which revealed just how predictably our expectations do shatter in relationships. We interviewed thirty-seven couples three weeks before the delivery of their firstborn child and again three weeks after delivery. During our first visit, we asked both mothers and fathers how actively involved they expected to be, given their available time, in taking care of their infant—changing diapers, feeding, playing, washing, and so on. During the second visit, we asked them how active they *actually* were with their newborns.

Prior to delivery, we found that mothers expected to be more involved in caretaking than fathers to a significant degree. No surprise, right? What happened after delivery, however, was somewhat surprising. Following delivery, the mothers ended up doing significantly *more* caretaking than even they had expected, while fathers ended up doing significantly less than they expected. We called this the "funnel effect," since actual caretaking behaviors became more and more skewed between the mothers and fathers over time. If we had followed these same families for a while longer, we would have discovered, no doubt, many reality shock experiences occurring around childrearing issues.

Most people are able to document a variety of annoyances they experience with their love partners. Can you relate to this client's list of frustrations and disappointments in her marriage?

Things He Does That Bother Me

1. Takes off socks in a wad.

2. Leaves underwear where company can see it.

3. Hogs bed covers.

4. Must have air conditioning on and cold at all times, even though I have a cold or my hair is wet.

5. Wears tennis shoes with a dress shirt and slacks.

6. Clears his throat grotesquely.

7. Leaves toilet lid up.

8. Leaves bathtub mat down and shower curtain open, allowing them to mildew.

9. Blames all sexual problems on me, but doesn't make an effort to be appealing to me.

10. Only washes his hair if we go someplace ... not just for me.

11. Only takes a shower if he's been hot and sweaty.

12. Dumps dishes and food in sink instead of scraping and stacking neatly.

13. Kills roaches and leaves them there.

14. Breathes heavily with a lot of mucus.

15. Appears callous towards things that are special to me.

16. Keeps curtains closed and house dark.

17. Defends anyone I complain about.

18. Drinks Tab all day (caffeine) and can't understand why he doesn't feel sleepy; he then misses work!

19. When he does not feel well, he takes the whole day off.

20. Expects me to go braless with a sheer shirt, but that is not me.

21. Complains that I don't clean the house; yet when he takes a day off he does not lift a finger to help.

22. Wants to do certain things with me sexually because some girl in a magazine "loved it," even though I may find it uncomfortable.

23. Whenever there is extra money in the bank, he spends it on himself rather than me or old debts.

24. He saves every issue of his *Playboy* magazines but bugs me about keeping my six romance novels.

25. He tells me that what I read in my romance novels is make-believe, but that his fantasies from Playboy are real.

26. He doesn't open up to me.

27. I get the silent treatment when he gets mad.

28. He has become weak and succumbs to every obstacle.

29. He complains about my mother constantly.

30. He has no will power or self-discipline.

31. He talks loudly.

32. He explains things in a tone of voice that makes me think I'm stupid.

33. Although he has made an effort to wear a seatbelt, I don't think it had anything to do with his concern for me.

34. If I'm upset, he tells me I'm upset over nothing.

35. He never seems to be serious.

36. He doesn't like dancing anymore.

37. He is not patient.

38. He wants a lot of material things but does not seem willing to work and sacrifice to obtain them.

Sure sounds like she lives with adversity, doesn't it? Because she is so unhappy, her husband has come under microscopic scrutiny. So long as these situations occur infrequently, she will remain in the reality shock phase of her disenchantment. However, if these behavior patterns reoccur often enough to become predictable patterns, this couple will find themselves fitfully struggling with the moody black and blues.

With a modicum of effort, most of us could create a similar list of annoyances. Two points should be remembered.

First, we perceive these sources of annoyance more selectively at times when we are unhappy. Remember that all of us are busy scientists collecting data to confirm our biases and are especially active in searching out the positive or negative in our lives. Real sources of frustration do pop up in our lives unexpectedly. However, we contribute to our discomfort by selecting what to focus on and how long to maintain our focus.

Second, there is a significant difference between focusing on a specific *behavior* and focusing on the *person*. Disenchantment at the reality shock phase is situational and focuses on specific behaviors. Notice that most of the 38 annoyances listed above describe specific behaviors of the woman's husband. As she gets into it, however, she begins to build themes or character profiles about her husband. Let's restate a few of these themes:

15. He is callous.

26. He does not communicate feelings.

28. He is weak.

30. He has no will power.

33. He is not a caring person.

35. He is not serious.

37. He is not patient.

These themes suggest that she has bridged the gap to the moody black and blues. Each theme represents a basic core structure which supports her negative views of her husband. By now, it takes very little to trigger volatile reactions in regard to these views. They had been built up over years, but can be sparked in milliseconds!

Themes are always ad hominem attacks. They are angry, polarized views of one another that are intended to be global truths. They always occur when the frustrating and disappointing situations of reality shock repeat themselves often enough to become painful patterns. "George, you *never* come home on time."

Our expectations will *always* be shattered. Our relationships will be much healthier and happier if we can deal with our frustrations and disappointments by focusing only on the situation and not indicting the person or setting. This is the key. Behaviors can change in a day, while personality characteristics may take a lifetime to alter. And some very loving and successful people also clear their throats grotesquely.

Phase Two: The Moody Black and Blues

The moody black and blues is a time of volatile emotions, sleepless nights, and physical symptoms. People get rip-roaring mad during this phase. They feel ripped off, abused, unfairly treated, and oftentimes ready to leave their partners. Always, underneath the anger, they are experiencing a great deal of hurt or fear. Most of us are more willing to express *anger*, the surface emotion, rather than tell someone that they have *hurt* us.

So many frustrating situations have been endured by this time that patterns begin to emerge. How many times can your husband or wife delay coming home for dinner without calling before we label him or her "inconsiderate"? How many times can your wife forget your birthday or anniversary before you label her "uncaring"? We begin to build themes about our partners when our own needs are compromised too often.

During the moody black and blues, we are resentful and angry, and our behaviors show it! *Resentments are not feelings*—even though we may say that we "feel" resentment. Resentments are memories of all the situations which have occurred that have contributed the themes we perceive in our partner's character. Some people have an uncanny ability to recall painful memories from the past—as if they are accessing a computer file. Different therapists have referred to this phenomenon as gunnysacking, stamp collecting, or playing "old tapes." They sound like this:

- On January 4, 1983, you stood me up for a date.
- You never introduced me to your friends from Michigan when they visited.
- You did not take me with you to the 1984 Democratic National Convention in San Francisco.
- You had an affair while I was pregnant.

And then it happens. They hurt us again. We experience a gush of feelings. Our muscles tense, our pupils dilate, our blood vessels constrict. We spew out an angry litany of charges against them that makes a cross-examination by F. Lee Bailey pale in comparison. Of course, they don't know what to respond to, since they are being deluged with indictments against them which date back to the signing of the Magna Carta. In our anger, we can be quite aggressive as we verbally—and perhaps physically—strike out against our "enemies."

During this angry phase, our thinking becomes quite polarized. We think only in extremes, only in black and white. We shift the power of our attention from the purity of our original romantic illusions to the shattered remnants which remain. The themes of the moody black and blues are those shattered remnants. Think about it: One moment you believe "He loves me." The next moment you *know* that "He doesn't give a damn!" You may actually shift your attention back and forth many times a day, believing first that he loves you, and then that he doesn't. And as we have seen, this process can unfold in milliseconds!

A particularly clear example is provided by a professional couple I worked with recently. Harriet was a lawyer, and Bill was a teacher. You will easily note Bill's theme building and categorical thinking:

> We were sitting around one dreary day watching TV. Harriet volunteered to do the food shopping for the week. This is a chore we have shared during the ten years of our marriage. On her way out the door, I asked her to pick me up an apple pie. I know she heard me because she stood still when I yelled to her.
>
> She returned forty minutes later. As I was helping to put away the groceries, I found myself salivating as I imagined bingeing on apple pie, vanilla ice cream, chocolate syrup, and cream. I soon discovered that there was no apple pie—only a peach pie!
>
> I got pissed as hell! She has done this kind of crap too many times for me to take it in stride. She *never* listens. She's just a space cadet. She heard me ask for apple pie, but she spaced out on me. To top it off, I don't like peach pie, never have, and never will. I think she is a lousy listener and I don't really believe she cares about me!

Bill writhed in angry protest for at least two reasons. First, he has developed a theme that Harriet is a poor listener. So much so that he has labeled her a "space cadet" over the years. Second, he wonders how special he is! How, after ten years of marriage, can Harriet not know that he likes only one kind of pie? Apple pie! She obviously doesn't care. Once established, these two long-standing themes are likely to erupt volcanically whenever they are triggered by a related situation.

Resentments are always stored in our memories—and are easily triggered by experiences that confirm for us that our most potent themes are undeniably valid. Resentments built up over time are so powerful that I believe that *90 percent of all expressed anger has nothing to do with the immediate situation.* In fact, this may also be true of other powerful emotions such as guilt, anxiety, and even joy. Think about the implications of this! Imagine pulling into the driveway after a sweaty, conflict-laden day at work. Traffic was sluggish for miles. In a daze you ram into your son's shiny two-wheeler—which happened to be lying in the driveway, waiting for you. As you are about to fling his bicycle into the deep recesses of outer space, remember that he merits only 10 percent of your anger. The other 90 percent has nothing to do with this situation at all.

Intense resentments carried over time can account for many different kinds of responses—ranging from extramarital affairs, to murder, to racial violence. Probably nine out of ten affairs occur because of resentments which have built up toward one's partner. We may find a lover in order to get even or to replace the idealized image of what we were looking for in our marriage. Every day there are thousands of incidents of domestic violence that mirror the pent-up anger and resentments of disenchantment—some fatal. Just this week, a man was arraigned in Austin for shooting his wife to death for refusing to have sex with him on his birthday. Family disturbance calls are considered the most dangerous for police officers and result in more police fatalities than even narcotics!

The relationship between the illusory dreams we create during romantic love and their obliteration during the moody black and blues is an important one. Whether this process is gradual or sudden, we must realize that the intensity of our pain may reach an unendurable level. One of my clients, who eventually left her husband, documented the disenchantments she had endured for fifteen years of marriage. At the same time, she identified the early illusions her husband was responsible for shattering! From an original list of over forty examples, seven stand out:

1. He hit me when I was pregnant. (I am safe and loved.)

2. He snipes at me in front of others whose opinion I value. (I am respected.)

3. He raises hell every time I travel. (I am supported.)

4. He does not respect the professional work I do. (I am respected and valued.)

5. He insists on sleeping in the "master bedroom" because of the designation "master." (I am an equal partner.)

6. He will not take the children to the doctor or stay home with them when they are ill. (He is an equal partner.)

7. He won't initiate dates or spend money on fun. (I have romance, love, and excitement.)

Most people simply will not tolerate this kind of pain forever. If relationships like these don't improve, partners will either use divorce to extricate themselves from their source of pain or numb themselves in order to endure it. This brings us to phase three of the disenchantment cycle—burnout.

Phase Three: Burnout

If we cannot find a healthy pathway through the anger and pain of the moody black and blues, we may choose to become petrified, freezing into deadened symbols of a past life form. We allow our feelings to atrophy toward the person who hurt us so much. In effect, we go numb. There are numb people everywhere who have decided that it is better not to feel, not to get excited, or not to dream dreams—because it is not worth getting hurt again.

You may be one of them. You may be in a "dead" relationship, simply going through the motions in a patterned way, acting like an automaton. You may appear to be an expressionless, faceless partner who participates in a well-orchestrated but ritualized marital dance. Your partner's needs, wants, and spiritual growth may no longer be of any interest to you. You may find yourself to be indifferent and apathetic.

One of the more puzzling questions of the day is, Why do people stay in self-defeating, empty relationships? Anxiety? Fear of the unknown? Security and image? Duty? Fear of facing even more pain outside the relationship? Possibly. But what do they get from these relationships? Occasional companionship? Sex? Food at predictable hours? Another set of hands to transport the little bumpkins to school? Sure. And, of course, they are reinforcing their world views. They assure themselves each day that their very worst illusions about life and love have come true. The world can really be a despicable place if you help keep it that way! We will review the ways we "stay stuck" in the next chapter.

When you reach the point of burnout in the disenchantment cycle, you may be clinically depressed. If you are experiencing some of the following symptoms of depression, seek assistance from a qualified helper (if you haven't already).

1. A profound loss of pleasure

2. A personal sense of inadequacy and loss of self-esteem

3. Chronic fatigue

4. Sleep disturbance/appetite disturbance

5. Decreased productivity at home or work

6. Diminished activity and social avoidance

7. Pessimism and hopelessness about the future

8. Confusion and difficulty remembering things

9. Guilt

10. Possible thoughts of suicide

Other symptoms, such as irritability and tearfulness, may have already diminished by this phase. In effect, we are all cried out. In order to get angry or cry we must still want something or someone. At this point, we have given up such hope.

(Remember that only a competent professional can help you determine if you are clinically depressed. Most of us experience some of the above symptoms from time to time.)

Let's step back a moment. I must emphasize that the phases of disenchantment do not reflect static, fixed states. Over longer periods of time, we progress through them in a predictable manner, although when viewed from a distance, we appear to be in one phase for the most part. It is akin to looking at the Mediterranean Sea from an airplane. At first glance we see a constant-level body of water. Closer scrutiny, however, reveals the ebb and flow, the constant change in motion that prevails. During the course of a day or week, we can pass through joyful heights, valleys of despair, and sheer-rocked chasms which seem to separate us from the whole of humanity.

Three points should be highlighted at this time.

First, phase two (the moody black and blues) and phase three (burnout) tend to be closely associated. In this case, people vacillate between hope and despair. One minute we desperately cling to a cherished need; the next we are resigned to throwing in the towel. The tearfulness and irritability of one moment are soon replaced by a ghostly remoteness. Most of the time we want to hang onto that sliver of hope. "Maybe she really does love me." "Maybe he can meet my needs."

Second, our sense of burnout can be isolated—only affecting our reactions toward one person—or it can be a generalized world view. If the burnout is isolated, you feel numb only when you are with your partner. The rest of the time you may even be a bubbling brook. Your friends might never know that your heart turns to cast iron when you pass through the doorway to your home.

Third, therapy is easier when burnout is isolated to one person or event and more difficult when generalized. People lack energy or the motivation to change in so many areas of their lives. An example here may be helpful.

The Case of Kate

Kate reacted as if burned by a molten iron rod if anyone touched her, even a co-worker's pat on the back. In most conversations, she realized she could only respond to initial hellos or light jokes. Anything personal would clamp down a thick steel door upon her ability to communicate. She would blush and tears would well up whenever she recognized the bewilderment in others' eyes in these moments. Such panic and desperation could not evolve over night.

Kate's withdrawal began when her husband of four years was having an affair during her second pregnancy and refused to let her touch him in bed. She became desperate for support as she tried to mother two toddlers who shared one ear infection or bout of diarrhea after another. There were many other layers of family pain as well. After her father died of leukemia, her mother soon became an alcoholic, who in one frenzied revelation told Kate that she "had resented her all her life." With these words, Kate felt that her mother had viciously killed her childhood.

Kate's lack of trust turned global. She became self-destructive and fatalistic, but turned to working seventy-hour weeks as a means of survival and self-preservation. She had little, if anything, to do with her husband.

This case points out the hopeless withdrawal, apathy, and disinterest that can occur in relationships. It does not detail the repeated frustrations and disappointments, nor the stored resentments and anger, which most definitely preceded this burnout. The pain this person endured in her marriage further scorched her soul and isolated her from warm human contact. Over the years, she learned to avoid her friends as well, convinced that they too would hurt her. Renewing her trust in others was key to this client's progress—a process that required patience from her husband and forgiveness from my client. However, they were able to progress through the RENEW program and, as of this writing, have a much healthier relationship.

A number of summary points can be made regarding the disenchantment cycle. Think about them in light of your own experiences. I offer them as food for thought.

1. All disenchantments are metaphors. Situations that trigger disenchantment are symbolic representations of the themes or illusions which govern our lives. They include positive situations such as a job promotion or a kiss which metaphorically mean "I am special" to negative symbols such as the forgotten Christmas gift which metaphorically means "He doesn't care about me."

2. The disenchantment process can be triggered at warp speed. I call this "mushrooming," since a cloud of debris will follow the innocent spark in milliseconds. When we mushroom, we allow a situation at phase one to trigger a long-standing theme in phase two. An unloving glance, a sarcastic tone of voice, or the lack of an expected stroke can trigger an avalanche of anger and resentment. I must emphasize that the long-standing themes are always there. They can be triggered so quickly that the disenchanted are often left feeling guilty about their sudden loss of control.

3. The harder we push, the harder we fall. The more idealistic we are, the more shattering are our incongruent experiences.

4. Disenchantments are reciprocal. It doesn't take long for two lov ers to share each others' disgust for one another or to develop reciprocal themes. There are always enough resentments to go around. Likewise, if you are a disgruntled employee, chances are good that there is a supervisor unhappy with you!

5. Situations are not disenchanting of and by themselves. They are given meaning through the eyes of the beholder. Situations which are viewed as merely frustrating by one person may instead create intense anger for another person.

6. Somewhere, in some way, someone will find something disenchanting about you. Your lovely home will disenchant someone because it is too garish. Wearing your hair too long, your skirt too short, being too thin or too fat will strike a chord with someone. Clearly disenchantment is a part of the human experience and we must learn to cope effectively with it.

7. The source for disenchantment ultimately lies within and reflects our own expectation levels. One angry client stated that she expected her husband to provide more adequately. She complained often about his level of income, compared to other successful businessmen. When we got right down to it, this client admitted that she never wanted to work outside the home and resented her husband because she had to.

8. Ninety percent of all expressed anger has nothing to do with the situation at all. This tremendous outpouring of emotion has more to do with the long-standing themes and resentments which actually preceded this situation. This may mean that the person you are pissed off at is not only getting the 10 percent that he or she deserves, but also the 90 percent that belongs to every son-of-a-bitch you have hated along the way.

9. The disenchantment cycle is not static. It is a dynamic model for understanding our needs. We do not remain stuck in the moody black and blues indefinitely. For one thing it is too painful. More importantly, most of us strive to find more joy and meaning in life. Fluctuating between the moody blues and burnout just does not cut the mustard. Most of us, instead, exercise the right to dream and strive to find the enchantments worth having. Some of us, however, do remain stuck much too long. The next chapter will look at this process in some detail.

8

Getting Stuck

The trouble with steeling yourself against the harshness of
reality is that the same steel that secures your life against being
destroyed secures your life also against being opened up and
transformed by the holy power that life itself comes from. You
can survive on your own. You can grow stronger on your own.
You can even prevail on your own. But you cannot become
human on your own.

Frederick Buechner

People are inclined to preserve what is known, rather than to face un-
charted waters. No matter if the "known" is positive or negative, we are
likely to maintain stability—the status quo—under any circumstances.
When threatened with something new and different, we often go so far as
to *distort* the new in order to safeguard the old. Although I have known
of this phenomenon for some time as a therapist, I recently had an
opportunity to experience it as a parent.

When my son, Erik, was in fourth grade, he happened upon my own
fourth grade report card from the once stately Vanderveer Elementary
School in Easton, Pennsylvania. During this memorable year, I had not
only managed to maintain my steady C average, but had reached a new
high—or low, as it were—by securing an F in arithmetic the first marking
period.

Flabbergasted, Erik ran to Claire. "Mom, look what I found! Can you
believe Dad got all C's *and* an F! By the way, what's arithmetic?"

"Arithmetic is what you call math these days. And isn't it wonderful
to see how Daddy worked real hard to improve himself over the years?
You can see how hard work can pay off."

When I arrived home and learned of Erik's discovery, I acknowledged
Claire's very astute observation about how far I had come and complimented Erik for being a much better student than I. No further mention
of the grades occurred for three weeks. Then one night while I was rocking
Erik, I felt curious about whether his high opinion of me had been lowered
by the clear, undeniable data that I had had a fling with failure.

"Erik, do you remember my fourth grade report card?"

"Oh, yes, Dad. You mean the one with all the C's?"

"Uh, yes, the one with all the C's. Is there anything else you can remember about it?"

"Well, you sure liked C's, Dad, and learned to work hard too!"

I left well enough alone. Erik wanted to maintain a positive belief that his dad was smart and not stupid, a success and not a failure, and hardworking and not lazy. Erik had his own "personal constructs," and he had me pegged at the positive end of these continuums. A measly old F would not displace my very cherished stature of being "smart," "successful," and "hardworking."

Embedded beliefs about human relationships have this kind of resiliency, whether they are positive or negative. They must, for if we are to make sense out of our lives, we must learn to see the world in a predictable fashion. As a little scientist, Erik was busy collecting data to support his theory that I am smart, successful, and hardworking. As resilient as his *beliefs* appeared to be however, there are two additional factors which contribute to his *maintaining* these beliefs: (1) his behavior toward me and (2) my behavior toward him.

Erik often asked me difficult questions in science or social studies at times when his homework would confuse him. I wish I had a dollar for all the "why" questions he asked over the years. Why does the moon change shape? Why do people stop growing? Why do we dream? Somehow I learned to fashion appropriate answers, from my own confusion, about these issues. There were other moments when he would hear me give a speech or talk to clients on the phone. He also had plenty of opportunity—during skiing vacations to Colorado or when we built the family entertainment room onto our house—to appreciate the lifestyle that Claire and I had made for our family. These positive indicators were data which also supported his belief that his Dad acted intelligently, worked hard, and seemed to be successful. He, in turn, acted toward me "as if" these observations were true.

These three elements of personal beliefs, behavior toward others, and others' behavior toward you are the basis for romantic love, disenchantment, and mature love. Of these three elements, our belief systems are the most important, since they anchor our behavior toward others, which thus influences their behavior toward us. Any changes in our belief systems have wide-ranging effects intrapersonally as well as interpersonally.

Psychologist Milton Rokeach (1960) made this point decades ago when he pointed out that

- All persons are assumed to have belief systems and each belief system contains tens of thousands of beliefs.
- Beliefs vary along a continuum of importance. Some are more important, or central, than others.
- The more important a belief, the more it will resist change; and the more trivial a belief, the more easily it can be changed.

- The more important a belief which is changed, the more widespread the impact throughout a person's belief system.

Erik knew this quite well and would not permit poor academic performance during my formative years to unlock the powerful notion that his Dad had his act together. I celebrated his belief in me and crossed my fingers that his adolescence would not do me in!

A Healthy Triangle (Romantic Love)

Romantic love is grounded upon three factors: (1) the belief that you have found a beloved upon whom you may project every fantasy, every need, and every requirement in order to be "completely" happy; (2) personal behaviors on your part which support this belief; and (3) the behaviors of your beloved toward you which support this belief.

Romantic beliefs must be fueled by actions and reactions between two lovers. Beliefs of any kind do not stabilize unless experiences—or our perception of experiences—support them. Beliefs are not static. They are vibrant, vacillating constructions that require "food for thought." In the case of romantic love, this nourishment comes from the courting behaviors that are choreographed by the two passion-intoxicated lovers.

We believe that our beloved will complete us—will make us more whole. Our partner has the power to do so because we have given him or her license to do so. We have allowed ourselves to "fall in love." But now, in order to maintain this ecstatic state, we must strive to sustain those behaviors that characterize true lovers in love. So long as our actions, as well as our beloved's actions, support our romantic beliefs, a state of "perfect" congruence exists. We seek perfect congruence because romantic love is based on perfection. Nothing less will do!

It is possible to fashion an interpersonal balance model that reflects these three components:

An Interpersonal Balance Model

POSITIVE BELIEFS

PERSONAL BEHAVIOR ⟷ BEHAVIOR OF OTHERS

Romantic love is characterized by a perfectly congruent matrix. Our positive beliefs about our beloved are supported by loving behaviors, both expressed and received. That is, we act in loving ways when we believe we are loved and we are the beneficiary of loving behaviors when we are loved. As a result, our belief that we have found that "one in a million" is maintained. All three elements are in "perfect" agreement. And this is just what romantic love feels like—perfect! But how can such perfection—such a healthy triangle—possibly be maintained indefinitely? It can't!

We often encounter situations where others do not support our matrix of love—when "perfect" agreement is lacking. Parents may not accept a beloved because of religious, cultural, or educational differences. Just today I heard a client describe how her potential son-in-law was not good enough for her daughter because "he was beneath her" due to his learning disability and his lack of clear career goals.

When these outside rejections occur, a threat to congruency exists. Two lovers, enthralled with one another, want to continue to view each other positively—usually to an exaggerated degree. They also want to sustain their sense of exclusivity—to preserve their special bond without interference. An intruding parent or a critical friend will be dealt with accordingly, since lovers will always strive to maintain congruency. When their sense of congruency is threatened by outsiders, they will pursue the following strategies:

1. Romantic lovers will continue to focus only on the behaviors of their partner which reinforce their positive beliefs about them. ("He is the only one who truly cares enough to call me every day. No one has ever devoted themselves more to me than he has done for the past six months!")

2. Romantic lovers will elicit more behaviors from their partners which fit their positive beliefs. ("I am able to get him to smile and laugh. Even his mother tells me he is normally very somber.")

3. Romantic lovers will distort or misinterpret the behavior of their partners in order to maintain their positive beliefs. ("It doesn't matter that he has dropped out of school four times. I know that he has a great mind.")

4. Romantic lovers will behave in ways that reinforce their positive beliefs about their partners and their relationship. ("Even though he gets drunk and threatens to hit me, I am always able to sober him up with enough love and patience. He always thanks me the next morning.")

5. Romantic lovers will misinterpret their own behavior in order to sustain positive beliefs. ("Even though my performance at work seems to be deteriorating, I now know that love is the most important thing in my life. Nothing else matters.")

6. Romantic lovers will interact only with those people who happen to share their positive beliefs. ("My parents and one of my friends think that he is a jerk, but what do they know! As long as I avoid them I don't have to hear their crap any more!")

Any of these strategies may be used in order to reestablish congruency when someone *outside* the exclusive bond threatens it in any way. In fact, the foundation for these strategies has been well established within social psychology for years (Secord & Backman 1964). A trademark of romantic love is the unified effort which *both* lovers exert to counter these negative forces. The sanctity of early love will be defended at all costs. But what happens when the threat to the bond arises not from without, but from within the relationship itself? What happens when your own beloved begins to act incongruently?

The Negative Shift

The inevitability of disenchantment is heralded by incongruency. Behaviors and beliefs no longer share a common bed. Their wondrous overlap, so characteristic of early love, now begins to be eaten away. What you once thought was rock-solid about yourself, as well as your beloved, now begins to rattle with uncertainty. How can you maintain beliefs that have fewer and fewer actions to support them?

The tarnishing effect, eye-opening effect, distraction effect, and existential effect begin to erode our extreme romantic visions. Personal constructs that once seemed absolutely true are now shaken by personal experiences which stun us—which blur our vision. He is no longer always "sweet" and "merciful." She is no longer "diligent" and "suave." Their actions, or inactions, are now telltale signs which warn us that the positive glow of romantic love is about to be displaced by the negative pallor of disenchantment.

Consider for a moment that you believe you are a "sexually attractive" person. You also believe that your partner is "passionate." Two of your personal constructs are :

1. I am sexy (and not repulsive).

2. He is passionate (and not lethargic).

You have behaved as if these constructs are true by frequently initiating sex or wearing sexy clothing which enhances your feelings about yourself. So far so good! Two elements—a personal belief and personal behavior— are in balance. But now what happens if your partner begins to lose interest in you and seldom initiates sex with you? Or even worse, your partner begins to rebuff your enticements!

Congruency now no longer exists. Your partner's behavior has upset a perfectly balanced matrix. This poses a serious threat not only to your self-concept, but also to your relationship. Your personal belief about yourself (I am sexy) and your belief about your partner (he is passionate) are likely to be in jeopardy. The matrix now looks something like this:

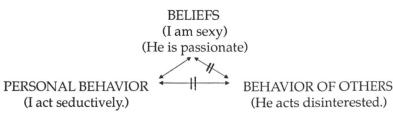

BELIEFS
(I am sexy)
(He is passionate)

PERSONAL BEHAVIOR   BEHAVIOR OF OTHERS
(I act seductively.)   (He acts disinterested.)

Your partner is neither reciprocating your positive actions nor reinforc-ing your positive beliefs about yourself. Unless you can modify your partner's behavior—unless he becomes more passionate—you are likely to begin altering your sexy behavior toward him *even if you maintain the positive belief that you are still sexy*. Because belief systems are so wedded to self-concept, they are much more likely to resist change *even* when we have already begun to alter our behaviors.

You may continue to see yourself as "meticulous" even if you stop cleaning the house. You may view yourself as "reliable" even though you fail to meet your partner on time. You may still describe yourself as "responsive" even though you refuse to return your partner's phone call. And you may certainly believe that you are "sexy" and "passionate" even if you have turned off to your partner! Behavior changes, prompted by the anger and hurt of disenchantment, will not easily destroy integral parts of your identity. Let's look more closely at this negative shift.

An Interpersonal Balance Model

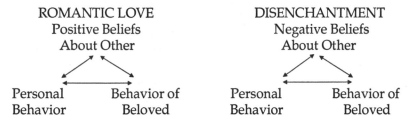

ROMANTIC LOVE
Positive Beliefs
About Other

Personal
Behavior   Behavior of
Beloved

DISENCHANTMENT
Negative Beliefs
About Other

Personal
Behavior   Behavior of
Beloved

The left side of the model suggests that we initially strive to maintain positive beliefs about our beloved. Early romantic love is based on ideal-ization and we will do anything to stay in love. Anything which threatens this adoration will be distorted or ignored in some way.

But when our illusions about one another begin to shatter, we shift to the negative side of the model. Now, instead of viewing our loved ones as complementary to our personal beliefs, we see them as incongruent threats. Our world suddenly begins to be shaken. In order to make sense of this chaos, we develop an entirely new matrix based on our "new" beliefs about each other. *This new matrix is negative, and once it is established, we make efforts to maintain it as well!* It is these very efforts to maintain negative matrices that keep us so stuck during disenchantment.

The new matrix is built upon the disenchantment "themes" described in earlier chapters. These basic core structures support the negative views we have constructed about each other. Once established, it takes very little to trigger volatile reactions in response to these themes.

The key point is that the new negative model is also designed to protect your sense of self-worth. Romantic love enhances your positive self-image in a deep and very personal way. After feeling so good for so long, it is normal to feel threatened now that your special someone is violating your trust by behaving incongruently.

When we recognize, with warp speed, that our beloved has shattered our illusion, we want to cast him or her far into the outer reaches of space. Themes represent the "encapsulation" necessary to accomplish this jetison. If we label someone an "insensitive son-of-a-bitch," it is much easier to detach from him in order to save ourselves. Our self-worth is somehow protected if we can devalue and disown this other person who appears to be threatening our self-image. Negative themes allow us to remove the threat and maintain stability.

Take the case of Linda. She and her husband, Clifford, had been in marriage counseling for eight weeks. Linda had come to believe that Clifford was insensitive (and not caring) and found herself steeped in anger and resentment most of the time. She claimed that this once caring man would now persist in watching TV when she was upset and would seldom alter his plans when emergencies arose for her.

Clifford had his own protest under way. His once "meticulous" partner had now become a "slob." He described the house as a pigpen, not suitable for habitation let alone entertainment. He wasn't about to give into being "sensitive" until his resentments about a messy house were cleared up. Likewise, Linda wasn't about to clean the house more carefully until she got some sensitivity. Linda's matrix looked like this:

PERSONAL BELIEF
(I need a sensitive partner.)
(Clifford *is* insensitive.)

LINDA'S BEHAVIOR ⟷ CLIFFORD'S BEHAVIOR
(I won't waste my   (He rarely speaks
time cleaning the house.)   to me after work.)

She had constructed a negative belief about Clifford—that he is "insensitive." Not only did many of his behaviors support this contention, but Linda had a "knack" of finding data to support this belief!

"What do you mean I ignored you this afternoon!" Clifford would shout at her.

"Just what I said. You came in the door and walked directly over to the TV set without saying hello."

"But how can you forget that I called you twice today just to say hello!" he would shout back again.

Linda treats Clifford "as if" he is insensitive. He is guilty as charged so long as she acts "as if" he is! She ends up with a perfectly congruent matrix—all negative! She believes that he is "insensitive." He acts "as if" he is "insensitive" whenever he forgets to say "hello." And she treats him "as if" he is "insensitive" by selectively finding examples to support her belief.

Sessions later, I had occasion to ask Clifford if he had been more "sensitive" during the past week. He said yes. I then asked Linda if she had put forth effort to straighten up around the house. She also said yes.

Since each of them appeared to get more of what they wanted, I asked each of them if they were ready to shift their views of one another toward the positive end of the continuum: Was Clifford now more "sensitive"? Had Linda become more "meticulous"?

Both said no! You might think that two yes's would actually mean yes, but I have discovered that two yes's can still mean no! Linda was quick to point out that when she had called him during the week, he had taken almost three hours to return her call. "Didn't he know it was important?" Likewise, Clifford volleyed back, "Even with the living room now fit for the living, her side of the closet still looks like a bomb shelter!"

What went wrong here? Linda and Clifford had each changed some personal behaviors. Wouldn't you think that such changes would record more impact on their partner's emotional Richter Scale? Predictably, each disenchanted spouse was maintaining a negative belief about the other— in spite of the new data being provided.

Once we painfully fling someone from our holy graces, we endeavor to maintain this status in order to maximize our well-being and to mini- mize our emotional distress. This is why theme building can be so calam- itous to a love relationship. Once some people are locked into negativity, they are stuck there in perpetuity.

In summary, we can note a number of points about the "negative shift." Each of us wants to maintain a positive self-image and will attempt to make our own behavior, as well as the behavior of others, congruent with this belief. When another person threatens this self-enhancing matrix, a second matrix is set up to deal with our wounds. This second matrix is entirely negative and its congruency is maintained with equal fervor. Congruent matrices, once established, are very resistant to change—par- ticularly negative ones!

The methods we use to maintain a "negative shift," once established, must be understood before we can make progress toward renewing our bond. So long as we continue to invest time and energy into maintaining negativity, we will not be able to establish a mature, covenant bond as a couple. Let's take a closer look at this process.

Forces That Maintain Stability

We have seen that many people, once they have developed disenchant- ment themes, eagerly search for more data to support their views, tena- ciously hold onto these views, and doggedly resist those who attempt to change them—even therapists!

If experienced therapists are likely to need alligator boots for such an endeavor, can you imagine what it is like for lovers who may be en- trenched in jungle warfare with one another? In time, lovers must learn that their partners resist changing in order to maintain stability. This resistance, for most lovers, is quite baffling. How is it possible to be so horribly maligned—when one is truly trying to make positive changes? Without realizing it, we maintain the painful but "safe" status quo in our relationships in six ways:

1. We selectively focus only on the behaviors of our partners which reinforce our negative opinions about them (*selective focus*).

2. We elicit behaviors from our partners that fit our negative opinions (*evoking congruent behaviors*).

3. We distort or misinterpret the behavior of our partners in order to maintain our negative opinions (*misinterpreting one's partner*).

4. We behave in ways that reinforce our negative opinions about our partners and our relationships (*self-fulfilling prophecy*).

5. We misinterpret our own behavior (*misinterpreting oneself*). For instance, we think we are loving when we may actually be controlling.

6. We selectively interact with only those people who happen to share our negative opinions (*selective interaction*).

Let's take a closer look at each of these strategies.

Selective Focus

Being positive or negative requires hard work. We actually make a decision to be positive or negative hundreds of times each day. How long do you focus on the sunny day outside or the broken dish in the sink? How about your scheduled lunch with a friend or your son's unfinished homework? Many of us would spend an entire lunchtime bitching about a son's incompleted homework, a wife's dental floss in the sink, or the dog's urinary tract infection! One heartache after another.

Events by themselves have no meaning. We give them significance. Take the example of your son's unfinished homework. Why did it bother you and not your wife? Why did your wife attribute his difficulties to an upset stomach while you attributed it to laziness? Perhaps you have developed a theme about your son? "He's unmotivated (and not ambitious). He'll never make anything of himself. Why can't he put his nose to the grindstone like I did?" You can collect data to support your negative themes about your son or wife or husband all week long, if you want to!

We selectively focus on the positive or the negative in order to make sense out of the world we live in. We all are interested in prediction and control. As you recall, this is true of all scientists. We achieve this predictability and controllability by creating "personal constructs"—our own personalized, rose-colored glasses!

You might think that a bad theory will be thrown out if the data does not support it. At least this is what an objective scientist would do! Unfortunately, love partners are not objective scientists. Love mates, instead of discarding a theory that seldom predicts events, will selectively focus on events which fit the theory. This can be done easily by invoking the "principle of superstition."

The principle of superstition requires only that an event occur occasionally—perhaps even rarely—in order for it to be considered a true happening. This is hardly the stuff on which science is based, yet it is preferred by many people. How many of you will walk under a ladder? Normally, you might have no problem doing so, unless you heard of the woman from Toledo whose garage burned down in 1942 after she walked under one. And then there was the gentleman from Pittsburg who stepped on a crack and broke his ....

Here's a typical example: Harry believes that June is more devoted to her career than to him. In fact, he believes that he is ranked fourth behind (1) her career, (2) the kids, and (3) her athletic club! Though June has tried to curb Harry's gripes about her hectic schedule, she finds that it only takes one incident to trigger the oft-stated comment: "June, you'll never change a goddamn thing about our relationship. I'll always be dead last on your hit parade." If Harry really wants to indict June, he only needs to notice a random event—coming home ten minutes late—to invoke his theory that "she doesn't give a damn!" and that he is "number four on her hit parade!"

When you selectively focus on your partner's negative qualities, you are committing yourself to an illusion rather than a real person. You are devoted to a process which needs only occasional support in order to discredit, devalue, and discount. Instead of loving your partner, you are committed to annihilating your partner. Annihilation is to disenchantment as idealization is to romantic love. Both require undying surrender to an illusion rather than a real person. It is only during mature, covenant love that we are able to abandon useless theories and see our partners for who they really are.

Evoking Congruent Behaviors

Once you establish that your husband is an uninvolved (and not involved) parent, you will be able to predict how he will act in many situations on the basis of this belief. In fact, if you are really talented, you will be able to evoke these undesirable behaviors from him very easily!

Suppose that your husband has been keeping up with current articles on the father's role in childrearing and has made a decision to put the pedal to the metal. He announces to his colleagues and support staff that he will be leaving work promptly at 5:00 p.m. in order to spend more time with the family. He expects you and your three-year-old, Jessica, to welcome him with open arms.

At 5:30 he parades through the front door, briefcase in one hand and a newspaper clipping for honey chicken and rice in the other.

"Look sweetheart," he beams. "I have a new recipe which Jessica and I can prepare tonight."

"Let me see that!" you stammer. "That's too sweet for me and Jessica, Bill. I'm surprised that you would pick out something that most of us don't even like!"

Somewhat taken back, your husband slides the now tainted recipe under the kitty litter and prepares to eat what you have prepared—fried chicken! Undaunted, however, he asks Jessica if she would like to help Daddy load the dishwasher after dinner. As he begins to do so, he suddenly hears a loud screech from somewhere behind the kitchen table.

"Don't put the plates in like that!" you howl. "They will never get clean at that angle."

This contest of point-counterpoint continues throughout the evening until 9:10 p.m. when you accuse your husband of keeping Jessica up too late. After all, this is hardly the time of day to be stimulating her with card games.

Feeling very compromised, your husband puts Jessica to bed and stalks off to his study, where he sits down in his favorite chair. It is now 9:28 and he has made an important decision. Beginning tomorrow, he will *not* leave work at 5:00 p.m. sharp. It just isn't worth it. Everything he has tried to do has been vetoed or ridiculed by you.

"Why should I get more involved in parenting if I don't have a partner who will support my involvement?" Bill wonders.

During the days and weeks that follow, Bill continues to withdraw more and more from family life—a distant position he knows well. As you begin to notice this withdrawal, you conclude, once again, that he isn't good for very much around the home—that he is indeed an "uninvolved" parent. Unfortunately, what you don't see is that you *selectively evoked* this behavior from Bill! You sabotaged his positive attempts to such a degree that he decided not to try anymore. Negative reinforcement decreases behaviors rather than increasing them. Instead of motivating Bill, you have only reinforced a negative belief about him by coercing him into behaving in accord with your personal construct about him.

Many of us are very adept at selectively evoking congruent behaviors about our lovers, as well as from ourselves! For instance, a woman who sees herself as unassertive may elicit dominance from both men and women in her life. In this way, the behavior of others is congruent with the belief she maintains about herself.

Misinterpreting One's Partner

Maintaining negativity may be an art form in itself. One of the best ways to remain stuck is to distort the way you *think* about your partner. All through life we are encouraged to "think straight," "be reasonable," "be logical," "keep our wits about us," and "to keep our priorities straight." Baloney! Sometimes we just want to be as irrational and illogical as we can be.

Distorted thinking can become addicting. Some people actually become so stuck, so negative, that they achieve "tolerance"—that is, they need more and more negativity to feel bad! This is similar to what happens with certain drugs. If we stay on opiates or amphetamines too long, we actually need more and more of them to maintain the desired drug effects.

It is ironic that our own resistance will meet its own resistance! That is, we resist change by maintaining negativity. As we continue to think negatively or distort illogically, a resistance to our resistance actually occurs. We must double our efforts to distort in order to resist change and stay in our self-contained ruts.

For instance, if you believe that your husband is a "jerk" (and not a "cool guy"), you must put out energy to think this negative thought. If he begins to change positively so that he becomes more of a "cool dude," you must resist these efforts by discounting them in a negative way, thereby doubling the amount of negativity required to maintain the status quo. As you can see, it is actually much easier to maintain negativity if your partner refuses to put forth any effort to change.

Many helping professionals have described the many ways we distort the world so we can readily digest it. You can find good summaries in David Burns' book, *Feeling Good* (1980), or Matthew McKay's work-book, *Thoughts and Feelings* (1981). Dr. McKay and his colleagues have identified fifteen styles of "distorted thinking" that all of us can use to maintain our negativity:

1. *Filtering.* You have the capability to take all the negative details about yourself and your partner and magnify them—while at the same time forgetting about the positive. Try this right after your partner returns from the grocery store with seven bags of groceries. Instead of noticing the 147 items he did remember, go after him for the Clorox he forget. In this way you can maintian a negative belief that he is "absent-minded" rather than "reliable."

2. *Polarized thinking.* You have seen this one throughout the book. When you think in extreme, all-or-nothing terms—avoiding the gray tones of life—you are using polarized thinking. You maintain negativity when you believe that your wife is *always* "indifferent" or "callous" and that your husband is *never* "punctual" or "kind!"

3. *Overgeneralization.* Try arriving at a conclusion after only a single incident. In order to stay stuck in negativity, you must be able to blow one happening out of proportion. If your wife tells you that she does not want to make love one night, you must remember to label her "frigid." Jumping to conclusions will usually help to keep you trapped here!

4. *Mind reading.* Be assured that you know what others "really" think. Don't be fooled by their point of view. Trust your assumptions over your partner's well-meaning intentions. If your beloved tells you that she cared about you a great deal today, even though she didn't call, you won't believe her because you pride yourself in a natural ability to divine the truth somewhere inside your head—no matter what others tell you.

5. *Catastrophizing.* You expect the worst from your spouse because it is bound to come. You expect your children to mess up, your health symptoms to worsen, and your husband to fall off the wagon—even if he has been sober for three years! You somehow manage to elude a more hopeful outlook whenever the promise of better times is right before your eyes.

6. *Personalization.* Some people are not satisfied just blaming their partners during disenchantment. They must also blame themselves—somehow believing that they are the reason things have fallen apart. Some people believe that every relationship they have ever known has been doomed because they were "losers." We maintain negativity here by comparing ourselves to every other successful relationship we can think of.

7. *Control fallacy.* You can remain stuck forever if you believe you are a helpless victim who is totally at the mercy of others around you. And if you do convince yourself that you have some power or control, you go to the other extreme—believing that you must be responsible for the happiness of everyone around you.

8. *Blaming.* You may refuse to take *any* responsibility for things which are wrong in your life. You will definitely stay stuck indefinitely if you *always* put the blame on your partner, your family, fate, or God. Blaming allows you to attack the person without even looking at the problem.

9. *Fallacy of fairness.* You know in your heart of hearts that you are getting a raw deal. Despicable others, who happen to inhabit the planet with you, are ripping you off or somehow getting better deals. You convince yourself that you have a "right" to be resentful!

10. *Shoulds.* You assume that you know the rules for good living and others do not. You are amazed that people make the choices they do and you take it upon yourself to straighten them out. They should do this ... and that ... and so on. You become a tyrannical enforcer in the eyes of others. You will certainly stay stuck here because others will definitely resist your control of them.

11. *Emotional reasoning.* If you have a tendency to base your self-worth, as well as your judgment of others, on feelings only, you rely on emotional reasoning. If you "feel" it is true, it must be! If you feel stupid, you must be. If you feel angry at your wife because she was late, then she must be "unreliable." If you feel embarrassed, then you must be a worthless fool.

12. *Fallacy of change.* Since your hopes for happiness depend so much on others, you make sure you get them to change in order to meet your needs. Regrettably, you may expect little of yourself!

13. *Global labeling.* This is the ultimate of overgeneralization. You don't just assault your partner, you go after his entire family, or her religious or cultural denomination. Somehow, when we are

angry and resentful, there seems to be more satisfaction if we can annihilate an entire ethnic group in one fell swoop.

14. *Being right.* There is too much at stake if your partner discovers that *you* have some imperfections. So you make sure that you are right in all situations. By never owning up to your share of the problems, you actually do more to keep your relationship stuck than your partner—even if you do think you are right!

15. *Heaven's reward fallacy.* You convince yourself that the family is hanging together *primarily* because of your efforts. Your spouse, in your opinion, contributes nothing! You therefore conclude that you have a great deal coming to you as a result of your sacrifice and self-denial. So, after starting out getting few of your needs met, you end up with exceedingly high expectations on the basis of your just due!

Each of these fifteen styles of distorted thinking is an example of how we can throw healthy continuums out of balance. In each case, we either indict our partner while negating our own contributions to the problem, or we create personal constructs which are categorical extremes. As extremes they are caricatures at best and offer us little hope of working through our difficulties.

Self-Fulfilling Prophecy

It has been said that if people define situations as real, they are real in their consequences. Implied in this belief is the recognition that people respond not only to the objective features of a situation, but also to the meaning that the situation has for them. Furthermore, once they have assigned a certain meaning to a situation, their resulting behavior—as well as the consequences of that behavior—are determined by the assigned meaning.

This phenomenon has been termed the "self-fulfilling prophecy" by social scientist Robert Merton (1957), who believed that a false definition of a situation in the beginning somehow evokes a new behavior which makes the originally false conception come true.

We sustain our own destiny by acting in accord with our negative beliefs. For instance, if we believe that others see us as weak, we might feel ashamed. Consequently, whenever we are around these people we may slump our shoulders, speak in hushed tones, avoid eye contact, and generally appear indirect. Our own actions perpetuate the problem.

A typical marital situation looks like this: Jana is convinced that Steven is the wrong partner for her. Sexually, their relationship has become a parched wasteland during the last few years. Typically, they might make love every other month. Steven is often impotent—losing his erection soon after foreplay ends.

Jana often daydreams about a previous lover, Jim, whom she had found very sexually exciting. Unfortunately, Jim also enjoyed having two or three girlfriends on the side—a situation which eventually led Jana to conclude that he was not the right man for her. Now, years later, she wonders if she should hunt him down and have a passionate affair with him.

Many other factors contribute to their difficulties. Jana is the adult child of an alcoholic and was physically and emotionally abused as a child. She needs to be in control and trusts no one but herself. Early in the relationship, she discovered that her husband had lied to her. This further wounded her and further strengthened her need to control events. Her response was to develop and promote a line of hair salons in Austin—an endeavor which not only brought her many financial rewards, but removed her further and further from her husband.

Though their case was far more complicated, we do see how Jana's belief that "Steven is the wrong partner" becomes a self-fulfilling prophecy. Over the years she begins to (1) avoid him sexually, (2) daydream more and more about a prior lover, and (3) compulsively devote herself to her career sixty to seventy hours per week. Steven, sensing this rejection, becomes impotent, which further reinforces Jana's belief that she is stuck with the wrong guy.

What she refuses to see is how *her own actions*, by being congruent with her negative beliefs, actually foredoom the relationship. Her own behaviors toward Steven guarantee that her worst fears—her most negative beliefs—will be fulfilled. The noted psychologist William James once stated that each person has as many "social selves" as there are classes of people he or she cares about. In order for Jana to renew her love bond, she will need to recognize that the "self" she presents to Steven forecloses a successful outcome rather than promotes one. Mature love is an impossibility given such behaviors.

Misinterpreting Oneself

We have seen that there are at least fifteen ways we can misinterpret or distort the behavior of others. It is also possible that we can misinterpret or distort our own behavior. This can occur for three reasons: (1) confusion regarding our needs, (2) a blurred distinction between "situational feedback" and "personal indictment," and (3) denial of our feelings. Let's look at each separately.

Many times we think we are expressing one need when, in actuality, we are expressing another. This often happens with parents who believe they are expressing "affection" when, in fact, they are "controlling" the living daylights out of their children. These parents will often persist in firmly directing all decision making for a child, in the name of love, even into the college years. I am aware of one instance in which the parents would call their twenty-one-year-old every day, supervise college class work, and regulate dating behavior from a distance of 200 miles! When asked why they had such tight reins on their daughter, they responded firmly by pointing out that they were simply loving parents. Their daughter, of course, had another perspective which had something to do with "being controlled!"

A similar thing often happens to couples. One partner may think that she is merely being "inclusive" or "affectionate" when she may be controlling. Take the case of Bill, mentioned earlier in this section. Bill had made a decision to arrive home sharply from work by 5:30 in order to parent his daughter, Jessica. If you, as the wife, were to hover over him like an eagle in flight, there would bound to be trouble ahead. Certainly you might defend your vigilance by explaining how important it is for the entire family to do things together. But there may be a deeper explanation.

You may have a belief that Bill is "irresponsible" or "neglectful"— necessitating very close oversight on your part. You may not even be consciously aware of this personal construct, yet your controlling actions toward Bill are unmistakably manipulative. On the surface your needs appear to be "inclusive" in nature, yet closer review suggests the need to "control" the situation. So long as you persist in misinterpreting your own behavior, you will remain stuck and possibly sabotage your hope for renewal.

A second way you may distort your own behavior is to blur the distinction between "situational feedback" and "personal indictment." Many times you believe that you are just giving your partner some straight talk about "what's wrong around here!" For instance:

> Sandra, you are the laziest person I have ever known. Why don't you get off your ass and help me clean up around here? You really are an inconsiderate bitch!

> Barnie, all I asked you to do is take Charlotte to school this morning. I am really frustrated hearing this song and dance about your busy day. What about my busy day? I would really appreciate some help this morning and will gladly pick Charlotte up for you later this afternoon.

Notice the difference between the two statements? The first is clearly a personal indictment about Sandra. She is getting creamed and will no doubt have quite a retort coming back. This kind of theme-oriented communication is destined to keep any relationship stuck at the level of the moody black and blues. Anger and theme building only begets more anger and theme building.

In the second example, note the use of the word "frustrated." Whenever we use the words "disappointed" or "frustrated," we are much more likely to be giving feedback at the situational level rather than indicting the person. It is important to remember that ad hominem attacks, on the basis of negative beliefs, accomplish only one thing: the relationship stays frozen in the darkness of disenchantment.

A final way we can misinterpret ourselves is to deny what we are actually feeling. Often our negative beliefs are so embedded that we are not even aware that we fuel these beliefs with anger, hurt, revenge, or fear.

As we grimace, frown, grit our teeth, ball our fists, and squirt acid into our stomachs, we may not even be aware that we are quaking in our boots.

Our partners may tell us that they are tired of our boiling and snarling and growling over an endless list of complaints. Innocently, we tell them that we are just paying attention to them and have no idea what they are talking about. We deny being upset and tell them *they* are the angry ones, *they* are the vengeful ones, and *they* are the ones responsible for ensuring the inevitable death of the relationship!

Denial of feelings is often the result of negative beliefs which have become fossilized over time. You may be so convinced your partner is "introverted," "sullen," or "gross" that you are not even aware that you accompany these negative thoughts with negative feelings which are equally virulent. You maintain a congruent matrix which is quite negative without even being aware of the elements that comprise it. Unless you can learn to recognize both your negative beliefs and the negative feelings that accompany these beliefs, you and your partner are destined to remain stuck.

Selective Interaction

Social psychologists have demonstrated that people have a need to affiliate with others, especially during times of increased emotional arousal. Disenchantment is such a time. When you are hurt and angry, you are likely to seek solace in the company of others who agree with you. I have seen clients turn continuously to their mothers, their fathers, their best friends, their neighbors, and their work colleagues *instead* of turning to the only person who really matters— their partner!

This is one reason why affairs are so common during the disenchantment phase of a relationship. We not only want our needs met, we want our beliefs affirmed, our psyches restored, and our actions reinforced. Extramarital lovers are affirming in that a wounded self-concept is assuaged, anger and hurt are temporarily forgotten, and negative beliefs about one's spouse are validated. All the elements for a perfectly negative matrix are thus kept locked in place.

You tell your extramarital lover bad things about your spouse, knowing that he or she will agree with your negative beliefs. Furthermore, by selectively meeting important needs elsewhere, your actions support your negative belief that the bountiful resources which truly matter in life lie outside your marriage, rather than in it! Finally, by not permitting your spouse to meet your needs, you predetermine that his or her actions are destined to fail.

Gossiping during coffee breaks can also be understood as a selective interaction that somehow buttresses your position. If you are among the many people who congregate over small tables with hunched, taut shoulders, you are not there for open debate. You are looking for accordance, unity, and agreement. You want to tell your story and hope that others will tell you to give 'em hell.

As a therapist, I know that when clients first come for counseling the last thing they want is to be cured or changed in any way. Clients first want to be understood before any change is possible. If I were a lousy listener, I wouldn't make the grade for very long. Clients would selectively seek out other mental health providers with whom they were able to find some agreement that they are indeed suffering. This is always the starting point of therapy. Mental health professionals are not selectively sought out because clients are feeling good. Quite the contrary.

You can stay stuck by endlessly seeking out like-minded souls who will agree with your woeful tales. By doing so, your relationships are destined to crash and burn—for the only way the smoldering embers can be put out is by going directly to the person who has ignited the fire. You must learn to move toward the heat, not away from it. Unless you learn how to face your partner, you will forever be faceless with your partner.

The Evolution of B-S

Addiction to negativity is so profound that "relief from adversity" is the best that some people hope for. The following continuum represents this simply:

Negative Thoughts and Feelings				Positive Thoughts and Feelings
	$-$	Peace	$+$	
	100	0 100		
		Relief		

This marriage sucks!   *I am well loved!*

Most of us are stuck on the left side of the continuum where negativity fluctuates between zero and an intensity level approaching 100. As you journey along toward the negative end of the continuum, your stomach may begin to churn, your heart may begin to crash through your chest wall, and your blood pressure may begin to balloon your arteries dangerously. If "peace of mind" and "relief" are the best you can hope for, you have successfully joined the ranks of millions. You have somehow managed to be brainwashed into believing that the best you can hope for is an overstuffed easy chair, one cable ready, remote-controlled TV, and a bottle of beer. Meanwhile, your spouse wants to go dancing, your kids want to play frisbee, and your friends are excited about planning one hell of a weekend!

This sludge of negativity infiltrates our lives so pervasively that, for many of us, church or synagogue is our only salvation. This one Sunday rest stop allows for a quiet and reflective interlude amidst our usual backbiting, skin-pricking, soul-scorching attacks on one another. We depend on our ministers, rabbis, and priests to spiritually reawaken our "positivity." We hunger for this manna from heaven that we refuse to search for on earth!

A year or so ago, I was flying back to Austin following a conference in New York. It became a shoulder-to-shoulder flight as we dipped down to Atlanta to fatten up on both passengers and baggage. Taking the only seat available around me was a smiling fellow, probably no more than thirty-three years old. He greeted me warmly, but then retreated into a polite reticence which seemed to respect my need for private space. As I continued to review my notes from the conference, I would occasionally hear my new-found neighbor quietly chuckling to himself as he read a novel. I was struck by his apparent easy-going nature.

Within a short time, our token beverages were being delivered by the team of flight attendants. Suddenly, to my neighbor's surprise, he found his long-awaited 7-Up being poured down his tweedy brown sportscoat. He looked the stewardess in the eye, smiled, and noted that "This is not a cost-effective use of resources given our country's current recession!" In seconds, laughter was flowing throughout the cabin as effortlessly as the 7-Up had moments before.

My neighbor seemed to have a good sense of humor. I liked him immediately. Many other people would be yelling their favorite four-letter epithets by now or considering a law suit for damaged property. As I found myself thinking about his healthy attitude about his minor incident, I realized that I had unwittingly stowed one of my bags under the seat in front of him. This, of course, meant that his leg room was cramped. His feet would soon take on the appearance of contorted pretzels if I kept my mouth shut during the entire flight. But why hadn't he said anything?

I quickly apologized, offering immediately to move my stuff. "That's not necessary," he reassured me. "I have more than enough leg room. And if I do find myself cramped in any way, I promise I will let you know."

Again, I was very surprised. Where was this man's territoriality? Why wasn't he staking out his personal space like other members of the animal kingdom? Who was this masked man anyway?

I couldn't resist any longer. I started with small talk, but very little was needed to get Donald going. After informing him that I knew something about stressful life experiences, he mentioned that he, too, had similar interests. Donald was just returning from a V.A. Hospital in Virginia—a hospital, he emphasized, which specialized in heart transplantation.

"Oh, so you are one of the members of the health care team?" I guessed.

"Not quite!" he grinned. "I am one of the recipients. The medical team was a bit concerned that I might be showing signs of rejection or infection, so I let them give me a mileage check."

My jaw dropped somewhere down around my camera bag, which happened to be on the floor. My God, this guy had somebody else's heart in his chest and it was efficiently pounding away, just like it was supposed to do! I shuddered to think of how I would be coping under such conditions. I also had one of those "real world" experiences in which I realized that I knew diddly squat about stress compared to this guy. I truly had more to learn from him in sixty minutes than he could learn from me in three days. I couldn't stop myself from asking one question after another.

Donald, it seemed to me, had every right to bitch and moan about his fate. Why did he have to be the one with congestive heart failure? Why did he have to abandon a chosen career path due to physical restrictions? Why did he have to endure a bloating body, just one of many side effects from needed drugs? But still, no bitching. Indeed, he seemed to relish moments of humor and joy!

I suddenly had a new cut-off level for "acceptable" bitching. It was somewhere between your "run-of-the-mill heart transplantation" and radical brain surgery.

What are we to make of these observations? On the one hand, we search out negativity among smoke-filled gossip rooms and television-oriented family rooms when we have equal opportunity to be feeling positive. On the other hand, there are folks maintaining a positive outlook on life at a time when they might understandably be angry or embittered. This leads me to the following conclusion. There are two basic, though extreme, life orientations which characterize most people:

1. LIFE IS A BITCH.
2. LIFE IS A STITCH.

This is the evolution of "B-S." If you believe that life is a bitch, you have designed a coherent and enduring illusion about life which assumes that people are essentially pernicious and that you will predictably receive far more than your share of troubles. You have probably (1) developed negative themes about yourself and others, (2) convinced yourself that others believe as you do, and (3) selectively orchestrated your life experiences to ensure that the future will be as bleak as the past and present have been.

If you believe that life is a bitch, you will primarily know negative feelings like anger, anxiety, hate, or sadness. You will not be able to describe a positive thought, nor will you take any positive actions next week. You will also discount any positive moment that you or anyone else you know experiences.

On the other hand, if you believe that life is a stitch, you eagerly preserve an illusion that a world of pleasure and meaningful surprises awaits your active discovery. When you believe that life is a stitch, you have discovered that (1) diverse experiences provide diverse opportunities for pleasure and meaning, (2) there are many other people around who share this same desire for surprise, and (3) you must actively search for life's surprises in order to find them.

"Life is a stitch" equates with the positive matrix presented earlier, while "life is a bitch" equates with the negative model. Many others have endeavored to clarify the importance of positivity. In his book, *Health*,

Stress and Coping, Aaron Antonovsky describes the well- adjusted person as possessing a "global orientation that expresses the extent to which one has a pervasive, enduring dynamic feeling of confidence that one's internal and external environments are predictable and that there is a high probability that things will work out as well as can reasonably be expected" (Antonovsky 1979, 10).

If we choose negativity over positivity, we are destined to remain stuck—perhaps dooming our relationship forever. I like the idea that things will work out—if I have reasonable expectations or beliefs. The choice to move in this direction is ours.

PART IV

DISENCHANTMENT
A Passage

Passing through disenchantment to reach mature, covenant love depends upon a reorientation of our ways of seeing and responding to our partner and the events in our relationship. First of all, *we must recognize that both romance and disenchantment are illusions*. The feelings and attitudes we experience during disenchantment are no more "real" than those we experience during romance. We create enduring, life-enriching covenant love by integrating the beautiful and difficult truths that underlie both romance and disenchantment. This section of the book introduces the basic concepts and techniques that are employed in the love renewal process.

9

The Secret of Survival

God grant me the serenity to accept the things I cannot
change, the courage to change the things I can, and the wisdom
to know the difference.

Reinhold Niebuhr

Our feelings of pleasure and pain in our relationships aren't caused by
changing events, but rather by the ways we perceive and then respond to
those events. In other words, it's not what happens to us that counts, but
how we *look* at it and what we *do* about it. *The way to create a mature loving
relationship is to learn how to perceive and respond differently to disenchantment.*

The emotional poles of ecstasy and resentment, of passion and aliena-
tion, can be transcended through a very practical set of strategies which I
will call *coping*. Coping isn't a "grit-your-teeth-and-bear-it" form of endurance arising from the attitude of "I have to settle for this, it's all I can
get." On the contrary, it is an enlivening, empowering approach to life that
allows us to experience true fulfillment, not only in our relationships but
in *all* areas of our lives.

The currently most accepted model for coping in the social and behavioral sciences today includes three strategies which can help us renew
our love relationships—no matter what the problem might be.

- We can modify the *source of the problem* itself.
- We can modify the *we think* about the problem situation.
- We can modify *the way we emotionally respond* to the situation.

For instance, a woman who has just argued with her husband over a
bounced check can suggest alternatives to prevent the mishap from happening again. She can remind herself that her husband is imperfect but
lovable anyway. Or she can go jogging to cool off.

Each of these strategies requires some conscious effort. Mature love,
because it is *conscious* love, requires work to be sustained. It is distin-
guished from romantic love and disenchantment by its "willfulness." Both

falling in love and falling out of it simply *happen* to us! We are not in control. In contrast, mature, covenant love requires will—the will to love—which involves a *conscious act of commitment*. Only through commitment, through the making of a covenant with one another, can a couple renew their love. That commitment is challenged every day by the illusions of disenchantment—and must be reaffirmed every day by the powerful strategies of coping.

Coping involves more than just dealing with the challenges of adversity, whether these challenges arise in a marriage or elsewhere. We also must cope effectively whenever we choose to *enhance our well-being*. Sometimes just getting out of the house to see a movie requires ingenuity that far surpasses what we must have to balance an overdrawn checkbook. Getting a babysitter, putting out night clothes for the kids, and rescheduling other commitments may all be necessary before our fun out on the town can begin. *Coping is an active, continuing process which we all engage in to maximize our sense of well-being and to minimize our emotional distress* .

This Thing Called Coping

Newspapers, magazines and journals abound with descriptions of how to cope with everything from visiting in-laws to mid-life crises. These prescriptions are usually an assemblage of unrelated helpful hints: find a friend, keep a journal, take a risk, or list everything in your marriage you consider unfair. Few social scientists have attempted to find a central theme in these prescriptions, primarily because mental illness—rather than mental health—has been the central focus of study for the better part of the last century.

However, for over two decades Richard Lazarus has been one of a handful of social scientists who have studied how healthy people process their experiences. His early investigations led him to distinguish two types of coping processes. The first process he called "direct action," which described behavioral efforts to deal directly with an annoying problem situation. The second process was called "palliation," which represented efforts to reduce unsettling emotional states that occur whenever we are unable to deal directly with a problem situation. I refer to each, analogously, as taking action and seeking balance.

Taking action represents our attempts to prevent or extricate ourselves from the plight we face. We may choose to attack a threatening situation head on or avoid it. Jumping out of the way of an oncoming car or getting a divorce are examples. We may also choose to modify the threatening situation, as two bored lovers do when they agree to read a sex manual in order to learn new ways to stimulate one another.

Strategies for taking action are aimed at a sense of mastery and preparedness through active interaction with our environments. All coping by direct action is an attempt to deal with the problem situation itself.

In contrast, *seeking balance* entails efforts to control our emotional response to problem situations. Joan, a frustrated wife, may choose to take tranquilizers, drink eight martinis a day, reduce body tensions through exercise or muscle relaxation, or seek frequent reassurance from her doctor about psychosomatic symptoms. Little, if any, effort may be directed to the problem situation itself. Joan's efforts are intended merely to reduce the emotional distress that ebbs and flows through her days.

Other researchers, including Leonard Pearlin from the National Institute of Mental Health, have emphasized a third category that we must consider as part of coping. Put simply, there are times in our lives when our attempts to modify situations may be limited. We must go with the flow. We may not be able to significantly alter our wife's professional work schedule or the course of our husband's diabetes. We may not be able to stop foreclosure on our family home or even bankruptcy proceedings! In situations like these, the stressful impact of a situation can be buffered by *neutralizing* the threats *cognitively*—that is, by *thinking about the threats in a different way.*

I refer to this third category of coping as *gaining perspective* and believe that it is the most important of all our strategies. One form of this coping strategy is called "making positive comparisons." This strategy could be used this way to cope with the foreclosure of a home:

> There are many others who have been through this. And let's remember that we have a beautiful family to focus our energies on while many others may not be so fortunate.

Other examples of gaining perspective include "selective ignoring," whereby we concentrate on something positive while at the same time minimizing the negative. Noticing your husband's playfulness with the children while ignoring his messiness in the bathroom is one such example. Romantic love is based on "selective ignoring" of undesirable qualities—even thought we are "on our best behavior" anyway in the early going!

We may also "reprioritize our values" as a way of gaining perspective. Have you ever noticed that when you have had a peak experience—like climbing a mountain or seeing the birth of a child—you are likely to reaffirm what's *really* important in your life—being with people you care about, doing things you value? For some, it takes a "near death" experience—like having a heart attack or surviving a severe accident—to come to the realization that life is too short and too precious to fritter away on addictions to work, alchohol, or negativity.

Well, some of us are capable of making such value shifts without such drama as a backdrop. Most couples who have navigated the choppy waters of disenchantment and found mature, covenant love have reconciled themselves with what's missing in order to appreciate what they have and to affirm the importance of a shared history, children, grandchildren, an abundance of leisure time, or other meaningful parts of their lives.

In summary, when we attempt to maximize our meaning and pleasure or to minimize our emotional distress, we have three useful strategies that we can use to cope and to stay in control of our lives:

1. We can *take action* to actively modify the situation itself.
2. We can *gain perspective* by modifying the way we think about the situation.
3. We can *seek balance* by modifying the way we react to the situation.

Let's take a look at how these three strategies look in a typical "crisis" situation.

My Crisis in Dallas

Have you ever watched your car being blown up by a hotel garage attendant? I have! It may be hard to believe that the explosion of a six-volt battery can compare to the outburst of one lover toward another. However, in both situations disenchantment requires *creative coping*.

Let me set the scene. The cast of characters includes one tired conventioneer (yours truly), one hotel garage attendant, one hotel assistant manager, and two Houston-based psychologists, also attending the conference in Dallas. Add to this a 1963 white 356 Porsche in very good condition, as well as a nationally recognized hotel chain, and we are all set.

I was fond of that little car. I had purchased it for $2,000 from an eccentric lawyer who was simply tired of it. I seldom took it out of Austin, for fear that the car might have a panic attack if it were to stray too far from its mechanic. But I ventured northward despite this concern on the condition that supervised garage parking was available. I was told, "No problem."

Due to a strange wiring problem in the starter, my little toy occasionally needed a bit of priming, a lot of loving, and a prayer or two before turning over. On this Friday evening, after two days in a musty garage, none of these strategies seemed to work. However, I usually carried jumper cables for such emergencies. I asked the garage attendant to help jump start my cranky vehicle. "No problem," he reassured me. A few minutes later he drove up to my Porsche in a large, souped-up tow truck. "I'll just hook this baby up and we'll have you out of here in no time!" he said.

"But," I protested, "don't you think the big 12-volt battery in your truck will wipe out my little 6-volt car?"

"No problem," he again reassured me. "I do this all the time."

Cable hookup and counting. One second, two seconds, three seconds, four seconds, five seconds, and then POW! As dangerous battery acid dribbled over the lip of my bumper, I noticed that miniscule parts of my battery were now deposited on a few Chevys and Fords parked nearby.

"That fool blew up my car. I can't believe it!" ricocheted from one side of my head to the other.

"I guess the little feller couldn't take it," mused the eager attendant. "No problem, though. Why don't you follow me upstairs and we'll get the assistant manager to take care of the situation."

As in many other moments of crisis, I suddenly found myself overcome with frightful images and considerations. How would I get home? What other damage would be found? Where was my mechanic when I needed her? I was upset. I believed this could have been prevented, but was determined to cope well. Time for a deep breath as the elevator drifted upward from the darkness of the parking garage below.

The eager garage attendant quickly explained the situation to the assistant manager, a middle-aged woman whose cold, piercing eyes and lack of facial expression gave me the eerie impression that somehow a slab of granite had been brought to life. Unfortunately, the garage attendant's memory was less than photographic. He remembered that I had a 12-volt battery, that I attached the cables myself, and that he quickly turned his engine off after starting.

The assistant manager, doing her best impression of a marble wall, looked me in the eye and told me I had two options: I could either stay in the hotel overnight for free, or they would take full responsibility for all costs relating to the battery and any other damages.

What a dilemma! They would replace the battery the next day, if I elected to sleep on the street that night. Or I could rest comfortably overnight and then face the problem on my own the next day. After brief consideration, I decided to buy myself some time to creatively cope with this situation. Since I also knew that the assistant manager was operating well above her level of incompetence, I quietly reminded myself that there were higher authorities who could correct any errors on the part of the lower level hotel staff.

Feeling frustrated with the situation, I decided to tell the assistant manager that she was handling this very poorly, that she did not represent my image of this hotel's management reputation, and that she would probably have to answer to follow-up actions I planned to take. She looked at me kind of funny when I told her that I was disenchanted and that she was shattering my illusions! With that pronouncement, I asked for my room key and proceeded to the lounge for a beer and some quiet music.

My efforts to cope with this "crisis in Dallas" may be summarized in terms of *taking action, gaining perspective,* and *seeking balance.* Throughout this dilemma I was continually attempting to maintain a balance among my three options: What could I do to influence the situation itself? What could I do to view the situation differently? What could I do to calm down? A partial list follows:

Strategies for Taking Action

8:30   Try to start the car.
8:35   Try again.
8:40   Request help from the hotel garage attendant.
8:50   Caution garage attendant about possible dangers.
9:00   Request to see assistant manager.
9:15   Request that incident report be changed to reflect the *correct* facts.
9:30   Request a copy of the incident report.
9:40   After being refused a copy of the report, request that my request for a copy be documented.
9:45   Request that a witness be present to verify that I was given a choice between a room or battery.

Strategies for Gaining Perspective

8:32   Don't worry. A little persistence usually does the trick.
8:35   No problem, let's try again.
8:45   Well, jumper cables ought to take care of this problem.
8:55   Relax. A hotel chain of this reputation will obviously be responsible for the damages and inconvenience.
9:00   Things are going to be fine.
9:12   She's really putting it to me now. I'd better document everything and assume that she reports to administrators more sensitive to public relations.
9:35   One thing at a time. I can handle this situation.
9:46   I have done as much as I can do tonight. Now it is time to enjoy the amenities of one of the nicest hotels in Dallas.
10:00 I'll call Claire—she'll support me in this "crisis."
10:10 There are bound to be a number of people in a city this size who will be willing to help me on Saturday. People do care about others who need help.
10:15 In 24 hours I will be laughing about this. One day I might even write about this in a book!

Strategies for Seeking Balance

8:52   Make time for a quick ten-second calming technique.
8:55   Request that my two psychologist colleagues remain with me for a while for support.
9:01   Take deep cleansing breaths as I ride the elevator upstairs.
9:15   Look at my colleagues for support as I request that the incident report be changed to reflect the facts.
9:45   Make time for a quick ten-second calming technique when I realize how rigid the assistant manager is being.
10:10 Enjoy the music and atmosphere in the lounge.
10:17 Enjoy a drink with my colleagues before bidding them adieu. Thank them for hanging around beyond their departure time.

Lenny Bruce once said that tragedy plus time equals humor. Well, this was hardly a tragedy and humor seemed hard to find that evening. But a happy ending did result a day or two later. When I contacted the hotel's corporate office in Chicago, the division chairperson told me that he would check into the situation and call me back in two hours. Two hours later, on the button, my phone rang.

Dr. Bugen, we have really blundered and ask for your understanding. Nothing can be said to justify the assistant manager's actions and we will have Personnel take appropriate steps. We would like to reimburse you for your flight back to Austin, for your battery, and for any other damages associated with the incident. We also would like to drive your car to Austin for you, at your convenience.

I graciously accepted his apologies and his offer. "I always knew that things would work out," I beamed. "And by the way, Mr. Division Chairperson, the music in the lounge was wonderful and the bed was very comfortable."

Although I had my share of frustration and disappointment that evening in Dallas, I am convinced that my level of emotional distress was *significantly* reduced as a consequence of using the three coping strategies. While my "crisis in Dallas" may seem somewhat removed from our focus on love, let me assure you that coping skills are universal. My ability to manage a testy situation in a strange city is very much akin to my ability to handle an upsetting incident with Claire. Let's take these universal skills and apply them to a marital situation.

Nikki's Fiasco in Uvalde

When our best laid plans go awry, we often get stuck in the mire of our own anger and hurt and blame our partners (or hotel personnel!) for messing up our lives. As a therapist, it is rare for me to hear clients accept complicity in their own hardships at home. Most of us are content to recycle old data and old theories about one another. It is much too easy to simply bitch about the louse who lives with you rather than to generate new ways to act, think, and feel about one another. Creative coping requires an active stance.

Nikki is a good case in point. After visiting her in-laws in Uvalde, Texas, Nikki returned to tell me what a lousy time she had had.

"You wouldn't believe it," she groused. "This was supposed to be a relaxing weekend! Instead, the baby gets diarrhea, my mother-in-law insists that I join her on a nonstop shopping expedition, and my husband thinks it's fine to play golf with his father on both Saturday *and* Sunday. That is just like him, too! Well, what about me?"

Who is taking care of Nikki's needs? Nobody ... including herself! Prior to her weekend in Uvalde, I had asked Nikki to visualize one positive feeling, thought, and action she might enjoy experiencing over the weekend. They were:

Feeling: Excitement.
Thought: I like discovering new things.
Action: I will make time to take creative pictures in the nearby
               park.

As she sat in my office that day, I asked Nikki what had happened to her plan. She quickly reminded me that the baby got sick, her mother-in-law had dragged her elsewhere, and her husband was not around to help out. She seemed to be blaming these *other* people for *her* lack of pleasure and meaning. What an irony! As her husband, mother-in-law, and father-in-law were happily zooming around, taking care of their own needs, Nikki was stalled out with her own misery for company. Her weekend had been so outrageous that she had already told three of her friends about it and had been salivating to tell me since Sunday night.

Nikki found it easier to complain about others than to implement a creative coping plan. She reinforced her negativity by:

- Focusing on the behaviors of others that reinforced her negative opinions about them. (As she did by dwelling on the fact that her husband played golf on both Saturday and Sunday.)
- Eliciting behaviors from others that fit her negative beliefs. (Bitching about her husband's golf on Saturday so much that he went out on Sunday for spite.)
- Distorting or misinterpreting the behaviors of others. (Believing that her mother-in-law never thinks of anyone but herself.)
- Behaving in ways that reinforced her own negative beliefs. (Lethargically moping around most of the weekend.)
- Misinterpreting her own behavior. (Thinking that she was being a "good" wife and daughter-in-law just by being there, when in fact she preferred exclusion to inclusion and emotional distance to emotional closeness.)
- Interacting with others who will support her negative views. (Telling three friends about her dreadful weekend fiasco.)

I pointed out to Nikki a few "taking action" coping strategies that she could have used during the weekend in Uvalde:

- She could have told her mother-in-law that she didn't want to go shopping this particular weekend.
- She could have told her husband before the trip that she would like to take an afternoon for photography. He could play golf on Saturday and she could go out on Sunday.
- She could have joined her husband in asking her in-laws to take care of the baby for a short while so that he could play nine holes of golf while she shot a few rolls of film in the park.
- She could have hired a babysitter for three hours—or a home health nurse, if all else failed.

- She could have taken the baby with her to the park for a short walk and possibly a few pictures.

Of course, there were other coping strategies Nikki could have used—ways of gaining perspective and seeking balance—that would have completely changed her weekend in Uvalde, as well as her relationships with her husband and his family.

Nikki's dilemma is our dilemma. Our best-laid plans get sabotaged by others who impose their will upon us—that's what family and organizational life are all about. Sure, there are times when we must give in to the needs of others. This is what "other-directedness" truly means. But then there are those times when we must cherish our own needs enough to stick by them. This process of identifying and satisfying our needs requires effective coping—a process that Nikki abandoned on her weekend trip to Uvalde.

Let's take an even closer look at each of these coping strategies— all three of which are indispensable for anyone attempting to renew his or her love relationship.

Taking Action

We are an action-prone species, always shaping, carving, or wielding great forces toward one purpose or another. Yet, when it comes to our marital bonds, we soon relinquish all this power and choose negative resistance instead. We make a commitment not to fix something that is actually very malleable. But why?

When we are consumed by negativity, we often choose to stew in our agony rather than reach for new solutions. We may secretly wish to withdraw, fearing that we will be hurt again. Or if we have already tried to fix things and failed, we may have learned to feel helpless or hopeless, somehow believing that we do not possess the wherewithal to achieve desired goals. In times like these we believe that our disenchantments are beyond renewal and that our cherished dreams are beyond our control.

The most direct way to regain control over our love relationships is to fix something—anything!—that is broken. It doesn't really matter where you begin—just fix something together, as a team. Agree to get the children to bed by 9:00 p.m., to straighten out your checking account, or to plan your first weekend getaway in three years. Begin solving problems together. Consider the following questions:

- How can my "will to love" empower me to find new solutions to old problems?
- What alternatives have I honestly explored?
- What alternatives are left to explore?
- What risks are associated with these alternatives?
- Which alternative is the next best to choose?
- What consequence can I expect from each alternative?

- How will I evaluate the effectiveness of each?

Taking action requires a logical and reasoned approach that modifies the presence of a problem: (1) We may change something about ourselves which contributes to the problem, or (2) we may alter the circumstances around us in some way.

Let's consider Nikki and her husband, John. These two were locked into a negative, downward cycle that surfaced in more places than Uvalde, Texas. Put rather simply, he was a lousy listener who downplayed her needs, while she had become unassertive about those needs. Their plight is a common one. Unless they both were willing to modify something about themselves that contributed to their communication problems, no permanent changes would occur. John would have to learn how to listen more effectively, while Nikki would have to become more forceful in asserting herself, instead of shredding John's character with her friends and therapist.

When we take action, the best plan is designed with small steps in mind. The plan should be ambitious enough so that some change, small though it may be, can be seen, but it should not be so grand that failure is likely. If you really want to see your partner succeed, it is easier to suggest little steps than it is to cut back on big ones. Plans are not final. Most of us know that there are many different approaches to solving a problem. If our first plan does not help us, try successive strategies until one is found that does work.

When we experience problems in love, we arrive at a crossroad where we must make plans for where we want to go in the future. It has been said that if you don't know where you are going, you'll never get there. You might think of planning as a five-step problem-solving process:

Step One: Specify and define the nature of the problem. For instance, Jim and Ann, two new parents, find themselves fighting more and more frequently. They have begun to question their suitability as partners for one another. In actuality, the demands placed on them by their new son may be depriving them of much needed time together.

Step Two: Analyze the nature of the problem by finding out the facts. Once a problem has been specified, pertinent data must be gathered in order to prevent misunderstanding. For instance, Jim and Ann will need to assess how much time they spend together, when they spend it, when they argue, and when they don't.

Step Three: Create goals that describe potential solutions and criteria for a successful solution. This step, more than any other, determines the success of an action plan. When we plan our lives effectively, we have the facts, causes, and effects clearly in mind so that we can determine a goal that is reasonable and reachable. Jim and Ann may set the goal of hiring a babysitter two evenings a week in the hope that this goal will afford them the time they need together.

Step Four: Implement the solutions you have selected. Our young parents may actually try using a babysitter two evenings a week as well as getting up together an hour earlier each morning.

Step Five: Evaluate the effectiveness of your implemented goal. Did the solution meet the criteria established for the goal or does the problem still remain? It may be necessary to recycle this entire process by reestablishing new goals or implementing other alternatives. Jim and Ann may discover that the cost of a babysitter two evenings a week is prohibitive or that one evening out a week is sufficient.

At its worst, taking action is a desperate draw from the hip—too impulsive, too short-sighted. At its best, it is a monument of labor (a labor of love) carved out of bedrock by two industrious workers. And, as is true of any act of creation, extraordinary things are possible only when we have taken that lonely journey into our hurts, needs, and wants. Solutions for the many inevitable dilemmas you will face in love are there.

You will find many more detailed suggestions for taking action in chapter 14 on negotiating problems, a crucial component of the RENEW process.

Gaining Perspective

We encounter a sobering realization during mature, covenant love: *We are able to love someone in spite of their incompleteness.* This is a remarkable shift from the quest for completion that marked romantic love! As our relationships mature, we learn to balance what we *want* to have with what we *do* have. In the words of Howard Mumford Jones, "Happiness is wanting what you want, getting what you get, and hoping the two will coincide."

During mature love, we learn to shift our perspective in order to balance love with work, leisure, health, finances, and spirituality. We learn to balance pleasure with meaning. We learn that every viewpoint, every attribute, lies on a continuum—rather than at a fixed endpoint. Our partners are not good or bad, warm or cold, or vibrant or boring. They move along these continuums, always changing, always responding to forces in their lives as well.

During mature love, we become more active in constructing what we need and want rather than expecting it to just be there. This requires vision, which is the essence of gaining perspective. Unless we know where we are going and truly believe we can get there, we will never be satisfied in any loving relationship.

Commitment requires this combination of vision and effectiveness. Vision represents the ever-evolving, ever-dynamic creation I call mature love, while effectiveness is having the *will* and *competence* to get there. The beauty of this process is captured by the late Carl Rogers, who stated:

A marriage which is continually being transformed by the development of each spouse is without a doubt one of the greatest sources of security a man [or woman] can know. From it he can venture into daring, innovating, challenging, behavior, can work freely to change his world, can take risks because he knows he can return to his secure relationship. Even this is security in change and process, not in something static. But a core of this continually blossoming security is, to me, marriage at its best. (Rogers 1972, 198)

There is no way to demonstrate the eight elements of mature, covenant love if you lack perspective. Without perspective, how can you:

- Balance your needs with those of your partner?
- Be other-directed?
- Possess realistic values and expectations?
- Be tolerant?
- Yearn to be known?
- Express all emotions?
- Recognize your partner's separate identity?
- Be able to transcend the separateness of two separate selves by becoming one shared identity?

I believe that we have two powerful ways to gain perspective: (1) We can develop deep-set values which guide our lives powerfully (and sometimes unconsciously) or (2) we can learn to change the specific thoughts that we have about a situation. This latter approach is often called *cognitive restructuring* by mental health professionals. In this approach, the emphasis is on *thinking style*, rather than on embedded values or beliefs. But let's briefly appreciate the importance of deeply held, embedded values as a coping tool.

Consider Aaron Antonovsky's perspective about coping presented earlier: "a pervasive, enduring though dynamic feeling of confidence that one's internal and external environments are predictable and that there is a high probability that things will work out as well as can reasonably be expected" (Antonovsky 1979, 10). THINGS WILL WORK OUT! This deeply embedded belief allows us to buffer the impact of very upsetting disenchantments in our lives—if we are willing to shift perspective.

Taking perspective at this level usually embraces both existential and spiritual realms. It is the successful search for meaning, throughout the most shattering of experiences, which marks the resiliency of the hearty life traveler. Our best-laid plans, our most cherished dreams, and our most desired goals sometimes don't come to fruition. It is during these critical moments that gaining perspective has meaning.

Things really will work out! This can be hard to believe when you are entangled in the throes of disenchantment. I recall Laura and Jerry, a couple who found themselves very stuck in a downward, negative cycle. Laura needed much more affection than she was receiving. This was a profound need for her, given the lack of nurturing she received from her father during her childhood years. In particular, she wanted to be held by her husband at social gatherings, to be kissed warmly in front of friends, and for her husband to arrange family gatherings in which all family members had fun.

Jerry, in turn, needed to be accepted. He had been so wounded during his own childhood years by an overcritical father that whenever his wife criticized him, he withdrew with the same hurt feelings he had felt years before. Now they found themselves stuck. The more criticized Jerry felt, the more he withdrew, and the less affection Laura received. The more emotionally neglected Laura felt, the more critical she would become about Jerry's work schedule, parenting, and so on, and the more he would withdraw.

Though they both admitted that they wanted to take direct action to fix this problem, neither was willing to initiate an action until each believed that "things really could work out" and that his or her partner "really cared." This was a problem for each of them because neither had been able to remedy a similar problem within their original childhood families. This is a common experience that leaves us ill-prepared to believe that our adult relationships are any more malleable than those we experienced in early childhood.

Once Laura and Jerry gained the perspective that "things could work out" if both of them worked simultaneously to renew their bond, a transformation occurred. Instead of viewing their relationship only as a painful steel trap, each was now able to envision a more loving, a more peaceful bond.

As powerful as this coping strategy appears to be, we are less inclined to gain perspective within our love relationships because we have *too many* choices, rather than too few. Our dilemma is that we have too many escapes. A divorce rate approaching 60 percent suggests that many of us are encouraged to take action to rid ourselves of suffering in our relationships, rather than gaining perspective to stay in them!

Gaining perspective is a coping strategy that can be useful at both the situation level and the thematic level of disenchantment. When we alter our specific thoughts about a situation, we are gaining perspective. We do this when we say "Joanna was subdued last night, but I know she is working to become more outgoing" or "Roger still hasn't taken on more of the housework, but he has been more help with Jenny. And he's sure been affectionate and fun to be with!" We can do the same for the more embedded themes of disenchantment.

When you employ gaining perspective as a coping strategy, you might begin by asking, Is this all I have wanted out of this loving relationship? When you gain perspective, you face yourself squarely as though you were looking directly in the mirror. You might imagine asking yourself ten consecutive times, What do I really want from this love relationship? When you are finished, try rank ordering your ten answers according to their importance. Any surprises?

Chapter 15 on exploring new perspectives is devoted to a deeper analysis of this coping skill.

Seeking Emotional Balance

What do we do when our attempts to directly modify a situation or to view it differently fail? For most of us the answer is undeniable—we get angrier than hell! We tell our partners that we aren't going to take it any more! And, if we are in a typical relationship, the sequence goes something like this (according to Carol Tavris (1984), author of *Anger: The Misunderstood Emotion*):

- A precipitating event leads to ...
- an angry outburst characterized by ...
- shouted recriminations and ...
- screaming or crying, which builds up to ...
- a furious peak (sometimes accompanied by physical violence), followed by ...
- a feeling of exhaustion and ...
- a sullen apology, or perhaps just sullenness.

This cycle may be repeated the next day or the following week, depending on the circumstances. This emotional arousal is usually accompanied by a physical arousal as well. (See the appendix for discussion of the body's physical reaction to anger and hostility.) Yet we engage one another in battle, somehow expecting that these emotionally charged exchanges will extinguish the flames of anger within us. This is not surprising, according to Tavris, because of a number of assumptions we are likely to make:

- We often believe that emotional energy is a fixed quantity that gets dammed up or floods our physical system.
- We believe that anger and aggression are interwoven and are biologically linked. That is, anger is a feeling while aggression is an overt action. Both are considered to be instinctual, somehow primal to our species.
- We believe that anger is an instinctive response to threat and to the frustration of our needs and wants.
- We believe that if we are blocked from expressing this anger, it turns inward—into depression, shame, guilt, anxiety or psychosomatic symptoms.

If these assumptions are correct, then we must do three things in order to prevent ourselves from blowing up or further wounding ourselves when angry. First, we must have a catharsis—a sudden release of this poison which so painfully taints our systems. Second, we should find others who will listen to our negative tales of woe— people who will ask the right questions to open us up even more. And third, we need to have a good tantrum from time to time, because an occasional rage is a healthy expression of anger which somehow prevents us from becoming neurotic.

According to Dr. Tavris, none of these assumptions and their corresponding behaviors is supported by the findings of study after study. If we truly seek balance, we will not find it by having an emotional catharsis, gossiping about our unfair partner, or throwing a tantrum. Yet we do these things endlessly, even though there is no evidence that they resolve our marital disputes or make us feel better in any way.

Clinically, as well as personally, I have seen that when people "ventilate" all over each other, they don't feel better afterwards. They feel more angry. This seems inevitable because the recipient of this barrage gets pissed off, and then says or does something to get even. Cathartic release also excites us physiologically. Rather than calming ourselves, we actually work ourselves up into a hormonal frenzy. And we consider this ventilation beneficial!

If expressing our anger does not calm us down, or resolve the problem, why do we do it? Experts in the field have suggested that its one benefit (if any exist) is retaliation against a wrongdoer for some injustice. However, Tavris, in summarizing the work of psychologist Vladimir Konecni, warns us that three conditions must be met in order for retaliation to be truly cathartic.

First, you must retaliate *directly* against the person who has made you angry. This is why angry gossiping with friends does not work. You miss the real target of your concerns. All we do when we gossip is *rehearse* our anger—we don't resolve it. Likewise, hitting pillows, kicking the cat, or shouting at the kids will not work either.

Second, the amount of harm that you inflict on your target must be the "right" amount—the *just* amount—to release your fury. Neither too much nor too little will do. Only "an eye for an eye" will do.

Third, your retaliation must not be reciprocated in any manner. You can see why: if your retaliation is met by angry resistance equal to your own, you will not be absolved of your anger—only more incensed. This is why angry, revengeful treatment of one spouse toward another is destined to fail. Who in his right mind is going to let a marital partner ax his psyche to pieces without some sort of revenge in his own right—be it active or passive aggression!

If we intend to seek balance in our love relationships, we must choose methods that take the mind and the body into consideration, since both are aroused during disenchantment. One such program for doing so was developed for couples by Gayla Margolin (1977). Her program is based on these three principles: (1) Verbal and physical abusiveness is learned, rather than instinctual behavior. (2) Abusiveness is a mutual problem for both partners, rather than being one person's fault. (3) Since abusiveness is only one way to try to solve a problem, couples can be taught other more effective ways to do so. Her approach has four steps:

1. Couples first learn what specific things each partner does to trigger anger in the other.

2. Couples then determine which ground rules they will follow regarding arguing. A victim may say, "If you make a fist and approach me, I will move out tomorrow."

3. Couples develop a plan to resolve emotional buildup in the moment. Couples are often encouraged to disengage immediately when tempers flair, then make an appointment to reschedule a discussion later when the initial flair-up has subsided. The emphasis is always on preventing an escalation of emotional and physiological arousal. Certain cue words, such as "Not now!" or nonverbal signs, such as raising a hand in a sign of peace, may be helpful.

4. Couples learn new ways of thinking about each partner's triggering actions. Instead of saying "That bastard ignored me again!" they are encouraged to look for other explanations, such as "He did have a headache earlier, maybe he is still in some pain!"

Persisting in any argument is not likely to pay many dividends. As Carol Tavris reminds us: "A common fallacy is believing that the future of a relationship rests on being able to resolve this argument right now. The future of a relationship (actually) rests on the confidence that there will *be* a future, and giving both partners a cooling-down time" (Tavris 1984, 225).

Montaigne has said, "there is no passion that so shakes the clarity of our judgment as anger." Chapter 16 on weathering the storm describes five strategies that every loving couple can learn to use in order to seek balance when angry. These techniques need to be a part of our coping arsenal, since there are times in every loving relationship when our best efforts to negotiate problems or to explore new perspectives have failed.

Our Capacity to Cope

As I defined it earlier, coping is an active, continuing process which we all engage in to maximize our sense of well-being and to minimize our emotional distress. Both a sense of well-being and emotional distress are continuing features of our ever-changing lives. We are always coping with something. Nikki may be wondering how to squeeze in her photography one minute and how to fix her malfunctioning dishwasher the next! During her morning run to the supermarket, she may discover she has no checks. Before her afternoon luncheon, she may discover she has no babysitter, and during the evening hours, she may discover that her husband has no sexual desire. In each of these situations, Nikki is attempting to either maximize her pleasure or to minimize her pain.

The way each of us actively copes with the events that make up our lives is a complex issue which reflects these variables:

Our personality make-up. Type A's like to control the external events in their lives and often feel helpless when other forms of coping are required.

Our prior history of coping. Some people have not had much adversity in their lives and have not had the opportunity to learn to cope during difficult times.

The variety of coping skills we know. Some people may have a very limited repertoire of coping skills, and end up relying on alcohol or other drugs as a way to get through difficult times.

The variety of coping skills we are willing to use. Many times we know what to do in order to maximize our pleasures or minimize our pain, but we are not assertive enough to use our strategies. For instance, you may be a good negotiator with colleagues at work, but give in too easily to your spouse because you fear abandonment.

The variety of environmental resources available. We often need some backup resources in order to cope well. These resources may be financial in one situation, spiritual in another, or emotional in others. The availability of social support is widely regarded as an important buffer for stressful life events.

The amount of emotional distress experienced. Whether we perceive a situation as a challenge or a threat determines how much distress we feel. Stress can mobilize us to action. But when *stress* becomes *distress*, our capacity to function may become impaired. We may not be able to draw on those coping skills we *do* possess.

Since stress—including disenchantment—is an ongoing aspect of human existence, we cannot measure our coping effectiveness by the extent to which we eliminate stress from our lives. We must remember that even *positive* events in our lives—having a child, planning a vacation, or going home for Christmas—can be stressful. We can curtail some stressors (the *source* of stress itself) and avoid others. But we are bound to face *some*.

The real measure of our coping effectiveness is the extent to which we have maximized our meaning and pleasure or have minimized our emotional distress. Mary may not be able to change the fact that she is carrying twins, but the way she copes will greatly determine the extent to which childrearing is a meaningful experience or a traumatic one. Bob may not be able to forestall his divorce proceedings, but he can affect the course of his emotions or life planning from this point on.

Clearly it is not the changing event—or even the *event* of change—that causes our pleasure and pain, but rather the ways we handle the change. This is an intriguing notion: Not only do we create our own disenchantments by having expectations that are too high, but we also influence the emotional impact of these disenchantments by the manner in which we cope with them! The next chapter takes a much closer look at the factors that have an impact on our capacity to cope with the challenges that life and love offer us.

10

Personal Resources

Use the talents you possess. For the woods would be very
silent if no birds sang except the best.

Author Unknown

Coping skills alone aren't enough to survive disenchantment. Even when
we have a large repertoire of coping skills, we *simply may not use them to
renew our relationships*. Our actual capacity to cope depends upon our
"inventory" of personal resources—those life assets that empower us to
enhance our well-being and reduce our distress. Without the right combination of resources, we don't even make the attempt—or if we do, we
give up too soon, undermined by feelings of helplessness or hopelessness.
The truth is ... whether or not we succeed at renewing our relationships
actually *depends more upon our particular inventory of resources than upon any
of our partner's qualities.*

These resources are best expressed as beliefs:

A belief in who one is ... self-worth.
A belief in what one can do ... self-efficacy.
A belief in what will be ... hope.
A belief in what one has ... quality of life.

The two *inherent* resources—self-worth and hope—propel us forward
to *initiate* coping strategies. The two *achieved* resources—self-efficacy and
quality of life—*sustain* our efforts to cope over time. The two *internal*
resources—self-worth and self-efficacy—are essential building blocks for
our identity, our sense of who we are. The two *external* resources—hope
and quality of life—link us to outside support systems which, in turn, help
us to transcend our present problems.

Coping Resources

	Internal	*External*
Inherent	Self-worth	Hope
Achieved	Self-efficacy	Quality of life

Imagine that you have decided to run in a 26-plus mile marathon race. You wouldn't even begin training for such an ordeal unless you believed in yourself. Self-worth is the powerplant that feeds you this motivation. Next, you'd compete in lesser races, completing 5K and 10K events to build up your confidence that you can compete and do well. Achievements build confidence in your ability—your self-efficacy—in this way. Next, you must believe that proper training, good conditioning, and a positive attitude will get you past "the wall" to the finish line. You must trust or hope that you will transcend the pain in order to reach your final destination. Finally, you must have other resources in place in order to complete the race. Water stops, supportive fans, and proper racing equipment are quality of life factors you need to sustain your efforts for such a distance.

Think of a committed marriage as a marathon race. If you have experienced loving relationships throughout your life, you have come to appreciate yourself as lovable—as someone who likes being intimate and is worthy of being loved. You know more about what goes into a successful relationship than others who have never loved or been loved. You are aware that relationships have peak moments of exhilaration as well as moments of despair that can be survived through persistence and goodwill. And finally, you know that love is never enough—that satisfying leisure activities, sufficient finances, physical well-being, productive work, and fulfilling spiritual practice also contribute to your sense of happiness.

Psychologist Ethel Roskies has suggested that our *coping skills* are a currency we spend on specific situations, and thus our *coping resources* constitute the bank account from which this currency is drawn. This chapter is about that banking system.

Self-Worth

I have heard it said that we waste precious time in believing that we aren't as good as we really are. These simple but prophetic words penetrate to the heart of an issue that continuously affects our loving relationships. Nathaniel Branden, in his book *The Psychology of Self-Esteem*, declares that no value judgment is more essential to humankind—no cornerstone more important in psychological development and human motivation—than the estimate one places on oneself. He goes on to say:

> Man experiences his desire for self-esteem as an urgent imperative, as a basic need. Whether he identifies the issue explicitly or not, he cannot escape the feeling that his estimate of himself is of life-and-death importance. (Branden 1969, 104)

When we believe in ourselves, we bring an inherent resiliency to our encounters with life's surprising bumps and bounces. When we believe that we are worthwhile, we believe that we are entitled to have what is worth having. We strive more actively to reach for things we want and to side-step hazards along the way. A colleague of mine, denied tenure after seven years of superior teaching and publishing, remarked that the university was merely one vehicle through which she could express her ideas. "I bring my uniqueness with me wherever I am," she beamed. "The kitchen table is sufficient enough for me—if need be!"

As we noted in chapter 4, a sense of self-worth is based upon receiving undivided attention and affection from others during childhood. When we have experienced enough warmth, touching, and physical closeness from others during our earliest developmental years, we know an undeniable truth—we are *special*, we are *worthy*. We are special enough that significant others are willing to be diverted from their own important orbits to penetrate our private space of private needs.

Expectancy is born of self-worth. If you are special, you can expect that special moments will occur in all of your relationships. If you feel unworthy, you expect little and usually get little. Many people who have considered themselves unlovable their entire lives will not believe that another adult loves them. They will test and retest this love until they believe that it is real. Unfortunately for some, the responses to their challenges are never sufficient, and they remain the victims of a painful, self-fulfilling prophecy —"I am unworthy of being loved!"

If you tacitly believe that you are unlovable, you will sabotage all efforts at renewal in your relationship. Not only will you not initiate efforts on your own, but you will resist your partner's efforts as well, declaring that he or she doesn't *really* care about you. Blame is often a miserable coverup for our own feelings of inadequacy.

One of my clients, Denise, came to me to learn relaxation skills and biofeedback. At the time I met her, Denise was engaged to be married. She was also suffering from colon spasms and marked abdominal pain, pains that had always been more severe for her when she was involved in an intimate relationship. Years of psychotherapy and psychoanalysis had helped her to realize that she was "insecure." After reviewing her life history, I remarked that her physical symptoms certainly were real, but actually were a red herring.

The real problem was that Denise was practically bankrupt in self-worth and hope. She described her father as "cold, dignified, pro forma, and judgmental." Mother was "passive-aggressive, overly dependent, and hysterical when disappointed." Does this sound like a family likely to develop a radiant sense of self-worth in children? After teaching Denise skills to deal with her physical symptoms, I suggested that she tell her fiancé about her symptoms and trust that he would accept her and find her worthy—even if she did not find herself so! At first she resisted this idea, believing that he would be as judgmental as her parents. She was soon surprised to discover that she did not have to hide from him as she had done in every previous relationship. It is never too late to entrust ourselves to others for validation.

Perfectionism is one possible byproduct of diminished self-worth. In order to compensate for self-doubts, you may create a force within you, a "false self" that drives you and others to meet impossible standards and reach impossible goals. Only by achieving these impossibilities can you reassure yourself that you truly are OK. The irony, of course, is that these goals cannot be achieved, which further destines you to a personal sense of failure and self-contempt. Self-confident people create reasonable and achievable goals.

A hunger for power, control, achievement is another possible by-product of low self-worth. Those driven souls who scramble for every higher rung on the career ladder or every unclaimed parcel of organizational turf all do so to enhance their feelings of self-worth. Their quest for power and control makes life hellish for others and belies the real emptiness within. Others, instead of riding the fast track for success, spend much of their life worrying about how others evaluate them. Only if they manage to escape the close scrutiny of a vigilant boss or spouse do they feel OK. The "tyranny of the should" dominates their lives.

Low self-worth almost always originates within the childhood family unit. In her book, *For Your Own Good*, Alice Miller describes a rigid set of parenting rules as "poisonous pedogogy." Often children are raised to be seen and not heard or to speak only when spoken to. A child's self-worth is lost amidst a barrage of overly strict rules and regulations that convey an insidious message: we, the parents, are the powerful ones, while you, the children, are (or should be!) meek, compliant, and obedient. Even parents who are less rigid often confuse *positive reinforcement* with *encouragement*. Children learn that if they bring home wonderful grades or perform superbly at a recital, then they may be rewarded. Socialize with the right friends, join the right clubs, or choose the right sports and then you may get stroked.

Rewards for *performance* are fine, as long as the *person* is encouraged along the way. The real measure of love and worthy attention is when we receive warm encouragement to choose wisely or to continue to work toward our goals. Anyone can cheer for a champion, but how many strong shoulders are there when we have struck out for the third time or been stumped for the nth time by that fourth grade math problem? Encouragement during times of vulnerability convinces us that if we are OK in the eyes of others when we are feeling the *least* OK, then we must *truly* be OK!

There are three pathways for rebuilding self-worth when it is not well established in childhood and adolescence.

First, we can rely on achievements to augment our inadequate self-regard. By accomplishing important objectives in life, we usually do come to consider ourselves worthy. Completing college, building your own business, rearing five children, or becoming an associate director in your firm may all compensate for inadequate self-worth. These accomplishments are beneficial and contribute to self-efficacy, as we will see in the next section. However, because they are *compensatory*, they require constant reinforcement as a source of self-worth. That is, we must always be doing something which proves to ourselves, as well as to others, that we have worth.

A second way to buttress sagging self-worth is by acting "as if" we are worthy. Assume the virtue and it is yours. Once we act kindly, creatively, or sexily, others begin to see us that way. Eventually, after hearing others describe us as kind, creative, or sexy, we begin to see ourselves that way as well. When we behave "as if" we are special, we actually can begin to believe it after awhile. Since everything we experience in life includes some form of illusion, we might as well create more positive illusions of our own to live with!

The third way we can supplement our self-worth is the subject of this book—a loving relationship in adulthood. Relationship renewal is the doorway to *self*-renewal! Being loved and accepted as an adult, even with our inadequacies, can restore the most debilitated psyche. This is the magic of a loving bond that endures.

Self-Efficacy

Can you remember the first time you were able to stay "on point" in ballet? Or how about that first home run you hit at summer camp? Or that rapid you were finally able to shoot, that go-cart you were able to construct, or that tree house that you, your brother, and your father were able to piece together with old scrap wood? As adults, we trade in those ballet shoes, baseball bats, go-carts, and tree houses for more symbolic achievements. Managing your family's investments profitably, resolving your department's personnel crisis, or mastering the power serve in tennis are adult versions of these much-needed sources of achievement.

Competitive swimming did it for me personally. My entry into tenth grade was marked by a nine-year history of mediocre C's. These grades were perfectly acceptable in my family but, as of yet, I had not excelled in anything. But a new high school, a two-year competitive swimming program at our local YMCA, a naturally beautiful stroke, and *voilà*—I was a double winner in the first swim meet ever held in our new natatorium. Can you imagine my delight at hearing my name broadcast on the local radio or seeing my name headlined in the newspaper? The local kid had made it! I had taken the beautiful stroke that Mrs. Prim Mathews taught me and traded it in for something big—an accomplishment beyond words. My high school years were now truly golden.

I have had many moments of pride and mastery throughout my life. But something especially significant happened that January day in our high school pool. I realized that I had the capacity, the skill, and the know-how to make my wildest dreams come true. An attitude of "I can do it!" has been with me ever since. It is not enough to possess the *skills* of a creative coper; one must also *believe* one has them. Psychologist Albert Bandura expresses this quite well in his definition of self-efficacy:

Expectations of personal mastery affect both initiation and persistence of coping behavior. The strength of people's convictions in their own effectiveness is likely to affect whether they will even try to cope with given situations.... People fear and tend to avoid threatening situations they believe exceed their coping skills, whereas they get involved in activities and behave assuredly when they judge themselves capable of handling situations that would otherwise be intimidating.

Not only can perceived self-efficacy have directive influence on choice of activities and settings, but, through expectations of eventual success, it can affect coping efforts once they are initiated. Efficacy expectations determine how much effort people will expend and how long they will persist in the face of obstacles and aversive experiences. The stronger the perceived self-efficacy, the more active the efforts. Those who cease their coping efforts prematurely will retain their self-debilitating expectations and fears for a long time. (Bandura 1977, 193-194)

Think back to the disenchantment model proposed in chapter 7. Lovers eventually burn out if the triad of anger, hurt, and resentment continues unabated. We become indifferent, apathetic, and numb when repeated efforts to improve our relationships fail. "Why should I try to do anything anymore? Nothing I do makes any difference to me or anyone else!" In short, we feel helpless.

In order to initiate change and to sustain our efforts to cope, we must believe that a modicum of effort will be beneficial. When we have a history of mastering small things, we eventually take on bigger things. If my son can call his soccer coach in order to ask for a larger uniform, I believe he will be able to call the Governor one day to complain about fiscal mismanagement. Self-efficacy gives us the sense that we can attain the outcomes we desire.

Without early mastery experiences, people will not attempt to renew adult disenchantments. Many, many people have never experienced the satisfaction of renegotiating or revitalizing relationships in their lives. If you have never been able to improve your relationship with your mother, father, or anyone previously close to you—how can you expect to do so now? Yet, you must! For your best opportunity for mastery lies not in reconstructing the dysfunctional patterns of the past, but in renewing the problems of the present.

Renewal is a metaphor that conveys the belief that you, as a couple, can do whatever is necessary to maximize your meaning and pleasure or minimize your pain. Every challenge courageously faced builds this belief even more. While efficacy is built upon success, success is built upon mutual, sustained effort.

Hope

So far, I have extolled the importance of possessing an inherent belief that one is truly special (self-worth) and of achieving a personal sense of mastery (self-efficacy). Both, in their glorification of the self, as it is, may be considered internal resources. Hope, in contrast, transcends what is in order to exalt what can be!

Hope is a transcendent experience which acknowledges that we have read only a few chapters in the book of life. There are many chapters yet to come. My dear friend, the Reverend Chuck Meyer, reminds me that Paul says in Romans 8: 24-25, "For hope that is seen is not hope, for who hopes for what he sees? But, if we hope for what we do not see, we wait for it with patience."

Hope is an inherent personal resource that relates to a world of unknown possibilities. How can we possibly know if we will fall in love today, be forgiven tomorrow, or be recognized for our work at any time? How can we be assured that our efforts to lose twenty pounds, eliminate cigarettes, or lower our cholesterol level will improve our health and lengthen our lives? How can we be certain that learning to touch and communicate with our dejected and angry lovers will bring us closer? And how can we possibly know if the loving devotion we give to our children for decades is sufficient to prepare them for life? *We can't know. We can only hope for the best.*

If hope is truly transcendent, then we must look beyond "what is best" and accept "what will be." Things don't always work out as we would like them to. We lose our jobs, our husbands forget our birthdays, our wives may put the children first, or our loved ones may die. To be able to look beyond the immediate pain and sorrow is what makes gaining perspective the most important of all the coping strategies. By acknowledging that there is yet more to come, we give ourselves hope for tomorrow. Without hope, the will to live and to love withers and dies.

In his wonderful book, *Existential Psychotherapy*, Irving Yalom reviews the contributions of Viennese psychiatrist, Viktor Frankl. In contrasting Frankl's work with the work of Freud and Adler, Yalom states:

> Frankl is careful to distinguish between drives (for example, sexual or aggressive) that *push* a person from within (or, as we generally experience it, from below) and meaning that *pulls* a person from without. The difference is between drive and strive. In our most essential being, in those characteristics that make us human rather than animal, we are not driven but instead actively strive for some goal. Striving, as opposed to being driven, implies not only that we are oriented toward something outside of self (that is, we are self-transcendent) but also that we are free—free to accept or deny the goal that beckons us. Striving conveys a future orientation: We are pulled by what is to be,

rather than pushed by relentless forces of the past and present. (Yalom 1980, 445) (basic test)

It is this sense of the future, of what is to be, that characterizes hope. Frankl knew this well as a prisoner in Auschwitz during World War II. Frankl believed that he alone was equipped to fulfill a meaningful mission in life: to write a book about man's search for meaning—even in the harshest of conditions. All of life is filled with the possibility that, if it is approached creatively, meaning can be found. What matters, according to Frankl, is not the size of the radius of one's activities, but how well one fills its circle.

Frankl believes that we may transcend our immediate experiences to find meaning in three ways:

- What we accomplish in life or give to the world in terms of our own creations.
- What we take from the world in terms of our experiences.
- What our stand toward suffering is, that is, toward a fate which we cannot change.

It is this last category that, perhaps more than the other two, connotes the true essence of hope. What can be more hopeful than to believe that current suffering in a love relationship can have meaning if it changes one, or perhaps one's partner, for the better.

If you have an inherently embedded sense of hope, then you know that there is much more to coping once your efforts to change the source of a problem have failed. You know well the importance of gaining perspective, which allows you to change your perspective toward the problem, as well as seeking balance, which allows you to change your reaction to the problem. Hope, you see, transcends the problem itself. A friend, Alan Groveman, once put it this way: "There is hope if we cope." It is also true that if we hope, we can cope!

Closely aligned to hope is courage. We possess courage when we believe in renewal. It is courage that fuels the possibilities in love. It is courage that propels us forward as we risk in one way or another. To reach out to your partner when you have been rejected and hurt takes courage. To advocate a point of view when dissidents abound takes courage. Even those of us who have never considered ourselves spiritual can be excellent models of faith; we possess the hope and courage to continuously reach out for what is unknown, for what is uncommon to our lives.

Quality of Life

The relation of this final resource to coping is very direct. Satisfaction with love, work, leisure, health, finances, and spirituality contribute much to our experience of happiness. People with high satisfaction in each of these areas are far more likely to think of themselves as happy.

Imagine two different couples, each of whom is having marital difficulties. The Smiths have successful careers, many friends, good health, sufficient savings and income, and a close relationship with their pastor. After a few sessions with their pastor, they decide to pursue marital counseling with a highly recommended therapist who charges $75 per hour. Since money is not a barrier, they begin immediately. During the course of therapy, they balance the pressures of realigning their priorities by enjoying time with friends and accomplishing career-related tasks.

The Joneses, in contrast, are depleted in most quality of life domains. They are in debt for $12,000, due to a lengthy hospital stay for Mr. Jones. Their income is low because of Mr. Jones's continued disability. Mrs. Jones has a low-paying job in a company that does not value her work. Their closest friends recently moved to another state and they have no church affiliation. They cannot afford therapy.

The Smiths are far more likely to persist in their efforts to cope. Social support, financial assets, and access to helpful community resources correlate directly with health and well-being.

Just recently I heard of a minister who repeated the same liturgy on the same day for two different funerals. In the first instance, it was evident to him that strong, loving community ties had existed for the entire family. Family and friends sat shoulder to shoulder, leaning on each other for support throughout the service. In a later service, he noticed the frightened estrangement of the few family members in attendance. The bereaved wife sat alone, with a few neighbors two pews away. The same service, yet so striking a contrast.

Quality of life is not a consideration during romantic love. When we fall in love we are only concerned with love. Work, leisure, health, finances, and spirituality are not in focus—and are often viewed only as distractions. As one client recently recalled:

> I probably knew from the beginning that it wouldn't work with Betty. Our honeymoon was a disaster from my point of view. She wanted to take dancing lessons, eat, swim, meet people, and play shuffleboard while I wanted to stay in our berth making love for 72 hours. This has been her story all along. Now, instead of shuffleboard, it's her job and the kids. What about our relationship?

No loving relationship will endure unless both parties learn to celebrate the importance of each quality of life domain—each pillar of happiness. Happy couples learn how to play, to save and budget money, to respect each other's work and responsibilities, to expand their network of friends, and to find something greater than themselves to believe in—a common cause, a societal need, children, etc. Mature love is expansive, not restrictive.

When our lives are in balance, we are much more immune to the stinging effects of our day-to-day frustrations. Remember that problem solving, perspective taking, and emotional balancing are all fostered by the presence of these buffering resources. Regardless of whether we are changing something outside of us or within us, the process is made easier when we have built a framework of support around ourselves.

Let's conclude this chapter with the recognition that there are resources available to us which, to a large extent, influence the nature, the persistence, and the creativity of our coping. Self-worth, self-efficacy, hope, and quality of life each potentiate inner strength and ensure that spirit prevails and that coping strategies are well-grounded.

Now that we understand the underlying resources, it is time to focus on the coping skills themselves. And we might as well begin with you! The next chapter will allow you to profile your own repertoire of coping skills.

11

Getting Down to It

If all our misfortunes were laid in one common heap, whence
everyone must take an equal portion, most people would be
content to take their own and depart.

Socrates

There are three ideas we must understand if we are to grow beyond
disenchantment into mature, covenant love. First, each of us possesses the
capability to renew our love relationship by learning coping skills. We are
not simply born with the capacity to cope, we must learn how to do it.
Second, no single coping skill is so effective that it alone can buffer the
impact of disenchanting experiences. In other words, the more coping
skills we have, the more capable we are of getting past disenchantment.
Third, effective coping is a result not only of what we have (our resources)
or what we do (our skills) but also of where and when we employ our
resources and skills. Clearly, different patterns of response are needed for
different situations.

Cynthia's case provides a good example. She and her husband were
stuck at an impasse in deciding whether to have a child. Cynthia desperately wanted to have a baby, but her husband believed that they must first
decide whether to build on to their present home or to purchase a new
one. For him, financial concerns outweighed the urgency of Cynthia's
desire for a child. Cynthia "clammed up" her emotions, causing her to
experience numerous physical symptoms.

Cynthia could have been content to stay stuck, but she didn't. Why
should she prolong her pain when other more effective means were
available to her? As we have seen, Cynthia and her husband could:

- Take action to modify the source of their problem.
- Gain perspective to modify their views of the problem.
- Seek balance to modify their reaction to the problem.

Their first course of action was to address the vexing financial issues
that consumed her husband. Cynthia arranged for two independent
construction bids on adding another bedroom while her husband con-

sulted with a realtor regarding comparable homes. Three weeks of taking action yielded a very clear direction: It would be far cheaper to add on to their current home than it would be to buy something new. Their next action was to consult with their banker on construction loan rates.

A concurrent course of action was to have nightly discussions about the meaning of having a child in their life. Cynthia talked about the inevitability of cutting back on her teaching career while her husband addressed his fears about compromising his financial security as well as his exclusive bond with Cynthia. These discussions led to a much needed reaffirmation of their shared goals and a reprioritizing of their values—a shared sense of what was truly important to them both in life. Clearly, they had both gained perspective.

Finally, both of them realized that they had been building up much anger and resentment toward each other over the previous months. Their plan was to use exercise, relaxation, and continued open communication to seek balance during a stressful time of uncertainty. They planned nightly walks, a midweek movie date, and continued discussions about their fears.

Taking action, gaining perspective, and seeking balance are global, general coping *strategies*. Within each of these strategies, there are specific coping *skills*. My colleague Ray Hawkins and I identified these skills while we were on the faculty at the University of Texas. In a series of preliminary studies, we identified clusters of coping skills that seemed to hang together both statistically and intuitively. Our studies revealed that taking action is composed of two factors that we called "problem solving" and "personal compromise." All of the gaining perspective items hung together as a single factor called "reprioritizing values," though we certainly recognized a more specific category which I am calling "attitiude shift." The seeking balance items broke down into seven different factors: athletic release, nature, image diversion, meditation, emotional support, chemical dependence, and denial.

TAKE ACTION	GAIN PERSPECTIVE	SEEK BALANCE
Problem solving	Reprioritizing values	Athletic release
Personal compromise	Attitude shift	Nature
		Image diversion
		Meditation
		Emotional support
		Chemical dependence
		Denial

Taking Action

When we take action, we use one of two methods to modify conditions around or within us so that stressful situations occur infrequently, do not occur at all, or dissipate soon after their appearance. The "cause" of the problem will always be modified in some way whenever we take action.

Problem solving. Whenever we collect as much information as possible about a problem, evaluate this information, plan alternative strategies, and anticipate future consequences of a decision, we are using problem solving as a coping technique. The focus of problem solving is good planning, and the solution usually involves making some kind of change in your environment. Working a second job during Christmas in order to buy those special gifts would be an example of this kind of taking action.

Personal compromise. Sometimes we may choose to alter a personal behavior, belief, or attitude that contributes to the source of a problem. Learning to be more assertive with an overbearing spouse serves as an example in which taking action can prevent a disenchantment from reoccurring over and over again.

Gaining Perspective

This coping domain involves many different cognitive processes both conscious and unconscious, which we continuously use in order to maximize our well-being or to minimize our emotional or physical distress.

Attitude shift. This occurs when we learn more tolerant, less extreme ways to think about our relationships and partners. Transforming our negative thoughts into more positive thoughts is a common way in which this occurs.

Reprioritizing values. Essentially, this coping skill involves more global thinking processes that minimize the impact of upsetting events *after* they have occurred but *before* emotional upset. Paying attention to other aspects of our life that are going well or intentionally minimizing the importance of a problem are examples of this process. When we reprioritize our values, we recognize that even when we cannot control the occurrence of certain life events, we can control the *meaning* these events have in our lives. Preliminary data suggests that this may be the most important coping skill, since it causes us to reorder our larger sense of what's important in life.

Seeking Balance

This coping strategy consists of seven specific skills for reducing emotional arousal after an upsetting situation has already occurred.

Athletic release. One of the more important things we can do to ensure emotional balance is physical activity, like walking, jogging, tennis, or aerobics.

Nature. Time spent appreciating our oneness with nature is a powerful recentering technique for many of us. For instance, we can go for walks by the lake or lie in the park watching clouds or leaves blow by.

Image diversion. Most of us can visualize the upsetting people and places in our lives quite well. Using image diversion, we substitute more pleasing images to help ourselves relax. For instance, we sit and daydream or go browsing in a shopping mall.

Meditation. Many different relaxation techniques are available for enhancing our lifestyles as well as coping with specific problem situations that upset us. Among the most popular are breathwork, yoga, TM, and biofeedback.

Emotional support. We get emotional support by communicating openly with both our friends and partners. Talking about it can help assuage some of the intense pain, anxiety, or depression that may accompany our disenchantment.

Chemical dependence. At times people seek balance during upsetting times through external substances, such as alcohol, tranquilizers, and other drugs. Prescription drugs may be useful in the short term.

Denial. Putting things deliberately "out of our mind" is another useful coping mechanism for the short term. Feeling our emotional distress or thinking about a problem may be so difficult that we simply choose to ignore the situation as much as possible.

All of the coping skills outlined above reflect three general themes currently seen in the self-help movement: (1) an emphasis on what people do in everyday life situations, (2) an acceptance of more responsibility for one's situation, and (3) a recognition that life is experienced in a multi-sensory fashion. We are best able to help ourselves by using a full range of techniques—our senses, thoughts, imagination, and physical movements—in ways that allow us to meet the unique challenges or threats that we encounter in our lives.

Please answer the questions on the *Coping Assessment Inventory* that follows as honestly as possible. Since you are the only one who will know your scores, you need not be concerned about how others will evaluate your coping style. (Note that any tendency on your part to bias your responses indicates inadequate coping from the start!) Please answer all the questions.

Coping Assessment Inventory

Directions: We all experience situations in our lives that represent either challenges or threats. People differ in their responses to problem situations. This questionnaire will profile your general responses to problems.

A variety of statements are presented below. Think only of how you generally or ordinarily respond. Indicate how true each statement is for you generally by putting a circle around one of the numbers.

Never = 1, Sometimes=2, Often=3, Usually=4, Always=5

Whenever I have a problem:

1. I modify my personal behavior that is contributing to the problem. (2)   1 2 3 4 5

2. I know the various alternatives that exist before taking any direct action. (1)   1 2 3 4 5

3. I know the relative amount of risk I am willing to take in dealing with any problem.(1)   1 2 3 4 5

4. I learn any new skill or behavior needed to deal with the problem. (2)   1 2 3 4 5

5. I collect and evaluate much information needed to deal with any problem. (1)   1 2 3 4 5

6. I determine which information is reliable and valid in dealing with any problem. (1)   1 2 3 4 5

7. I change any attitude needed to deal effectively with the problem. (2)   1 2 3 4 5

8. I predict possible outcomes to various solutions.(1)   1 2 3 4 5

9. I estimate the probability that a certain outcome or solution will occur. (1)   1 2 3 4 5

10. I modify my outlook on things. (2)   1 2 3 4 5

11. I normally place possible outcomes in rank order according to their desirability. (1)   1 2 3 4 5

12. I narrow down the number of alternatives to a few that have a good chance of obtaining the desired outcome. (1)   1 2 3 4 5

13. I determine both the short- and long-term consequences of any action. (1)   1 2 3 4 5

14. I tell myself not to worry about it. (3)   1 2 3 4 5

15. I remind myself that life has its ups and downs. (3)   1 2 3 4 5

16. I pay more attention to other aspects of my life that are going well. (3)   1 2 3 4 5

17. I minimize the importance of the problem. (3)   1 2 3 4 5

18. I tell myself that the problem is not worth getting upset about. (3)   1 2 3 4 5

19. I remind myself that things could be worse. (3)   1 2 3 4 5

20. I try to notice only the good things in my life. (3)   1 2 3 4 5

21. I tell myself it will be over in a short time. (3)   1 2 3 4 5

22. I refocus my attention on other personal values. (3)   1 2 3 4 5

23. I remember that my worth or happiness as a person can never depend on any one problem. (3)   1 2 3 4 5

24. I go shopping or browse. (6)   1 2 3 4 5

25. I ignore it as much as possible. (10)   1 2 3 4 5

26. I find someone special to "lay it on." (8)   1 2 3 4 5

27. I daydream or fantasize. (10)   1 2 3 4 5

28. I turn to physical activities for an outlet. (4)   1 2 3 4 5

29. I try to put it out of my mind. (10)   1 2 3 4 5

30. I use alcoholic beverages. (9)   1 2 3 4 5

31. I play sports. (4)   1 2 3 4 5

32. I use mind-altering drugs. (9)   1 2 3 4 5

33. I calm myself with breathing exercises. (7)   1 2 3 4 5

34. I use tranquilizers or sedatives. (9)   1 2 3 4 5

35. I listen to the sounds of nature. (5)   1 2 3 4 5

36. I look for a person who might understand my situation. (8)   1 2 3 4 5

37. I watch the sky, clouds, or leaves. (5)   1 2 3 4 5

38. I work it off by physical exercise. (4)   1 2 3 4 5

39. I meditate. (7)   1 2 3 4 5

40. I use sports arenas, hike and bike trails, or other settings to work it off. (4)   1 2 3 4 5

41. I reach out to someone. (8)   1 2 3 4 5

Scoring your profile is easy. You will notice that every question is followed by a number in parentheses. Each of these numbers corresponds with a different specific coping skill. All you need to do is add up your score for all the number ones, then the number twos, the number threes, and so on until you have a total score for all ten coping skills.

For instance, notice that questions 14 thru 23 all have a number three in parentheses after each question. Coping skill three is "reprioritizing values." If you ranked your use of this skill at the high end of the scale (by circling five for "always") for all ten questions from 14 thru 23, then your total score for "reprioritizing values" would be 50.

Take a few minutes now to figure a total score for each of the ten coping skills and write your score on the appropriate line below:

(1) Problem solving   _____

(2) Personal compromise   _____

(3) Reprioritizing values   _____

(4) Athletic release   _____

(5) Nature   _____

(6) Image diversion   _____

(7) Meditation   _____

(8) Emotional support   _____

(9) Chemical dependence   _____

(10) Denial   _____

Understanding Your Score

Now that you have total scores for each of your coping skills, you are probably wondering what they mean. In order to understand each score, you will need to compare it to some norm or standard. The fastest run, the longest kick, or the most beautiful sunset means little unless we have a comparison point from which to judge.

Most of us are pretty good at looking for comparison points since we do it so often. Usually we feel worse for making the comparison: "He is more creative than I am!" "She is more attractive than I am!" "He makes more money than I do." "She has a more appealing home than I do." Let's try something new here and emphasize the positive instead of the negative.

First, identify and appreciate the coping skills that you tend to use before identifying the skills you don't use. Let me highlight a few key points before going on:

- All of these skills, with the possible exception of chemical dependence, are best viewed as positive strategies.
- Our goal is always to maximize our use of as many coping skills as possible.
- It is helpful to distinguish between short-term versus long-term coping.
- All coping skills, because they are skills, can be enhanced over time with some committed effort.

In an effort to identify a comparison group, Dr. Hawkins and I sampled 137 women and 57 men from a variety of helping professions. These included staff from an educational facility for the deaf, nursing staff from two area hospitals, and vocational counselors employed by a state agency. Means and standard deviations were then computed for each of the ten scales.

"Means" allow us to understand what the average score is when we pool both the men and women together. No sex differences were found on any of the coping skills. That is, when viewed separately, men and women had the same means or averages.

"Standard deviations" allow us to understand what a normal range is for each coping skill. A "normal" range, as defined here, is that middle range in which 68 percent of our sample fell. Scores that fell in the top 16 percent were considered high, while scores that fell in the bottom 16 percent were considered low.

Comparison Scores for 194 Helping Professionals

	Low	Average	High
Problem solving	25	30	35
Personal compromise	10	12	14
Reprioritizing values	22	29	36
Athletic release	7	10	13
Nature	3	5	7
Image diversion	3	5	7
Meditation	2	4	6
Emotional support	5	8	11
Chemical dependence	2	4	6
Denial	3	5	7

Let's look at a few examples. If your total score for "problem solving" is 23, consider it a low score. By comparison, 68 percent of the people in our sample scored between 25 and 35 on problem solving. The average score was 30.

If your score is 11 for "personal compromise," consider it an average score. By comparison, 68 percent of the people in our sample scored somewhere between 10 and 14. The mean score for practicing this skill was 12.

If your score is 37 for "reprioritizing values," consider it a high score. By comparison, 68 percent of our sample scored somewhere between 22 and 36 on this item. Since your score is higher than 36, it is in the upper 16 percent when measured against our sample of helping professionals.

Most people who complete the inventory have some high scores and some low scores. What accounts for your high scores? Your low scores? Do you recognize a few coping skills that require a larger investment of your personal resources?

For instance, if you are low on 'emotional support" or "athletic release," do you understand why you are reluctant to use these skills? If you are low on "reprioritizing values," do you realize that you are forsaking the most important of all coping skills? Such low scores are common among the people who attend my stress management classes.

It is interesting to note also how "special" populations cope. In a series of studies, Dr. Hawkins and I administered the inventory to hospitalized alcoholics, prison inmates, correctional staff, and students at the University of Texas. A number of interesting trends were noted:

- Alcoholics reported significantly less use of "problem solving," "personal compromise," "reprioritizing values," "athletic release," "nature," "meditation," and "emotional support." As expected, their use of "chemical dependence" and "denial" were high.
- Inmates tended to rely on "reprioritizing values," "chemical dependence," and "image diversion."
- Correctional staff tended to rely more on "personal compromise," "reprioritizing values," and "image diversion".
- Undergraduate students appeared to be the best copers of all with high scores for "problem solving," "personal compromise," "reprioritizing values," "athletic release," "nature," and "image diversion."

Coping Use and Useful Coping

In order to become a better coper within your love relationship, you must learn to *read maps better*. This may sound strange to you, but try to envision a large topographical map that details a point of origin, a destination, and various routes for getting there. Our task is to choose the most suitable route. We accomplish this task with surprising ease at times, as though our choices were archetypal. Often, however, our dilemma in choosing a route for our relationship can be as imposing as deciding on the destination itself.

My clinical and investigative interests lead me to the following observations regarding this dilemma of choice:

- An unlimited array of coping strategies is available to us in any single situation we might encounter, no matter how frustrating or disappointing it may be.
- The same person may choose different coping strategies to fit different situations.
- Different people, coping with the same situation, will choose very different strategies.
- Different situations may call for different strategies, no matter who the person is.

An unlimited array of coping strategies is available to us in any situation. First, let's imagine that I am driving along Congress Avenue, one of the busiest streets in downtown Austin. I am on my way, through the gridlock of rush hour traffic, to a lunch date with my wife, Claire, who has cleared her busy calendar just for me! Pop, bam, a flat tire makes my day! Nails from a downtown construction site were carelessly thrown in the street right in the path of my right front tire. A disenchantment and a hassle all rolled into one.

But what an opportunity to cope! Like a computer doing a rapid document search or a VCR on fast forward, my mind takes off looking for a strategy. What do I do first? Well, I could sit in the middle of the street and practice deep breathing. That ought to calm me down until I'm arrested for unlawful conduct on a public thoroughfare. "But officer, don't you see the benefits of seeking balance?"

Taking action strategies emerge: change the tire, call AAA, hitch a ride to the restaurant, call the restaurant, take a cab. Any of these might work to modify the source of my problem, but which one do I choose? And what perspective can I grasp which will ease my immediate tension?

"Claire would prefer that I get there late rather than not get there at all!"

"Claire has probably had a busy day and will appreciate some quiet time alone."

"Claire has been in my shoes before and will understand my lateness once I explain what happened."

"Claire and I are both committed to increasing our quality time to-gether—one botched lunch date will not affect us one way or the other."

These are difficult choices to make. How persistent should I be in attempting to get to the restaurant? When can I relinquish my search for a solution, let go, and consider it "a good try, but no banana today!" When do I abandon my goal, laugh at my predicament, and reason to myself that there will be another day?

Every disenchantment you face has this same menu of choices. You have just mailed $600 worth of bill payments and your husband tells you that he forgot to deposit his check. Your family's vacation plans depend on your upcoming raise, and your boss has just informed you not to expect a raise for six months. What are you to do now? You might begin a two-month struggle to reverse the decision, you might reason that job security means more than any vacation, or you might begin an exercise program to deal with your frustration.

The exclusive use of one coping strategy may have very harmful effects upon other coping domains, not to mention a marriage. This is often the case with people who demonstrate the Type A behavior pattern, a hard-driving profile that often increases the risk of coronary heart disease. (Recent research suggests that hostility or anger when things don't go according to plan seriously jeopardizes our cardiovascular health.) Such a person may insist on getting into his favorite restaurant, even though you remind him that there are several others that will do. They'll never do for him, so he continues to badger the hostess, bitch about the line, and try to wish the wait list away—all of this, while you urge him to blow it off since you both could be happy elsewhere. In this situation, you have gained perspective, while your Type A partner is stuck with a tunnel-visioned action plan.

On the other hand, imagine having a husband who relies almost exclusively on gaining perspective. He may be so passive and unassertive that tasks are never completed! In the beginning of the relationship, you appreciated how calming his viewpoints were, but now procrastination has become his trademark. The lawn or the income tax can wait, since there is always tomorrow. As much as you pester him, he always has a good reason for putting important things off. You begin to believe that you cannot count on him for anything!

I advocate a *balanced* approach to the use of coping skills. The more balanced our repertoire, the more prepared we are to choose wisely when confronted with one of life's challenging opportunities or overwhelming threats. When attempting to choose a coping strategy, I suggest the following sequence of strategies:

1. Always begin by attempting to modify the source of a problem. Prevention is usually better than remediation. Instead of continuously practicing calming techniques when we argue with our partner, we should learn to *prevent* arguments by communicating our needs more clearly.

2. Remember that gaining perspective is the most important of all coping strategies because it can accompany all the other coping strategies. When we achieve a meaningful perspective in a situation, no matter how tumultuous, we are in control of the situation.

3. When our efforts to maximize our well-being fall short, we have a responsibility to minimize our emotional or physiological distress in order to reduce our risk of illness and even death. We must know how to seek balance when our best laid plans go awry.

The same person will regularly choose different coping strategies, depending upon the situation. A very dynamic and enterprising young attorney may be quite assertive—even aggressive—in taking action in her courtroom litigation battles. In contrast, she may be quite withdrawn whenever she is around her father or husband. She may see them as overcritical, stubborn, and insensitive to her career goals. She convinces herself that it is easier to go along with what they say than to risk their disapproval or rejection. Instead of confronting them, she seeks balance by retreating to her legal briefs or a novel to relax.

In therapy, she may learn that she makes these choices to withdraw because she fears abandonment—a painful consequence of her father's abusive drinking pattern many years before. Since she could not count on family stability then, why should she do so now? This kind of reasoning restricts her use of the coping skills that she does possess and use in other circumstances when the loss of love is not at stake.

Or consider the devoted mother who enthusiastically embraces her parenting role. She is well-read and eagerly buys puzzles, creative toys, and lots of children's books, because she understands the developmental tasks that children must negotiate. Whenever a "crisis" occurs, like a broken finger or a stomach virus, she knows what options exist and promptly initiates an effective action. Yet this same woman feels out of place meeting her husband's business associates. At parties, she copes by nursing too many drinks in remote corners of the room in order to lessen her anxieties. Strategies for taking action dominate her parenting style, while strategies for seeking balance typify her social life.

Whenever we realize that we tend to always cope the same way in specific circumstances, we need to consider what is happening. Can you think of any patterns in your life? Perhaps an inventory of your personal resources will help to explain your repetitive patterns. For instance, the mother in the example above might be impoverished in the resource of "self-efficacy." This woman may have had few dates and other successful experiences meeting men and women other than her husband. This woman might easily learn both anxiety management techniques or social skills training which would help her restructure an old pattern.

Different people, coping with the same situation, will choose very different strategies. I remember one situation in which a scheduled airplane flight was delayed and eventually canceled due to icy conditions on the runway. This meant being stranded in Chicago overnight, as well as having my itinerary broken. What an opportunity to observe coping behaviors!

Strategies for taking action were in full force. Some people dashed to other airlines, attempting to squeeze onto other flights. One man actually took out his American Express card, held it up to the airline's representative, and asked, "Do you know who I am? See what you can do—I'm in a hurry!" Many others just sat calmly in well-cushioned chairs, either reading or talking to their family members. They minimized the importance of the situation, accepting it as a temporary inconvenience. As for me, I was looking forward to seeing downtown Chicago for the first time and already knew that the airline would put us up in a nice hotel for overnight lodging. I figured you can't beat Chicago on the house!

Still, there were others who were so upset by this dilemma that they found it necessary to practice enunciating every four-letter word they knew. One woman, obviously quite disenchanted, replayed every lost piece of luggage and spilled drink she had ever experienced while flying with this airline—as well as every other airline. Getting her anger out was very important. We all heard her sagas, whether we wanted to or not. Other folks sought balance by darting for the nearby lounge to "down a few." Humor was also used a great deal to relieve tension. Every joke you wanted to hear (or didn't!) about airlines was told and retold that evening in Chicago.

These observations simply illustrate the infinite possibilities that await us at every turn in life. Whether facing predictable marital disenchantments or the blow of a sudden, unexpected loss, we can choose from a smorgasbord of coping options. This point is driven home whenever we witness mankind experiencing collective hardships: POWs, hostages, disaster victims, and patients experiencing the same chronic illness can all attest to the varied coping strategies that are employed.

Some life situations may call for specific coping strategies, no matter who the person is. When Barbara Felton and her colleagues at New York University studied the structure of coping among middle-aged and elderly people faced with one of four chronic illnesses, her 1980 study yielded six different statistically derived coping strategies. In order of their empirical significance, they are:

- *Cognitive restructuring*—emphasizes the positive search for meaning as well as the need to redefine personal values.
- *Affective expression*—emphasizes the need to vent feelings, primarily anger.
- *Wish-fulfilling fantasy*—emphasizes the need to alleviate emotional distress by finding a respite in fantasy.
- *Self-blaming denial*—emphasizes that the illness is not a problem, which thus reduces anxiety.
- *Information seeking*—emphasizes problem solving.
- *Minimization of threat*—emphasizes a tendency to put all distressing thoughts about the illness aside.

Information seeking is similar to the technique I call taking action, while cognitive restructuring is an example of gaining perspective. The other four strategies mentioned above seem to be examples of seeking balance.

The key question addressed in this study was whether different strategies were routinely used with different chronic health problems. The results showed that rheumatoid arthritis patients tended to use "cognitive restructuring," "affective expression," and "wish-fulfilling fantasy" more than any other illness group. None of the other illness groups demonstrated characteristic coping patterns. "Minimization of threat" was used the most by all groups, while "self-blaming denial" was used the least. The authors reason that chronic pain combined with severe limitations on daily physical functioning causes rheumatoid arthritis patients to rely on strategies for gaining perspective and seeking balance.

Other researchers, such as Leonard Pearlin and Carmi Schooler (1978), believe that our efforts to cope are most effective when dealing with problems within the "close interpersonal role areas" of marriage and child-rearing and least effective when dealing with the more "impersonal problems" found in occupations. They are convinced that forces affecting our lives on the job are simply not within our control. To rely on taking action in such settings is not effective according to Pearlin and Schooler. Stating this even more strongly, they believe that to rely on individual efforts, rather than interventions by collectivities, in occupational arenas may be foolhardy.

The work of Pearlin and Schooler is significant because it focuses on "normal" coping responses to "normal" life problems in four common areas: marriage, parenting, household economics, and occupation. In the areas that are difficult to change immediately—such as economics and occupation—strategies for gaining perspective were clearly found to be the most effective. If lack of money is a disenchantment, then "demeaning the importance of money" is effective coping. Or if work lacks intrinsic worth, then "valuing extrinsic rewards, such as pay and fringe benefits," may be helpful.

Marriage problems call for more taking action strategies than balance seeking strategies. Pearlin and Schooler state, "It is the reflective probing of problems, rather than the eruptive discharge of feelings created by the problems, that is the more effective response. Similarly, the most effective type of response to parental strains is not resigned helplessness, but the conviction that one can exert a potent influence over one's children" (Pearlin and Schooler 1978, 10).

The RENEW model espoused in this book requires that you and your partner empower yourselves to actively cope with the problems in your relationship. Passive resignation, angry protests, and painful withdrawal are merely the predictable symptoms of disenchantment which will disappear once *both of you* make a commitment to RENEW.

Independence, Codependence, and Dependence

Before concluding this chapter, I would like to reflect a bit on the work being done in the areas of addiction, codependency (including the adult child of alcoholic syndrome) and dysfunctional families. Millions of us have identified with this body of literature, and for good reason—most of us come from dysfunctional families!

One sign of our early wounds is an over-reliance on one of the three coping modes we have been discussing: taking action, gaining perspective, or seeking balance. As we have seen, an over-reliance on taking action is often associated with the Type A behavior pattern. If your scores for taking action on the coping questionnaire were particularly high on "problem solving" but low in all other areas, the following comments may apply to you.

Individuals who fit this pattern seem to pride themselves on their independence, their autonomy, and their capacity to control the events in their lives. These hard-driving, goal-oriented people seem to be problem solvers by nature and find themselves very frustrated when they cannot control the source of their problems. They readily admit to becoming impatient and hostile when things don't go according to plan. Seldom do they make accommodations within themselves, change their perspectives, or take responsibility for contributing to their problems. This is why they are so stressed out or disenchanted. They just keep hammering away, trying to find a solution *outside* of themselves. Often, these are the people who insist that their partner "get fixed," since he or she obviously is the source of the problem.

In effect, these people are distressed because they overuse taking action strategies and underuse gaining perspective and seeking balance strategies. What they know, they know well. But they are not using the full spectrum of coping skills available to them. If this pattern fits you, read on.

Much of the early work on the Type A behavior pattern was done by two San Francisco cardiologists, Meyer Friedman and Ray Rosenman, who got into this whole business in quite a fascinating way. While they were having their waiting room furniture reupholstered, the decorator was puzzled to discover that only the outer three inches of each chair seat was worn out. He questioned Friedman and Rosenman about a clientele who would demonstrate such peculiar seating habits. The rest is history!

Friedman and Rosenman hypothesized, and later found, that their heart patients were very keen and ambitious, with engines at full throttle—so much so that their risk of coronary heart disease was twice that of less intense individuals (the so-called Type B's). What they discovered was a distinquishing behavior pattern that they defined as "an action-emotion complex that can be observed in any person who is aggressively involved in a chronic, incessant struggle to achieve more and more in less and less time, and if required to do so, against the opposing efforts of other things or other persons" (Friedman and Rosenman 1974, 67).

The relationship of the Type A behavior pattern to our focus on coping should be quite clear: taking action strategies are outcome-oriented. Individuals with excessively high scores are constantly pushing, shaping, coercing, always trying to control events in their lives to conform with their preordained notions or expectations. This usually makes life on earth hellish for other family members. Such individuals are so self-reliant, so independent, that mature love is often impossible. These partners are selfish, stubborn, and rigid. How can mutuality, other-directedness, and tolerance be achieved within such a delimited, tunnel-visioned world?

Next, it occurs to me that an over-reliance on gaining perspective may reflect a "codependent" pattern for many people. The spotlight for most codependents is on their "significant other" rather than on themselves. Codependents are not happy unless their partners are happy. Codependents will not give to themselves, but rather are driven to please others and to live through others. Codependents typically become so absorbed by the needs and concerns of others that they have no time to identify or remedy their own. Such a life orientation is not possible unless a person is able to maintain a value system (through *distorted* perspective gaining) to the point where he or she is truly living a lie. Such individuals use positive thinking to a fault, somehow seeing a half-empty glass when barely a drop can be found. In her book, *Women Who Love Too Much*, Robin Norwood identifies this pattern with exquisite clarity. If you are a codependent woman, then these characteristics may describe you.

1. You may have come from a dysfunctional home where emotional needs were not met.

2. You may have received little real nurturing, so you try to fill this unmet need by vicariously becoming a caregiver to men who appear needy.

3. Because you were never able to change your parents into the warm, loving caregivers you longed for, you continuously seek opportunities with men to complete this unfulfilled part of your life.

4. Because you are terrified of abandonment, you do whatever is necessary to keep a relationship going.

5. Almost nothing is too much trouble or takes too much time if it will "help" the man you love.

6. Since you are accustomed to a lack of love, you are willing to wait, hope, and try harder to please.

7. You are willing to take on far more of the responsibility, guilt, or blame in the relationship than your partner.

8. Because your self-esteem is so low, you do not believe you deserve to be happy.

9. Because you experienced little security growing up, you have a desperate need to control "your man."

10. In your relationship, you are much more aware of your dream of how it "could be" than with the reality of "what is."

11. You are addicted to men and emotional pain.

12. You may abuse drugs, alcohol, or certain foods.

13. By being drawn to people who need "fixing," you avoid focusing upon yourself.

14. By clinging to the excitement of an unstable relationship, you avoid depressive episodes.

15. You find kind, stable, reliable men who are interested in you to be boring.

Women and men who maintain this addiction to love can do so only by distorting their thinking and their value systems. To love and care for others is natural. To do so in order to be loved or to feel more secure or to survive one's fear of abandonment is misguided. To compromise one's needs for the sake of another is often the mature thing to do. However, to do so repeatedly is to abandon oneself for the sake of another. Mature love is impossible under these circumstances, since mature love requires us to *balance* our own needs and wants *equitably* with those of our partner's. Addicted lovers cannot do so!

Codependent lovers are stuck—stuck because they believe in a set of rules that prevent the open expression of feelings and thoughts, as well as a direct discussion of problems and issues. By adhering to implicit rules and assumptions, most codependent people are unable to extricate themselves from patterns of living that only meet their partner's needs and not their own. Distorted thinking and misguided values lie at the base of these implicit rules.

Each of the six ways of staying stuck, discussed in chapter 8, contributes to codependent patterns. Our perspectives become codependent because our thinking and our actions are distorted. We learn to:

- Focus only on the behavioral needs of our partners, rather than our own.
- We elicit behaviors from our partners which reinforce our belief that they need us.
- We constantly misinterpret their needs, their wants, and their feelings for our own.
- We consistently behave toward our partners in ways which maintain their neediness.
- We misinterpret our own behavior as loving, when we are actually manipulating and controlling.
- We interact with our partners in codependent ways rather than interdependent ways.

It is ironic that the energy we expend buoying our old, distorted perspectives prevents us from gaining new perspectives that work. Melody Beattie makes this point quite well in her book, *Codependent No More:*

> Worrying and obsessing keep us so tangled in our heads we can't solve our problems. Whenever we become attached in these ways to someone or something, we become detached from ourselves. We lose touch with ourselves. We forfeit power and ability to think, feel, act, and take care of ourselves. We lose control. (Beattie 1987, 52-53)

Finally, it occurs to me that an over-reliance on seeking balance may characterize "dependence." In our need to feel secure, safe, or calm, we may depend excessively on (1) alcohol, (2) other drugs, (3) food, (4) cigarettes, (5) a love relationship, (6) sex, (7) work, or (8) exercise. In fact, we can get addicted to any of these things in order to feel good and avoid further pain (whether the pain be fear, hurt, or anger).

Dependence is similar to codependence in that both are fueled by a vast neediness which reflects the huge emotional void left by our earlier family life. The spotlight is different, however, for the two of them. Codependence, as I stated earlier, is marked by focus on a significant other. Our survival seems to depend on first making another person happy. For this reason, codependents are often seen as exceedingly responsive and responsible. However, dependence is marked by a focus on ourselves. When we are dependent, we face an urgent imperative. *Our* needs must be quieted, *our* pain arrested. NOW, not later! Middle-of-the-night phone calls, time demands, and other forms of impulsive reaching out reflect dependent behavior.

Outlets that normally balance people's lives are used to the point of imbalance. Instead of viewing exercise, visualization, recreational drinking, friends, loved ones, and denial as additional tools, we distort their importance by "having to have" them. We become addicted—we want more and more of them and withdrawal from them is painful. Life seems intolerable without them. Once again, Melody Beattie guides our understanding. She believes that dependent people:

- Don't feel happy, content, or peaceful with themselves.
- Latch onto whoever or whatever they think can provide happiness.
- Feel terribly threatened by the loss of any thing or person they think provides their happiness.
- Don't love themselves.
- Feel they *need* people more than they *want* people.
- Don't take time to figure out if they love or like someone.
- Look to relationships or other substances to provide all good feelings.
- Worry other people will leave them.

Often, dependent people do not understand why they compulsively rely on people, substances, or other things to provide relief from their pain. This is a mystery that often requires therapy to unravel, but if you do find yourself over-relying on balance seeking, you may have a strong indication that some outside help is advisable. Mature love may be impossible unless you do. Each week I see at least two or three couples in which one partner refuses to give up a crutch, refuses to communicate openly, and refuses to commit to therapy—or to the relationship! How can such a person possibly solve problems and shift perspective if he or she is content to seek out one quick emotional fix after another?

The situation is often more complicated when a codependent person is emotionally tied to a dependent person. The codependent person, whose script involves pleasing others, often will reach out endlessly to meet the unending needs of the dependent partner. By meeting the needs of his or her dependent partner, the codependent person is led to believe that he or she is very special, very loved—that is, until no longer needed. Her world then falls apart! He then feels duped! It is in these painful moments that the codependent can see more clearly that the dependent partner's urgent need to "connect" had little to do with his or her specialness. Instead, the codependent must admit that the dependent partner's vision does not extend beyond his or her own neediness—a tragic admission, if it is ever made!

We have seen, then, that an over-reliance on any strategy may indicate a false sense of security, diminished self-esteem, and dysfunctional relationship patterns that must be changed. The key to effective coping is not exclusive use of any one coping strategy. Rather, effective coping relies on a well-rehearsed, broad repertoire of skills and resources.

It is important to note that anything can be abused—even coping skills. Throughout this book I have stressed the need for balance and moderation. Perhaps these points will be made even clearer in the next and final section of the book. Reflect on your coping inventory scores as you consider these points:

- It is clearly better to be armed with *both* personal resources and a reservoir of coping skills than to have either alone.
- Personal resources (self-worth, self-efficacy, hope, and quality of life) may be more helpful in *sustaining* people who face disenchantments over which they have little control.
- No single coping skill is so effective that its possession, alone, can buffer the impact of disenchanting experiences.
- Having a particular coping skill or resource at one's disposal is significantly less effective than having a broad repertoire of skills and resources.
- The complete story of coping efficacy must include not only what people have (their resources) and what they do (their skills), but also where and when they use them. Clearly different patterns of responses are needed for different situations.

It is now time to RENEW your love relationship. The following five chapters are intended as a self-help guide for this purpose. If you have read this book to this point, you understand that your relationship is a complex arena that reflects your influence—both positive and negative— as well as your partner's. If you are fair-minded, willing to change, and can enjoy a cool mountain stream, you are ready to begin.

PART V

PAST DISENCHANTMENT
Renewing Your Love

Disenchantment isn't an experience confined to any particular period in a relationship. Whether we have been with our partner seven months, seven years, or seventeen years, we can find ourselves painfully trapped in the destructive cycles of disenchantment. Often we feel helpless to save our relationship ... we don't even know where to begin. And often—when our present hurt and anger override our memories of earlier joy and hope—we aren't even sure we want to try. However, by engaging in the RENEW process, we can not only save our relationship, we can transform it into the enduring, deeply fulfilling bond that we have always hoped for.

The five steps of the RENEW process are:

R = Release Resentments
E = Express Caring
N = Negotiate Problems
E = Explore New Perspectives
W = Weather the Storm

The process begins with the two steps that prepare us for implementing the coping strategies presented in Part IV. We must first break through the wall of resentment that has built up over time. Then, after our resentments have diminished, we must reintroduce genuine caring into our interactions. When our negative responses to each other have been re-duced and our positive responses enhanced, we then can begin to apply the three coping techniques: taking action, gaining perspective, and seek-ing balance.

This is an important point. Why would any partner choose to change anything about themselves unless two conditions are met? First, we must be assured that our partners understand *our* resentments. Second, we must believe that our partners still care about us. Only then will we be willing to change. Only then will we be determined to cope with our disenchantments.

12

RENEW: Release Resentments

The hardest thing to learn in life
is which bridge to cross,
And which to burn.

David Russell

We obstruct our own renewal by stockpiling resentments toward our partner. These resentments become a lethal arsenal of anger, hatred, and disdain that ignites instantly whenever a problem arises between partners. Resentment—and the anger that underlies it—blocks the flow of caring, inhibits resolution of problems, denies the possibility of mature love, and can damage physical health and well-being. It is also impossible to recognize the fullness of our lives when we are angry and resentful. Releasing resentment is the first crucial step of the love renewal process.

Release from our inner torment is possible only if we learn to forgive one another. Ironically, the refusal to forgive is the ultimate cause of resentment, and the true victim of resentment is always the one who refuses to forgive. The two concepts of resentment and forgiveness are distinctly similar in that neither is a *feeling*. Both are willful *choices* that lead to decisive actions. We make a choice to resent, or to forgive. Yet resentment drives us away from one another, while forgiveness draws us toward each other to commitment.

Forgiving is not synonymous with forgetting. When we forgive, we accept character flaws, differences of opinion, and separate identities, as well as the inevitable frustrations and disappointments that accompany situations that do not go according to plan. When we forgive, we arrive to work things out. We share our feelings, we share our thoughts, and we share our solutions.

Forgetting has a very different outcome. When we forget, we reject our partner. We ignore him. We refuse to communicate, eat, or even sleep with her. Instead, we choose work, TV, friends, and other lovers. Rather than work things out, we leave our partner. We don't just forget the issues, we forget the whole person. We blunt our feelings, we repress our thoughts, and we seldom reach any solutions.

We must forgive if we are to love maturely. This process is ongoing, requires continual communication, and must become a daily part of our lives. Many people will warehouse their resentments for years before cashing them in, usually by dumping a huge pile of bitterness and complaints. Harboring resentments seems only too natural, but there is a better way. All we need is the courage to talk with one another. Yet this basic requirement is surprisingly painful for many people.

I recall working with one couple who resisted revealing their resentments as strenuously as any couple I had ever seen. Each requested individual therapy, believing that the other's problems needed fixing first. This is a common ploy. In their case, there were indeed inner problems, problems arising from childhood wounds. The wife, Marlene, admittedly was a codependent whose early family life was marred by an angry, alcoholic father. The husband, Darrell, an ex-football player, had learned during his West Texas youth that feelings were totally unacceptable and that the only way to settle a score was somewhere between the goal posts. As our work on releasing resentments proceeded, Darrell— who was in obvious pain—bellowed out his feelings:

> I'm clamming up. I've said way the hell too much. I have the feeling that I have been drawn way off sides and am very much at risk of being trapped, blindsided. I am getting back behind the line, sitting up, ready. I'm not talking until you talk. I feel very exposed. I don't really know what's going on, where we are, where we are going. I want to sit where I can get to my feet quickly, not squatted down in that couch, on my back practically, like a damned flipped-over turtle. I must be able to see both of you so that I will not get knocked on my ass.

Talking about resentments is not easy, but Marlene and Darrell learned how to do it. They learned to understand that it is natural to have resentments, but unnatural to hold them. By learning how to communicate their most carefully guarded secrets, they actually reached a level of intimacy they had never known before. This is a crucial point. Communication is so integrally related to intimacy that *even the sharing of negative resentments can bring people closer together*. This couple's renewal can be your renewal if you possess the same courage. Let me reassure you in two ways.

First, don't be discouraged by your hurt and anger. Feelings go away. It may not seem that way when you are upset, but they do. You may be so discouraged by your negative feelings that you have little confidence that this section can help you. The format may seem too simple or too slick. Don't let your present anger get in the way. When you are angry, the future looks bleak and happy moments of the past cannot be remembered. When your anger subsides, your mood will improve. So will your memory! Research has clearly shown that people remember far fewer pleasant events when they are upset. Once your anger and hurt do diminish, you and your partner will be able to work through the more enduring resentments that trigger these feelings over and over again.

Second, your anger will diminsh as your needs get met. You are angry because your needs are not met. If you are like most people I see, you probably don't know what your needs are! You may be so busy blaming, labeling, or yelling at your partner that you miss this point. Like a kneecap tapped by a doctor's hammer, your relexes may snap you forward into a fury whenever you feel let down. But let down about what? Most of the time you may not even know. Instead, your instincts in these moments is to look at your partner as if he or she were some alien with evil intent. You must eventually focus on your own unmet needs if you are to successfully reduce your anger.

The cold boulders of resentment that form barriers between you and your partner must be removed before safe passage is possible. If you are like most couples, your partner must first understand what your grievances are before you will be more caring, or before you will change anything about yourself! But before we begin this process of blasting away these boulders of resentment, we need to examine the ground where they lie a bit more closely.

Things To Know About Anger

1. The events of the world don't make you angry. Your own thoughts about these events create your anger. Nothing can be construed as stressful or upsetting unless you perceive it as such through your own eyes.

2. Anger will not help you. If there is a solution to the problem, anger will keep you from finding it. If no solution is readily available, anger will only keep you stewing in your own juices.

3. Angry thoughts nearly always contain distortions. Correcting these distortions will reduce your anger.

4. Angry thoughts often involve issues of fairness. If you learn to look at things through other people's eyes, you will often find that their actions are not unfair from *their* perspective. You are not the only judge of fairness in the world.

5. Getting even seldom gets you what you want. It usually provokes counterattack or withdrawal.

6. Accepting the idea that you are responsible for your anger is ultimately to your advantage, because it gives you the opportunity to achieve control and change how you feel.

7. Anger usually results from built-up frustrations. If you learn to express these frustrations earlier, you will often prevent yourself from experiencing anger.

8. Frustration results from unmet expectations. If you change your expectations, you will be less frustrated.

9. Anger often results from a sudden loss of self-esteem. When you find yourself getting angry, look inside to identify how you believe you have been humiliated.

10. Letting go of anger gets you closer to love—if that is what you truly desire!

Anger Self-Assessment

You may find it helpful to gauge just how susceptible to anger you are. The following scale will help you determine how your expression of anger compares to others. If you score relatively high on this scale, you may reasonably conclude that your typical responses tend to make matters worse. Use the scale below to indicate the most truthful answer to each of the following questions.

0	1	2	3	4
NOT AT ALL	VERY LITTLE	SOMEWHAT	QUITE A BIT	EXTREMELY OFTEN

1. I am easily annoyed or irritated. _____

2. I have temper outbursts I can't control. _____

3. My heart pounds or races. _____

4. I feel tense or keyed up. _____

5. I have urges to beat up, injure, or harm someone. _____

6. I have urges to break or smash things. _____

7. I get into arguments. _____

8. I shout or throw things. _____

9. I feel that people will take advantage of me. _____

10. I never feel close to another person. _____

Now add the numbers and put the total here. _____

Compare your total score to the scale below to get a general idea of the extent to which your anger and aggressiveness may be a problem.

    0 - 5 = AVERAGE
    6 - 15 = MODERATE
   16 - 25 = SERIOUS
   26 - 40 = SEVERE

Are you surprised?

Are you willing to admit that *you* may be contributing to the problems in your relationship?

Are you willing to read on so that you can learn how better to deal with your anger and resentments?

Thoughts Can Create or Dissipate Anger

There is no doubt that loving couples, in the course of living together, develop many patterns of behavior that frustrate and disappoint one another. Identifying and modifying these patterns is a prime focus of this book. Explosive anger is another story. Events by themselves cannot *make* us throw temper tantrums, break furniture, call each other filthy names, or tear apart the family photo album. We must accept that we create every last drop of anger we feel by *choosing* to interpret events in very negative ways.

For example, being ignored by your husband need not necessarily make you angry. You might think, "He's busy and will probably make time for me later."

By viewing your husband's behavior as situational—as the result of a bad day—you manage to keep a positive perspective. Thoughts like these have very different results:

That jerk! He doesn't give a damn about me. I won't stand for being treated like that!

He never takes time to understand my needs, but he's always ready to perk up for his damn friends.

Thoughts like these feed the fires of anger and resentment through *negative theme building*. Three kinds of distorted thinking characterize the theme-building process.

1. Labeling. You call your partner "a jerk," "deceitful," or "uncaring." These labels allow you to explain his or her behavior. Of course, you continue to search for data to support your theory, and you find it! As the data rolls in, you continue to justify your anger by blaming your partner repeatedly. Of course, the picture you've created destroys your motivation to strive toward resolving the problem. (After all, how can a "deceitful, uncaring jerk" possibly help in modifying a problem!)

2. Mind reading. You conclude that "He has definitely lost interest in me," or "He's got it in for me." By assuming that the other person has mean intentions, you justify your anger and your impulses to get even. The problem is that your asssumptions usually are wrong! Remember that when you *assume* things, you make an *"ass"* out of *"u"* and *"me."* You also discourage yourself from seeking a solution to the problem.

3. "Should" statements. You tell yourself, "He shouldn't ignore me after an entire day apart." Or "If people really love each other, they should be able to communicate." These distorted thoughts are based on the assumption that you are *always* entitled to what you want, whenever you want it. Your sense of being deprived is thus magnified.

Let's take a closer look at how thoughts can either create or dissipate anger. One way to determine whether your anger and resentment are useful (or useless) is to weigh their advantages and disadvantages. You are likely to sustain your anger and resentments if you think that doing so has advantages. The opposite is also true. If you think that there are disadvantages associated with your anger, you are far more likely to let go of it. Here is one example:

> *Thoughts:* George didn't give me the help I wanted with landscaping the yard. He's an uncaring jerk!

Advantages of Anger	*Disadvantages of Anger*
1. It feels good.	1. It will make my relationship with George worse.
2. George will see that I disapprove of him.	2. George will want to reject me.
3. I have the right to give him hell.	3. I feel guilty and stupid when I blow up at someone.
4. I'll get even.	4. He will get angry and retaliate since he does not like getting hurt any more than I do.
5. He'll see that I am not weak or someone he can step on.	5. My anger will block solving the problem.
	6. Living with him will be hell for the next three days.
	7. If I am in an angry mood, no one will want to be around me.
	8. I'd be coping better if I tried to solve the problem.
	9. I feel miserable and tense when I am angry.

As you can see, the disadvantages far outweigh the advantages of being angry. Most of the stated advantages are actually fallacious as well! Note that the disadvantages of anger can also help us to recognize the positive reasons for resolving our resentments and managing our anger. Let's summarize them:

1. My partner, as well as others, will like me better.
2. I will be more predictable.
3. I will be in better control of my emotions.
4. I will be more relaxed.
5. I will be more accepting of myself.
6. I will be less judgmental as a person.

7. I will be able to influence others in a more positive way and, therefore, get more of what I want.
8. I will be more productive.
9. Life will be more pleasurable and meaningful rather than painful and empty.

Anger as Helplessness

So why do we persist in clinging to our anger and resentments when emotional distance and high blood pressure are the only consequences? Clearly, it is not for our health! The answer may have more to do with helplessness than anything else. When most of us are confronted with a problem, we attempt to fix it. This is certainly true with disenchantments in love relationships. If you don't like your husband's dependence on alcohol, you will try to dissuade him from drinking. If your wife's gray flannel nightgown, bequeathed to her by grandmother, does not turn you on, you will try to get her into silk.

What happens when all your resourceful strategies come up short? You get more and more resentful by the day. Each time you fail to meet a personal need, your emotions rise one step higher on the "Richter Scale" of anger. Ralph Kantor, a human relations consultant, has expressed this process very well in a four-stage model. According to Kantor, verbal and physical aggression mount in the following manner:

1. Irritant + inability to remove = Frustration
2. Frustration + inability to remove = Anger
3. Anger + inability to remove = Rage
4. Rage + inability to remove = Fury

This inferno of aggression is fueled by our feelings of powerlessness and futility in the face of unmet needs. We often become incensed when we can't "make" our loved ones change. Loving couples who are able to effectively express frustration and then find solutions forego the blistering heat that emanates from the fires of unmet needs.

We represent most of our adult needs symbolically, communicating them to other members of society by means of the abilities lodged in the cerebral cortex, that very intricate brain telemetry which has propelled us, as a species, from the Stone Age to the twentieth century. The need for self-esteem, pride, creativity, and reciprocity in relationships all depend upon our capacity to construe and communicate very abstractly. The irony is that our cortex, the most *sophisticated* part of our brain, triggers the most *primitive* part of the brain, the limbic system, when we get angry.

From an evolutionary perspective, it seems that we first had to learn how to deal with our frustrations before we could advance as a species. I doubt if we would have learned how to use flint and steel, fashion candles from wax, or invent the light bulb had we not experienced—and somehow transcended—the bitter frustrations of the Cro-Magnon era. Perhaps the same is true of loving couples, who must also learn to articulate their resentments and their helplessness to one another *before* more pleasing and elaborate transformations can take place. The six-step process for releasing resentments is an absolutely imperative first stage in the renewal process.

Releasing Resentments

Step One: Assumptions

Unstated "shoulds," "oughts," and other misguided "assumptions" often worsen our marital headaches. In the absence of effective communication, partners are left to imagine, to mind read, what's going on. In order to begin working through your anger and resentments, you must now begin to check things out through dialogue with your partner.

Sit facing each other and maintain eye contact throughout this exercise. This is most important. If you begin to look away, your message will become more and more diluted until it means nothing to your partner. Take turns alternately completing the following sentence for at least three minutes:

I assume that you ...

As you go through this exercise, please remember the following guidelines:

1. Maintain excellent eye contact.

2. Pause ten seconds before taking your next turn.

3. Do not respond to anything you hear. Once again, DO NOT RE-SPOND to anything your partner says to you. Your job is to listen and understand, rather than to agree or disagree.

4. If you run out of things to say, just repeat the words "I assume that you ..." You will often find more assumptions if you stay with it.

Now tell each other what you learned or experienced while doing step one. Were your assumptions correct? Were you already aware of your partner's assumptions? How wrong were you about your partner's assumptions? Take up to thirty minutes to discuss this exercise.

I am continuously amazed at how wrong loving couples can be when they make assumptions about one another. One recent couple missed on all eight of their assumptions.

He: I assume that you want out of this relationship.
(*The truth* is that she actually was afraid that he was going to abandon her.)

She: I assume that you prefer your career to me.
(*The truth* is that he turned more and more to his career because he detested conflict at home.)

He: I assume that you don't like my body.
(*The truth* is that she adores his body but feels so detached and unloved that she does not allow herself to be turned on by routine sex.)

She: I assume that you think I am stupid.
(*The truth* is that he respects her knowledge of management techniques and politics but refuses to give her any credit because he is so angry.)

He: I assume that you prefer talking more to your friends about our problems than to me.
(*The truth* is that she desperately wants to speak with him but fears his judgments.)

She: I assume that you felt obligated to marry me.
(*The truth* is that nothing mattered more to him than making the commitment to marry.)

He: I assume that you don't care about me.
(*The truth* is that she is too resentful to let her caring be known.)

She: I assume that you don't care about me.
(*The truth* is that he is too resentful to let his caring be known.)

Reality is often elusive. You must begin to recognize that your despair is usually affected more by the way you think about things than by the circumstances themselves.

Step Two: Resentment Lists

Resentments are inherently neither good nor bad. They are stored information that inevitably influence the way we think about our experiences with each other. We are blessed with a capacity to remember—and we do! In this exercise, you and your partner must each write down fifteen resentments. Both of you must agree on fifteen. If you believe that ten will be enough, then BOTH of you must write ten. I learned this the hard way. I once worked with a couple where the husband brought in four resentments and his wife arrived with eighty-four!

No partner is more victimized than the other. If you believe otherwise, you will not forgive nor move forward in the renewal process. Sharing the same number of resentments is a way of proclaiming that *both* of you have been wounded, that *both* of you have grievances, and that *both* of you have contributed to being stuck!

There are three stages in this process.

1. Construct your lists without talking to one another.

2. Take turns sharing the items on your lists. Partner A tells partner B his first item. Partner B waits a few moments and then tells partner A her first item. Partner A then waits a few moments and proceeds with his second item, and so forth until your lists are exhausted. Once again, *you both must share an equal number of items*. If one of you is short of items, then you may repeat some from your list. This will give your partner his or her chance to be heard completely. Don't agree or disagree with your partner's resentments at any time. This only leads to confrontation.

3. When you have finished, each of you must summarize any three resentments you heard *to your partner's satisfaction*. This step will convince your partner that you really listened and understood.

Begin each resentment statement with the phrase:

_____(Name)_____, I resent you for ...

Note four things about this simple phrase:

1. It is important to begin with the *name* of your partner. In this way you focus your resentment directly at him or her.

2. You focus on "resentments," which are thoughts, rather than on "anger," the emotion. Resentments are remembered, feelings are not!

3. You are resentful "about" something. You must specify the behavior, the actions, of your partner. Otherwise, he or she will never know what to change.

4. All resentments are best expressed in the present tense.

You may find that it is much easier to remember resentments when you are angry. Since we become consumed with negativity when we are upset, it is often much easier to retrieve stored-up resentments from the past. You will also find that making a list of your resentments when you are angry will actually help to *diminish* your anger. This was the case with Johanna, whose list of ten follows:

1. Phil, I resent you for so putting me down about my weight that I have gained almost 30 pounds.

2. Phil, I resent you for talking to me in a condescending way.

3. Phil, I resent you for telling me that I talk too much and then cutting me off in conversation as if what I had to say were unimportant.

4. Phil, I resent you for believing that you have given me everything I have and that my salary offers nothing to the family coffers.

5. Phil, I resent you for playing "master and ruler" of the household.

6. Phil, I resent you for making it necessary for me to quit my job because of your career move.

7. Phil, I resent you for assuming that I will follow you anywhere.

8. Phil, I resent you for resenting me for being clean.

9. Phil, I resent you for pushing people and situations on me when I desire to go at my own pace.

10. Phil, I resent you for calling *my* mother, who then called me to straighten me out on how to handle myself as a "professional's wife."

As an alternative to an unstructured, "stream of consciousness" listing, you may prefer to do year mapping, in which you write down two major resentments for each year you have been together as a couple. Think back over the years of your life together and create a road map of the resentments you have experienced since meeting.

The following brief example illustrates this method. If you are inclined, you may list more than two resentments for each year.

Year	Resentment
One	1. Janice, I resent you for being late to our wedding.
	2. Janice, I resent you for clinging to your mother's advice the first three months.
Two	1. Janice, I resent you for dropping out of your academic program after wasting so much money.
	2. Janice, I resent you for not being sexually responsive when you were a student.

The process of disclosing long-held resentments is akin to a dentist revealing tooth decay. In both cases, because neglect has created the problem, a probing drill bit may be required before restoration can begin.

Step Three: Theme Building

Without knowing you have done so, you have labeled your partner for each of his or her transgressions. You are quite familiar with this process from earlier sections of the book where we described the theme-building process. You will remember that all themes (1) represent ad hominem attacks, (2) are extreme polarized views, and (3) begin with "You are ... " As you move to this next step, be aware of the emotions that well up. All themes engender upset. So that you may begin to see this more clearly, follow these suggestions first on your own.

Sit in a hardback chair with your legs uncrossed. Get a very clear image of your partner in your mind. Now go over each resentment that you listed in step two. As you read each resentment, clench your fists and transform each one into a "you are ... " statement. Be sure to convert *each* resentment into an angry "you are ... " theme. Imagine telling your partner each theme, eyeball to eyeball. You will probably see a pattern of similar themes emerge if your list of resentments is long enough.

Now look at one another and share your themes aloud. The following example uses the resentment list from step two to illustrate this technique.

1. Phil, you are a critical son-of-a-bitch.
2. Phil, you are an egotistical, conceited man.
3. Phil, you are insensitive.
4. Phil, you are arrogant.
5. Phil, you are egotistical and arrogant.
6. Phil, you are an intrusion into my life.
7. Phil, you are egotistical and arrogant.
8. Phil, you are unappreciative.
9. Phil, you are insensitive to my needs.
10. Phil, you are untrustworthy.

These are painful admissions to make to one another, yet we must do so. These negative constructs that underlie all stormy protests must be understood as the real source of our anger toward one another. Once again, it is not the precipitating situation itself which triggers our upset. Frustrating and disappointing situations trigger long-standing themes, which, in turn, trigger emotional upset!

$$\text{Triggering Situation} \longrightarrow \text{Negative Theme} \longrightarrow \text{Anger}$$

But we must go even deeper in order to understand why we get so angry with one another. Let's turn to that process now. [A reminder: If you find that you are unable to move past your hurt, anger, or avoidance, contact a mental health professional for additional assistance.]

Step Four: Hurting and Retaliating

All anger rests on a foundation of hurt. This fundamental emotion must be acknowledged before we can work through our anger, Much of our anger, which we are all too willing to express, becomes unnecessary when we dare to become more open about our basic hurts. You will see this very clearly as we progress through the three phases that comprise step four.

Once again, face your partner with excellent eye contact. If you don't maintain eye contact, you will water down your message until it becomes nothing more than a vaporous mist. Now tell your partner how you feel hurt. Use one of these two sentence structures:

I feel hurt by ...
I feel hurt when you ...

Feel free to make a very long list of hurts. Remember that all hurts represent unmet needs. This is your chance to identify all your unmet needs. If you get stuck and are unable to think of another hurt, just pause for a moment. You will probably find that you will be able to continue.

Next, allow your partner to describe one of his or her hurts. Pause again for ten seconds or so. Now you repeat the statement "I feel hurt by ... " one more time. As you purge yourself in this manner, be aware of your body posture and your tone of voice. Note how different both are when compared to your vehement expression of anger! If you and your partner alternate in this fashion, four or five minutes should be sufficient to express your many hurts. Consider the following examples.

Partner A: I feel hurt by your continued put-downs.
Partner B: I feel hurt when you rebuff my hugs.
PartnerA: I feel hurt when you come home so late without any explanation.
Partner B: I feel hurt by your harping about how little money I make.

Now go back over your list of hurts and convert them into accusations. Be assertive in telling your partner how he or she hurt you. Instead of saying "I feel hurt by ... ," say "You hurt me by ... " or "You hurt me when you ... "

Notice your body posture and tone of voice again. What do you notice? Is there more animation? More muscular tightness or looseness? What happens to your eye contact? Four or five minutes should be enough. Note the following examples:

Partner A: You hurt me by putting me down.
Partner B: You hurt me when you reject my affectionate hugs.
Partner A: You hurt me when you stay away from home without calling me.
Partner B: You hurt me when you humiliate me about my earning potential.

Now it is time to link your anger more directly to the hurt that underlies it. Your goal here is to get in touch with your anger verbally, not physically. Verbal aggression, by itself, is sufficient retaliation. You are attempting to accomplish two things here. First, you are clearly letting your partner know just how angry you are. Second, you are identifying the consequences of anger. Use the following words for each of the accusations you made earlier:

_____(Name)_____, there are times I get so fed up with you that I want to hurt you by ...

Once again, please note your body posture and voice tone as you complete this last phase of step four. Honesty here will reveal the self-defeating, negative cycles that couples create for themselves. Here are some examples.

Partner A: Bill, there are times I get so fed up with you that I want to hurt you by not taking care of the house.

Partner B: Jean, there are times I get so fed up with you that I want to hurt you by *not* moving to Houston.

Partner A: Bill, there are times I get so fed up with you that I want to hurt you by embarrassing you in front of the kids.

Partner B: Jean, there are times I get so fed up with you that I want to hurt you by not coming home on time.

By acknowledging retaliation you admit your part in what has become a very painful, downward cycle for both of you. Tit for tat! An eye for an eye! Retaliation has been with us throughout the ages. Bare your swift sword now, quickly, and be done with it. The time has come to put down your weapons! There is usually more to your hurt and anger, however. Let's go even deeper.

Step Five: Releasing Your Inner Child's Anger and Hurt

Ninety percent of all anger or hurt has nothing to do with the immediate situation that seems to trigger it. This anger and hurt represents the painful, sometimes traumatic experiences we had in childhood relationships with our mothers and fathers. Step five addresses the need to free our partners from these vendettas of the past. Our partners surely have enough to contend with without being culpable for our childhood pain— pain that preceded them.

As you learned in chapter 4, we each hope to find in one another the fulfillment of past longings. These longings are driven by three powerful needs: (1) the need to belong, (2) the need for control over our lives, and (3) the need for affection. When any of these three needs is frustrated, we are very likely to experience anger or hurt. This angry or hurt "child of the past" lives on within us, emerging years later in our adult love relationships. Six patterns typically evoke this anger and hurt.

Evokes Anger	Evokes Hurt
1. Too many demands or expectations	1. Too little attention
2. Too much imposed control or criticism	2. Too little appreciation or approval
3. Too much smothering or overprotection	3. Too little affection

There are a number of stages in step five. First, you must go back to the fifteen resentments of step two in order to classify them according to the six categories above. Then share your thoughts and feelings, alternating back and forth using one of these two formats:

_____, when you do _____, I find you excessive in (1) your demands, (2) your control, or (3) your affection. (*Choose one only.*) I feel angry because of this.

_____, when you do _____, I find you neglectful in providng enough (1) attention, (2) appreciation, or (3) affection. (*Choose one only.*) I feel hurt because of this.

If we use Johanna and Phil from step two as examples, you will be able to see this more clearly. Here's how Johanna stated her first three resentments using this format:

1. Phil, when you put me down about my weight, I find you excessive in your criticism of me. I feel angry because of this.

2. Phil, when you talk to me in a condescending way, I find you excessive in your criticism of me. I feel angry because of this.

3. Phil, when you cut me off in conversation, I find you neglectful in providing enough appreciation of me. I feel hurt because of this.

By tying your partner's deeds, or misdeeds, to these six basic needs, you are now better positioned to truly talk about your most deeply embedded wounds. You must now acknowledge this level of pain by sharing your insights using one of the following formats:

_____, let me be clearer with you. When you are excessive in your demands, control, or smothering of me (*choose only one*) by ___
_____, you trigger much anger from my early childhood since my mother or father (*choose one, or both*) treated me that way. Please understand that this is a deep pain that I must not project onto you. I hope you will help me by being more aware of how sensitive I am in this need area.

_____, let me be clearer with you. When you are neglectful in providing enough attention, appreciation, or affection (*choose only one*) by _____, you trigger much hurt from my childhood since my mother or father (*choose one, or both*) treated me that way. Please understand that this is a deep pain that I must not project onto you. I hope you will help me by being more aware of how sensitive I am in this need area.

Here is how Johanna restated her third resentment.

Phil, let me be clearer with you. When you are neglectful in providing enough appreciation, by cutting me off in conversation, you trigger much hurt from my childhood since my mother treated me that way. Please understand that this is a deep pain that I must not project onto you. I hope you will help me by being more aware of how sensitive I am in this need area.

At this point you must realize that many factors have contributed to your anger and hurt. If you both have endeavored to listen to each other with compassion and patience, each of you now feels more hopeful because you have been understood. Remember that you do not have to agree with what you are hearing in order to be an effective listener. You merely have to understand!

There is no benefit in holding onto your resentments. As excess baggage they weigh you down, preventing you from moving on in your journey to renew your love. Now is the time to let go!

Step Six: Forgiveness Fantasy

Forgiving is possible even when forgetting is not. Our memories are full of resentments simply awaiting the call of feelings of anger and hurt. These memories, as powerful as they can be, become mere skeletal remains when the taut muscles, swollen blood vessels, and sizzling, chemical messages are put at ease. This happens only when we are able to forgive.

The Jewish Day of Atonement, Yom Kippur, offers the hope of atonement for transgressions against God. This same Day of Atonement, however, cannot atone for transgressions of one person against another until each has forgiven the other.

We have come to our final step in releasing resentments. You have had an opportunity to express both anger and hurt, resentment and retaliation. To hold onto such venom can only extinguish what life remains in a relationship that is much too fragile already. The choice between life and death, growth or stagnation, joy or despair lies with you.

Find a time and a place where you are alone and won't be interrupted for at least half an hour. Sit in a comfortable chair and close your eyes. Become aware of your breathing. Notice how you inhale and exhale. Gently focus on your next few breaths, noticing the movement of life-giving air through your nostrils, down your trachea, and into the tiny alveoli of your lungs. How good it feels to be alive.

Pay close attention to the movement of your belly, your abdomen, as you breath in and out. Notice how much more you relax each time you exhale. Take in all the air that you want. Breathe in and out in an easy, gentle manner. Slowly inhaling, slowly exhaling. There is no need to force yourself to breathe. Breathing is a natural, life-giving force which we can only interfere with. Let go. Just relax and enjoy a few moments of relaxation.

Your awareness may drift. You may begin to think about unfinished work, grocery shopping, or the sound of traffic outside. It is natural for your awareness to wander. When this happens, merely return your attention back to your breathing. As you do this repeatedly, you will begin to note more and more sensations, sensations like heaviness or warmth. Just continue to notice these sensations for the next few minutes as you allow yourself to breathe naturally.

Good, now that you have relaxed a bit more I would like for you to think of a time when your partner did something that upset you. You may have become angry or you may have felt hurt. Just let your memory drift back in time, as far back in time as you like.

Develop a clear mental picture of this moment in time. Actually see yourself in this picture. Notice how upset you are. Notice how angry you are at your partner as well. Your muscles may be tightening and your breathing may be getting faster and faster. Now repeat the following phrase to yourself. Do not repeat this out loud. This is only for you.

_____, I forgive you for not meeting my needs as I wanted. I am willing to let go of my anger, hurt, and resentment about this moment so that we can feel love for one another as we once shared. I remember how good this love once felt and I want us to be that close again.

Notice your breathing once again. Allow yourself to breathe naturally, slowly inhaling and exhaling. Be aware of yourself as you are now: comfortably seated, with feelings of heaviness and warmth flowing in. How good it feels to just let go. Just continue to relax this way for the next few minutes.

Now try to remember another moment in time when you experienced hurt, anger, or resentment. Form a clear picture of this moment and then repeat the above process. Remember that your focus will always return to the gentle, easy way you are now, if you let yourself go. Let go and appreciate what you have!

Now complete this exercise by recalling a positive moment that you have shared at some time in the past. Remember one of these special moments. Close your eyes, feel the warmth and heaviness within. Just allow yourself to drift back in time. Go as far back as you like. Grasp that special moment. What do you see? Where are you? What do you smell, see, hear, or feel? Enjoy, knowing that you can create more of these special moments very soon. Continue relaxing this way for a few more moments before opening your eyes.

Critical Impasses

Most of you have smashed those boulders of anger and resentment into manageable pebbles and are now ready to move on to RENEW: Express Caring. A number of you, however, will have discovered that there is one resentment that is so profound, so significant, that there is no way to move forward until this grievance is more carefully explored. If this is your situation, you may need professional assistance to unravel these resentments in order to proceed with your renewal. Let me take a few moments to identify some of the impasses that I have seen over the last few months—impasses so profound that I don't believe each couple would have been able to make progress without professional help.

Normally, when a couple initiates therapy, one partner is more invested in the process than the other. This partner usually has a major axe to grind and anticipates winning me over as an ally. In order for therapy to progress well, I must make one essential point very early: disenchantment is a *reciprocal* process in which *both* parties must be represented. Since themes are universal, I must encourage both parties to be heard. Although this process must be bilateral, often one partner has issues that are so troubling that progress is impossible until this critical impasse is resolved. Let me briefly elaborate on a few of these issues in order to make this point.

The Alcoholic Husband

Substance abuse is often an impasse for a couple. This was the case with one couple who had been married for thirteen years. Initially, the wife had tolerated her husband's daily consumption, believing he needed to relax after his stressful workday. Over the years, however, his behavior became much more erratic, unpredictable, and embarrassing. Finally, his drunken stupors at social gatherings, repeated work absences, and abusive language led her to withdraw from him physically and emotionally.

Though her list of fifteen resentments included a mixed bag of hurts, she wanted her husband to understand how upset she was over this particular resentment. We spent two sessions on this item alone. She simply was unable and unwilling to go on to express caring until this item was more fully elaborated. Ultimately, by exploring her personal constructs (see chapter 5), she was able to help her husband understand why she was so upset. Though his wife's overarching construct was "sober versus *alcoholic*," there was a number of embedded constructs that she wanted him to see.

Sober versus Alcoholic

1. Responsible versus irresponsible
2. Entertaining versus embarrassing
3. Dynamic versus stagnant

This couple actually dropped out of therapy for a month because the wife felt that I was progressing too slowly. She would later admit that she had tunnel vision about this one concern and felt impatient about changing it. She didn't know why she had to "listen to his crapola" when there was only *one* issue that really mattered! Once she confronted me, as therapist, she was able to settle into a more extended process.

A Marriage Without Sex

Sex problems in a marriage are usually symptomatic of other concerns. When sexual issues emerge as resentments, it is often a signal to go hunting for other things. This was the case with one recent client couple. During step two of the resentment release process, this husband was to summarize three of his wife's stated resentments. As he was about to begin, he tearfully looked at me (instead of his wife) and said, "There is only one real issue that brought us into therapy." Curious, I asked what that was. He replied, "I haven't been up for sex for six months and she is frustrated with me." (Although his assumption was partly correct, his wife actually felt rejected more than frustrated.)

After this emotional moment, the need to elaborate on one of his resentments became abundantly clear: "Susan, I resent you for not understanding the pressures I am under!" Since he was in obvious emotional pain—and opening up for the first time—I decided to break out of the structured process in order to give him an opportunity to talk about the impact of these "pressures" on his sexuality. He described a variety of business and financial obligations that he feared he could never meet. Silently he had been plodding along, hoping to right a sinking financial ship. To make matters worse, he had kept all of this a secret from his wife, whom he didn't want to worry. As he tearfully put it, "I haven't failed at anything in my entire life. I just don't know how to face it all!"

Two sessions and many hugs later, we were able to get back to the structured RENEW program. In this couple's case, it was first necessary to fully uncover the mystery of a troubling symptom—a case of diminished sexual arousal. Parenthetically, once this wife understood that her husband's loss of sexual interest was more related to his work stress and fear of failure, her anger and resentment diminished greatly.

A Failure To Nurture

An even more intriguing case involved a couple who had recently given birth to twins—both boys. This normally happy event was marred by a postpartum depression so severe that the wife was unable to nurture her newborns properly. Once her depression was stabilized, the wife requested couples therapy, since she believed there were issues between her and her husband that contributed to her depression.

The mystery behind this woman's depression began to unfold once we began the RENEW process. The first obvious clue was a resentment phrased, "I resent men!" This puzzled me. Why would a woman, after fourteen years of marriage—not to mention the birth of two delightful boys—suddenly manifest a resentment toward men? During her husband's summary of her resentments, the wife pointed out that this resentment was so all-consuming that she was not prepared to go any further in this process without being understood. This led to a series of four sessions, all directed at uncovering the root of her resentments toward men.

The wife had come from a family of four daughters, no sons. Now, with the birth of her two little boys, she found herself overwhelmed by the presence of three males! What a stark contrast to the female-dominated household within which she was reared. She saw this was a problem because she believed that once *women* could be a source of nurturance, warmth, and compassion. She would suffocate in this jock-laden realm of three males. Where would the warm fuzzies come from?

During our side journey of four weeks, the wife learned that her husband not only possessed many "feminine" nurturing qualities, but was also eager to demonstrate them. She would not have to provide the "softer" values in their family all by herself. Their marital issues turned out to be gender issues. Once certain stereotypes were dismantled, this couple was prepared to discover mature love.

A Blended Family's Dilemma

This final vignette captures a common pattern in blended families—jealousy over perceived alliances among family members. In this case, the husband had a daughter from his first marriage, while the wife had two sons from hers. Though they had been married for only eight months at the time of therapy, Steven was convinced that his wife, Betty, made decisions by consulting her oldest son, rather than him.

All of Steven's resentments were unified by a common theme: "I resent Betty because she aligns too closely with the kids—even my own!" Betty, in turn, resented Steven because of his "unruly, self-righteous, and rather intense anger." It was not uncommon for each member of the family to run for cover in their respective bedrooms whenever he became upset.

This couple could not express caring until they elaborated on the husband's resentment theme. This required an understanding of each partner's "wounded child of the past." In Steven's case, he had been sorely neglected as a young boy. His solution was to become a self- sufficient and a self-proclaimed hero—someone who knew how to influence people and climb high peaks. His desire to achieve worked well in the business world—where he was boss—but failed miserably at home. There he overpowered and dominated other family members simply because he felt so left out. Instead of being able to get close to the children, his overpowering style only alienated them.

Betty's story was painful as well. Being the daughter of an alcoholic father certainly propelled her into a responsibility mode. However, the death of her first husband brought home another frightening reality—that life and limb are fragile possessions which require a protector or gate-keeper. She thus took it upon herself to always be vigilant and somehow make sure that all was well, particularly with her surviving flesh and blood. Once this couple understood that they each carried out a role—as hero and gatekeeper—which contributed to the problem, they were able to begin caring and eventually carved out other solutions as well.

This chapter has given you an opportunity to assess your current level of anger and to complete exercises to take you through a six-step process of releasing your resentments. If you have reached an impasse, you may need to consider geting outside help. As a first step, however, you might go back to chapter 8 on getting stuck. By rereading this chapter, you may be able to circumvent your current impasse. With forgiveness in mind, let us now proceed to the next chapter, RENEW: Express Caring.

13

RENEW: Express Caring

You can give without loving,
But you can never love without giving.

Author Unknown

During disenchantment, we come to expect conflict, and this expectation
cuts off the expression of positive, loving feelings toward each other. Once
we have discharged the resentments that block our loving feelings for one
another, we must demonstrate to one another that we still care ... so that
we both can trust that it is safe to be open and vulnerable once again.

But what do we mean by caring? For one couple, caring may mean five
decent conversations during the coming week—times when you actually
sit down and look at one another while you talk! For another couple,
caring may connote a soothing back rub or loving touches upon request.
For yet a third couple, caring may be as basic as a concerned telephone
call or a pat on the back after a trying day.

"Caring" and "intimacy" are inextricably woven together. To be cared
for means to be special. To be intimate means to be close. To be cared for,
in an intimate way, means to be touched in a special way. When ethologists
like Desmond Morris refer to intimate touching, they mean bodily or
physical contact. Though I am indebted to Dr. Morris, whose work I shall
profile in some detail, I do not believe that caring is in any way restricted
to just physical contact. As a symbolic species, we are quite capable of
feeling special when we are cared for in nonphysical ways as well.

Yet there is something profound, something primeval and archetypal,
about physical caring. The profound comfort we experience from physical
caring probably has its unspoken origins in the womb itself. Morris
describes this quite well in his classic book, *Intimate Behavior*.

The very first impressions we receive as living beings must be sensations of intimate body contact, as we float snugly inside the protective
wall of the maternal uterus. The major input to the developing nervous
system at this stage therefore takes the form of varying sensations of
touch, pressure, and movement. The entire skin surface of the unborn

child is bathed in the warm uterine liquid of the mother. As the child grows and its swelling body presses harder against the mother's tissues, the soft embrace of the enveloping bag of the womb becomes gradually stronger, hugging tighter with each passing week. In addition, throughout this period the growing baby is subjected to the varying pressure of the rhythmic breathing of the maternal lungs, and to a gentle, regular swaying motion whenever the mother walks. (Morris 1971, 14)

We don't live in such close, intimate quarters without becoming imprinted to its sweet music and gentle, swaying motions. We become used to it, unconsciously yearning for more of it throughout the remainder of our days. Satisfying this need for intimacy is relatively easy during the first months of childhood. Being tightly swaddled, suckling a breast while listening to mother's heart beat, and feeling the gentle pat for that necessary burp are all early ways of experiencing intimacy. What can be more comforting than to be rocked and swayed as one is attempting to release a bubble of distress!

These comforting actions by a caretaker ensure normal development and serve as an early template for intimacies later on. Other parenting behaviors that serve the same purpose include fondling, kissing, hugging, stroking, cooing, and humming while playing or washing an infant. The pat which eventually replaces the hug becomes a signal that tells the child to relax: "I will take care of you and comfort you in your distress!" Who among us does not like such reassurances during the storm and stress of our daily lives?

Courtship allows us to reexperience many of these tender, intimate behaviors that we unquestionably cherished during our childhoods. Desmond Morris, along with other ethologists who study animal behavior, believes that there are twelve distinct stages of courtship, all of which entail a progressive unfolding of caring behaviors from lesser intimacy to greater intimacy.

1. *Eye to body.* In that fraction of a second when we first set our eyes upon one another, we begin to "size" each other up. Shape, height, animation, and other attributes all begin to contribute to the selection process. If we don't like what we see, we won't pursue any further.

2. *Eye to eye.* While we first connect with others, they are also connecting with us. Our eyes must eventually meet. In this moment, we may either look away in embarrassment or we may smile, thus removing the first barrier to intimacy.

3. *Voice to voice.* In the beginning, our conversations are somewhat trivial as we attempt to break the ice. This small talk, which often details interests, pastimes, hobbies, and likes, is often done without other people being around. By keeping the conversation at a super-

ficial level, it is possible to make a polite exit if other, more substantial signals, do not materialize.

4. *Hand to hand.* Beginning with a handshake or an effort to help, we may touch hands. These first touches may take just seconds. Later, within the context of a growing relationship, these hand to hand touches may become undisguised intimacy, as in more sustained hand-holding or arm-holding.

5. *Arm to shoulder.* Now, for the first time, two bodies may come into contact. In this uncommited posture, two partners look ahead rather than *at* each other. There is an air of ambiguity in this safe posture which exists somewhere between friendship and romantic love.

6. *Arm to waist.* This posture more romantically conveys intimacy, since friends are unlikely to walk together in this fashion. Each lover's hand is now closer to the beloved's genital region as well.

7. *Mouth to mouth.* When kissing is combined with a full frontal embrace, a significant commitment toward intimacy has been achieved. Both partners have acknowledged a willingness to accept the other and may begin to experience sexual arousal.

8. *Hand to head.* As an extension of passionate kissing, two lovers may begin to caress each other's hair, neck, and face. Their embrace now becomes more entranced and more prolonged as each seemingly finds tremendous comfort in the other. Since we rarely touch each other's heads in this culture, this is a true sign of emotional commitment.

9. *Hand to body.* One partner's hands may now begin to explore the other's body in an escalating display of emotional and sexual arousal. Lovers may now squeeze, fondle, and stroke one another's genitals or breasts.

10. *Mouth to breast.* At this point, two lovers have become so aroused that privacy is necessary in order to be intimate with one another. If for no other reason than to obey the law, two lovers must now seclude themselves.

11. *Hand to genitals.* As manual and oral exploration of the body continues, the genitals are eventually stimulated. Gentle actions eventually give way to rhythmic rubbing and inserting that simulate pelvic thrusts.

12. *Genitals to genitals.* The full stage of copulation is reached with orgasm. Each stage, leading to this one, has served to further tighten the bond of emotional and sexual commitment. In the case of heterosexual love, this final consummation also signals the possibility of fertilization, which permits this cycle to renew itself in later generations.

In a healthy courtship, intimacy and caring proceed slowly, somehow embracing each of these twelve steps. Oftentimes, however, this is not the case. Lovers may quickly find themselves in the throes of orgasm on the first date without ever knowing if their partner has the capacity to look softly into their eyes, to tenderly touch and be touched, or to hold without demanding anything more. These lovers often develop patterns in which only the last four stages are experienced.

When this over-reliance upon sexual intimacy occurs during the disenchantment phase, we witness the irony of the "intimate shift." To understand this shift, consider the first eight stages described by Dr. Morris as representing "emotional intimacy" and the latter four stages as representing "sexual intimacy."

The Intimate Shift

During early romantic love, we are sometimes led to believe that we are "special" only when intimacy develops *beyond* "hand to hand," "arm to waist," or "mouth to mouth" (steps one through eight). To be truly "special" during early love, many lovers believe they must experience sexual intimacy—"hand to body," "mouth to breast," "hand to genitals," and "genitals to genitals."

This intense level of sharing, which often bypasses the earlier steps, distinguishes a sexual relationship from any other relationship occurring at the time. You assume: "Though you may be hugging, touching, or even kissing other people, I know that you are not having intercourse with anyone else at this time. Therefore, I must be special to you. You must care about me if you are making love to me." Sexual intercourse thus becomes the keystone for true commitment and for real intimacy. What better underpinnings for disaster? You must crash and burn!

Later on, when the magic of romantic love gives way to the bitterness of disenchantment, you and your partner make a tragic discovery: the *only* basis for intimacy now appears to be sexual passion, that natural and alluring sexual dance whose siren song still beckons. The potent swell of arousal, the gush of hormones, still sweeps you away on Saturday night. The real tragedy for many men is that encasement within a vagina is the only way they will permit themselves to retain the intimate comfort of their lost womb. These men are conditioned to believe that penile engorgement is the only permissible standard for fullness within a relationship.

The tragedy continues! Often, because of the demands of our lives, we have little time to invest in the emotional intimacy of steps one through eight. We may be working long hours, away on repeated business trips, up with the kids till ten doing homework, or just too preoccupied during the day to think of calling one another. This constant pattern erodes a feeling of closeness or specialness in many relationships. As a result, we may begin to turn away, or turn off, from partners who seem too distant to care. At this point, sexual intimacy may decline along with emotional intimacy. Many people will simply not turn on sexually, given a few moments to do so, when emotional and physical distance has prevailed during the week.

Neither disenchantment, nor divorce for that matter, necessarily extinguishes our passion for one another, though its frequency may indeed diminish. Even when sexual intimacy is maintained, we often miss the basic caring, the tenderness, and the feelings of specialness. Where is the emotional intimacy that our nine months of comfort in a warm, snuggly womb promised we would receive in life? It is practically our birthright! Somehow, even when we maintain our sexual passion, there is a void, an empty pit of longing.

This is the "intimate shift." While sexual intimacy seems to be the benchmark for "specialness" during romantic love, emotional intimacy soon emerges as the urgent imperative during disenchantment. At this point, though there may still be orgasmic release, you desperately find yourself yearning for some good old TLC, some basic caring. This closeness has somehow been lost in the inevitable transition from romantic love to disenchantment. You notice other couples hugging, touching, and snuggling and feel the painful void even more! You may find that you have forsaken the very behaviors that bonded you together in the first place.

There is an expression I have heard here in Texas: "You gotta dance with the one who brung ya." Well, say hello to the first eight steps of intimacy building once again. You "gotta" learn how to look into each other's eyes again, how to talk to one another again, and how to tenderly touch again! You must reclaim those actions that once ensured exclusivity. Whether it be handheld walks in the park, jogs on a misty Sunday morning, or discussions over the morning paper with a cup of coffee, these are the moments which "brung" us together in the beginning and these are the moments that can rejoin us now.

Each summer, as our children are whisked away by bus to overnight camp, I am struck by a phenomenal observation. At that moment, a jubilant round of cheers breaks out from the same adoring parents who, just moments before, tearfully squeezed every last hug out of their embarrassed children. How can we break out in song, wildly cheer, and perform a grandstand "wave" as the bus pulls away? In fact, the loving parents of two or more children seem to be the ones who are the most intoxicated with joy. Are we living a lie? Hardly! As couples we are clearly celebrating a two- or three-week window of exclusivity, a time for restaurants, movies, and emotional reacquaintance. This is our time for renewal.

I have heard it reported that the average couple makes eye contact with each other for less than twelve minutes each week. Think about that! Instead of looking at each other, we bury our faces in the newspaper, the TV, our novels, our kids' homework, our unpaid bills, and under the hoods of cars, which are appropriately placed outside the house or in the garage. We will go to great lengths to avoid looking at, talking to, or tenderly touching one another. This may be due to the excessive demands of our over-extended lifestyles, or perhaps to resentment. Is there any wonder that so many of us are so hungry for basic warmth, caring, and comforting? We possessed these gifts during our infancies, our child-hoods, and then during our courtships. But now these gifts may seem lost forever.

To fill this void, many people search for substitutes for real intimacy and caring. Since we are not getting it with our partners, we seek it elsewhere in one of four ways, according to Desmond Morris:

1. We seek out *specialists*. We turn to doctors and nurses who are "licensed to touch." Many of our physical complaints are actually symptoms that allow us to get the emotional reassurance we lack elsewhere. We also seek out priests, ministers, and rabbis, all of whom may offer only a mixed blessing. There are many others who soothe and comfort us in their brief moments with us: masseuses, hairdressers, beauticians, manicurists, and shoeshine attendants each pamper us in special ways.

2. We seek out *live substitutes*. We may find lovers who provide the eye contact, the touch, and the warmth that we have lost at home. We may go dancing with other couples where "friendly" body contact is permissible. We may acquire one of the 5,000 million pets in the United States, which include over 90 million cats and dogs. If we pet or hug our cats and dogs three times daily, Dr. Morris believes we can experience over 150,000 million intimate contacts per year with just these little furry creatures. We may also receive much warmth or even adulation from our colleagues and subordinates at work.

3. We seek out *objects*. Though it is OK to start out our lives with a pacifier for comfort, we must eventually give it up. In place of this oral gratifier we often seek out cigarettes, food, chewing gum, warm coffee (symbolizing milk from the breast), warm beds with down-filled pillows, waterbeds (which rival mom's amniotic fluid), cars with luxurious upholstery, tight clothing, electronic massagers and chairs, vibrating dildos, and even inflatable rubber partners to mimic the forms of a live human embrace.

4. We may also indulge in *self-intimacy*. We may touch ourselves in a manner that comforts, stimulates, or reassures. When all else fails, we have our own bodies to hug, embrace, clasp, and fondle. We can soothe away our fears and loneliness. Though we might believe that our genitals are most frequently touched, ethologists have dis-covered that the head region is the most important area for receiv-ing these comforting touches and the hand is the most important organ for giving them. Over 650 different types of hand to head actions have been categorized! In descending order, the most com-mon hand to head self-intimacies are (1) jaw rest, (2) chin rest, (3)

hair clasp, (4) cheek rest, (5) mouth touch, and (6) temple rest. (Where is the mustache stroke—one of my favorites!)

If we are to find our way back from this parched land, we must turn to our partners for renewal—for real intimacy. The remainder of this chapter is designed to instruct you in this process. This journey begins with the "comfort hug." As you will note from the diagram, it is important to literally put yourself in your partner's hands for a while. There are four components to a comfort hug.

1. You comfortably rest your head on your partner's chest so that you can hear his or her heartbeat.

2. Your partner supports your head or shoulders with the palm of his or her hand.

3. As you lie on your side, you draw your knees up toward your chest in a fetal position.

4. As you lie facing your partner, you extend your arms around his or her waist for additional comfort.

I don't know why so many of us are afraid to hug. My clients like hugs, therapists like hugs, kids like hugs, Leo Buscaglia (author of *Love*) and Bernie Siegel (author of *Love, Medicine and Miracles*) like hugs. You'll like hugs too!

There is something wonderful about this simple posture, but one you may be inclined to avoid because it appears to be so infantile. We live so much of our lives trying to appear strong and decisive. What a relief it is to be vulnerable for a change, to let someone else nurture us. This is particularly true for us men. Let's not be so easily dissuaded. Real men like quiche and hugs.

Usually fifteen minutes is sufficient for a comfort hug, though many couples, once they overcome their initial resistance, continue for up to forty-five minutes or so. You will discover that your conversations will become increasingly more personal in this posture.

If you resist this position, consider resting your head on your partner's lap while you talk or watch TV. From this posture your partner can still stroke your hair, neck, or face. Feel free to instruct him or her. Remember, you are trying to renew emotional intimacy, which consists of light touches, hugs, eye contact, and personal communication. Try hard to get past your own barriers to intimacy. We all need much more than we are receiving!

Ten Principles You Should Know About Caring

Caring is not love, and yet it undergirds love. You cannot fall in love with someone who does not care, yet you can care for someone you do not love. When you choose to care for another, you are making an emotional commitment to that person. Such emotional intimacy can be achieved in so many ways, both physically and nonphysically. You are a person who deciphers symbols, you know how to detect when someone is emotionally reaching out to you. There are a number of principles to keep in mind.

   1. Act as if you care. Influencing your partner's belief that you care is one of the most important stepping stones in renewing your love. Loving couples convince one another that they are willing to do whatever is necessary to improve their relationship. You bolster this belief by acting "as if" you care. In the words of Shakespeare, "Assume the virtue—even if you have it not.... For use almost can change the stamp of nature."

   2. Actions speak louder than words. Beliefs about caring are based solely upon human behavior. What your partner does is infinitely more important than how compatible you think he or she is! Why wait for a personality change (they are hard to find!) when you can wake up tomorrow and begin to act differently.

   3. Think small. Caring behaviors that are bite-size, specific, and positive go just as far (maybe farther) than winning the Publisher's Clearinghouse Sweepstakes! Why wait to win it all once a year, or once in a lifetime, when you can get some goodies every day. Think small and get big payoffs immediately! Tell your partner you want a hug today rather than a trip to Hawaii tomorrow. Avoid generalities. Think small. Don't ask for more affection (in general) when you want a hug (in particular).

4. Accelerate, rather than decelerate. Caring is *never* demonstrated by decreasing negative behaviors. Caring is *always* demonstrated by increasing positive behaviors. Contrary to popular belief, your lover does not display caring when he or she stops throwing clothes on the floor, stops leaving the lights on, and stops calling you bad names. Caring is more accurately displayed when we increase desired behaviors like telephone calling, meal preparation, and eye contact instead.

5. Likes attract likes. You are far more likely to be strongly attracted to others who have acted toward you in a positive way. Common sense, as well as experimental research, suggests that you will begin to like your partner much more when he or she begins to act more positively toward you—and vice versa!

6. Learn to anticipate pleasure and meaning. Loving couples start off caring and go downhill from there. You eventually learn to suck in your belly, bite your tongue, grit your teeth, whiten your knuckles, mumble four-letter epithets under your breath, and take on the appearance of rigor mortis whenever your disenchantments are triggered. With the advent of caring behaviors, you can learn to reverse this degenerative process. You can learn to look forward to being in each other's warmth once again.

7. Something for something. Your happiness as a loving couple depends upon your ability to meet each other's reciprocal needs. There are no free rides, contrary to public opinion. Quid pro quo—something for something—sets the standard. Your partner will not want to care about your needs until he becomes convinced that you care about his needs.

8. Zap your partner with power. Your partner once had tremendous powers to light your fire! The dark ages of conflict have dampened her ability to please you. It is in your interest to help your partner reestablish this power. Teach her how to be more caring.

9. Lead the way. You must assume responsibility by taking the initiative in changing your own caring behaviors before changes can be expected in your partner. Angry power struggles have burned out both of you. Rather than engage in a prideful but senseless control struggle—to see who cares first—both of you can assume equal responsibility and equal initiative. When you feel like a victim, you are more inclined to wait for the antagonist to make amends. Don't wait! Initiate!

10. Caring is a two-way street. In order for battle-weary couples to change negative patterns, both partners must be willing to demonstrate caring behaviors simultaneously. Couples who "care" half-heartedly often watch one another with piercing eyes, as if each were defenseless prey being stalked by some carnivore. Remember, if one of you bails out, the other is sure to follow. Be mindful of this as you treat each other gently. In the words of songwriter Bob Dylan:

> I was burned out from exhaustion, buried in the hail,
> Poisoned in the bushes and blown out on the trail,
> Hunted like a crocodile, ravaged in the corn.
> "Come in," she said, "I'll give you shleter from the storm."

Prescriptive and Nonprescriptive Strategies for Caring

Richard Stuart and Robert Weiss have made significant contributions to our knowledge about couples therapy. Each of these authors has taken the best of behavioral psychology and applied it to the very murky world of marital interaction. This is no small feat, given the traditional analytic approach to the study of relationships within the social sciences. We have been content for years merely to conjecture about the motives and personalities of marriage partners. Yet it is often more efficient to spark *behavioral changes* that can alter a relationship in hours or days. This chapter will present two different approaches that will enhance your intimacy as a couple quickly and dramatically. The first approach is a "prescriptive" one that entails turning the word CARING into an acronym for specific caring behaviors that must be performed every day:

C = *Communication* - talking to one another, calling one another, telling what's on our mind, sharing our feelings.

A = *Affection* - touching one another, holding one another, buying special things for one another.

R = *Responsibility* - taking the lead in completing tasks and helping one another do projects.

I = *Interest In* - asking how the other feels, inquiring about the other's day.

N = *Noticing* - carefully observing and interpreting clues to each other's feelings, then discussing them with each other.

G = *Greeting* - physically acknowledging each other's presence following a separation due to work or sleep.

The prescriptive approach does not require much discussion with your partner before trying it out. Each of you will simply review the scripted behaviors, agree to implement the plan for one week, and off you go. Couples are often skeptical at first. How can anything so simple be effective? One or two days is often enough to settle these concerns once partners experience the good feelings that accompany emotional intimacy. I often hear couples say:

I feel closer to him than I have in years!

What a change! It's nice not to be fighting, but to be going out of our way for one another is wonderful. It makes me wonder how we could have lost it!

Other couples will tell me that they do these things anyway. Why is it necessary to formalize a process that already occurs so naturally? In such cases, I encourage you to feel good about what you already do, but simply to try a different format.

A second approach to renewed caring is a "nonprescriptive" approach that requires each of you to first tell your partner what feels good in each of twelve designated categories. Rather than assuming that an across-the-board script fits all, this approach individually tailors caring to meet the unique wants and desires of each partner. After all, there is no sense dispensing M&M's if your partner does not like chocolate!

Before describing each of these plans in more detail, let me dispel a common myth: "My partner is not a caring person!" Everyone is potentially a caring person who may have stopped caring because of resentment, hurt, and anger. There are four reasons why this may happen:

1. *Lovers don't know what to do.* Many people have not had enough experience being in caring relationships with others. Or they have not had suitable models to learn from. Or the special needs of a current partner rule out prior learning. A little knowledge, in these situations, will go a long way.

2. *Lovers don't do it correctly.* Even if your partner knows that you like to kiss or have your back rubbed, he or she may not know how to kiss or touch to your satisfaction. A little "show and tell" will be helpful here.

3. *Lovers may not want to do it.* The likely problem here is resentment. As you so well know, as long as the boulders of resentment are fueled by anger, little caring can be exchanged. In this case, you must go back one chapter and try again to express the venom. If repeated efforts fail, professional help is clearly warranted.

4. *Lovers forget to do it.* People often become distracted by other tasks and relationships. When this happens, you become convinced that your partner does not care. You want your lover to walk around the house thinking about your needs as much as you do! Since this is impossible, a gentle reminder will go a long way.

A Prescriptive Approach to Caring

Consider for a moment the benefits of being in a loving relationship. Your partner can renew your energy when it is depleted, bolster your ego when it is sagging, and arouse your libido when it is shriveling. When you feel belittled, anxious, alone, or sad, you want to know that a sanctuary exists where you can be cared for and where you can feel special. You want to know that someone special will take time to listen, to touch, to probe, and to help you feel better. These are benefits of being in a love relationship.

Most caring behaviors are naturally occurring phenomena that herald the beginning of any new relationship. Think back to your first few months as intimate partners. You greeted one another warmly. Smiles and hugs were commonplace. You often called each other. You talked more than you do now. You paid more attention to each other's needs. It makes sense to prescribe the same plan now, when you feel so distant from one another!

I offer you a simple prescription for caring. The prescription that follows is not a cure-all. Though your problems will not be solved by caring alone, your *desire* and *motivation* to solve problems will dramatically increase in one week if both of you make a heartfelt commitment to this plan. After all, these are things you did in the beginning of your relationship. Why not resurrect them now? First, let's recall the acronym:

C = *Communication*

A = *Affection*

R = *Responsibility*

I = *Interest In*

N = *Noticing*

G = *Greeting*

Implementing this plan is simple. Each of you will be in charge of caring three days a week. One of you will be Monday, Wednesday, and Friday. The other will be in charge on Tuesday, Thursday, and Saturday. As with the comfort hug, Sunday will be a day of rest and reflection or mutual sharing. On your day you must choose at least *one* of the following three choices in each CARING category. You must choose at least one.

There is only one way this plan can fail—if *you* refuse to do it. Even if your partner does not follow the plan, *you must follow the plan for the entire week*! Only then will you know for sure who is holding on to the boulders of resentment. You will be making a diagnosis of sorts. Even if you are ready to renew the relationship, you will now know whose foot is on the gas pedal and whose foot is on the brake!

Directions: Choose at least one of the following, from each category, for each day of caring.

Communication

1. Call your partner on the phone one time. Talk about anything you like.

2. Mail drop. Write your partner a short note that expresses your hope, excitement, and optimism about a more loving relationship. Drop it in the mail box during the day or leave it in some conspicuous place where it can be found.

3. Talk time. Take fifteen to thirty minutes to initiate a discussion with your partner. Take responsibility for the content. Talk about your day, your fears, your dreams. If you cannot think of anything, consider selecting one of the following phrases to elaborate:

> "I hope that ..."
> "If I took a risk with you, it would be ... "
> "I feel excited by your ... "
> "I particularly like ... "
> "I am afraid you might think that I ... "
> "I would like to give you ... "
> "If I were truly honest with you right now, I would like to talk about ... "
> "I try to please you by ... "
> "What I want more than anything in this relationship is ... "
> "I keep you from getting close to me by ... "

Affection

1. Create or select a card or flowers to give your partner.

2. Give your partner a fifteen-minute massage. (After five minutes, ask your partner what feels the best.)

3. Give one spontaneous hug sometime during the day.

Responsibility

1. Complete, or continue working on, one project that has been on your "should do" list for a while.

2. Reverse roles. Do one of your partner's tasks. For example, you might do the laundry, the gardening, the shopping, or take out the garbage.

3. Plan a full weekend's entertainment for the two of you. This might include making a reservation at your favorite restaurant.

Interest In

1. Ask your partner, "How are you feeling?" (Make sure you stick around for the answer!)

2. When you know that your partner has an important meeting or scheduled activity, ask how it went.

3. Ask your partner, "What are you doing that I can help with?"

Noticing

1. Say to your partner, "I notice that you are quiet this evening. Is there anything that you are thinking about?" (As long as you check out your hunches, it is good practice to make inferences about the nonverbal behavior of your partner. You are likely to do this anyway. At least now you are validating them. Make sure you allow your partner the freedom to modify these hunches, however.)

2. Say to your partner, "I notice that you are quiet this evening. Is there anything that you are *feeling*?"

3. Tell your partner about a time, earlier in the relationship, when you were so tuned in that you surmised correctly what he or she needed. For instance, you may have intuited correctly that your partner needed to see his or her family—a situation you promptly took care of at the time. Reinforce the notion that you really do tune in!

Greeting

1. Greet your partner in the morning with a hug in bed.

2. Greet your partner at the end of the day with a hug. (Do not read the paper, turn on the TV, or do anything else before giving this hug.)

3. Whenever you meet your partner in any room of the house, smile and look into his or her eyes.

I have seen the above prescription work wonders in a short time span, even for very troubled relationships. The key to success is simple. Most people tire of the anger and conflict that mark their daily lives. If a mutual agreement can be reached in which partners begin to anticipate caring, rather than war, a new belief becomes manifest: that your partner cares enough about you to do whatever is necessary to improve your relationship. This belief is critical if problem solving is to be successful in the next chapter.

A Nonprescriptive Approach to Caring

The nonprescriptive approach to caring consists of three phases: (1) creating a menu, (2) choosing, and (3) checking. These three C's enlist the involvement of both partners. One partner creates a "caring menu," the second partner chooses which items to give, and both partners check on their mutual progress.

The caring menu uses twelve areas of marital interaction developed by Robert Weiss and associates at the University of Oregon (1977). Many of the twelve areas were borrowed from a "happiness" scale originally developed by Nathan Azrin and associates in 1973. The twelve categories are as follows:

Appetitive	*Instrumental*	*By-products*
1. Companionship	7. Child care	11. Personal habits and appearance
2. Affection	8. Household management	12. Self and spouse independence
3. Consideration	9. Financial and decision making	
4. Sex	10. Employment and education	
5. Communication		
6. Coupling Activities		

Categories one through six consist of the "appetitive," or sought-after, goals which most intimate partners expect to receive from a loving relationship. Categories seven through ten relate to the "instrumental," or task-oriented, aspects of a loving relationship. The final two categories, called here "by-products," relate to secondary aspects of relatedness. You may assume that increasing satisfaction in the above categories, particularly one through six, will result in more pleasure and meaning for intimate partners. You might also note the similarity between categories one through six and those categories presented in the previous section on prescriptive approaches to caring.

The procedure is fairly straightforward. Each of you will review the following smorgasbord, or menu. Your purpose will be to select items, or equivalents, that you would like to receive from your partner at various times during the week. Your partner will then have the freedom to choose which of the smorgasbord items he or she prefers to give you each day. Finally, both of you will review your mutual satisfaction as you go along. Let's begin.

Directions: A list of five activities, within each of the twelve categories, will be offered to you below. You may tell your partner which two of the five activities you would enjoy experiencing during the upcoming week. If none of the five activities appeal to you, you may write in your own two items. Remember, you will be selecting items that you believe will make a difference in how you feel. You want to experience more closeness, and you must choose items that are likely to enhance this bonding.

Affection

1. Partner initiates a shower (or bath) with me.   _____

2. Partner holds my hand.   _____

3. Partner cuddles close to me in bed.   _____

4. Partner gives me a massage.   _____

5. Partner hugs me when we greet each other.   _____

6. _____   ____

7. _____   ____

Companionship

1. We listen to music on the stereo.   ____

2. We sit and read together.   ____

3. We prepare a meal together.   ____

4. We walk or exercise together.   ____

5. We go out for a nice meal together.   ____

6. _____   ____

7. _____   ____

Consideration

1. Partner thanks me for doing something.   ____

2. Partner says he or she loves me.   ____

3. Partner asks how my day was.   ____

4. Partner listens attentively to one of my problems.   ____

5. Partner complies in a friendly manner to one of my requests.   ____

6. _____   ____

7. _____   ____

Sex   .

1. Partner admires my body.   ____

2. Partner sets a mood for a sexual experience.   ____

3. Partner lets me know that he or she enjoyed our sexual experience.   ____

4. Partner engages in other sexual behaviors that I especially like.   ____

5. Partner reads something pornographic that I like.   ____

6. _____   ____

7. _____   ____

Communication Process

1. Partner initiates a good talk about our relationship.   ____

2. Partner talks about something troubling outside of our relationship. _____

3. Partner asks for my opinion. _____

4. Partner shows interest in what I am saying by agreeing or asking relevant questions. _____

5. Partner talks about a show we have seen. _____

6. _____ _____

7. _____ _____

Coupling Activities

1. Partner initiates an evening out with friends. _____

2. Partner invites a couple over to our house. _____

3. We write a letter to friends together. _____

4. Partner arranges for a visit to relatives. _____

5. Partner makes a good impression with my friends. _____

6. _____ _____

7. _____ _____

Child Care and Parenting

1. Partner initiates a discussion about the children. _____

2. Partner takes the children out to play. _____

3. Partner cares for the children when they are sick. _____

4. Partner disciplines the children. _____

5. Partner arranges for babysitting. _____

6. _____ _____

7. _____ _____

Household Management

1. Partner runs an errand for me. _____

2. Partner helps with shopping. _____

3. Partner helps with meal preparations. _____

4. Partner cleans or straightens up house. _____

5. Partner arranges for one household repair. _____

6. _____ _____

7. _____   _____

Financial Decision-Making

1. Partner works calmly on the budget.   _____
2. Partner balances the checkbook.   _____
3. Partner agrees on a purchase.   _____
4. Partner pays the bills—on time.   _____
5. Partner agrees to splurge on something.   _____
6. _____   _____
7. _____   _____

Employment-Education

1. Partner discusses future employment opportunities with me.   _____
2. Partner figures out new ways to meet job demands.   _____
3. Partner assists me in work I bring home.   _____
4. Partner reads something I write.   _____
5. Partner consults me about a decision.   _____
6. _____   _____
7. _____   _____

Personal Habits and Appearance

1. Partner uses a new cologne.   _____
2. Partner dresses nicely for me.   _____
3. Partner hangs his or her clothes in the closet.   _____
4. Partner buys a new outfit that will appeal to me.   _____
5. Partner takes a shower before being with me.   _____
6. _____   _____
7. _____   _____

Self and Partner Independence

1. Partner encourages me to schedule independent activities.   _____
2. Partner supports my going to a different show.   _____

3. Partner supports my spending an evening out without   _____
him or her.

4. Partner supports an independent activity of mine.   _____

5. Partner supports my having lunch with a friend of the   _____
opposite sex.

6. _____   _____

7. _____   _____

Once you have selected two items from each category, your partner has the freedom to choose only one item to respond to at some point during the week. Caring will be demonstrated when each of you has been able to respond to one of your partner's requests in each category during a seven-day span. A total of twelve caring behaviors will then be received by each of you.

Finally, you will arrange to have a debriefing at the end of the week. At this time, you will check to see if your response to any item can be improved upon. Before you begin, let me ask each of you to repeat these statements aloud:

1. I agree to give these gifts to you independent of your gifts to me, or any arguments we might have along the way.

2. I appreciate your gifts and will tell you so throughout the week.

3. I am invested in improving our love relationship and will not sabotage our progress by playing the "You don't know how to please me" game.

You are now ready to begin! Either the prescriptive or nonprescriptive approach to caring, when combined with a comfort hug, will renew the emotional intimacy in your love relationship. This is extremely important to do, for neither one of you will be motivated to make personal changes unless you believe that your partner truly cares about you. The next chapter will show you how to transform those long-held resentments into cherished solutions to your most embedded problems.

14

RENEW: Negotiate Problems

> In real love you want the other person's good,
> In romantic love you want the other person.
>
> Margaret Anderson

If you have come this far, you have come a long way. Your two accomplishments are very significant. First, in chapter 12, each of you has learned to forgive one another for wrongdoings in the past so that the two of you may pursue together the promise of your future. Second, in chapter 13, you have found a reservoir of caring, a framework for renewed intimacy, that will serve you well in the years ahead. Your relationship is probably feeling much better. Your anger may be diminished, but your resentments are not gone. In many ways, your work is just beginning. There are still nitty-gritty, long-term problems with which you must now cope.

Although you are touching more, you may still be concerned that your wife rarely undresses in front of you. You may consider her a "prude" or "frigid." Though you are talking more, you may still be perturbed that your husband's daily fund of knowledge comes only from work. You may consider him "shallow" or a "workaholic." And, although more time for intimacy occurs, you may be concerned that your thirteen-year-old daughter still sleeps in the "master" bedroom whenever storm clouds move into the county. You consider your wife "permissive" and "overprotective." Note how "thematic" these thoughts and feelings are.

In order to further renew your bond, you must now shift your focus from a "theme-oriented" perspective to a "problem-centered" perspective. As you have seen throughout this book, themes are negative, insidious indictments that only perpetuate anger and revenge. You must be willing to forego your assualt on your partner's character and personhood and choose instead a more specific focus on his or her behavior that troubles you.

These more embedded problems require creative coping strategies. Remember that coping is an active, continuing process that we all engage in to maximize our sense of well-being or to minimize our emotional distress. There are only three things we can do to cope with specific problems:

1. We can modify the problem situation that produces the emotional upset.

2. We can modify our perspectives about an upsetting experience, once it occurs, in order to minimize our emotional distress.

3. We can modify the emotional impact of an upsetting situation after it has occurred.

I devote this chapter to those techniques that will *modify the problem situation itself*. Chapters 15 and 16 will help you work through the other two coping strategies.

While resentments are usually expressed in *"decelerating"* terms, problems are always best modified in *"accelerating"* terms. Take a moment to appreciate this point. When you are angry at your partner, you want him or her to stop doing something that annoys you. Stop drinking! Stop watching TV! Stop coming home late! Stop demanding sex! Stop bitching! On and on you two go.

If you yell loud enough, you probably will get your way. Unfortunately, getting your own way reinforces your yelling even more. This is a short-term solution at best. Three long-term problems usually accompany this short-term solution.

First, couples reciprocate the negative treatment they receive from one another. Yelling begets yelling. Name calling begets name calling. Withdrawal begets withdrawal. Loss of sexual interest begets loss of sexual interest. Punishment begets punishment.

Second, couples learn to intensify their efforts to punish one another over time. A lover first protests, then gossips, and finally has a fling. Another lover first gets swallowed by the TV, then by Jack Daniels, and finally, in a frenzied display of disgust, squanders the last of the family's hard-won savings on a financial long shot.

Third, positive ways of relating which once occurred become blurred memories as a "make a demand/be spiteful" cycle wipes out all remaining vestiges of caring. Partners give less and less, out of spite, when a litany of endless demands are delivered. They talk less, play less, touch less, and accompany each other less. Can there be any doubt that this degenerative process produces ever-increasing anger, hurt, and resentment? Surely there must be a better way to change things!

Such decelerating efforts to cope do not remedy problems over the long term. These momentary respites only reinforce avoidance and detachment. Though problems may appear to be modified for the moment, as when the sharp shrill of anger subsides, the underlying source of anger will continue unless more positive approaches are discovered.

Clients have adamantly insisted that I am wrong about deceleration. One client recently accused me of "siding" with her husband because I did not agree with her that he should stop smoking pot.

Liz: How can you not advise Sam to get rid of the pot when the pot is the problem?

Dr. Bugen: I think your unmet needs and wants are the problem for you, not the pot.

Liz: What do my unmet needs have to do with Sam barricading himself in the back bedroom one hour each day *ignoring me*...

Dr. Bugen: Ah, do I detect an insight?

Liz: Yes, but, but...

Dr. Bugen: Liz, you just identifed one of *your* needs. You have a need for attention, which is quite normal in relationships. And you want Sam to spend more time with you each day. This is a very important need for you since we already know that Sam is reluctant to talk about his thoughts and feelings.

Liz soon realized that her needs for attention and communication were slighted each time Sam went into the bedroom and closed the door. It was necessary for Sam, in this relationship, to *increase* attention-giving and conversation time with Liz. If he also needed to *decrease* pot smoking to meet her needs and wants, so be it! But the pot smoking of itself was *not* the real issue.

In this chapter, I will outline a five-step approach to *acceleration* toward meeting our needs. But before I get started, I want to set forth the seven basic premises upon which I base my approach.

Seven Basic Premises for Problem Solving

Premise 1. *Disenchantment exists due to unmet needs.* You may need more inclusion, more control, or more affection. You may need more security or responsibility from your partner. Whatever these needs may be, you must be able to satisfy most of them, most of the time. Unfortunately, most people cannot identify their needs or the desired behaviors they want from their partners. We instead get angry at our partners for not "knowing" what we need. How should they know if we don't know?

Premise 2. *Problems (which are really unmet needs) are solved by accelerating positive behaviors, rather than decelerating negative behaviors.* Problems will not be solved until we begin doing *more* of what each other requests.

Premise 3. *Battles to decelerate unwanted behaviors only deplete existing caring resources.* Telling your partner to "stop coming home late" only invites an angry defense and blocks whatever flow of caring may still exist. You must learn how to motivate your partner to give you more of what you need, not less of what you *don't* need!

Premise 4. *Efforts to decelerate unwanted behaviors usually mask the real problems.* Couples may fight over jealousy, alcohol or drug abuse, or children. "Stop spending time with so and so," "Stop drinking," and "Stop obsessing over the children" are frequent complaints. Under all these complaints lie the real needs for more honest communication and more intimacy, the two most common needs expressed in therapy.

Premise 5. *Partners mirror each other's efforts, whether the focus is positive or negative.* We already know how reciprocal theme building and resentment sharing can be. The same is true of problem solving. Partners can actually delight in the renewal of their bond if the renewal is a simultaneously shared process. It is a simple truth that no problem in a relationship can be solved unless both partners share in the effort.

Premise 6. *The more specific you are about what you want, the more likely it is you will get what you want.* Research continues to show that improved outcomes result when partners are able to communicate their needs and wants clearly and directly.

Premise 7. *Your success in problem solving depends more on changing each other's behavior patterns than on changing each other's personalities.* Ad hominem attacks are not necessary. There is no human need that cannot be met, by any personality, if the will and commitment to meet that need exist. If the will to love exists, the know-how can be acquired.

SPIRO: A Five-Step Approach to Problem Solving

Do you remember the television program "Mission Impossible"? Each week we would be thrilled by an intrepid group of scientists who repeatedly faced incredible challenges in order to accomplish their espionage goals. Your mission, though not so thrilling, is just as important. You must find ways to identify and then meet your needs and wants. You will learn how to do so by following a tried-and-true model for problem solving called **SPIRO:**

> **S = Specificity** (What are you trying to accomplish?)
> **P = Performance** (What behavior is implied?)
> **I = Involvement** (Who is going to do what?)
> **R = Realism** (Can it be done?)
> **0 = Observability** (How successful have you been?)

There is nothing complicated about SPIRO. Its purpose can be understood simply if you keep the following in mind: there are no absolutes in life. Everything imaginable exists on a continuum. It is only when you are angry that you make extreme statements like:

> He *never* hugs me.
> She *never* is home on time.
> He *always* messes up our monthly finances.
> She *always* spends too much.

Each of these issues is more a matter of degree than absolute truth. In effect, they represent either high- or low-frequency behaviors that need to be modified. Each can be put on a continuum somewhere between one and one hundred. For instance, instead of saying "My partner never hugs me" or "He never puts money into the checking account on time," you might say "My partner hugs me only about 10 percent of the time I need one" or "The checking account is funded properly only 50 percent of the time."

Obviously, you will be happier when you are hugged closer to 70 or 80 percent of the time. These are imaginary points to be sure, but they represent direction. You don't need to get to 100 percent of the hugs you want to be happy. First of all, it is impossible for any partner to be so tuned in and responsive. Second, true happiness is found in the gray, not in the black and white extremes. Third, you don't need to walk around with a calculator to figure out when you are getting *more* hugs.

"Funding a checking account" is on a continuum which ranges from *never* putting money in on time to *always* putting money in on time. SPIRO allowed one of my clients to take her resentment theme that her husband was "irresponsible" regarding family finances and convert it into an important need: "I need to be able to depend on you." Better yet, she was able to *specify* a specific "want" using SPIRO:

Specificity: I want you to put $1000 in our checking account on a regular basis each month.

Performance: I want you to deposit the $1000 by the fifth of each month so that I have five days to pay the bills.

Involvement: If you put the money in by the fifth, I will then pay the bills as we agreed upon. If you don't make enough this month to fund the checking account, let's agree that you will then go to the savings account to supplement the shortfall.

Realism: I know you can be fiscally responsible because you have done your own business accounting for eleven years and have done our personal income taxes for seven years.

Observability: Let's agree to review this plan on a month-to-month basis. We'll find out if you need more time for your deposits and whether $1000 is enough to meet our expenses. I will also let you know how much I appreciate this with lots of smiles, hugs, and—if you're real responsible—your favorite cheesecake!

Now that you understand the SPIRO model in general, let's take a much closer look at each step.

SPIRO: *Specificity*

Your first step in problem solving will be to specify what you want. Begin by recalling your resentments. Resentments are always the starting point for problem solving. This may sound strange to you. Why would we dredge up old garbage at a time when we are trying to positively change our course? The answer is simple. The most direct way to understand what you want is to listen to what you most complain about!

Do the following. Using your resentment list from chapter 12, transform each *resentment* into a *need*, then a *want*. Let me first distinguish a need from a want:

- A *need* is an unmet, generalized drive within each of us that requires some course of action in order to be satisfied.
- A *want* specifies the course of action required to meet the need.

Remember that needs are *general*. Wants, on the other hand, are very, very *specific*. You might be used to thinking that wants are frivolous and not necessary. (For example, *I want* a new ten-speed bike, but I really don't *need* one.) Wants, as I refer to them, are *absolutely necessary* in order to meet your needs.

Take a look at your most important ten resentments and see if you can identify the needs and wants that they represent. (You can go back later to examine the others, if you like.)

RESENTMENTS	NEEDS	WANTS
1.		
2.		
3.		
4.		
5.		
6.		
7.		
8.		
9.		
10.		

Let's work together on one example. Do you remember Johanna's resentment list from chapter 12? Look back for a moment to refresh your memory. Let's see what happens when we transform her resentment list to needs and wants:

RESENTMENTS	NEEDS	WANTS
1. I resent you putting me down about my weight.	I need to be accepted as I am.	I want you to compliment me about my body.
2. I resent your condescending talk.	I need to be respected as an equal.	I want you to change your voice tone.
3. I resent your cutting me off in conversation.	I need to express what I am feeling.	I want you to let me finish my sentences.

4. I resent you putting my salary down as insignificant.

I need to have recognition for my contributions.

I want you to acknowledge my payment of the grocery and daycare bills.

5. I resent your playing "master" of the house.

I need to clarify my role.

I want joint decisions for all purchases above $200.

6. I resent quitting my job.

I need to have a professional identity.

I want to find a job as soon as we relocate.

7. I resent your presumption that I will follow you anywhere.

I need to have choices in our relationship.

I want you to ask me what my preferences are about relocation.

8. I resent your resenting my cleanliness.

I need to keep things neat and orderly.

I want you to help me clean the kitchen.

9. I resent your pushing me at your pace.

I need to be "laid back."

I want you to ask me about our social calendar prior to making plans.

10. I resent your using my mother as a confidant.

I need honesty in our relationship.

I want you to talk to me directly and not through others.

This exercise is not an easy task. In fact, it usually takes me up to a full hour just going over the first need and want for a couple. If you find yourself getting discouraged, please keep the following in mind:

- It is normal to have difficulty identifying a need from a pool of emotionally charged feelings and long-held resentments. Be patient and work together as a team to do this.
- Wants are usually expressed too vaguely. Most wants, when first stated, resemble general needs. Most people do not have much experience telling other adults what they want in specific terms.
- You may feel dejected or hopeless as you clarify your needs and wants. You may experience a sense of futility—a belief that you have told your partner these things before to no avail. Remember that you have never tried to mutually change at the same time in such specific ways.
- Finally, you may be discouraged to notice that attaining all your and your partner's wants requires a "giving in" from each of you. That is, you must now begin to *give* your partner more than you ever have in order to *get* more than you ever have. This is known as quid pro quo.

You must specify your wants in order to successfully work through the succeeding steps of SPIRO. Talking about your needs and wants may seem quite foreign to you. Given our egocentric natures, this is quite peculiar. Listen to children talk some time. They make it look easy. "I want to go to the movies." "I want popcorn." "I want that doll." "I want to spend the night at Stephen's house." Over time, as we become socialized, we seem to lose this capacity.

Sit down with your partner and review each other's lists. It is in your interest to help your partner distinguish his or her needs from wants in a helpful, pleasant manner. You will not be helpful or pleasant if you call your partner a "jerk" if he or she has not stated needs and wants clearly. Take turns reviewing items on each other's lists.

Here's the pattern you should follow: Present a need and want to your partner. Your partner then must simply state that he or she understands the need and want. If he or she *doesn't* understand, then attempt to state it more clearly. If two attempts to reach clarity are not successful, consider one of the following possibilities:

- Your resentment has not been clearly converted into a general need and a specific want. Try not to blame your partner for not understanding. Instead, try to restate your need and want a different way.
- Once you do understand his or her need, you may find yourself getting angry with your partner. You may feel that the need and want is unreasonable or you may be so angry that your own needs and wants have not been met that you cannot respond positively. Tell your partner that you are having a difficult time with this item and come back to it later.

SPIRO: Performance

Once you have stated your needs and wants clearly, it is time to specify what behaviors are required to reach your need goals. The key word here is *behavior*. Even well-stated wants will appear vague until performance behaviors are clearly stated. Let's look at Johanna's first five wants as an example:

1. I want you to compliment me about my body.
2. I want you to change your tone of voice.
3. I want you to let me finish my sentences.
4. I want you to acknowledge that my salary covers the grocery and daycare expenses.
5. I want joint decisions for all purchases above $200.

There was every reason to believe that Johanna would be much happier in her loving relationship if her partner would comply with her list of wants. But Phil needed more information. Let's look more closely at Johanna's first request: "I want you to compliment me about my body."

A maze of wrong turns awaited Phil if he assumed that he knew what to do here. We discovered this in therapy. He had complimented her on her eyes, hair, and breasts whenever he saw her dressed up during the day. In return he received more and more anger. Appearing quite exasperated, he wondered, "What the hell does Johanna want from me?"

Johanna finally had to "fess up." She really wanted Phil to be more verbally expressive during their love making. She described Phil as an "emotional masked man" during sex. Two or three of her lovers, prior to marriage, had been very verbal during lovemaking, which was a real turn-on for her. Phil's silence was particularly painful for her since he had been complaining about her weight. She found herself more and more distracted during sex, wondering if his silence meant he was disgusted with their intimacy in general and her body in particular.

A downward negative cycle had resulted for them. The more weight Johanna gained, the more repulsed her husband felt, and the more sexually disinterested and silent he became. This cycle had to be broken by both of them.

You can see how inextricably tied their resentments, as well as their needs, seem to be. One feeds the other. Both agreed that each would have to change in order to get their own needs met. Once this principle was understood, it was relatively easy to enable them to be quite specific about the respective "behaviors" each wanted from the other.

Johanna wanted:

- Phil to tell her during foreplay which of her touches, and other sensual acts, turned him on most fully.
- Phil to look her in the eyes and tell her how he felt during sex.

Phil wanted:

- Johanna to lose one pound each week for the next twelve weeks.
- Johanna to walk or run with him each Sunday morning, to be followed by a breakfast away from the kids.

Now it is your turn. Sitting down facing each other, take turns discussing each of your partner's wants. Begin as follows:

(*Partner's name*), you would be meeting my want for _____ if you would do the following:

I would like you to _____.
I would like you to _____.
I would like you to _____.

Remember to describe your behaviors very specifically in observable terms. One more example may help. Looking at Johanna's list above, let's review her desire to "find a job as soon as she relocates."

Phil, you would be meeting my desire to find a job if you would do the following:

1. I would like you to check with your personnel office to see if they have job listings throughout the city.

2. I would like you to review the want ads in the paper with me.

3. I would like you to go over my vocational tests one night next week.

It is important to understand that each want may require as many as ten specific behaviors from your partner in order to be satisfied. Please take your time with each want. Efforts to modify problems in love relationships require much patience and much clarity. Most of us are conditioned by the media and by illusions of love to expect too much, too easily. Be prepared to labor for what you most want. Relationship renewal requires this!

SPIRO: Involvement

Johanna's husband had been relocated to another city due to career advancement opportunities. As you know from her lists, she is resentful that she had to relinquish her job, salary, and social network. Who should have the say in such matters? How should a couple balance their respective needs to control such decisions? Or what about Johanna's current need to jointly decide on all purchases above $200? Will Phil agree with her on this?

Other examples of involvement issues are easy to find:

- The school nurse calls Mrs. Cline. Little Johnny is ill and needs to be picked up from school. Who should take off from work—Mrs. Cline or Mr. Cline?
- Mr. and Mrs. Copeland own a racehorse that has been doing quite well. Someone offers to buy the horse from them for a handsome profit. Mr. Copeland wants to sell immediately. Mrs. Copeland wants to hold on to the horse for both investment and emotional reasons. Who has the authority to make a decision here?

Every loving couple faces many problems where authority and control must be allocated. Mature love cannot be found unless couples discover how to mutually balance their respective needs for power and influence. Whether it is moving, rearing children, sex, or family finances, some equitable distribution of power must occur which allows a couple to function well. Each of these problem areas represent a potential quagmire where needs and wants will conflict. Even when partners are able to specify their own wants, as well as the needed performance behaviors, problems cannot be modified so long as the partners are struggling for control.

Though most couples would like to believe that their marriages are based upon egalitarian principles, most studies of power distribution within loving relationships suggest otherwise. Common findings are:

- Males have been found to have greater influence in marital decision making than females.

- Males seem to gain greater power as the number of children increases.
- Females seem to gain more power with employment.
- Many decisions that are made by males and females appear to be culturally based.

This last point is most interesting. Studies have shown that men seem to have more influence regarding decisions that involve buying cars, life insurance, and liquor. Females, on the other hand, seem to have more say when the decisions involve how much money to spend on food each week and how to handle housecleaning. Shared decision making has been found in such areas as who to invite over for dinner, the purchasing of household furnishings, and which bank to use.

Dr. Richard Stuart (1980) has done much to clarify this whole area of decision making, problem ownership, and partner involvement. Stuart believes that three possibilities exist for couples attempting to distribute control equitably:

1. Each partner may make certain decisions independently of one another, with little or no consultation with one another at any time.

2. All decisions may be made jointly with consensus always being the rule.

3. Some decisions might be made separately by each partner, some might be made in consultation with one's partner, and some might be made jointly.

Most couples find it impractical, if not impossible, to make many decisions jointly. For one thing, mutual decision making is very time-intensive. And who has that much time? Second, delegation for loving couples works well when there is healthy communication between the partners.

Stuart has develped a very effective technique that allows us to continue enhancing the power of SPIRO. Your wants list, reviewed earlier, assumes that you are delegating power to your partner to meet your needs and wants. This kind of power delegation assumes that you have the power to delegate and that your partner is willing to assume the responsibility which accompanies the delegation. Sometimes this will be true and sometimes it won't be true. It is important to find this out.

Following is a list of twenty problem areas that Stuart believes most couples make decisions about. Review each item carefully. You will note that most of the conflicts you have as a couple will fit into one of the twenty areas. After reviewing the list, add additional items that fit your relationship. (Add only those items that reflect important needs or wants for you. For instance, taking out the garbage is unlikely to be a major item.) Then review your expanded list of items. With the following categories in mind, rate each item in terms of who "should" have responsibility for making this kind of decision:

1. *Always* you.
2. You, *after* consulting with your partner.
3. Both share *equally.*
4. Your partner, *after* consulting with you.
5. *Always* your partner.

DECISION-MAKING PREFERENCES

Item	Category (1)	(2)	(3)	(4)	(5)
1. Where couple lives	—	—	—	—	—
2. What job you take	—	—	—	—	—
3. Hours you work	—	—	—	—	—
4. What job your partner takes	—	—	—	—	—
5. Hours your partner works	—	—	—	—	—
6. Number of children	—	—	—	—	—
7. Praising or punishing children	—	—	—	—	—
8. Amount of free time together	—	—	—	—	—
9. How to spend free time together	—	—	—	—	—
10. Amount of free time apart	—	—	—	—	—
11. How to spend free time apart	—	—	—	—	—
12. Which friends to see	—	—	—	—	—
13. When to see friends	—	—	—	—	—
14. Which relatives to see	—	—	—	—	—
15. When to see relatives	—	—	—	—	—
16. How to spend money	—	—	—	—	—
17. When and how to spend vacations	—	—	—	—	—
18. Which religion to follow	—	—	—	—	—
19. When to have sex	—	—	—	—	—
20. How to have sex	—	—	—	—	—
21.	—	—	—	—	—
22.	—	—	—	—	—
23.	—	—	—	—	—

It would be wonderful if each of you agreed upon your ratings for every item listed. Unfortunately, this is impossible. Disagreement and conflict are inevitable. Such disagreement must be settled in an equitable manner. If there are two or more disagreements over items, you might arrange a tradeoff. One of you might accept more responsibility for one behavior, while the other accepts more responsibility for another.

Please keep in mind that you are attempting to find solutions that benefit both of you. There is no sense in trying to "win" with any item. The inevitable control struggles that surface in any relationship must be handled in a collaborative manner that enhances your self-esteem as a couple. This point has been made by many writers. Thomas Gordon, for instance, describes a "no-lose method" for resolving conflicts in his *Parent Effectiveness Training*:

> Parent and child (or husband and wife) encounter a conflict-of-needs situation. The parent asks the child to participate with him in a joint search for some solution acceptable to both. One or both may offer possible solutions. They critically evaluate them and eventually make a decision on a final solution acceptable to both. No selling of the other is required after the solution has been selected, because both have already accepted it. No power is required to force compliance, because neither is resisting the decision. (Gordon 1970, 196)

Unless the two of you are able to find creative and equitable solutions to conflicting needs, you are likely to rekindle old resentments and anger. Remember that this is a time for "accelerating" your own behavioral repertoire!

SPIRO: Realism

Okay, now you know what you want. You can describe the necessary behaviors, and you and your partner are prepared to delegate authority needed to accomplish what you want. It is time to make sure that what you want can actually be done!

I recall working with a couple in which the husband had previously been married to a glorious athlete. She had been so gifted athletically that she had qualified for the Olympic trials some years before. The husband, who appeared to be an adrenalin-saturated jock himself, wanted his current wife to be a clone of his first wife. No matter how hard she tried to meet her husband's specific wants, this current spouse could not run fast enough, far enough, or often enough. The only thing this couple found waiting for them at the finish line was angry disenchantment.

Your wants must be realistic. Consider these three criteria for realism:

1. Are my partner and I both motivated to meet each other's needs and wants?
2. Have we removed all restraining forces that might block us from achieving our wants?
3. Have we selected wants that are bite-sized enough to accomplish?

At this point in your problem solving, you must believe that your partner is as motivated to reach desired needs and wants as you are. Otherwise, you would not have gotten this far! Nonetheless, couples often find that efforts to change are met with a variety of resisting, or restraining, forces. This is true with all decisions and wants in life. Consider the following case.

Harry wants to move into a larger three-bedroom home in a very desirable neighborhood in the city. His wife, Judith, has been arguing against such a move for over a year. She does the accounting in the family and believes the financial strain would be unbearable. Both are frustrated and weary of the debate. This problem combines the enchantment of finding a dream home in a dream neighborhood with the disenchantment of finding a spouse who does not share the dream. Harry used a process called "force field analysis" to check out how realistic he was and examine forces working for or against this decision. In force field analysis, "driving forces" are those forces which promote action, while "restraining forces" are those forces which inhibit an action. Here's what Harry's analysis looked like.

Driving Forces	Restraining Forces
In Myself	
1. I want a third bedroom as a study.	1. I sometimes overextend myself financially.
2. I feel cramped in our small master bedroom.	2. I know I am being influenced by two other friends who are moving "up" in the world.
3. I want a new home to landscape.	3. Once I get an idea into my head, I sometimes miss the larger issues.
In Others	
1. My mother has never liked the house we are in.	1. Judith is definitely against the idea from a financial perspective.
2. The realtor says that it is a good deal.	2. I know a couple who got divorced partly because the husband worked two jobs to pay the mortgage.
3. We will have another child one day who will need her own bedroom.	
In the Situation	
1. The school district is supposed to be great.	1. We have not had the extra money needed to pay off our MasterCard in six months.

2. I think larger interest payments will be a better tax write-off.

2. We will definitely have a cash flow problem.

3. I will be closer to work. There have been layoffs at my job during the past six months. My own job could be in some jeopardy.

3. Judith will be farther away from her job.

Harry decided not to buy the house at that time, once he analyzed the "driving" and "restraining" forces in the situation. Since the problem involved a want that proved to be unrealistic, the problem resolved itself once Harry modified his want. This process is also a good example of the coping strategy of taking direct action, since Harry was willing to engage in active problem solving in order to choose the best option for the entire family.

Once you have (1) affirmed your motivation to help one another and (2) reviewed the restraining forces that might block a good decision, you must also be certain that (3) your wants are stated in such a manner that they can realistically be achieved by your partner. You can usually be certain in those situations in which your partner had behaved in the past in the way you desire. For instance, "I want you to kiss me passionately as you did when we were courting."

However, when your partner must learn a new behavioral repertoire in order to satisfy your want, you must be realistic enough to think small and start small, knowing that an accumulation of small behaviors actually produces a profound change. An apt analogy for this process is in the way movies work.

What do you think would happen if you slowed a movie projector down to its slowest speed? Well, we all know that the smooth flow of scenes would soon become nothing more than a series of halting stills, each capturing some frozen particle of movement. We would be left with nothing more than one singular frame after another.

This phenomenon, known decades ago as *flicker fusion* to experimental psychologists, provided an opportunity to study human perception in well-controlled laboratory settings. By controlling the speed at which eidetic, or previously seen, images could be recognized, psychologists were better able to understand unconscious processes, such as repression. For our purposes, let us say that *all* continuous motion can be broken down into individual frames.

So, you are wondering, what does this flicker fusion stuff have to do with the direct action needed to problem solve? The prospect of any change seduces us into fantasies that have a full-length feature film quality to them. We want our husbands to be romantic figures, the Clark Gables of the world. We want our wives to be sexual goddesses or nurturing mother-earth symbols who greet us with unconditional love at the end of the day.

A key to realistic and successful problem solving is to think and act small. Take one frame at a time rather than expecting a complete production. Remember that every complete movie that mesmerizes us is nothing more than a compendium of individual frames. Through the process of flicker fusion, the frames appear to run together. The same is true of any small changes that we and others make. If we continue to add one small frame to another, we will soon have a complete picture that is more satisfying.

For this reason, your wants must be narrow in focus and your heart must be full of understanding. In your zeal to shape your partner's behavior, you must not overshoot his or her capacity to give you what you want—one frame at a time! This is where tolerance, the sixth element of mature, covenant love, has its most profound importance. What more gracious gift can we give one another than loving patience as we try on our new ways of relating?

Flicker fusion is a regular part of my therapy. If a wife believes that her husband does not care about her, we begin immediately with small frames of behaviors that provide new data for her. The husband might be asked to call his wife once a day, buy her a card during the week, give her a back massage, hug her upon greeting her, and tell her "You are special to me" at least once each day.

Each of these behaviors is a metaphor which conveys a larger and more embedded special message to the wife: "I care about you!" Eventually, these behaviors form a meaningful full-length film, featuring the husband and wife in starring roles.

If you or your partner are willing to change even one small frame of behavior, you will be well on your way to creating realistic wants that both of you will enjoy. This is particularly true when your partner is trying to learn brand new behaviors to satisfy your wants. Remember to start small!

SPIRO: Observability

Our final step of problem solving requires that you find some observable way to check on your progress. Without this final step you will never know if your "get-up-and-go" ever "got-up-and-went"! You both will need data. Feedback is most effective when it is:

- Immediate
- Specific
- Verbal or written

If you have wanted your husband to kiss you more passionately, it is wise to tell him after *each* kiss what you liked and what you would like even better! This is true of all desired wants. Don't hold back now. You have come too far for that. If you don't plan on giving immediate feedback, then make a date each evening to do so. The longest any loving couple should ever go without reviewing their progress together is one week.

Johanna's husband needs to know if he has behaved in the ways Johanna wants. For instance, has Phil

... become more emotionally and verbally expressive during lovemaking?
... changed his voice from a burly, condescending tone to a more laid-back, warm, accepting tone?
... let Johanna finish sentences?

Scientists have known the importance of valid and reliable data for centuries. Since each of you is a scientist in your own right, you must also collect observable data which either confirms or questions your basic hypothesis: that you can get your needs and wants satisfied in this relationship.

One last example will make this point clear. I recently worked with Margaret and Hal, whose principal problem concerned their child's lack of discipline. Each blamed the other for the problem. After working through their respective resentments and revitalizing their much-needed caring behaviors, both were ready to problem solve. Parenting, for many couples, is often a source of much marital strain. Not surprisingly, Margaret's and Hal's wants were quite similar.

In our efforts to love our children, we sometimes lose control of them. We may gradually realize that their behavior is out of control and we don't know how to work the brakes. At such times, we may frantically search for one haphazard means after another that might straighten them out. Inconsistency and anger are usually the only two consequences of these actions.

This frustrating state of affairs is a problem for both parents and child. Parents may feel helpless in managing their child's behavior, will probably spend too much time warning and then reprimanding their child, and may punish their child rather severely. Children, in turn, feel constantly pestered and are usually deprived of desired activities or things without warning. This often leads to more defiance, anger, hidden feelings, blaming, submission, and a need-to-win attitude—which usually only leads to defeat for both parents and child. Even if we parents win a skirmish or two, we are destined to lose the war!

Parents often confuse punishment with discipline. Very clear differences exist between the two. Consider the following distinctions described by psychiatrist William Glasser (1969):

Punishment	Discipline
Expresses the arbitrary power of an authority figure. May be painful and based on resentments.	Based on natural consequences which reflect rules that had been agreed upon.

Is imposed or done to someone. The punisher assumes responsibility.	Responsibility is assumed by the child. It comes from within.
Options are closed.	Options are kept open so the child can choose to improve behavior.
A teaching process which usually reinforces failure, a negative experience which emphasizes one-shot reprimands.	An active teaching process which involves close, sustained, personal involvement.
Open or concealed anger.	Friendly.
External controls.	Internal controls.
Breaks involvement.	Maintains involvement.

The solution to this dilemma is the *token economy* system of discipline described by behavioral psychologists. The token economy system is based on the assumption that children must understand two things in order to behave properly. First, they must know what is expected of them. Second, they must know what consequences will follow either compliance or noncompliance with these expectations. Pretty simple, isn't it? Not quite.

We parents usually screw it up. I am convinced that most children, because of their need to feel special, are looking for acceptance rather than angry rejection, which is what punishment feels like. We parents screw it up by not communicating our expectations clearly, by not consistently restating our expectations, and by not consistently providing natural consequences. Children need to know what "goodies" will come their way if they successfully comply and they need to know what goodies will *not* come their way if they don't comply. This is certainly true for us adults, isn't it? Our paychecks reflect this very nicely. Money is one of those nice "tokens," or natural consequences, which we earn by complying with certain expectations. We then trade in our money for the things we want. No work, no money, and no play.

A token economy is a perfect solution since it depends on problem solving as a coping strategy. If children can comply with parental expectations and parents can be firm and consistent with their expectations, both parents and children come out winners. Here's how it works:

- First, establish and share your expectations with the child verbally and on paper (pictures are a great idea for preschool children).
- Then decide what positive consequences will follow when each behavior is successfully achieved.
- Next, create and post a weekly chart that shows stars and checks for each expected behavior.
- Meet with the child daily to give the stars and other positive consequences.

- Determine how many stars are needed to earn a positive consequence. (All positive consequences are earned when the child successfully achieves a predetermined number of stars, happy faces, or checks.)

Margaret and Hal "wanted" their seven-year-old child, Lisa, to behave in the following manner:

Sit in the chair away from the TV.
Brush her teeth in the morning and before bed.
Put her toys away after playing with them.
Put her dirty clothes in the hamper.
Sit at the kitchen table until Mom and Dad finish eating.
Ask Mom or Dad before going into the pantry or refrigerator.
Feed the cat at night.

Lisa earned stars for doing each of these things. If she earned enough stars on a daily basis, she would earn "daily goodies." If she earned enough stars for the week, she would earn "weekly goodies." Here's what her stars would earn her:

Daily consequences
2 stars = daily bedtime story or extra sticker
3 stars = favorite drink that night
5 stars = get to do a workbook the next day
6 stars = eat her favorite dessert

Weekly consequences
21 stars (for the week) = bake a cake with Mom
28 stars (for the week) = a special art project
32 stars (for the week) = eat out at her favorite restaurant
36 stars (for the week) = go to the park or zoo

Here is what one week's star chart looked like for Lisa:

	S	M	T	W	Th	F	S
Sit in chair	X		X	X		X	
Brush teeth (a.m.)	X	X	X	X	X	X	
Brush teeth (p.m.)				X			
Put toys away	X		X			X	X
Put dirty clothes away			X		X	X	X
Stay at dinner table	X						X
Ask before going into pantry or refrigerator	X						
Feed the pussycat	X	X	X	X	X	X	X

The beauty of this system is that Lisa's parents did not remind her *one time* during the entire week. They let the natural consequences take over. They were consistent.

This particular week, Lisa earned her workbook and favorite dessert on two separate days. Her weekly total of 30 stars earned her a favorite art project, but not her favorite restaurant, the park, or the zoo. We note that Lisa was most compliant at doing something she enjoyed like feeding the cat. She soon learned that if she wanted to enjoy other goodies, she would also have to do things her parents expected as well.

This "observable" system worked well. A couple whose conflicts centered on their anguish over discipline soon learned to meet each other's needs. There was much more time for love when all family members compromised and learned to agree on the family rules. Each family member changed something about himself or herself in order to eliminate a problem situation that interfered with love and affection. Feedback was very observable, thanks to the star chart. It was immediate (nightly), specific (appropriate behaviors got stars), and both verbal and written (the star chart on the refrigerator door, along with each evening's discussion).

Obviously, loving couples will not go to this much effort to observe the attainment of *each* of their wants. However, if you do not find some way to capture your progress, it will escape from you! If you don't find ways to pat each other on the back, or other places, each of you will lose your enthusiasm. We need strokes, and lots of them, in order to sustain our efforts to change. It is sadly true that there are too few good words being shared throughout this land. But if they are to be heard at all, what better place than that place we call *home*?

This chapter has presented a five-step model for changing problems in our relationships. We learned that we must:

Specify what we are trying to accomplish.
Perform wanted behaviors needed to achieve our goals.
Involve both partners in the change process.
Realistically set attainable goals.
Observe and reinforce the changes.

All of this may seem overly structured and burdensome to you, particularly if you are burned out on your partner. You may not have the needed energy to think about your needs as hard as I am asking you to do. You may not have the capacity to forgive your partner for past mistakes in order to move on. You may lack visions for change which allow you to design a better future. Or, perhaps most tragically, you may have lost the "will to love," which is that undefinable, spiritual part of ourselves that truly unites us to one another.

If any of the above is true for you, the next chapter will help you find another perspective to cope. You will learn that the way you *think* about your problems may be the most important barrier to surmount. You will see that unless you learn to modify your attitudes about love, your patterns of loving will never change.

15

RENEW: Explore New Perspectives

True love is not a feeling by which we are overwhelmed. It is a
committed, thoughtful decision.

M. Scott Peck

Not all relationship problems can be negotiated. We often encounter
things in our lives that cannot be changed—a chronic illness, a lost job, a
child's death, a jail sentence, or a foreclosed homestead. Each demands a
different kind of coping in order to go on with our lives. The same is true
of love. There are limits on how much our partner's personality, body, or
lifestyle can be changed. Yet we often grasp and tear at our partners "as
if" we have no time or "as if" our survival somehow depends on their
changing.

When life is viewed as a journey, the urgency for change is diminished.
Since covenant love—perhaps our most meaningful life journey—requires time to "mature," we must learn to view its course in a curious and
patient manner. To do so we must implement the second coping strategy—gaining perspective. Unless we learn to modify our attitudes toward
love, our patterns of loving will never change. There are four reasons for
this:

**Reason 1: Life, because it is unpredictable and imperfect, can be
painful.** The part in each of us that cherishes stability is often overwhelmed when change (whether desired or undesired) occurs in the six
domains of life—love, work, leisure, health, finances, and spirituality. A
job promotion, change in health, or difference in spiritual growth will
impact a loving bond as well as other areas of our lives. In just a moment
you will have an opportunity to inventory change in your life and to
recognize how you can prioritize the domains of your life in response to
these changes.

Reason 2: Love, because it is a part of life, can be painful. The part
in each of us that yearns for completeness grasps for a partner who will
fulfill all that has ever been unfinished or wrong in decades of human

relationships. This endless search for a perfect union is futile. You will soon learn, through a series of exercises, that all is just fine in your love relationship—all is wonderfully pleasurable and meaningful, without being "perfect."

Reason 3: Unconsciously, we make our love relationships more painful than they need to be. This is true because our love lives are guided by deeply embedded beliefs and values that are largely unconscious. By reacquainting yourself with your "child of the past," you will see more clearly how your life scripts—created many years before—seriously impact your perspectives about love today.

Reason 4: Consciously, we make our love relationships more painful than they need to be. We often add to our pain by thinking about our partners in very critical and defensive ways. The way we think affects the way we feel. When we learn to identify these filter screens, we can move from a negative focus to a positive focus before the emotional carnage that usually occurs.

Let's take a closer look at each of these four perspectives.

Life Is Painful

Suffering is our existential destiny. Sören Kierkegaard has suggested that we are a union of opposites. We are "soulish and bodily, half angel and half beast, transcendent and immortal in spirit, yet possessed by an animal finiteness that is doomed" (Kierkegaard 1954). This is a frightening paradox that fills us with suffering: glorious immortality on the one hand, and bodily decay on the other. We struggle to find meaning as we face this polarity.

We attempt to reconcile this frightening paradox—this painful struggle to find meaning—by choosing instead to find perfection! The perfect job, the perfect child, the perfect house and car, and certainly the most perfect mate! We think, "If only I could find this perfection, I might suffer less." We search, we crave, and we protest life's imperfections, rather than experiencing inner peace as we view the full spectrum of life before us.

You might strive to perfect your roles of mother, wife, accountant, and community volunteer—that is, until you hit an unforeseen wall. A sick child sent home from school may require caretaking. A frustrated husband may demand more time and attention. Income tax season or a job promotion may require tedious weekend work. Or a community board that values your membership may announce a mandatory retreat the same weekend that your son is to play in a regional soccer tournament. Perfect balance becomes impossible under these circumstances.

The need to alleviate our existential pain is felt even more strongly during critical times of marital separation, divorce, bankruptcy, cancer, or death. In his autobiographical book on surviving the concentration camps of World War II, *Man's Search for Meaning*, Viktor Frankl states:

> ... man's search for meaning may arouse inner tension rather than equilibrium.... There is nothing in the world, I venture to say, that would so effectively help one to survive even the worst conditions, as the knowledge that there is a meaning to one's life. (Frankl 1963, 164)

Each of life's major entrances and exits—marriage versus divorce, childbirth versus death, employment versus unemployment—is accompanied by tremendous adjustments that require compromise. The meaning of our lives must always be viewed as an amalgam of compromises. Our wedding vows remind us of this. We find happiness "for richer or poorer, through sickness and health ..."

Claire and I discovered this struggle much too early in our married life. Within four short years of our small marriage ceremony, 80 percent of the wedding party had either died or been divorced. Tragically, the deaths included my mother and father and Claire's two brothers and her grandmother. We found it painfully hard to balance bliss with tragedy in those early days.

We each are a system. When one part of a system is changed, a necessary impact—often painful—is felt throughout the entire system. Let's find out more about ourselves as a system.

Life Change

The concept of life change has been studied extensively by mental health professionals since Adolf Meyer advocated the "life chart" in the 1930s. Many notable research scientists have made contributions to the field in the years that followed Dr. Meyer's work. One group, spearheaded by Thomas Holmes and Richard Rahe, devised an instrument called "The Social Readjustment Rating Scale" to study the relationship between life changes and physical illness.

As impactful as life events appear to be, there is growing concensus that no life event—be it divorce, job loss, or foreclosure—has a harmful impact unless the event is perceived as harmful or threatening by the person who is experiencing it. We can't understand how painful an event is until we understand its impact, individually, from the eyes of the beholder!

Take a few moments to complete the Life Events Scale.

Life Events Scale

Directions: To determine your life events score, place a check on the line *before* the numbered value if you have experienced the event during the past twelve months. Place a check on the line *after* the numbered value if you will experience the event during the next twelve months. Place a check on both lines if you have experienced (or will experience) the event twice during a twelve-month period.

Add up the total number of points corresponding to the life events. Remember to double the point value if an event is experienced twice.

		PAST		FUTURE
1.	Death of spouse	_____	100	_____
2.	Divorce	_____	73	_____
3.	Marital separation	_____	65	_____
4.	Jail term	_____	63	_____
5.	Death of a close family member (except spouse)	_____	63	_____
6.	Major personal injury or illness	_____	58	_____
7.	Marriage	_____	50	_____
8.	Fired at work	_____	47	_____
9.	Marital reconciliation	_____	45	_____
10.	Retirement	_____	45	_____
11.	Change in health of a family member (not self)	_____	44	_____
12.	Pregnancy	_____	40	_____
13.	Sex difficulties	_____	39	_____
14.	Gain of new family member	_____	39	_____
15.	Business readjustment	_____	39	_____
16.	Change in financial status	_____	38	_____
17.	Death of close friend	_____	37	_____
18.	Change to different occupation	_____	36	_____
19.	Change in number of arguments with spouse	_____	35	_____
20.	Mortgage or loan for major purchase	_____	31	_____
21.	Foreclosure of a loan	_____	30	_____
22.	Change in work responsibilities	_____	29	_____
23.	Son or daughter leaving home	_____	29	_____

24. Trouble with in-laws _____ 29 _____

25. Outstanding personal achievement _____ 28 _____

26. Spouse begins or stops working _____ 26 _____

27. Begin or end school _____ 26 _____

28. Change in living conditions _____ 25 _____

29. Change in personal habits (self or family) _____ 24 _____

30. Trouble with boss _____ 23 _____

31. Change in work hours or conditions _____ 20 _____

32. Change in residence _____ 20 _____

33. Change in schools _____ 20 _____

34. Change in recreation _____ 19 _____

35. Change in church activities _____ 19 _____

36. Change in social activities _____ 18 _____

37. Mortgage or loan for lesser purchase _____ 17 _____

38. Change in sleeping habits _____ 16 _____

39. Change in number of family get-togethers _____ 15 _____

40. Change in eating habits _____ 13 _____

41. Vacation _____ 13 _____

42. Christmas _____ 12 _____

43. Minor violations of the law _____ 11 _____

Once you have totaled your scores, decide which of the following ategories seems to fit you.

_____ 1. Mild life crisis (scores below 150 points)

_____ 2. Moderate life crisis (scores between 150-300 points)

_____ 3. Major life crisis (scores above 300 points)

You may have noticed how important perception is with the Life vents Scale. *The scale does not allow for subjective ratings of distress for any ven life event.* Mary may score 744 points and not report debilitating stress. John may have only 160 points and feel like he is falling apart.

Any single life event will have a different personal meaning to different people. You may sink into a major depression following your divorce, while your neighbor—after years of verbal abuse—may feel relieved.

Psychologists, psychiatrists, sociologists, and physicians are more and more convinced that people who remain free from emotional and physical illness in the face of major life changes appear to have psychological characteristics that help to insulate them from the effects of these experiences. We seem to be more hardy when we possess these factors. Perspective taking is one such factor.

Getting Perspective: Who Am I?

If life events can have such devastating effects upon our health and our love relationships, what can we do to insulate ourselves? How can we buffer ourselves against the inevitable pain? There is no better elixer, no more effective antidote, than the perspective we take toward hardship and pain. Isn't this the foundation for spirituality itself: a deep conviction, sometimes certain, often fleeting, that one is part of a larger whole?

This capacity to transcend our immediate circumstances allows us to find other vantage points to explore new perspectives. Painful life events are only one subset of a larger sampling of experiences. A depleted marriage, a suffocating job, or a collapsed business venture are smaller domains with in a much larger array of domains affecting the quality of our lives.

I can remember my despair in leaving the University of Texas after three frustrating years of academia. As I repositioned myself professionally in the months that followed, I had an opportunity to discover a new perspective toward life in my role as a father to Erik. I spent endless hours hugging, playing with, and feeding him. Even though my professional life was in flux, I realized that I could feel great about myself, my family, and my life by concentrating on other things that were going well.

This often is the case. Even when one part of our identity is wounded, we can notice other aspects of our life that are just fine. Life events do not merely happen to us—we actually shape them ourselves. Whether it be our choice to marry, buy a home, have a child, or move to Colorado—we are active in realigning the priorities in our lives.

You can actively maximize your pleasures and minimize your pain by posing one of the most important questions of your life: "Who am I?" The following process is intended to help you transcend your immediate pain by reviewing who you are and what you need. People often experience a variety of feelings and insights during this process. Having someone to share these reactions with is often helpful. I strongly recommend that a significant and trusted person be with you during this activity.

This activity is one part of a larger life-planning workshop that I was introduced to in 1975 as a graduate student at the University of Missouri/Columbia. I am indebted to the Colorado State University Counseling Center, which originally shared it with us at that time.

Directions: Take five slips of paper and write down five different roles that you are active in now.

I use the word "role" here not as a superficial part that you play in your life, but rather as a meaningful aspect of your identity. People have unique ways of thinking about themselves—*attributes* (strong-willed), *relationships* (married), *responsibilities* (a corporate manager), *beliefs* (a Christian), *strengths* (a prolific writer), or *liabilities* (a diabetic). Try to list those things that are really important to your sense of yourself—things that, if you lost them, would make a radical difference to your identity and the meaning of life for you.

After you have identified your five different roles, arrange them in order of their importance to you. Which ones could you live without and that would be the hardest to do without? Ask yourself: Have I taken on this role for someone else? What satisfaction does it bring? Is it worth it? If some items in your list are aspects of yourself that you dislike and would like to be rid of, they don't necessarily fall in the lower end of the rank order. *The question is how big an adjustment you would have to make if you lost that role.* Some aspects of yourself that you dislike might be very hard to give up! Number your slips from one to five, with one being the most important and five the least important.

Now look at your least important role—role number five. Take a couple of minutes to think of yourself without that role. Now, take that slip of paper and ball it up! Try to imagine, try to *feel*, how it would be if that role were no longer true for you. If "wife" or "husband" is one of the items, what would the loss of your spouse mean to you? What would you do? How would you feel? After you have stripped away your first role, do the same with each of the next four, stripping them away one at a time.

Finally, when you have taken away your last and most important role, take about five minutes to fantasize who you are without any of your roles. Be alone with yourself, mentally apart from others, and feel how it is to be just you without any roles. After five minutes or so, share your feelings and fantasies with the person sharing this activity with you.

It is possible that you now feel more free to visualize new, more meaningful roles for yourself. It is also possible that you feel emotionally vulnerable. Giving up long-held roles may leave a hole in your identity that troubles you. Let someone know about these feelings and be open to the possibilities for change.

One lovely example of this process in action was shared with me by a client, Rebecca, who was attempting to meet the demands of three major roles in her life: (1) university professor, (2) mother, and (3) wife. Though each of these roles was deeply gratifying, she had experienced tension and insomnia since adding the role of mother. Underlying her response to these demands was an honest recognition that she contributed to this distress with "a responsibility fetish" and difficulty in relaxing.

> I seem to maintain a conviction that I must earn or merit my selfhood and my relationships by virtue of my efforts or work. In other words,

unless I am trying, the whole world will collapse and I will not be worthy of love. I know this is irrational.

Rebecca's happiness was based largely upon accomplishments. Her work fetish, in which success was measured so completely by outcome, blinded Rebecca to the process of living—the journey itself! The "Who am I?" process helped Rebecca clarify and reframe her roles to achieve a much-needed balance in her life. Rebecca's responses to the exercise were as follows:

1. A scientist—probing, inquiring, figuring things out; an observer, investigator, and pioneer.

2. A loving person—caring for people, a lover to my husband, a mom to my child, a neighbor and friend, a teacher, a gardener who cares for the earth, a warm and sensual being.

3. A secular rabbi—a teacher, a person who honors and acknowledges, makes ceremony, witnesses in work the values of Judaism and civil rights.

4. An artist—making the world beautiful, in landscape, cooking, home, presents; appreciating wilderness, art, music, and dance.

5. A Russian peasant woman—strong, healthy, agile, and passionate, with a sturdy body.

Rebecca's delightful ability to conceptualize so abstractly allowed her to create these new roles that cut across the compartmentalized tasks of being a teacher, mother, and wife. By reviewing herself anew, in terms of values and sentiments, she was able to create a more balanced identity. Though she had to abandon her illusion of a "perfect" life, Rebecca also jettisoned much of her pain as well. In Rebecca's own words, "To have grace in a world of disharmony is a gift to oneself."

Love Is Painful

Love, because it is a part of life, is painful. It has to be! As diligently as we attempt to plan and control and predict, things go wrong. But it is not critical life events that demolish our idealized images of one another in love, it is disenchantment that topples our holy sanctuaries. We grow apart, into separateness, which is where we started in the first place. Later, when we discover mature, covenant love, we grow to appreciate what Erich Fromm has called our "unified separateness."

In the process of discovering unified separateness, however, we demolish one another. Why is imperfection so intolerable? Why are individual differences so unsavory? If the answer lay in our need for completion, you would think that our differences would be more highly valued than our sameness, and that our hope for salvation would depend on finding the *missing* pieces.

The truth is that we often do find the missing pieces we need—we just can't tolerate the other stuff that comes along with them. You find the decisive partner that you've been looking for, but then blow a gasket when you discover she visits her mother too much. Or you want a sensitive partner, but refuse to tolerate his weekend tennis league. We fall in love because we like what we are getting, and then we conclude that we shouldn't take anything that we don't like!

Part of our dilemma is explained by the existential opposites referred to earlier in this chapter. In the course of our short spans on earth, we are likely to realize only a limited degree of our true potential. This is true of love as well. As a result, each sentiment, each emotion, each need becomes an urgent imperative. Endless visions of romance and completeness on the one hand compete with imperfection and incompleteness on the other. There is a way out, though.

True love is less having and more giving, in a way that writer Charles Hampden-Turner (1982) has described as "creating mutual abundance." Shakespeare's Romeo epitomizes this quite well when he turns to Juliet and says, "The more I give you the more I have." If we are to diminish our suffering in love, we must see our lovers not as goblets filled to the rim, but rather as incomplete vessels needing to be filled by us! In the words of author John Powell (*Why Am I Afraid to Love?*):

> Whatever else can and should be said of love, it is quite evident that true love demands self-forgetfulness.... As long as he continues to concentrate on himself, his ability to love will always remain stunted and he will himself remain a perennial infant.... If, however, a person seeks not to receive love, but rather to give it, he will become loveable and he will most certainly be loved in the end. This is the immutable law under which we live: concern for ourself and convergence upon self can only isolate and induce an even deeper and more tortuous loneliness. (Powell 1967, p. 105)

Pleasure and Meaning: An Affirmation

Our need for love must always be understood within the context of our overall quality of life. We don't give and receive love in a vacuum, though it may seem that way during romantic love. The context of our real lives is very different however. Now we must come to terms with the demands of work, family, financial pressures, and day-to-day responsibilities. Within this context, pleasure and meaning often get lost. We may be unable or unwilling to shift to a positive perspective in these circumstances. Our relationships may seem devoid of any pleasure and meaning.

The life events of my own family had quite an impact. My father never completed his education as a pharmacist, which was a source of unceasing unhappiness for my mother. She wanted a "professional" and instead got the owner of a "low end" men's clothing store. Her nightmare became our entire family's nightmare as she spewed an endless stream of negativity.

Few escaped her onslaught. The level of conflict was so destructive that I often cried myself to sleep. (Decades later I discovered that my sister, Shelly, had done the same, only twenty feet away from me, neither of us knowing of each other's pain.)

As dysfunctional as their relationship was, my mother and dad never divorced. They died instead, physiologically compromised by their hostile assaults upon one another. My quest for a perspective—a more positive way of life—has clearly risen from their ashes. It is also not surprising that I became the "professional" that my mother always wanted. Early life scripts unconsciously steer us this way!

The activity that you are about to experience accomplishes three goals: (1) it requires that you notice the positive occurrences in your life, (2) it helps you distinguish between pleasure and meaning, and (3) it invites you to affirm your partner in the most positive ways.

The procedure is simple enough. Divide sheets of paper into three columns. Any time you like what you are feeling, thinking, or doing when you are with your partner, write down the circumstances surrounding this experience in column one.

In column two, classify the moment you've listed as "pleasure," "meaning," or "both." (You may want to review chapter 6 on the pursuit of happiness before doing this section.)

In column three, affirm your partner in some way. Think about each moment and write down your appreciation for what your partner has contributed to this moment. Begin each affirmation with the statement, "(Partner's name), I appreciate ..."

These affirmations highlight delightful things about your partner that embellished the pleasurable or meaningful moment in time. The format will look like this:

FEELING GOOD MOMENT	PLEASURE, MEANING, OR BOTH?	AFFIRMATION

Some examples from a recent client, Melinda, demonstrate the renewing power of affirmation. Melinda kept her record for an entire week, which is what I usually recommend for this exercise. Notice the brief time span of her recollections. It's really the "delicate moments" like these that support mature, covenant love—not the weeklong Carribean cruises or Colorado ski trips.

FEELING GOOD MOMENT	PLEASURE, MEANING, OR BOTH?	AFFIRMATION
Made love to Sam.	Pleasure and Meaning	Sam, I appreciate your sensuality.
Went to church with Sam.	Meaning	Sam, I appreciate how similar our values are.
Cooked dinner with Sam.	Pleasure	Sam, I appreciate you as a companion.
Sam and I went out for dinner.	Pleasure and Meaning	Sam, I appreciate our lifestyle together.
Sam's dad told him how lucky he was to have me.	Meaning	Sam, I appreciate being so accepted by your family.
Sam and I were complimented on our appearance.	Meaning	Sam, I appreciate how handsome you are.

You would never know how far Melinda and Sam have come without understanding the venomous themes that existed when they initiated therapy. She considered Sam an "ogre," a "mama's boy," and "aloof." Clearly, he and his family have found a way back into Melinda's heart. These affirmations are practically impossible when the boulders of resentment are present. When this kind of focused experience is done regularly in a relationship, it helps keep the positive elements in perspective. If you find yourselves stuck in negativity, this exercise will also help to untangle your negative pattern.

Since perception and cognition are both selective processes, it is Melinda's choice to focus on either a *moment* that feels good or a *disenchantment theme* which feels bad. Her choice, as well as ours, is to live in the present, with its abundance of "delicate moments," or to live in a past where hurt, anger, and resentment smother the joy of life. At this stage in therapy, Melinda had made her choice. During a week filled with excessive demands, a business trip for Sam, and a sick child, Melinda still managed to notice and to treasure these very special moments.

If you can admit to yourself that you are preoccupied with negativity, I encourage you to try this technique. Take time to notice the smile you get from a co-worker, the excitement you have created in your child, or the barbecue dinner that you and your husband hosted for friends. Affirm the positive by documenting "feeling good" moments with each person with whom you are disenchanted.

Unconsciously, We Make Love More Painful

Our love lives are guided by deeply held, tacit beliefs that are largely unconscious. These tacit assumptions always reflect our most intense personal relationships of the past—whether they be childhood bonds that echo early family life or romantic bonds that reflect our first flights into the wondrous world of enchantment and disenchantment. Often these tacit beliefs will create pain many years after the original wound. Consider the following beliefs:

1. You believe that your current wife will be unfaithful to you because your first wife was.

2. You believe that your husband will leave you because your alcoholic father abandoned the family when you were a child.

3. You believe that you are unlovable because you were unceremoniously passed from one adoption home to another during your childhood.

4. You tense with anger when ignored as an adult because your parents were so aloof during your childhood.

The original wounds are painful enough, but then we add to our suffering by developing implicit notions about ourselves, others, and the world around us. These attitudes are largely unconscious in that we respond "automatically" or "reflexively" to triggering events. (The concept of unconscious, as I am using it, refers to these automatic response patterns, rather than to a Freudian view of uncontrollable and overpowering forces that are largely instinctual and species-specific.) Psychiatrist Hugh Missildine clarifies one aspect of this point very well:

> Somewhere, sometime, you were a child. This is one of the great obvious, seemingly meaningless and forgotten common denominators of adult life. Yet the fact that you were once a child has an important bearing on your life today. In trying to be adults, we mistakenly try to ignore our lives as children, discount our childhood and omit it in our considerations of ourselves and others. This is a basic cause of much distress and unhappiness. It is a way of mistreating ourselves. (Missildine 1963, 1)

Missildine describes the impact of our wounded "inner child" on our lives as adults quite well. However, it is important to note that these wounds can be incurred much later than childhood. A humiliating and deflating relationship in your twenties can have as serious an effect on your future bonds as the wounds of your childhood have.

Further, these tacit beliefs of adulthood—which leave their imprint on our relationships forever—are born not only from childhood wounds but also from childhood fairy tales, myths, and play. Fairy tales and myths encapsulate human experience. They represent vast sums of knowledge that help people perceive, organize, evaluate, and respond to human experience. Somehow all of the joys, fears, excitement, and tragedies of life are entwined in these stories.

Myths are to adults what fairy tales are to children. They magnify the milestones of human life from birth to marriage to death by giving us a portrait of how identity unfolds. The hero is usually born miraculously, is recognized for superior performance or accomplishment, obtains great notoriety and power, and then often loses it all. Often the perfection that he quests for is revealed to be a false goal, or merely a waystation on the road to some deeper meaning. The recovery of the Holy Grail marks the beginning of the end of King Arthur's court. Oedipus' pride drives him to discover the truth of his identity, and the shame leads him to blind himself and go forth into exile for the rest of his days.

What perspectives do we learn here? For one thing, Oedipus tells us that as human beings we are at times ignorant of our "true" natures—lacking insight as to who we are and what we are doing. (How can we trust our choice of loving partners after hearing about poor old Oedipus?) We also learn that it is painful to sometimes look too closely. (So much for self-help books!) Finally, we see how life events can be exaggerated into tragic extremes. It is important to remember that problems of living are always dimensional, rather than absolute.

While fairy tales and myths represent the "truths" of the past, *play* represents the "truth" of the future. I can remember how my daughter, Jessica, nurtured her future vision of motherhood. One day, years ago, our family was running late in the morning. (Things haven't changed!) Jessica, however, was attempting to feed her dolls and stuffed animals. Oblivious to our needs, she insisted that Claire, Erik, and I sit down and be fed some breakfast cereal and milk.

We took a few token bites and then hastened to grab lunch boxes, school bags, and a few pocket toys. With tears welling in her eyes, Jessica yelled, "I want a new family—a family that knows how to play with little girls!" My daughter found disenchantment in that moment. We had shattered her illusion of a loving and well-fed family. But we are an adaptive species, and illusions are often quite resilient. As the car backed down the driveway, Jessica asked me if I thought that her doll had gained too much weight. Without waiting for a response, she continued, "Perhaps tomorrow I should feed her less!"

Jessica did not abandon her need to be nurturing—she simply modified it. This is exactly what mature, covenant love requires. We must be willing to shift our perspectives and make mid-course corrections as our relationships and needs change. To accomplish these shifts in perspective, we must understand our most implicit and tacit assumptions about life and love.

My Hero

I am indebted to my dear friend Chuck Meyer for introducing me to this exercise, which most people consider delightful fun yet surprisingly revealing.

Do you often wonder why you keep doing the same things day in and day out, yet receive little satisfaction in doing so? Does your love life or work life seem "scripted" in some way? Remember Pavlov's dogs? They learned to salivate when they heard a bell ring prior to being fed. Such conditioned responses may govern your life as well. Without thinking about it, you respond to your partner in conditioned ways that may only perpetuate needless suffering. The following exercise will help you understand why this is so.

Directions: Take a few moments to think of someone alive or dead, real or imagined, who has influenced your life in a very meaningful way. Make this a person whom you revere, who has or had qualities that you admire. You may think of more than one person, but choose only one. Write that person's name below and continue to answer the questions that follow.

My Hero _____

1. A description of my hero:

2. My hero's best qualities:

3. My hero's least noteworthy qualities:

4. My hero's motto:

5. His or her marital status:

6. His or her age at death:

7. What is written on my hero's tombstone:

8. A regret of my hero:

9. What might be written on the *front* of a T-shirt my hero would wear:

10. What might be written on the *back* of a T-shirt my hero would wear:

11. A wish my hero had:

12. Unfinished business my hero never completed:

13. Something my hero would do over again:

14. A quality which is *both* a strength and weakness:

15. Advice my hero would give me:

16. Who is my hero's hero:

This exercise tells us more about ourselves than it does about our heroes! Our heroes occupy their lofty positions because they represent important dimensions that we value. We identify with them. We aspire to be like them in many instances. The most noteworthy feature of all heroes is that they represent important needs of the worshipper. We are actually projecting ourselves onto the very characters we cherish. Isn't this the basis for romantic love?

A recent client named Gloria had been obsessed with the attainment of extraordinary work goals. At the time she began therapy, she expected to make between $100,000 to $300,000 a year in sales. She owned her own business, had few employees, and believed that with enough discipline she could continue to be successful without needing anyone. She was twice divorced, had two children, and was living with a man she considered more an adversary than friend. She also had an ulcer, hemorrhoids, chronic headaches, and a history of depression that had resulted in hospitalization some years before.

Gloria feared dependency, resisted external influence, and carefully protected her autonomy. She displayed a brash willingness to risk harm and responded with rebellion to threats and punitive action. She was envious of other people, wary of their motives, and easily provoked to irritability or anger. Family members and friends often accused her of having a chip-on-the-shoulder attitude, which she of course denied.

Gloria's hero was Jane Fonda. She described her hero as "an activist who turned her life around. She used to be bulimic and was into drugs. She learned to take her strong convictions and channel them." The exercise revealed some other pertinent observations:

Best quality: Jane Fonda was her own person. She set goals and went after them. She will make a decision and not vary from its course.

Least favorite quality: Her anger and temper.

Motto: Fight to the end. If it is to be, it is up to me!

Regret: I believe Jane Fonda's mother committed suicide and that she may have wondered if she did everything possible to help her.

Unfinished business: There is always a cause, always a goal to seek, always a mountain to climb. If you think your work is finished, you are dead wrong.

Strength which is also a weakness: Her rebellion. This may have worked well against the establishment during the Vietnam War, but it was a hindrance in unifying a solid coalition needed to deal with ongoing challenges. She never learned how to develop relationships that would endure.

Advice: Don't let criticism bother you.

Hero's hero: Her father, Henry Fonda.

Once Gloria saw how she was trying to emulate her distorted image of her hero, she could understand why she had remained stuck for so many years. She was able to see that her obsession with work symbolized autonomy and a solitary, fighting spirit. As long as she could continue to make $200,000 a year, she would be able to validate her illusion of not needing anyone.

Gloria garnered other important insights as well. She had not seen her own father very often in the ten years prior to his death one year before. Afraid to mourn this loss of contact, she buried herself in her work instead. But Gloria did learn to grieve and soon understood that her rebellion had truly blinded her to the wonderful qualities her current beau possessed. He wasn't the enemy after all! With her focus on love now renewed, Gloria was eventually able to design a new T-shirt front that beamed, "I am fit for life!"

Inner Dialogue

A second way to understand our unconscious attitudes is commonly referred to as a "dialogue technique." This method encourages a process of self-talk. Keeping a journal is perhaps the most usual way to self-talk. When we keep a journal, we experience the power of emptying our thoughts and feelings onto a blank piece of paper. The more stream of consciousness, the better. By allowing a steady stream to pour out, we eventually speak to our unconscious self—that part of ourselves where tacit assumptions and beliefs reside.

Robert Johnson's 1986 book, *Inner Work*, is an excellent example of this technique in action. The idea is to identify two aspects of the self that need to talk to one another. These "sub-selves" may reflect important personal constructs such as those you learned about in chapter 5. You may want to have your "pure and innocent" sub-self talk to your "sexy and wild" sub-self, for instance.

To facilitate your dialogue, you can try expressing one sub-self through printing and another through cursive. Or if you use a typewriter, you can allow one sub-self to be lower case and another sub-self to be upper case. Don't worry about correct punctuation, spelling, or grammar in either case, since this will only slow down your process of free association—of getting to your unconscious voice.

A client named Miriam used this technique to work through some blocks concerning her sexuality in her marriage. She considered herself "bad" on the one hand (lower case) as well as "SENSUAL" on the other (UPPER CASE). Let me share a portion of her dialogue work with you.

> I'm going to the wall—it's tall and gray and black, like the obelisk in 2001. who built this wall? i've been coming up against it lately—last week in bugen's office i felt myself scratching at it—even clawing to climb over it but i couldn't make any progress. YOU'RE AFRAID TO FIND OUT ABOUT ME, YOU'RE AFRAID THAT IT'LL HURT AGAIN LIKE OTHER THINGS HAVE BEEN HURTING YOU LATELY. I'M NOT SURE YOU WANT TO KNOW ABOUT ME. you're right. i am afraid and scared but i've got to find out about you. i can't make any

progress until i can understand you. THERE IS A DOOR YOU KNOW—IT'S IN THE MIDDLE. yes i know but i have to have feelings for that, i have to have touch. TOUCH YOURSELF, GIVE YOURSELF WHAT YOU ALWAYS WANT OTHERS TO GIVE YOU. DO IT NOW. BE YOUR OWN FRIEND. GO THERE FOR YOURSELF. FEEL YOUR HAIR, SMELL IT. YOU'VE GOT TO LOVE YOURSELF UNCONDITIONALLY AND JEALOUSLY PROTECT YOURSELF. YOU'VE GOT TO WALK IN HOLDING HANDS WITH YOUR FRIEND. but that's really hard for me to do. HOLD ON TO YOURSELF. how? RELAX, ENJOY, SMILE. FEEL THE WARMTH INSIDE. i feel it but it feels fleeting. i'm afraid i'll lose it. YOU DON'T GIVE YOURSELF ENOUGH CREDIT. IF YOU WANT TO HOLD ON TO YOURSELF, YOU CAN. CREATE AN IMAGE OF YOURSELF BEING A FRIEND TO YOURSELF. REVEL IN IT—FEEL IT… . i want to argue with these instructions. YOU HAVE NOT FELT LIKE A FRIEND OF YOURSELF SINCE YOU WERE VERY YOUNG, TWO OR THREE YEARS OLD. YOU FELT LOVED AND NOURISHED AND WORTHY AS A BABY BUT WHEN YOU STARTED TALKING AND EXERTING YOUR INDEPENDENCE YOU WERE QUASHED … . what do you mean? … YOUR SENSE OF SELF WAS THINKING, VERY PRACTICAL… NOT WARM AND LOVING … . i don't want you to be with me but i keep reacting by pushing you down, even now. can you help me keep you with me? LOOK AT YOUR RINGS. YOU'RE THE DIAMONDS IN THE MIDDLE. no. YES YOU ARE. ONE OF THE GUARDS IS TOM, THE ONE ON THE OUTSIDE. THE OTHER ONE IS ME—YOU REST AGAINST ME. THE THREE OF US HAVE TO BE TOGETHER TO BE BALANCED. LOOK AT HOW MANY YEARS YOU HAVE BEEN UNBALANCED, SINCE YOU WERE TWO YEARS OLD. IT'S NO WONDER THAT IT'S HARD FOR YOU TO ACCEPT AND EMBRACE ME—BUT I AM A PART OF YOU. YOU HAVE TO TAKE ME WITH YOU TO GET ANY FURTHER ON THIS JOURNEY.

Miriam was able to integrate her "SENSUAL" side into her own identity as well as into her marriage to Tom. She learned that emotional and sexual abuse early in one's life do not necessarily result in a predestined life script. Miriam found her inner beauty and power in a place she called THE MEADOW. Through inner dialogue, you will be able to find yours as well.

Consciously, We Make Love More Painful

One of President John F. Kennedy's favorite expressions was "Some people look at things the way they are and ask why? Other people look at things as they might be and ask why not?" This is the power of positive thinking. It is also the power of conscious love.

Positive thinking and conscious love both share a common ingredient —vision. We must be able to transcend the immediate moment in time in order to cherish a more loving partner, a more luxurious lifestyle, or a healthy growing family. We have a tendency to hold on to moments of anguish as if they define our reality. This is foolish, since moments never define reality—only we do.

We always have a choice as to how we view our partner's behavior, our overall happiness, or the world at large. We have the power to preserve our resentments and themes about one another—to live our lives in conflict—or to free ourselves to love more fully. *We can love more fully only if we create a vision to do so.*

Visions are never cheap. We must invest much of ourselves in the process and put ourselves on the line. We must demonstrate a courage to see a better way of life at times when others—even our partners—refuse to do so. During the first stages of renewal, this can often be a lonely vigil. There are no guarantees for success, but there is *always* a guarantee for failure—the absence of vision!

We add to our pain or suffering in relationships by consciously obsessing about the inevitable frustrations and disappointments of love. We construct negative themes about one another as though these themes were monuments. When we think bad *thoughts* about one another, we will inevitably feel bad *feelings* about one another. Chapters 8 (on getting stuck) and 12 (on release resentments) have explored this notion at some length.

Negativity is a symptom of blindness. When we obsess about another person in an angry, vindictive manner, we have lost our vision. I am reminded of George Bernard Shaw's words:

Better keep yourself clean and bright;
you are the window through which
you must see the world.

But let's rejoice. You have come such a long way! You have managed to express your resentments, to demonstrate caring, and to specify your most vital needs and wants. You are almost there. You have regained much of your vision for a more loving relationship. You now see each other more truthfully, without pretense, without disguise. You have created a covenant—a vision—of what can be!

This positive focus requires that we diffuse the situations that disappoint us or frustrate us *before* they climax into thematic explosions. This conscious process is a hallmark of mature, covenant love (see chapter 3) and reflects our commitment to these eight elements.

1. A mutual balance of met needs. Both partners have needs of equal importance, they both understand and accept these needs, and they both are willing to meet these needs as often as possible.

2. Other-directedness. Each partner experiences meaning and pleasure from the other partner fulfilling his or her *own* needs—and actively helps him or her to fulfill those needs.

3. Realistic values and expectations. Both partners jettison stereo-types about men and women, husbands and wives, love and marriage. They make their assumptions explicit to each other and avoid extreme points of view.

4. Tolerance. Mature loving partners do not expect to find perfection in each other. Instead, they accept each other's attitudes, beliefs, and actions. They discuss problems on the situational level rather than on the level of personal indictment.

5. Yearning to be known. Both partners value the safe harbor of their relationship, the place where they can put aside their societal masks and truly be themselves. Mature relationships nurture this process of becoming fully known.

6. Freedom to express all emotions. Both partners encourage each other to express all their feelings, including sadness, remorse, anger, and hurt. And each is open about expressing these feelings.

7. Separate identities. The partners recognize that each has a unique set of personality traits, skills, and aspirations. They give each other freedom to explore their separate interests and friends without judgment or undue restriction.

8. Transcendence of two separate selves into one identity. Both partners in healthy relationships enjoy celebrating their "we-ness" through time spent together in shared activities, creating a shared identity. And with this shared identity comes a joint sense of worth, a shared feeling of self-esteem as a couple that goes beyond individual self-esteem.

These are your tools for conscious, mature love. Any situation that threatens our love for one another, no matter how frustrating, can be viewed more positively with the aid of these tools. Let me provide a personal example.

Early parenthood, as well as Claire's professional travel, were an admixture that created much disenchantment for me. I often felt over-whelmed when she attended professional meetings. For one thing, single parenthood—even just for four days—caused a great deal of stress. During my most pessimistic moments, I believed the only way to manage this stress was to assume that I had no rights and no needs and no time for myself as I devoted myself full-time to the kids. This was too high a price to pay! I also missed Claire as a companion. My needs for attention and affection were such that her absence did not make my heart grow fonder! I wanted to talk with her, hold her, and share family time with her.

I had many negative thoughts during those days of disenchantment, thoughts I am embarrassed to admit.

- If Claire really cared about me and the kids, she would cut her trip from four days to three days.

- I am pissed that she is having so much fun in Washington while I am conducting a fire drill here in Austin.
- Claire only called twice during her entire trip. That proves she never even thinks about us. What a selfish ingrate!

These were painful thoughts that only infuriated me further. I fell prey to obstructive themes like "Claire is selfish" or "Claire is uncaring." In truth, I was the one who was selfish and uncaring.

As I have matured over the years, I have learned to view these trips in a very different way, using the eight elements of mature, covenant love as a guide.

1. *A mutual balance of met needs.* Claire's professional world is as important to her as my professional world is to me. Conventions offer both of us an opportunity to learn and grow.

2. *Other-directedness.* I am truly proud of her. She is appreciated nationally for both her writing in the field of deaf education and for her leadership as President of CAID. I love seeing her honored.

3. *Realistic values and expectations.* There are times in every relationship when one partner carries more of the load than the other.

4. *Tolerance.* She only called twice because she got caught up with friends, colleagues, and organizational activities. When that happens to me, it certainly does not mean that I don't care!

5. *Yearning to be known.* The more I told Claire about my frustrations and nasty thoughts, the better we were able to plan together, as a team, for these interludes. We wouldn't have lined up resources to help me with the kids had I not been honest about my needs.

6. *Freedom to express all emotions.* I know I was often rude and sarcastic on the phone when Claire did call home. As much as I feel I was a louse in those moments, it is good to know that I am accepted by Claire even when I act like a jerk.

7. *Separate identities.* Claire has special skills and talents as a deaf educator and administrator. I don't think our relationship would be worth very much if she did not have opportunities to express these abilities.

8. *Transcendence of two separate selves into one identity.* We are wonderful role models for Erik and Jessica. In addition to being warm and loving, we introduce the kids to important problems and issues in society. We are truly special parents to be teaching the values we teach.

The above example is nothing more than an inner dialogue. Consciously, I am talking myself out of negativity and into positive, mature love. Using the standard triple-column technique, you will be able to talk yourself out of your negative reactions to situations quickly and lovingly.

The procedure is quite simple. In column one, describe the situation that upsets you. In column two, document the negative thought that underlies your disenchantment. Finally, in column three, choose one or more elements of covenant love that you can use to reconstruct your negative thought into a more loving, positive point of view. In parentheses, indicate which elements you used. You will find yourself becoming more positive just by deciding which element to use.

UPSETTING SITUATION	NEGATIVE THOUGHT	POSITIVE THOUGHT
Carl is late for dinner again.	He cares more about his patients than me.	Carl must practice medicine *his* way, not *mine*. (Separate identity.)
_____	_____	_____
_____	_____	_____
_____	_____	_____
_____	_____	_____

My clients have devised a helpful modification of this technique in that you document *your partner's* capacity to use the eight elements of mature love. The procedure is very straightforward. For one week, actively look for ways in which your partner demonstrates each element of covenant love. This process is surprisingly effective in getting both of you to focus on the positive. Marie's examples below bear this out:

1. Stephen decided to eat at the Olive Garden Saturday night (my favorite restaurant) rather than the Cadillac Bar (his favorite restaurant). (*Mutual balance of met needs.*)

2. Stephen encouraged me to take a photography course, knowing how excited I am about my new camera. (*Other directed.*)

3. Stephen and I talked honestly about having a third child. He was able to list both pluses and minuses. (*Realistic expectations.*)

4. Stephen was able to accept my anger toward his Dad, given his ridiculous intrusion into our lives. (*Tolerance.*)

5. Stephen told me that he didn't find parenting to be as rewarding as he had hoped it would be. (*Yearning to be known.*)

6. Stephen cried when we saw *Field of Dreams*. (*Freedom to express all emotions.*)

7. Stephen acknowledged that I enjoyed parenting much more than he did, but that it was not his intention to deprive me of my life's rewards. (*Separate identities.*)

8. Stephen revealed his wish that we continue to grow together as a couple, no matter what direction that might be. (*Transcendence of two separate selves into one identity.*)

In Closing

So what about this thing called mature, covenant love? Is it an ideal that can never be achieved? Are we not better off with the pursuit of pleasure—the fulfillment of our most passionate desires? I think not for one simple reason: "I've seen the sun!"

Emily Dickinson has said it best.

Had I not seen the sun I could have borne the shade;
But light a newer wilderness my wilderness has made.

When we experience the power of renewal, we cannot go on living routinely, much less hopelessly. Our relationships are transformed when we begin to forgive, to care, to tolerate each other's uniqueness, and to transcend the inevitable misgivings by finding our cherished common ground.

To see the sun, we must have vision. I have discovered that our capacity to have vision is severely impaired by the haze of commitments in our lives. We are so hurried, so overextended, so tired, that finding the opportunity to envision positive, covenant love seems impossible. Unless we as a culture abandon our obsession with busyness, we will continue to abandon each other at a startling rate.

We need more relaxed time with each other, to dream our dreams and live them. Both emotional and sexual intimacy depend on this time. The seeds of mature love cannot germinate unless we bask in the sunlight together.

16

RENEW: Weather the Storm

It's a gray, gray and gloomy day,
A strange and moody blues day.
Got to get through, got to get through
Another day!

Carole King

It is 6:30 on a Thursday evening. Nobody is home.
Nobody.
Your partner and the kids have vanished for the third evening in a row.
How can this be? You have told your partner how important a family sit-down dinner is to you. In an attempt to modify one source of the problem, you have started coming home earlier after work. You have even learned crockpot cooking yourself so that food can be prepared during the day while both of you are away. You have also tried to modify your attitude about sit-down dinners by realizing that life with children is unpredictable—occasional breaks in the routine are unavoidable. But three nights in a row? Instead of sharing a pleasant family meal of smoked turkey, steamed broccoli, and fried potatoes, you now find yourself smoking, steaming, and fit to be fried!

There are a million such stories in the American family. The issues may vary from too little money to too much booze, from too little sex to too much jealousy. The endpoint is the same no matter what the issue: *You are angry.* You have used your best coping efforts to modify both the source of the problem and your point of view toward it. And still you are boiling!

Stop for a moment before your stomach starts squirting acid and your forehead starts twisting into knots. Remember that there are three phases of creative coping. The time has come to seek balance.

The first step in weathering these unavoidable emotional storms is to *calm down.* Stress expert Charles Stroebel offers one example of a quick calming technique that, with practice, can relax the body in just ten seconds:

Step 1. *Clearly identify the actual source of your distress.* This prevents you from blaming your partner when you are actually angry at your boss or at traffic snarls on the way home.

Step 2. *Take a deep, cleansing breath.* This allows you to relax your respiratory system.

Step 3. *Drop your jaw.* This allows you to relax your skeletal muscle system.

Step 4. *Imagine warmth flowing into your hands.* This allows you to relax the smooth muscles in your vascular system.

Step 5. *Visualize a positive scene or think a positive thought about yourself or someone else.* This allows you to relax your brain—perhaps the most stressed out organ of all!

Well over two-thirds of all the couples that I see for marriage counseling have at least one member who is experiencing physical symptoms. Often they are referred to me by their family doctor because of these symptoms. These couples have clearly not coped well with the emotional impact of their disenchantments. It is likely that they are stuck in the moody black and blues where anger, hurt, and resentment breed.

This chapter looks at five coping techniques that modify the emotional and physical impact of disenchantment. In chapter 11, you completed a short assessment of your coping skills. You may want to review your scores in these areas:

1. Athletic release

2. Denial

3. Image diversion

4. Relaxation and meditation

5. Emotional support

Athletic Release

Two years ago I arrived home one evening with a tension headache. As my irritation and discomfort grew, I began to tear away at the family: first at Claire, who can hold her own with me ... then at Erik, who can't ... and then at little Jessica, who started to cry. As I began a second bloody round, Claire looked me straight in the eye and told me to "hit the road" (figuratively) and try my homecoming all over again. With jogging shoes in hand, I followed her advice ... with surprising results!

My headache disappeared somewhere between mile one and mile two. Granted, the first mile was a bit uncomfortable, but not as painful as you might imagine. Having been a jogger for ten years, I soon found my usual rhythmic cadence during the remaining three miles. Since that time, I have used jogging successfully to relieve stress-related pain *before* coming home! My family approves.

Exercise is becoming an integral part of many Americans' fast-paced lives. The benefits of exercise on weight and body fat are obvious, but the potential benefits for our emotional well-being are even more noteworthy.

Dr. Susan Jones, fitness instructor at UCLA, describes more than 100 ways exercise enriches people's quality of life. In addition to the physical benefits—such as improving digestion, enhancing the immune system, and decreasing triglycerides and cholesterol—she points out psychological benefits like increased self-confidence and self-esteem, increased energy, reduced tension and stress, enriched sexuality, and "high spirits." Many people who exercise aerobically report experiencing a "high" — similar to the euphoria associated with various opiate-like substances, such as morphine. These so-called highs seem associated with even moderate amounts of exercise and persist for *two to five hours* following exercise! Imagine ... if you get hot under the collar, you can cool off for five or more hours just by doing an aerobic exercise for thirty minutes or so.

A state-of-the-art conference dealing with exercise and mental health was sponsored by the National Institute of Mental Health in 1984. A number of very important consensus statements emerged:

1. Physical fitness is positively associated with mental health and well-being.

2. Stress symptoms, such as acute state anxiety, are reduced in association with exercise.

3. Exercise is associated with reductions in mild to moderate depression and anxiety, particularly when these symptoms reflect inadequate coping.

4. Long-term exercise is associated with reductions in certain traits reflecting neuroticism and anxiety.

5. Exercise is associated with reductions in various stress indicators such as muscle tension, resting heart rate, and levels of stress hormones.

6. Exercise is associated with emotional benefits across all ages and both sexes.

Keep in mind that exercise is *associated* with these benefits, but does not necessarily *cause* these benefits to occur. Research to date simply has not established an indisputable cause-effect relationship between exercise and emotional well-being. And yet, collectively, these statements emphasize that significant emotional benefits can be expected to be linked to exercise programs.

Why does exercise makes people feel good, even euphoric? Current knowledge suggests four possible explanations. The first two are more psychological in nature, while the last two are based on the assumption that biochemical mechanisms account for the development of altered states.

1. Distraction hypothesis. This view posits that it is the "distraction" from the source of stress, for instance your spouse, as opposed to exercise per se, that is responsible for your improved mood following exercise. In other words, getting your mind off the argument or irritant is the key. Being able to shift your attention to another, more positive activity allows your body to cool off.

2. Mastery hypothesis. This view is based on the belief that people feel accomplished when they are able to complete thirty minutes of exercise, run four miles, or swim one mile—particularly when they didn't want to in the first place!

3. Monoamine hypothesis. This view rests on the knowledge that our bodies produce powerful brain chemicals called neurotransmitters. Two in particular—norepinephrine and serotonin—have been linked to depression. It is hypothesized that exercise may increase these two hormones, which in turn reduces depression in moderately depressed persons. In effect, exercise complements the role of antidepressant medications.

4. Endorphin hypothesis. This notion is based on the belief that exercise creates a euphoric state based on changes in opiate-receptor sites in the body. These morphine-like changes have the ability to reduce the sensation of pain and produce altered emotional states. As with other drugs, these states may also be susceptible to withdrawal and tolerance effects.

Possibly all of these hypotheses are true. Whatever the reason, the fact remains that exercise has been shown to have a tremendous positive impact on people's emotional states. The bottom line is that you will cope better with the stress of disenchantment if you follow a regular exercise program. Consult your YMCA, church, or fitness center to find a program that suits your schedule and your interests.

Denial

Eric Hoffer has said that we feel free when we escape—even if it is just from the frying pan into the fire. The most basic response to change and distress appears to be the escape of *denial*. Out of sight, out of mind ... out of mind, out of misery!

As a coping strategy, denial has had quite a glaring history of unacceptability. As a member of the well-known Freudian family of "defense mechanisms"—that also include rationalization and projection—denial has had a tainted history. More recent trends, such as the encounter-sensitivity movement of the late 60s and early 70s, also questioned the value of denial in light of the emphasis on "awareness" as a steady state.

Evidence does exist, however, that documents the value of denial or avoidance as a coping response—if combined with other strategies. In one well-known National Institute of Health study, Dr. Wolff and colleagues (1964) studied parents whose children were dying of leukemia. These researchers found that those parents who denied the life-threatening significance of their child's illness no longer felt as threatened as parents who acknowledged the tragic implications. Denying parents also displayed lower levels of adrenal cortical stress hormones in blood samples. Psychologist Richard Lazarus and colleagues (1966) found that patients who approached surgery with avoidance strategies had faster and smoother postsurgical recoveries than more vigilant patients had. Not wanting to know about their illness and the nature of their impending surgery seemed to pay off for these patients.

As a coping response, denial is better thought of as a conscious process that somehow minimizes the impact of unpleasant events. Examples are plentiful. When Claire and I have an early morning skirmish at the breakfast table, each of us may quickly forget the conflict once we reach our respective offices, where either clients or school faculty are waiting for us. In effect, each of us has chosen to focus on other things that are more rewarding, more stimulating, and more fulfilling than conflict.

Effective denial requires that we find satisfying distractions that provide pleasure or meaning to our lives. Without such distractions, we are destined to stay stuck in our own negative thinking and emotional upset. Remember that denial:

- Attempts to extinguish all conscious thought of the problem.
- Does nothing to modify the problem itself.
- Represents only a short-term method of effective coping.

How often has your satisfaction in love been tainted by the awareness that there is "something better"? Perhaps you saw another couple passionately kissing. Or you may have experienced a wonderful sense of caring and warmth from a colleague at work. In these moments, you may have wondered if you were settling for much less than you should. Suddenly, what had been minor issues in your relationship mushroom into severe crises!

All loving couples walk in the shadows of denial constantly. To continuously face the imperfections in yourself, your partner, and your relationships is simply too painful. As La Rochefoucauld once said, "No man can look directly at the sun, or death, for too long." To face our partner's incompatibilities and inconsistencies day to day would drive us mad. Denying the negative while emphasizing the positive is our only hope.

Yet a further consideration relates to what psychologist Martin Seligman (1975) labels "learned helplessness." When we realize that our efforts to modify our partner's behavior are fruitless, we can begin to feel helpless. In situations where our partner's behavior continues to be independent of our input or desires, we may begin to believe that we are ineffective in changing things. So why try? Since there are aspects of every relationship that are not likely to change, we must admit that denial has its place.

How can we *intentionally* learn to put out of our minds what *unintentionally* has taken over our minds? There is a way. Any expert in martial arts knows that one should never attempt to oppose a great force with an equal or greater force. The key is to create a movement of your own that deflects, absorbs, or distracts. You must become distracted or absorbed by something else in order to ward off the impact of painful life experiences. Your goal is *not* to directly *resist* an oppressive force, but to *displace* it. Denial is essentially a conscious process of choosing a more pleasurable or meaningful experience over an unpleasant one.

Many people choose inappropriate distractions such as alcohol, cocaine or other drugs, cigarettes, gambling, a lover, or sleep as preferred altered states. Although these distractions óften help us to deny the unpleasantness of life, their benefits are usually short-lived and have consequences that often become more disruptive than the original problem. It is our responsibility to enrich our lives sufficiently so that we have a variety of healthy interests and pastimes to draw upon when we attempt to weather the storm.

Our range of healthy distractions is enhanced as our quality of life is enhanced. Love provides extended family to enrich the holiday season. Work provides challenging tasks that define a purpose to our lives. Leisure brings the sun, the stars, and the moonlight to assuage the dark moments of life. Health provides the stamina, strength, and resiliency we need to reach an aerobic high. Finances provide the currency we need to sail the seas, shop the malls, or lounge by the pool. And spirituality provides the written word, the loving congregation, or the transcendent beauty of nature as infinite resources for growth and comfort. All of these can be healthy distractions.

The DENY procedure consists of four steps that use the word D-E-N-Y as an acronym:

D. *Describe the event.* Specify the disappointing or frustrating situation.

E. *Eliminate stress.* Practice the quick calming technique immediately.

N. *Notice a distraction.* Choose a pleasant or meaningful alternative to get absorbed in.

Y. *Yearn for more distraction.* Become positively addicted to these more pleasant and meaningful alternatives.

A recent client named Linda successfully used denial during a Thanksgiving celebration at her in-laws' home in Dallas. Her husband, Herb—a man she described as "stubborn" and "unyielding"—had insisted that they stay two extra days at his parents' home instead of returning to Austin as originally planned. Linda had already made plans to go Christmas shopping with friends on Friday and Saturday and did not want to miss the great holiday sales that always accompanied Thanksgiving Day weekend.

As their skirmish escallated into a war, Linda soon realized that the entire day would be wasted if she did not calm herself down. Since she and her husband had learned a number of relaxation techniques, including the quick calming technique, she told Herb that they were stuck at an impasse for the time being and that she thought it would be better to resolve it later in the day. He agreed. With that, she got up, went into the den, took a deep, cleansing breath, dropped her jaw, imagined warmth flowing into her hands, and visualized a positive scene.

Linda was surprised at how quickly and vividly a scene developed in her mind's eye. She imagined her mother-in-law basting the turkey in the kitchen, with all the pungent smells that accent this part of the meal preparation. Soon this image of the turkey gave way to acorn squash and apple pies. Feeling more relaxed, Linda decided to turn her visualization into realization by helping her mother-in-law in the kitchen. Grabbing an apron from a hook in the pantry, she soon found herself rolling out two pie crusts from scratch. Two lattice-top delicacies were soon ready for baking.

Linda made a point to tell me that she was amazed at how quickly she was able to calm herself down and to extinguish her thematic indictments of Herb. She admitted that she did not even think of him once she started to knead the dough, smell the bread, and sample the stuffing. Distraction works, and she wasn't about to let go of her pleasant state! Once meal preparation was completed, Linda immersed herself in holiday decorations, playful activities with the children, and cleanup after the meal was completed. She and Herb eventually reached a compromise—they would stay one extra day, instead of two. (It is telling that they were not able to modify the source of their conflict until they were able to modify its impact!)

Denial is a tool that can be overused. Men, in particular, seem all too eager to walk away from conflict before it is resolved. The problem is not so much the walking away as it is the "never returning." But when our foundation and commitment to love is secure, there are very few critical problems that require immediate resolution. For loving couples, denial can be an effective prelude to effective problem solving.

Image Diversion

Do you see yourself as a hapless victim in your relationship? In your mind's eye, do you see yourself as the one with no control, the one unfairly treated? Does your belief system—as well as the belief systems of your family and friends—tend to indict your partner on numerous counts of harassment and abuse? If so, you probably spend a great deal of time visualizing very negative images about your partner.

You may see your partner hanging from a tall, gangly tree. You may see yourself pouring hot coffee down the front of your partner's new blue suit or burgundy dress. Or you may see your partner pounding on the locked front door until he or she gets bruised and bloodied knuckles. Visualizing negative images about our partners only accomplishes one goal: It intensifies our anger!

In fact, most of us are pretty good at creating full-length feature films about our partners—particularly when we are upset. You are the "good guy" and he or she is the "bad guy." There is a beginning, when you are helplessly tied to the railroad tracks. And there is an end, when the varmit is thrown out of the house. In between, there is colorful dialogue: "I want to tear your hair out," "bite your head off," or "rip your eyes out." These are the images of anger and rage.

When you are "chomping at the bit," you need another coping skill that diminishes, rather than intensifies anger. *Positive visualization* is another tool in your arsenal. To be successful you will need:

1. To avoid other people who want to create negative images about your partner.

2. To maintain a passive state of mind.

3. To maintain a relaxed body.

4. To create a pleasant mental scene.

5. To believe that you control your own thoughts.

6. To practice regularly.

In order to visualize, you will need to use all of your senses— seeing, hearing, feeling, tasting, and smelling. You will find that certain sense modalities are more vivid for you than others. Try to use as many as possible, but do not be concerned if some do not seem as clear as others.

Some people are more able to visualize than others. The following simple technique developed by Arnold Lazarus (1984) will help you to determine how well you can visualize. Try visualizing the twenty images below. After each one, rate the quality of your image in the following manner: on a scale of one to four, with four representing a very clear image, and one representing a very unclear image.

1. A close relative or friend in front of me.   _____

2. My relative or a friend laughing.   _____

3. His or her eyes.   _____

4. A bowl of fruit.   _____

5. Driving down a dusty, dry road.　　　　　　＿＿＿＿＿＿

6. Myself throwing a ball.　　　　　　＿＿＿＿＿＿

7. My childhood home.　　　　　　＿＿＿＿＿＿

8. A white sandy beach.　　　　　　＿＿＿＿＿＿

9. A shop window.　　　　　　＿＿＿＿＿＿

10. A blank TV screen.　　　　　　＿＿＿＿＿＿

11. The sound of a barking dog.　　　　　　＿＿＿＿＿＿

12. The sound of an exploding firecracker.　　　　　　＿＿＿＿＿＿

13. The warmth of a hot shower.　　　　　　＿＿＿＿＿＿

14. The texture of rough sandpaper.　　　　　　＿＿＿＿＿＿

15. Myself lifting a heavy object.　　　　　　＿＿＿＿＿＿

16. Walking up a steep stairway.　　　　　　＿＿＿＿＿＿

17. The taste of lemon juice.　　　　　　＿＿＿＿＿＿

18. Eating cold ice cream.　　　　　　＿＿＿＿＿＿

19. The smell of cooking cabbage.　　　　　　＿＿＿＿＿＿

20. Smelling a rose.　　　　　　＿＿＿＿＿＿

Add the ratings for each item to obtain a total score. Dr. Lazarus uses the following guidelines to evaluate the quality of your visualization skills:

60 or Higher = Good visualization skills
Between 30 and 60 = Moderate visualization skills
30 or Below = More practice needed.

How did you feel about these images? Did any have special significance? Were you surprised by your reactions to some? Were your images strong and clear? Was more than one sense (smell, sound, touch) involved? Were you able to create a number of details in some images?

Now let's use this tool to handle a hot situation that seems upsetting to you. Before using visualization, however, you must first relax.

As you sit comfortably on a soft chair or sofa, allow your mind to turn off. Focus your attention on the easy rhythm of your breathing. Slow and easy. Listen to yourself breathe for four or five breaths.

Now focus your attention on your upper body. Notice your trunk, shoulders, head, and neck. As you breathe slowly in and out, notice the heaviness in your upper body. Relax and let go as you feel heaviness. Allow yourself to sink lower and lower into the chair or sofa. Sink lower and lower with every breath that you take. Repeat this for three of four breaths.

Good, now for the next three of four breaths, focus on your entire body. As you exhale, feel your body let go. Feel your body relax. Feel your body become heavier and heavier with every exhalation, As you let go more and more, you become heavier and heavier. Allow the chair to fully support you.

Now that you are relaxed, it is time to use what many psychologists call an "imagery rehearsal technique." One example of this technique, from Dr. Lazarus's book, *In The Mind's Eye* (1984), is particularly well-suited for our purposes of reducing anger once it is aroused. This is called "running a mental movie":

Leaving the body completely relaxed, let your mind become a TV screen. Let a part of your mind be the "director" of the movie, detached enough so that you can "stop the action" or "change the script" when instructed. *(Pause.)* Now allow pictures to come to mind of a situation that has caused you to feel very hurt or angry. *(Pause.)* See very clearly the physical surroundings *(pause)*, who's there *(pause)*, and what's going on as the scene unfolds. *(Pause.)* Hear the words that hurt and anger, that are said to you and that you said back. *(Pause.)* Feel the tension increasing in your body, as you scan from head to toe to feel the tightness. *(Pause)*

Remember that the part of the mind that is the "director" will keep you in control as you continue to run this mental movie, letting the anger build until you are on the brink of losing control. Now put the scene in slow motion as the last trigger is pushed for the start of physical violence. What was this last trigger? *(Pause.)* Stop the action. *(Pause.)* Take a slow, deep breath, and let go of the scene. *(Pause.)*

Now it is time for a "retake." Again let's run the mental movie, except that this time the part of your mind that is the "director" will stop the action and "change" the script so that the angry scene gets resolved constructively, without violence. *(Pause.)* Once again let the scene unfold as before. See the situation clearly, hear the voices that begin to hurt and anger, and feel the tension in your body begin to rise. STOP THE ACTION! *(Pause.)*

Change the script so that you feel a calm, quiet strength in your body, and a clear confident, rational presence of mind. Take a slow, deep breath, feel the relaxation flow throughout the body. Tell yourself: "I can handle this. *(Pause.)* What do I have to prove? Let me tune in closely to how the other person is feeling threatened. What can I do to ease the tension? Can I agree with part of what they're saying or feeling to defuse the tension? Personal put-downs and shoulds won't help. Let's see if we can reason about one issue at a time. One step at a time. The tension is easing more and more. I can express myself without threats and get the job done pretty well.

I feel good about my self-control. *(Pause.)* It gets a little better each time I practice the anger control technique I've learned. *(Pause.)"*

Stop the action. Take another slow, deep breath, and let go of the scene completely. Let the TV screen go blank and just relax. *(Pause.)* The "movie" is going to be a success, thanks to the "director." Enough for now, until it's time for the next practice. Count slowly from one to five, feeling more and more alert and refreshed with each count: one, two, three, four, five, eyes open, wide awake, feeling alert, refreshed, confident, and in control.

It is not necessary to do an imagery rehearsal technique to benefit from image diversion. Why do you think the shopping malls are as crowded as they are? Surely you don't believe that everyone you see is spending their hard-earned money! Malls are wonderful places to browse through the windows for free. One scene, one image after another gives us some breathing space from all our trials and tribulations. Any time you are able to distract yourself by substituting a more peaceful image in place of an upsetting one, you are successfully using image diversion. Remember, however, that the true mark of success will be the emotional calm you create to replace your anger.

Relaxation and Meditation

We gasp in surprise. We sigh in relief. We constrict in anger. We hold our breath in anticipation. We feel breathless with excitement. No matter the emotional state, our breathing is inextricably intertwined with our emotional arousal. Breathing is not only essential for life, but may be the key to all relaxation as well.

Like all relaxation techniques, breathing counteracts the effects of the "fight or flight" response. Although our stressors may be different from those our ancestors experienced, the pathogenesis of our stress response remains the same. Instead of preparing ourselves for battle with our partners or escape from our annual performance review, we can learn to quiet our breathing, heart, and metabolic rates, blood pressure, and blood flow to the muscles.

Herbert Benson wrote a very popular book some years ago, entitled *The Relaxation Response* (1975), that devotes itself entirely to breathing. The book suggests a very simple procedure based on ancient meditation practices:

- Sit quietly in a comfortable position.
- Deeply relax all your muscles from toes to head.
- Breathe through your nose, becoming very aware of this process.
- Each time you exhale, silently say the word "one."

Dr. Benson recommends that we practice this breathing technique for ten to twenty minutes once or twice a day. (Never use an alarm to check the time.) When finished, first sit quietly with eyes closed, then sit quietly with eyes open.

There are numerous relaxation or self-regulatory strategies available to choose from. These include biofeedback, transcendental meditation, zen, yoga, self-hypnosis, autogenic training, progressive relaxation, and imagery techniques. Although most of these techniques have been shown to lower physiological arousal, no one technique has been shown to be more clearly effective than any other and none of these techniques has been shown to be consistently more effective than simple resting.

There is one inescapable conclusion, however. Relaxation techniques, with practice, will help to reduce physical and emotional arousal. It is not essential to know whether relaxation works because of "distraction" from the source of stress or, perhaps, because of direct physiological benefits. The point is that it works! When you are angry, it is to your advantage to possess relaxation tools that quiet the storm within.

Some years ago, my colleagues at the Austin Stress Clinic and I developed this calming technique that uses visualization, suggestion, and instruction to induce a deep level of muscular and visceral relaxation. Feel free to tape record and use it.

Get in a comfortable position, close your eyes, take a deep breath and let it out slowly. I want you to imagine that a warm and heavy liquid is flowing all the way down to your feet. Every place this warm and heavy liquid touches, it releases all tension and pressure completely as you sink into a deep level of relaxation. Allow that warm and heavy liquid to penetrate to every muscle and ligament in your feet. You can imagine and feel that heavy warmth flowing through the deepest muscles in your feet.

Allow that heavy liquid to flow up to your lower legs, flowing up your Achilles tendons, up your ankles, and into your calf muscles. Release and relax all tension and pressure completely. It is a very pleasant sensation to relax. Good. Now allow that heavy liquid to flow into your knees. Feel your knees relax as you feel and imagine that warm and heavy liquid flowing into the deepest part of your knee joints—relaxing tendons, ligaments, cartilage, and all the small muscles that connect your knees to your lower legs. Good!

Now allow that heavy liquid to flow into your thighs. Feel relaxation flow into each layer of muscle in your thigh. Feel and imagine that warm pleasant feeling of relaxation flowing into the deepest muscles in your thighs, all the way to the bones. Relax your thighs completely as warm and heavy relaxation flows into your hips and torso. Notice all the tension draining away as that warm and heavy liquid relaxes all tension and pressure completely.

Now feel a warm and pleasant sensation flowing across your lower stomach muscles, penetrating and sinking into all the muscles. Relax your stomach muscles completely. Now allow that warm and heavy feeling to flow in and fill up the bowl that your hips make. Feel the relaxation as the warm and heavy liquid sinks to the floor of your hips. Feel it flow into your genitals, organs, glands, and supporting tissues. Relax this part of your body completely as you sink deeper and deeper into a very pleasant feeling of relaxation.

Now allow that warm heavy liquid to spread out across your lower back. Really imagine and feel the tension and tightness flowing out of your muscles as the warm heavy liquid enters. Feel all the muscles in your lower back becoming soft and warm as you relax more and more with every breath you take.

Allow that warm liquid to flow around to your chest, spreading a warm and relaxing feeling across your chest, sinking into all the small muscles in your chest. Now imagine and feel the warm and heavy liquid begin to fill up your abdominal cavity. Allow that warm and pleasant feeling of relaxation to surround and penetrate your organs, glands, and smooth muscles. Take a deep relaxing breath as you release all tension and pressure completely from your chest and abdomen. Relax.... Good.

Now, just as that liquid warmth has filled up your feet, legs, hips, abdomen, and chest, it begins to flow over into your arms and all the way down to your finger tips. All tension and pressure are released completely in your hands. Feel your hands becoming very warm and heavy—so heavy that you can't lift them. Allow that warm liquid to fill up your wrists and forearms, releasing all tension as you relax deeper and deeper. Good, now imagine and feel that warmth and heaviness flow into your upper arms and shoulders, penetrating to the deepest part of your shoulder joints. Now feel the pleasant relaxing warmth flowing into the muscles that run across the top of your shoulders to your neck. Let go of all tension in your shoulders and begin to feel the warm relaxing liquid flowing up the back and sides of your neck.

Imagine and feel the relaxation penetrating deeper and deeper into your neck, releasing all tension. Let the warmth and relaxation continue all the way to the very top of your neck where the muscle connects to your skull. Feel each layer of muscle in your neck give up the tension as the warmth and the soft feelings of relaxation flow in. Good, now allow that warm heavy liquid to flow into your temples. Now just allow the warm softness to flow into your jaws and release all tension and pressure.

Allow your mouth to open slightly, as the warm heaviness flows down your jaw line to your chin. Feel that warmth spread across your face and flow into your lips, nose, cheeks, and eyes. Feel your eyelids becoming very warm and heavy as the liquid relaxes all the muscles and tissues surrounding your eyes and flows onto your forehead.

To help you relax even further, I'm going to count backward from ten to one. On every descending number feel yourself going deeper and deeper into relaxation. Ten ... nine, feel yourself going deeper ... eight ... seven ... six, deeper and deeper ... five ... four ... three, more and more relaxed ... two ... one, completely relaxed.

Now just allow yourself to feel your body all over. If you have any remaining tension, go to that place and bring in the warm, heavy liquid to relax.

Emotional Support

To express or not to express anger—that is the question! Should you ventilate your anger or suppress it? If you do ventilate, will you experience a catharsis—a purging? If you hold it in, will you experience physical symptoms of distress? Centuries ago, the Greek statesman Plutarch wondered about the same thing:

> For he who gives no fuel to fire puts it out, and likewise he who does not in the beginning nurse his wrath and does not puff himself up with anger, takes precautions against it and destroys it.

Turning to others when upset is a norm in our culture. Practically every self-help book ever written extols the need to talk out our problems! Fume with a friend, confess your sins, or enter therapy— whatever means you choose, you are asked to unload your feelings onto someone who will listen.

As essential as emotional support appears to be, a direct link to cathartic release is hardly a given. In her book, *Anger: The Misunderstood Emotion*, Carol Tavris argues against three prevailing myths within the mental health field:

1. Aggression is the instinctive catharsis for anger.

2. Talking out anger gets rid of it.

3. Tantrums and other childhood rages are healthy expressions of anger that forestall neurosis.

Tavris goes on to say:

> The psychological rationales for ventilating anger do not stand up under experimental scrutiny. The weight of the evidence indicates precisely the opposite: Expressing anger makes you angrier, solidifies an angry attitude, and establishes a hostile habit. If you keep quiet about momentary irritations and distract yourself with pleasant activity until your fury simmers down, chances are you will feel better, and feel better faster, than if you let yourself go in a shouting match. If you want to scream at your children, berate your spouse, or ventilate all over a powerless bureaucrat, you can't call on the medical profes-

sion to justify your actions. You may decide you want to behave this way, but you've made a strategic judgment, not a scientific one. (Tavris 1984, 144)

We must remember that there is a difference between emotional release and emotional support. The former has more to do with what we "put out" to others. The latter refers to what we take in from others. Anger is clearly an example of emotional release that puts us out in the middle of nowhere! The expression of intense anger is likely to (1) get you fired, (2) get you more angry, (3) get you divorced, and (4) get you lonely. In short, people have enough difficulty accepting negative feedback of any kind, let alone negative feedback that drops out of the blue like an incendiary bomb!

There may be only one set of circumstances in which we get away with the intense catharsis of anger. Consider the following situation recently reported to me by a client:

John, a 53-year-old accountant, had been fired from a prestigious accounting firm seven years before. Though he was at the height of his career at the time, a change in management resulted in a sudden loss of support for him. After struggling with his own business for three years, he finally resigned himself to a "menial" role in another well-established accounting firm. An angry depression lingered on, however. At the urging of his wife, John committed himself to therapy. Seven weeks into therapy, he was asked to go directly to the man who fired him and express his resentments. He did so with much relief. His depression began to lift soon afterwards.

This brief scenario points out that some benefit can be found for emotional release if three conditions are met:

1. Your retaliation must be directed to the person who made you angry.

2. Your method of retaliation must inflict *appropriate* harm to your target if it is to exorcise your anger.

3. Your catharsis must not be followed by any further retaliation from your target.

This technique worked well in John's situation, but it is destined to fail miserably in love relationships. Why? For one thing, you must be able to face your partner the next day! Also, retaliation only begets retaliation. Couples who express verbal or physical aggression do little to reduce their reservoirs of anger. If anything, by participating in a reciprocal pattern of barbs, you only increase anger.

Getting Emotional Support

The following diagram charts the full range of options that people use to get emotional support. Some of these options are obviously much more successful than others.

	TALK TO YOUR PARTNER	*TALK TO SOMEONE ELSE*
TALK ABOUT *SITUATION*	Best Option	Second Best Option
TALK ABOUT *PERSON*	Second Worst Option	Worst Option

Talk about the situation with your partner. The key in finding emotional support for ourselves is to talk about the situation with the person who shares responsibility for it—our partner. We manage disenchantment much better when we express disappointment and frustration at the *situational* level. Don't allow your feelings of frustration and disappointment to build into themes of resentment. Instead, describe and discuss your feelings about the situation with your partner. Avoid "you" statements when talking about the problem situation. Use "I" statements instead to express your needs and wants. You are most likely to find emotional support—and to work out a solution to the problem—if your partner doesn't feel personally threatened.

Talk about the situation with someone else. Talking to a third person about a problem situation is your second best option—particularly if you are unassertive or too intimidated to talk directly to your partner. However, this should be viewed as a temporary means of emotional support. This might be a time to rehearse what you want to tell your partner directly about a problem situation. For instance, if you are angry with your wife about bouncing checks, you might talk with a friend about the situation— *but not about your wife.* Your goal here is not to indict your wife, but to find an equitable solution to a frustrating situation.

Talk about your partner with your partner. Telling your partner what you think about him or her, as a *person*, is the second worst option. If you choose this option, you are actually seeking emotional release, not emotional support—and we've already established how unproductive that is! Though it is tempting to tell someone that he or she is selfish or unreliable, very little useful information is conveyed. And your partner is very unlikely to be receptive to a personal attack. That means little or no emotional support for you! Cancel this category, since it does not help your partner understand your needs, your wants, or the problem situation. By disparaging your partner, you only alienate your most important potential source of emotional support.

Talk about your partner with someone else. Gossiping to friends and others about your partner is the worst option available for finding emotional support. Again, this is a form of emotional release, not emotional support. Gossiping only rehearses the problem and perpetuates your anger. In such cases, people tend to define a "good friend" as someone who agrees with them. Otherwise, you wouldn't be wasting your time gossiping to him or her. If you are completely honest with yourself, you must admit that you want to believe that your lover is a louse, a no-good-nick, a real bastard! And the only way you can convince yourself is to buttress your point of view with like-minded "friends" who agree with your negativity. When you gossip about your partner, it is clear that you don't really want to change your situation.

Some people use therapists as gossip partners. They go doctor shopping over the course of many years, finding one therapist after another who will listen to them bitch about their spouses. When a therapist, in the name of change, pushes these clients too hard toward resolving their issues with their partners, the therapist is fired!

Giving Emotional Support

Since you are also a partner in your relationship, you must know how to give emotional support as well. What does giving emotional support look like?

1. *Give attention.* Attention refers to those nonverbal and verbal cues that tell your partner that you are focused, not distracted. Eye contact and body posture are very important here.

2. *Give understanding.* Be alert to and repond to the feeling being expressed, rather than attending solely to the content of what the person has said. By communicating that you can accurately sense the world as your partner is feeling and perceiving it, you are giving understanding.

3. *Give direction.* By sharing in the creation of possible solutions, you give direction. Direction has much more to do with problem solving than advice giving.

Behavior that demonstrates attention, understanding and direction helps establish a feeling of trust and support that encourages open and honest communication.

In providing emotional support, the importance of accurate listening cannot be overstated. Frequently, when one partner is telling his or her side of a story, the other person is not listening. Instead, he or she is making snap judgments, mentally composing a response, or cutting his or her partner off with defensive remarks. Instead, you should:

- Reserve judgment until your partner has finished speaking.
- Encourage your partner by nodding agreement.
- Check to see if you really hear what your partner is saying by rephrasing what he or she said.

Remember that communication takes place not only with words, but also with feelings and attitudes that are conveyed by nonverbal cues.

- Look at your partner talking to show him or her that you are listening.
- Maintain eye contact.
- Make positive facial gestures.
- Make responsive gestures such as leaning toward your partner and nodding affirmatively.

You show a *lack of interest* in what your partner is saying when you:

- Look away.
- Glance at your watch or the TV.
- Busy yourself with something else.
- Read or write when your partner is talking.
- Yawn.
- Tap your foot.

Now that you are aware of some of the verbal and nonverbal ways of facilitating or hindering communication, how do you actually ask for more information in a way that opens your partner up? Some ways of encouraging your partner to give more information are:

1. Ask open-ended questions rather than questions that have a yes or no answer. Ask "What makes you want to move to a new neighborhood?" rather than "Do you want to move because of the schools?"

2. Rephrase what your partner has said as a means of gaining still further information. "Let me see if I got what you were saying. You think I want a third child and we will need another bedroom?"

3. Build on what your partner has said by summarizing. "Let's see, you have mentioned my ignoring the kids' homework and my coming home late. Are there any other things I have done to upset you this week?"

4. Use phrases that ask for more information. "Could you tell me some more about that?" "What makes you think that may be so?" "What do you mean?"

5. Use responses that indicate you understand and are interested in what your partner is saying. "I see" or "Um-hm" are good examples.

6. Let your partner know you are aware that he or she is talking about a sensitive problem. Let him or her know that you are not judging him for what he or she has revealed. "You feel you have learned how to budget better now that we have been able to save for the last three months." "I know it has been difficult for you to manage with Marcy being home so much."

7. Be aware when your partner wants you to clarify a statement. "Let me try to say it another way. What I am trying to ask is...."

Remember that listening is an active process, as Carl Rogers called it many years ago. If you listen actively, your partner will experience emotional support for three reasons:

1. Your partner will know that you feel empathy toward him or her.

2. Your partner will know that you heard his or her feelings.

3. Your partner will see that you can express your empathy and caring without having to give advice or offer a solution.

This chapter has offered you five different strategies that will help to weather the storm. Each has its own unique benefits for managing emotional distress:

Athletic Release: We can work it out!
Denial: We can block it out!
Image Diversion: We can visualize it out!
Relaxation and Meditation: We can smooth it out!
Emotional Support: We can talk it out!

A common thread runs through each of them: Don't be a helpless victim, be a resourceful coper instead! So long as you take responsibility to quiet your upset, you will not burn at your own stake. Emotional upset is a predictable component of any meaningful relationship. You cannot avoid the experience. It is your responsibility to acquire skills, techniques, and perspectives that minimize the intensity and duration of these troubling times.

Appendix

Counting the Physical Costs

Angry conflicts with our love mates, unresolved over time, play an active role in increasing our chances of illness or death. It is now well established by both the American Medical Association and the American Academy of Family Physicians that most visits to a family physician are either caused or exacerbated by stress, much of this being family stress.

1. Migraine and tension headaches alone account for one-fifth of all complaints evaluated by doctors in general practice.

2. Nervous stomach and bowels "eat up" 20 percent of the population.

3. The three best selling drugs in the United States, all clearly stress related, include an ulcer medication (Tagamet), a hypertensive drug (Inderal), and a tranquilizer (Valium).

4. New fields such as health psychology, behavioral medicine, and psychoneuroimmunology are burgeoning in order to explore the ways emotional states affect the body's defenses or health in general.

Virtually all illness has emotional components. Maintaining biological equilibrium, much like a teetering seesaw, is what good health is all about. We strive to preserve a precious balance between too much and too little. As disenchantments upset this balance, our bodies seek ways to adapt by altering their hormones, nervous systems, and musculature. Psychosomatic disorders, as well as other diseases of adaptation, may be the painful byproducts.

Headaches, gastrointestinal disorders, heart disease, sexual disturbances, asthma, cardiovascular disorders such as high blood pressure, thyroid problems, and skin problems all may result from being keyed up. And let's not forget hyperventilation, which results in so many visits to the emergency room. We really believe that our "number is up" during such attacks as we begin to shake, sweat, and panic. We may become flushed and light-headed; our hands may turn cold while a lump grows in our throat; our breathing may become shallow and rapid as our pulse rate goes up.

Which of the following symptoms do you regularly experience?

Tension headaches	Burping
Migraine headaches	Gassiness
Jaw clenching	Acid stomach
High blood pressure	Palpitations
Low back pain	Irritability
Constipation	Butterflies in stomach
Diarrhea	Nausea
Cold hands	Sweating
Cold feet	Loss of sexual response

Chronic Activation

A frog, unsuspectingly placed in a cool vat of water, will eventually boil to death as the temperature of the water is slowly increased. A second frog, placed in a vat of boiling water, will quickly jump out of this deathtrap. The difference is plain to see. The first frog slowly accommodates to a stressful and dangerous environment without sensing the increased health risks that accompany this adaptation. This is also true for you as you continue to be swallowed by a dysfunctional love relationship which saps and debilitates you over time.

Disenchantment is a stress response. Unless we learn to cope effectively with our disenchantments, we are likely to become symptomatic, probably developing one or more medical problems over time. I cannot overstate how medically costly our anger can be. Physicians refer nearly one-third of my clientele to me for such reasons.

Chronic activation from disenchantments may lead to numerous medical complaints or diseases. Susceptibility to microorganisms, which bring on the common cold virus and flu, is one example. Ulcers, kidney damage, heart disease, and stroke are others. Even cancer may be linked to the harmful effects of stress upon the immune system. *Time Magazine* reported that "researchers have discovered that the body's production of its own cancer-fighting cells, including natural killer cells, T-lymphocytes and macrophages, is inhibited by chronic stress" (6 June 1983). A series of studies conducted by the National Institute of Mental Health has also revealed that parents of children who had died from cancer had elevated stress hormones two years after their children died.

There is ample evidence that anger has close ties to disease, especially heart disease. In three separate studies, researchers have found that high hostility scores correlate with an increased chance of dying early. At Rush Medical School, Dr. Richard Shekelle (1983) examined psychological data from 1,900 male factory employees which had been collected twenty-five years before. Higher hostility scores were associated with increased rates of coronary heart disease. It was also found that deaths due to all causes—including cancer, accidents, suicide, and heart disease—went up with hostility scores.

Dr. Redford Williams (1983) at Duke University studied the hostility of patients undergoing tests for blocked coronary arteries. Williams reported that individuals with high hostility scores were 1.5 times more likely to have a blocked artery. And finally, at the University of North Carolina at Chapel Hills, Drs. Barefoot and Dahlstrom (1983) studied the hostility scores of 225 doctors themselves, all of whom had been tested twenty-five years earlier as medical students. Those with high hostility scores were six times more likely to die by the age of fifty from all causes of diseases than were fellow students with low hostility scores.

A chain reaction within the body appears to be set off by anger and hostility. Anger stimulates the release of a powerful chemical called norepinephrine. This hormone acts to constrict blood vessels while at the same time it accelerates the heart rate. These two actions then raise blood pressure, which strains both the heart and blood vessels further. Let us track the chemistry of disenchantment a bit further.

A Two-Track System

Mankind has long been fascinated with the workings of the body, particularly that grayish, wrinkled organ in our heads. We seem to attribute certain aspects of the personality to various organs throughout our body: emotions to the heart, soul to the pineal gland, and intellectual functioning to the brain.

Every system of our body is capable of responding to disenchantment through a complicated response pattern which involves the brainstem, the limbic system, and the cerebral cortex. Let's think of these responses as a journey along two train tracks, one being nervous stimulation of "organs" and the other being nervous stimulation of the "endocrine glands." This mysterious journey begins in the hypothalamus, a pea-size collection of nerve cells located at the base of the brain.

The hypothalamus, along track number one, regulates the activities of the autonomic nervous system. This involuntary system regulates basic survival functions such as hunger, body temperature, thirst, rage, pain, and pleasure. Two subsystems comprise the autonomic nervous system: the sympathetic and parasympathetic systems. We are primarily concerned with the sympathetic branch, which researcher Walter Cannon described as the originator of our "fight or flight" responses.

The sympathetic branch generally tenses and constricts involuntary muscles and blood vessels, while stepping up the activity of the glands. The parasympathetic does the reverse by providing expansion and relaxation. We have many figures of speech which reflect the functioning of these two systems. We "warm up" to someone; people have "cold feet" or "warm hearts"; we get "frozen with terror" or "burst with happiness and joy"; we even "swell with pride." Figure 1 distinguishes these two areas by function.

Let's imagine a "fight or flight" situation. You have had recent talks with your wife about her "late night meetings." Once too often she has come home at 2:00 a.m. smelling like a brewery. You hope she understands your jealousy and need for fidelity. But alas, she has done it again! It is now 3:00 a.m. As you look at the clock, your heart suddenly quickens. It is beating more times per minute and pumping more blood per beat. At the same time, your body tries to make more efficient use of its available supply of blood by constricting blood vessels in organ sites where blood is not essential during the stress response. The stomach is a good example, since digestion is a nonessential activity during "fight or flight." Now the blood can be directed elsewhere, such as the heart, brain, or eyes, for the quick thinking or action that you will need when your wife arrives home.

Not all parts of our body are aroused when angry or fearful. Gastric secretions and stomach movements may actually *halt* during acute stress. In behavioral medicine, we are more concerned with the increased secretions and movements of chronic stress that brings about such conditions as ulcers.

Amidst your angry feelings, the bronchials, which carry oxygen into your lungs, expand. This allows your breathing to become deeper and faster. You may begin to sweat and salivate. The pupils in your eyes enlarge to better see that saber-toothed tiger in front of you when she walks through the door. Adrenalin is secreted by the medulla, which is located inside the adrenal glands. This, in turn, stimulates your liver to release more glucose to meet your energy needs. Next time you are upset and angry, think of figure 1, which demonstrates the host of sympathetic reactions likely to occur!

When we feel anger, we become energized, flushed, and pumped up. Research has actually found that while we are angry the mucous membranes of our nose and stomach swell and redden from increased blood flow. They may become congested to the point of hemorrhage. Gastritis can be a medical consequence.

The parasympathetic system, by contrast, does not have a mass reaction throughout the body when we get stressed. Its actions are relatively specific to single organs, promoting action in some organs while inhibiting action in others. It might slow down the beating of our heart while it expands the size of blood vessels. Although most organs of the body are affected by both sympathetic and parasympathetic stimulation, some are not.

SYMPATHETIC AND PARASYMPATHETIC EFFECTS

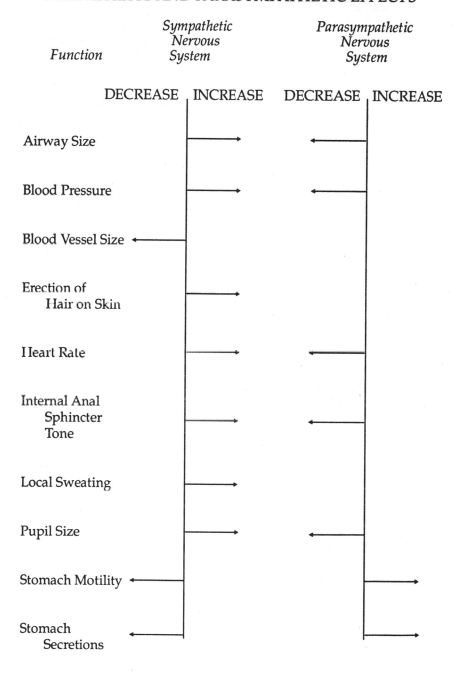

Figure 1. Effects of sympathetic and parasympathetic stimulation on different autonomic functions.

A Second Track

A second track becomes quickly operational at the same time you are fiercely staring at the clock, waiting for your wife. This is the *endocrine system*, which consists of ductless glands that secrete powerful substances, called hormones, into the bloodstream. Most activities of the body are influenced by these hormones. The pituitary gland and the adrenal glands are most directly involved during peak moments. It all begins when our gatekeeper, the hypothalamus, directly influences the pituitary gland through a portal opening in the brain.

The pituitary then obediently secretes ACTH (adrenocorticotropic hormone) right into the bloodstream. With instinctual know-how, the ACTH then circulates until it reaches its target gland, the adrenal cortex (the outer layer of the adrenal glands). The adrenal cortex then secretes many of its own hormones into the bloodstream to impact on the rest of the body. The process reminds me of July 4th fireworks, where one burst of light seems to ignite so many more.

The two primary secretions of the adrenal cortex are cortisol and aldosterone. Cortisol, much like a built-in power booster, speeds up our body's overall metabolism. In fact, cortisol can increase the liver's production of glucose tenfold. This excess glucose is the energy supply that any athlete depends upon. In its magical way, glucose transforms fats and proteins—which circulate freely in the blood—into powerful energy sources. But beware! Chronic mobilization of proteins, fueled by chronic anger, may compromise our ability to form mature white blood cells and antibodies. Our immunity may thus be affected in a big way. In addition, excess fats mobilized throughout the blood stream may promote atherosclerosis, due to the high levels of fatty plaque.

Aldosterone is also produced at higher levels during our response to stress. Acting like a built-in air-conditioning unit, aldosterone helps our bodies regulate heat and waste products more efficiently, as well as prepare us for vigorous muscular activity. To do so requires the retention of extra sodium (salt) which may then indirectly elevate blood pressure (yet another cost to our health).

Just to be clear, the two-track system being described affects two different areas of the adrenal glands, which sit on top of the kidneys. The sympathetic track, described first, influences the inner section of the adrenal glands called the medulla. The endocrine track influences the outer layer of the adrenals called the cortex. Adrenalin (sometimes called epinephrine) is released by the medulla when it is stimulated by the sympathetic nerves.

The pituitary-adrenal axis is remarkably sensitive to even subtle psychological factors. Even predictable events, where we have prepared ourselves for action, will exaggerate cortico-steroid output. Studies of cardrivers at the Indianapolis Speedway, parachute jumpers, and college students taking final exams reflect such increased levels. In many studies involving one kind of performance or another, just the anticipation of an event is enough to get our juices flowing. And surprisingly, we spectators may be generating as much physical excitement just by watching these events as the participants are creating themselves. This is quite a commentary on the level of "relaxation" we actually experience while watching a sporting event on TV!

Disenchantment and the General Adaptation Syndrome

A number of years ago I went to Dallas to hear Dr. Hans Selye speak on stress. Selye had published at least 30 books and hundreds of articles on the subject. This was to be an enchanting evening with the world's renowned expert—and indeed it was! He spoke energetically and extemporaneously for over two hours. A question and answer period then followed. I will always remember the somewhat brash graduate student who unabashedly asked Dr. Selye to summarize—in one sentence—what he had learned about stress during his decades of research. How, I wondered, would this brilliant scientist meet this challenge? Slowly he arose from his chair and limped to the front of the stage. Without hesitation, he simply stated: "It is not what happens to us that matters, but how we view it."

I sat back and pondered these words, as I have many times since. I knew that many years before, in 1926, Selye had wondered why the most diverse diseases produced so many common physiological signs and symptoms. During years of investigation, he observed a syndrome of physical damage which resulted to animals who were exposed to diverse sources of chronic stress. These symptoms included: (1) enlargement of the adrenal cortex, (2) shrinkage of the thymus, a growth-regulating gland in the upper chest, and (3) deep, bleeding ulcers in the stomach.

To Selye, disease was not just suffering, but rather the result of a process whereby the organism fights to maintain a homeostatic balance. Our bodies attempt to adapt to stressful situations in the best possible manner. This process occurs in three stages, aptly named the General Adaptation Syndrome:

1. The alarm reaction stage

2. The resistance stage

3. The exhaustion stage

The alarm stage is characterized by increased ACTH secretion from the pituitary, which we learned stimulates the adrenal cortex. The body is reacting generally at this point as the autonomic nervous system fires up. We also called this the "fight or flight" stage earlier. So far, no specific organ system is affected.

It is during the resistance phase that we see the so-called "diseases of adaption." Decreases in ACTH occur as the stress response is channeled into specific organ systems. It is this adaptation which, over time, contributes to stress-related illness. Organ systems become aroused, then fatigued, and then begin to break down. Chronic resistance may eventually affect the organ system's capacity to respond at all. During this phase, we may notice headaches, insomnia, sinus attacks, high blood pressure, gastric and duodenal ulcers, rheumatic and allergic reactions, and cardiovascular and kidney disorders. Sustained stress leads to the adrenal cortex hormones constricting the blood vessels in the kidneys. Hypertension and kidney damage thereby result.

The exhaustion phase is manifest when organ systems break down and even stop functioning. ACTH secretion may increase again at this point. The generalized damage I mentioned earlier is apparent at this point. That is, adrenal enlargement, thymus atrophy, stomach ulcers, and a compromised immunity are probable. Damage to secondary systems, such as the kidneys and heart, occur as a result of prolonged adaptation. Hypertension is an example. All in all, the wear and tear is quite formidable.

Disenchantment, as it moves through its phases, makes a striking parallel to Selye's General Adaptation Syndrome. The phases might be matched as follows:

Reality Shock   ⟶   Alarm Stage

Moody Blues   ⟶   Resistance Stage

Burnout   ⟶   Exhaustion Stage

During reality shock, one can imagine the sympathetic nervous system and endocrine systems firing up. ACTH and other hormones begin to course through our bodies as we become frustrated and disappointed, fighting against forgotten phone messages, neglectful lovers, and critical supervisors. Any of the reactions listed in figure 1 begin to occur as we attempt to cope with these shattered illusions.

Over time, we create the themes that underlie the moody black and blues. During this phase, the workers of America are arriving home each day with acid indigestion and tension headaches. Some people, anticipating a snake pit at work, actually wake up with their headaches and indigestion. In fact, some people are so chronically upset about conditions at work or in the home that they never go to sleep at all some nights. They become insomniacs.

At this point in our adaptation process, we are knocking on our doctors' doors for Valium, Dalmane, and Tagamet. We are angry, resentful, and still fighting back with a vengeance. Arguments, irritability, and emotional tirades are at their zenith. So are our hypertension, asthma attacks, and herpes. We can't go on too long at this fever pitch.

Apathy, disinterest, and withdrawal soon become ritualized states. We feel exhausted. A sense of futility exists. We may be depressed. Nothing matters. Why should I go on? Helplessness and hopelessness may blanket our thoughts. Motivation has ceased. We no longer believe that anything meaningful or pleasurable is possible, so why try. We may grow fat, muscles become weak and limp, and sex organs remain flacid. During the exhaustion phase, we lose the desire to help ourselves. Our will to live fades. Our bodies wither as our will to love dies. Disenchantment is indeed costly!

EPILOGUE

I recently heard tell of a beautiful, dynamic young woman whose husband insisted that she have a breast augmentation surgically performed. Though the surgery in itself is not medically significant, it is psychologically noteworthy. This couple, I discovered, had only been married for one year. When I allowed myself to be inquisitive about the reasons for the surgery, I discovered that her husband had lost sexual interest within six months of their wedding day. This decline in desire followed what had been a very torrid sexual time during their courtship. A pretty rapid burnout, I thought!

The tragic proportions of this situation were yet to be revealed. Not only had this woman consented to a surgical procedure which would enlarge her breasts from a B-cup to a D-cup, but she was later to find out (1) that there were painful complications to the surgery which would require more surgery, (2) that a constant barrage of whistles and hoots would greet her wherever she would go, and (3) that her husband would lose his sexual interest in her again three months later!

Hearing that this husband had reluctantly agreed to marriage counseling, I thought about the elements of mature love and wondered if this man would ever achieve them. Yes, he surely knew about the importance of passion. But what did he know about emotional intimacy, or spiritual transcendence, or reasoned commitment? Their marriage was sure to fail unless they, as a couple, were able to renew their bond maturely. D-cup-sized breasts may suggest a kind of abundance, but they will never be enough to sustain a loving relationship.

This couple would have to learn what I began to learn over twenty years ago when I gazed down at a young, gorgeous blonde sleeping so peacefully nearby. There, in Nova Scotia, where endless sea meets rugged coastline under the shimmering moon, I began learning my first important lesson in love: *Love must end before it can truly begin.*

I can honestly admit that Claire knew this important message long before I did. It is she who has had more patience, more tolerance, and has been able to view our problems as specific situations gone awry, rather than as indictments of her partner's failure. I am the one who has had to learn how to cope with disenchantment. I am the one who felt the need to look inward, knowing that my own childhood wounds had muzzled my capacity as a loving partner. I have had more to learn than Claire has about renewal.

Yet at this point in our journey I am prepared to say that both of us have found the necessary amalgam of compromises and have seen enough light to maintain our commitment—not to a fixed image of one another, but more to an ongoing process with one another. I offer the following covenant as a symbolic rite to this passage.

A Couples Covenant

_____, (YOUR PARTNER'S NAME) I am committed to you and our relationship. We have come a long way and have a great deal to be proud of. I now realize that successful relationships pass through three phases...romance, disenchantment, and finally mature, covenant love. More than ever, I appreciate your commitment to me and the process we have undertaken to RENEW our love for each other. This has not been easy for either one of us, but we have succeeded in getting past the disenchantments which entrapped us for a while.

I no longer see you as an unreal projection of my ideal fantasies. I realize now that the perfect person I was looking for...and tried to shape you into...does not exist. Though there are thousands, perhaps millions of other potential partners for me, I now believe that YOU ARE ENOUGH for me. I want you to know that I will demonstrate my commitment to you by:

1. Recognizing the importance of your needs and helping you to meet these needs as often as possible.

2. Experiencing joy and satisfaction whenever you seem to be fulfilling your needs.

3. Maintaining realistic values and expectations about you as my life partner.

4. Tolerating those attitudes, beliefs, and actions of yours that are different from mine.

5. Striving to reveal myself to you honestly so that you will continue to know who I really am.

6. Expressing my feelings to you openly and candidly in a manner which allows you to respond to me in a caring way.

7. Giving you all the freedom you need as an individual to pursue your own interests and relationships.

8. Celebrating our "we-ness" by privately creating an identity with you while publicly appreciating you.

I appreciate you for accepting my basic needs to belong, for control, and for affection. I know that I sometimes get angry or hurt when these needs are not fulfilled, but I now realize that a child of the past still lives within me who is often more responsible for these feelings than you are. I will take responsibility for these childhood imprints and will not blame you for wounds of the past.

I appreciate you for giving me time to modify my most embedded beliefs about you and others. I have learned that I sometimes view you and others in very rigid and extreme ways. Though this kind of extremism is typical of romantic love, as well as disenchantment, we have come too far to be frozen by such inflexible themes. Given our committed love, I will do my best to move my beliefs and feelings along a full continuum.

I appreciate you as my partner in life, but will not depend upon you to meet my overall needs for happiness. Though you enhance my satisfaction in love, work, leisure, health, finances, and spirituality, I cannot depend upon you to exclusively meet my needs in so many areas. I realize that the life I want can only happen when I learn to find a balance between work and play, as well as a balance between devotion to others and devotion to myself.

I know that our work as a loving couple will never be completed. I realize that we will encounter many situations which will fester over time or may seem to overwhelm us. I am committed to the RENEW process during these painful times and I recognize that each of these elements is essential to getting past disenchantment. You can count on me to:

Release my resentments. I realize that my resentments—and the anger that underlies them—block the flow of caring, inhibit resolution of problems, deny the possibility of mature love, and can damage my physical health and well-being.

Express my caring. I realize that we must demonstrate to one another that we still care, so that it is safe to be open and vulnerable once again.

Negotiate our problems. I realize that unmet needs contribute to our problems. Rather than blame you for these problems, I will work with you to find creative solutions.

Explore new perspectives. Viewing our relationship as a journey diminishes the urgency for change. The positive attitude I take toward you and our commitment is by far the most important thing I can do to renew our love.

Weather the storm. I know that things will go wrong occasionally. We will get upset. During these times I will take responsibility to lessen my upset.

Partner A:

Signed_____ Dated_____

Partner B:

Signed_____ Dated_____

This book has been dedicated to the renewal of love. We live in a day and age when time-urgency and expediency are benchmarks for living. Car phones, self-timing microwaves, and super-duper TV remote controls allow us to flip past anything that seems too sluggish or boring. Good cooks will tell us that there still is nothing like the old-fashioned sauce pan simmering at moderate temperatures to ensure a well-cooked meal that has not lost its essential nutrients. I urge each of you to taper your pace just enough so that your own special qualities can be prepared slowly enough for one another's tastes. I wish you all a full-course meal. And do remember that many cold platters need just a little reheating to taste wonderful again.

References

Antonovsky, A. *Health, Stress and Coping.* San Francisco: Jossey-Bass, 1979.

Azrin, N. H., Naster, B. M., and Jones, R. "Reciprocity counseling: A rapid learning-based procedure for marital counseling." *Behavior Research and Therapy,* 1973, *11,* 365-382.

Bandura, A. "Self-efficacy: Toward a Unifying Theory of Behavioral Change." *Psychological Review,* 1977, *84,* 191-215.

Barefoot, J. and Dahlstrom, G. In article by Sally Squires, "Anger's dark side: Researchers study rage, early death." Newhouse News Service, 1983.

Beattie, M. *Codependent No More.* New York: Hazelden Foundation, 1987.

Benson, H. *The Relaxation Response.* New York: Morrow, 1975.

Branden, N. *The Psychology of Self-Esteem.* Los Angeles: Nash Publishing Corporation, 1969.

Bugen, L. A. *Death and Dying: Theory, Research and Practice.* Dubuque, Iowa: William C. Brown, 1979.

Burns, D. *Feeling Good.* New York: William Morrow, 1980.

Campbell, A., Converse, P., and Rodgers, W. *The Quality of American Life.* New York: Russell Sage, 1976.

Cancian, F. M. *Love in America.* New York: Cambridge University Press, 1987.

Cummings, E. E. *A Selection of Poems.* New York: Harcourt Brace & World, 1961.

Dobson, J. C. *Love Must Be Tough.* Waco, Texas: Word Books, 1983.

Felton, B. J. et al. "Coping with Chronic Illness: A Factor Analytic Exploration." Paper presented at the annual meeting of the American Psychological Association, Montreal, September 1980.

Frankl, V. E. *Man's Search for Meaning*. New York: Simon and Schuster, 1963.

Freedman, J. *Happy People*. New York: Harcourt Brace Jovanovich, 1978.

Friedman, M. and Rosenman, R. H. *Type A Behavior and Your Heart*. New York: Knopf, 1974.

Fromm, E. *The Art of Loving*. New York: Harper & Row, 1956.

Gilbert, L. A. *Sharing It All: The Rewards and Struggles of Two-Career Families*. New York: Plenum, 1988.

Glasser, W. *Schools Without Failure*. New York: Harper & Row, 1969.

Gordon, T. *P.E.T.: Parent Effectiveness Training*. New York: Peter H. Wyden, 1970.

Grier, W. H. and Cobbs, P. M. *Black Rage*. New York: Basic Books, 1968.

Guggenbuhl-Craig, A. *Marriage: Dead or Alive*. Spring Publications, 1977.

Hampden-Turner, C. *Maps of the Mind*. New York: MacMillan, 1982.

Hoffer, E. *The Passionate State of Mind*. New York: Harper & Row, 1956.

Holmes, T. H. and Rahe, R. H. "The Social Readjustment Rating Scale." *Journal of Psychosomatic Research*, 1967, *11*, 213-218.

Jackson, D. 1965. "Family rules—marital quid pro quo." *Archives of General Psychiatry 12*, 589-594.

James, M. *Marriage is for Loving*. Reading, Massachucetts: Addison-Wesley, 1979.

Janero, R. P. and Altshuler, T. C. *The Art of Being Human*. San Francisco: Harper & Row, 1979.

Johnson, R. A. *Inner Work*. San Francisco: Harper & Row, 1986.

Johnson, R. A. *We*. San Francisco: Harper & Row, 1983.

Kierkegaard, S. *Fear and Trembling*. New York: Anchor, 1954.

Kopp, S. *An End to Innocence*. New York: MacMillan, 1978.

Kramer, M. *Reality Shock*. St. Louis: C.V. Mosby, 1974.

Langdon-Davies, J. *A Short History of Women*. New York: Literary Guild of America, 1927.

Larsen, E. and Hegarty, C. L. *Days of Healing, Days of Joy*. New York: Harper & Row, 1987.

Lawler, A. "The healthy self: Variations on a theme." Paper presented at the First Annual Southwest Regional Conference for Counseling Psychology, Houston, April 29, 1988.

Lazarus, A. A. *In The Mind's Eye*. New York: Guilford, 1984.

Lazarus, R. S. *Psychological Stress and the Coping Process.* New York: Mc-Graw-Hill, 1966.

Levinson, D. J. *The Seasons of A Man's Life.* New York: Ballantine Books, 1978.

Margolin, G. "A multilevel approach to the assessment of communication positiveness in distressed marital couples." *International Journal of Family Counseling,* 1977, 6, 81-89.

Margolin, G. In C. Tavris. *Anger: The Misunderstood Emotion.* New York: Simon & Schuster, 1984.

Maslow, A. H. *Motivation and Personality.* New York: Harper & Row, 1970.

McKay, M., Davis, M. and Fanning, P. *Thoughts and Feelings.* Oakland: New Harbinger Publications, 1981.

Merton, R. K. *Social Theory and Social Structure.* Glencoe, Illinois: Free Press, 1957.

Miller, A. *For Your Own Good.* New York: Farrar, Straus, & Giroux, 1983.

Missildine, W. H. *Your Inner Child of the Past.* New York: Simon and Schuster, 1963.

Morris, D. *Intimate Behavior.* New York: Random House, 1971.

Norwood, R. *Women Who Love Too Much.* Los Angeles: Jeremy E. Tarcher, Inc., 1985.

Peck, M. S. *The Road Less Traveled.* New York: Simon and Schuster, 1978.

Pearlin, L. I. and Schooler, C. "The Structure of Coping." *Journal of Health and Social Behavior.* 1978, 19, 2-21.

Perls, F. S. *Gestalt Therapy Verbatim.* New York: Bantam, 1971.

Powell, J. *Why Am I Afraid to Love.* Niles, Illinois: Argus Communications, 1967.

Rogers, C. R. *On Becoming A Person.* Boston: Houghton Mifflin, 1961.

Rokeach, M. *The Open and Closed Mind.* New York: Basic Books, 1960.

Schutz. W. C. *The Interpersonal Underworld.* Palo Alto, California: Science and Behavior Books, Inc., 1966.

Secord, P. F. and Backman, C. W. "Personality theory and the problem of stability and change in individual behavior: An interpersonal approach." In Harper, J. C. et al. *The Cognitive Processes: Readings.* Englewood Cliffs, New Jersey: Prentice Hall, 1964.

Seligman, M. E. *Helplessness: On Depression, Development, and Death.* San Francisco: W. H. Freeman, 1975.

Selye, H. *The Stress of Life.* New York: McGraw-Hill, 1976.

Shekelle, R. In article by Sally Squires, "Anger's dark side: Researchers study rage, early death." Newhouse News Service, 1983.

Stein, R. "When First We Met." *San Francisco Chronicle*, 14 February, 1977.

Stroebel, C. F. *QR: The Quieting Reflex*. New York: Berkley Books, 1982.

Stuart, R. B. *Helping Couples Change*. New York: The Guilford Press, 1980.

Tavris, C. *Anger: The Misunderstood Emotion*. New York: Simon and Schuster, 1984.

Weiss, R. L. and Margolin, G. "Assessment of marital conflict and accord." In A. R. Chiminero, K. S. Calhoun, & H. E. Adams (Eds.), *Handbook of Behavioral Assessment,*. New York: John Wiley and Sons, 1977.

Wensinger, A., (Ed.). *Paula Modersohn-Becker: The Letters and Journals*. New York: Taplinger Publishing, 1984.

Williams, R. In article by Sally Squires, "Anger's dark side: Researchers study rage, early death." *Newhouse News Service*, 1983.

Wolff, C. T. et al. "Relationship between psychological defenses and mean urinary 17-hydroxycorticosteroid excretion rates. I. A predictive study of parents, of fatally ill children." *Psychosomatic Medicine*. 1964, 26, 576-591.

Yalom, I. *Existential Psychotherapy*. New York: Basic Books, 1980.

Other New Harbinger Self-Help Titles

The Relaxation & Stress Reduction Workbook, 3rd Edition, $13.95

Leader's Guide to the Relaxation & Stress Reduction Workbook, $14.95

Beyond Grief: A Guide for Recovering from the Death of a Loved One, $10.95

Thoughts & Feelings: The Art of Cognitive Stress Intervention, $12.95

Messages: The Communication Skills Book, $11.95

The Divorce Book, $10.95

Hypnosis for Change: A Manual of Proven Techniques, 2nd Edition, $11.95

The Deadly Diet: Recovering from Anorexia & Bulimia, $10.95

Self-Esteem, $11.95

The Better Way to Drink, $10.95

Chronic Pain Control Workbook, $12.50

Rekindling Desire, $10.95

Life Without Fear: Anxiety and Its Cure, $9.95

Visualization for Change, $11.95

Guideposts to Meaning, $10.95

Controlling Stagefright, $10.95

Videotape: Clinical Hypnosis for Stress & Anxiety Reduction, $24.95

Starting Out Right: Essential Parenting Skills for Your Child's First Seven Years, $12.95

Big Kids: A Parent's Guide to Weight Control for Children, $10.95

Personal Peace: Transcending Your Interpersonal Limits, $10.95

My Parent's Keeper: Adult Children of the Emotionally Disturbed, $11.95

When Anger Hurts, $11.95

Free of the Shadows: Recovering from Sexual Violence, $11.95

Resolving Conflict With Others and Within Yourself, $11.95

Liftime Weight Control, $10.95

The Anxiety & Phobia Workbook, $12.95

Love and Renewal: A Couple's Guide to Commitment, $11.95

Send a check or purchase order for the titles you want, plus $1.50 for shipping and handling, to:

New Harbinger Publications
Department B
5674 Shattuck Avenue
Oakland, CA 94609

Or write for a free catalog of all our quality self-help publications.